Computational Methods for Medical and Cyber Security

Computational Methods for Medical and Cyber Security

Editors

Suhuai Luo
Kamran Shaukat

MDPI • Basel • Beijing • Wuhan • Barcelona • Belgrade • Manchester • Tokyo • Cluj • Tianjin

Editors
Suhuai Luo
School of Information and
Physical Sciences
The University of Newcastle
Newcastle
Australia

Kamran Shaukat
School of Information and
Physical Sciences
The University of Newcastle
Newcastle
Australia

Editorial Office
MDPI
St. Alban-Anlage 66
4052 Basel, Switzerland

This is a reprint of articles from the Special Issue published online in the open access journal *Applied Sciences* (ISSN 2076-3417) (available at: www.mdpi.com/journal/applsci/special_issues/ computational_methods_cyber_security).

For citation purposes, cite each article independently as indicated on the article page online and as indicated below:

LastName, A.A.; LastName, B.B.; LastName, C.C. Article Title. *Journal Name* **Year**, *Volume Number*, Page Range.

ISBN 978-3-0365-5116-6 (Hbk)
ISBN 978-3-0365-5115-9 (PDF)

© 2022 by the authors. Articles in this book are Open Access and distributed under the Creative Commons Attribution (CC BY) license, which allows users to download, copy and build upon published articles, as long as the author and publisher are properly credited, which ensures maximum dissemination and a wider impact of our publications.

The book as a whole is distributed by MDPI under the terms and conditions of the Creative Commons license CC BY-NC-ND.

Contents

About the Editors vii

Preface to "Computational Methods for Medical and Cyber Security" ix

Hamed Alqahtani, Saud S. Alotaibi, Fatma S. Alrayes, Isra Al-Turaiki, Khalid A. Alissa and Amira Sayed A. Aziz et al.
Evolutionary Algorithm with Deep Auto Encoder Network Based Website Phishing Detection and Classification
Reprinted from: *Appl. Sci.* **2022**, *12*, 7441, doi:10.3390/app12157441 1

Mohammed A. Alqahtani
Factors Affecting Cybersecurity Awareness among University Students
Reprinted from: *Appl. Sci.* **2022**, *12*, 2589, doi:10.3390/app12052589 17

Ghulam Qadar Butt, Toqeer Ali Sayed, Rabia Riaz, Sanam Shahla Rizvi and Anand Paul
Secure Healthcare Record Sharing Mechanism with Blockchain
Reprinted from: *Appl. Sci.* **2022**, *12*, 2307, doi:10.3390/app12052307 39

Mengtao Sun, Li Lu, Ibrahim A. Hameed, Carl Petter Skaar Kulseng and Kjell-Inge Gjesdal
Detecting Small Anatomical Structures in 3D Knee MRI Segmentation by Fully Convolutional Networks
Reprinted from: *Appl. Sci.* **2021**, *12*, 283, doi:10.3390/app12010283 61

Shanza Abbas, Muhammad Umair Khan, Scott Uk-Jin Lee and Asad Abbas
Columns Occurrences Graph to Improve Column Prediction in Deep Learning Nlidb
Reprinted from: *Appl. Sci.* **2021**, *11*, 12116, doi:10.3390/app112412116 77

Ansar Siddique, Asiya Jan, Fiaz Majeed, Adel Ibrahim Qahmash, Noorulhasan Naveed Quadri and Mohammad Osman Abdul Wahab
Predicting Academic Performance Using an Efficient Model Based on Fusion of Classifiers
Reprinted from: *Appl. Sci.* **2021**, *11*, 11845, doi:10.3390/app112411845 91

Madiha Khalid and Muhammad Murtaza Yousaf
A Comparative Analysis of Big Data Frameworks: An Adoption Perspective
Reprinted from: *Appl. Sci.* **2021**, *11*, 11033, doi:10.3390/app112211033 111

Adele Ossareh, Mohammad Saeed Pourjafar and Tomasz Kopczewski
Cognitive Biases on the Iran Stock Exchange: Unsupervised Learning Approach to Examining Feature Bundles in Investors' Portfolios
Reprinted from: *Appl. Sci.* **2021**, *11*, 10916, doi:10.3390/app112210916 137

Mengtao Sun, Hao Wang, Mark Pasquine and Ibrahim A. Hameed
Machine Translation in Low-Resource Languages by an Adversarial Neural Network
Reprinted from: *Appl. Sci.* **2021**, *11*, 10860, doi:10.3390/app112210860 159

Alhuseen Omar Alsayed, Mohd Shafry Mohd Rahim, Ibrahim AlBidewi, Mushtaq Hussain, Syeda Huma Jabeen and Nashwan Alromema et al.
Selection of the Right Undergraduate Major by Students Using Supervised Learning Techniques
Reprinted from: *Appl. Sci.* **2021**, *11*, 10639, doi:10.3390/app112210639 177

Adeel Nasir, Kamran Shaukat, Kanwal Iqbal Khan, Ibrahim A. Hameed, Talha Mahboob Alam and Suhuai Luo
Trends and Directions of Financial Technology (Fintech) in Society and Environment: A Bibliometric Study
Reprinted from: *Appl. Sci.* **2021**, *11*, 10353, doi:10.3390/app112110353 . . . . **197**

About the Editors

Suhuai Luo

Suhuai Luo is an associate professor in information technology at the University of Newcastle. He received Bachelor's and Master's Degrees from Nanjing University of Posts and Telecommunications and a PhD degree from the University of Sydney, all in Electrical Engineering. His main research interests include image processing, computer vision, machine learning, cybersecurity, and media data mining. His diverse research focus has led him to conduct studies in areas ranging from medical imaging for computer-aided diagnoses to computer vision for intelligent driving systems and machine learning for enhancing cybersecurity.

Kamran Shaukat

Kamran Shaukat received an M.Sc. degree in computer science from Mohammad Ali Jinnah University, Pakistan and is currently affiliated with The University of Newcastle, Australia. He is the author of many articles on machine learning and cybersecurity. He served as a Lecturer for the University of the Punjab, Pakistan, for seven years. He has also served as a Reviewer for many journals. He has attended international conferences, including the USA, the UK, Thailand, Turkey, and Pakistan. He received the Gold Medal for his M.Sc. degree.

Preface to "Computational Methods for Medical and Cyber Security"

Over the past decade, computational methods, including machine learning (ML) and deep learning (DL), have been exponentially growing in their development of solutions in various domains, especially medicine, cybersecurity, finance, and education. While these applications of machine learning algorithms have been proven beneficial in various fields, many shortcomings have also been highlighted, such as the lack of benchmark datasets, the inability to learn from small datasets, the cost of architecture, adversarial attacks, and imbalanced datasets. On the other hand, new and emerging algorithms, such as deep learning, one-shot learning, continuous learning, and generative adversarial networks, have successfully solved various tasks in these fields. Therefore, applying these new methods to life-critical missions is crucial, as is measuring these less-traditional algorithms' success when used in these fields.

Authors were invited to submit their papers focusing on but not limited to the following topics: machine learning, explainable machine learning, adversarial machine learning, cyber security, imbalanced datasets, bioinformatics, medical diagnosis, financial risk management, finance, asset return forecasting, stock exchange, educational data mining, learning analytics, student performance prediction, and intelligent tutoring systems.

It is our great pleasure to thank all of the participating authors, the referees, and the peer-reviewers for their invaluable contributions toward the remarkable success of each paper. We also appreciate the editorial and managerial help and assistance provided efficiently by Ms. Nicole Lian and associates in the Editorial Office of *Applied Sciences*. The dedicated and wholehearted support and help of all are greatly appreciated.

Suhuai Luo and Kamran Shaukat
Editors

Article

Evolutionary Algorithm with Deep Auto Encoder Network Based Website Phishing Detection and Classification

Hamed Alqahtani [1], Saud S. Alotaibi [2], Fatma S. Alrayes [3], Isra Al-Turaiki [4], Khalid A. Alissa [5], Amira Sayed A. Aziz [6], Mohammed Maray [7] and Mesfer Al Duhayyim [8,*]

[1] Department of Information Systems, College of Computer Science, Center of Artificial Intelligence, Unit of Cybersecurity, King Khalid University, Abha 62529, Saudi Arabia; hsqahtani@kku.edu.sa
[2] Department of Information Systems, College of Computing and Information System, Umm Al-Qura University, Mecca 24382, Saudi Arabia; ssotaibi@uqu.edu.sa
[3] Department of Information Systems, College of Computer and Information Sciences, Princess Nourah bint Abdulrahman University, P.O. Box 84428, Riyadh 11671, Saudi Arabia; falrayes@pnu.edu.sa
[4] Department of Information Technology, College of Computer and Information Sciences, King Saud University, P.O Box 145111, Riyadh 4545, Saudi Arabia; ialtraiki@ksu.edu.sa
[5] SAUDI ARAMCO Cybersecurity Chair, Networks and Communications Department, College of Computer Science and Information Technology, Imam Abdulrahman Bin Faisal University, P.O. Box 1982, Dammam 31441, Saudi Arabia; kaalissa@iau.edu.sa
[6] Department of Digital Media, Faculty of Computers and Information Technology, Future University in Egypt, New Cairo 11835, Egypt; amirabdelaziz@fue.edu.eg
[7] Department of Information Systems, College of Computer Science, King Khalid University, Abha 62529, Saudi Arabia; mmarey@kku.edu.sa
[8] Department of Computer Science, College of Sciences and Humanities-Aflaj, Prince Sattam Bin Abdulaziz University, Al-Kharj 16278, Saudi Arabia
* Correspondence: m.alduhayyim@psau.edu.sa

Citation: Alqahtani, H.; Alotaibi, S.S.; Alrayes, F.S.; Al-Turaiki, I.; Alissa, K.A.; Aziz, A.S.A.; Maray, M.; Al Duhayyim, M. Evolutionary Algorithm with Deep Auto Encoder Network Based Website Phishing Detection and Classification. *Appl. Sci.* **2022**, *12*, 7441. https://doi.org/10.3390/app12157441

Academic Editors: Suhuai Luo and Kamran Shaukat

Received: 27 May 2022
Accepted: 18 July 2022
Published: 25 July 2022

Publisher's Note: MDPI stays neutral with regard to jurisdictional claims in published maps and institutional affiliations.

Copyright: © 2022 by the authors. Licensee MDPI, Basel, Switzerland. This article is an open access article distributed under the terms and conditions of the Creative Commons Attribution (CC BY) license (https://creativecommons.org/licenses/by/4.0/).

Abstract: Website phishing is a cyberattack that targets online users for stealing their sensitive data containing login credential and banking details. The phishing websites appear very similar to their equivalent legitimate websites for attracting a huge amount of Internet users. The attacker fools the user by offering the masked webpage as legitimate or reliable for retrieving its important information. Presently, anti-phishing approaches necessitate experts to extract phishing site features and utilize third-party services for phishing website detection. These techniques have some drawbacks, as the requirement of experts for extracting phishing features is time consuming. Many solutions for phishing websites attack have been presented, such as blacklist or whitelist, heuristics, and machine learning (ML) based approaches, which face difficulty in accomplishing effectual recognition performance due to the continual improvements of phishing technologies. Therefore, this study presents an optimal deep autoencoder network based website phishing detection and classification (ODAE-WPDC) model. The proposed ODAE-WPDC model applies input data pre-processing at the initial stage to get rid of missing values in the dataset. Then, feature extraction and artificial algae algorithm (AAA) based feature selection (FS) are utilized. The DAE model with the received features carried out the classification process, and the parameter tuning of the DAE technique was performed using the invasive weed optimization (IWO) algorithm to accomplish enhanced performance. The performance validation of the ODAE-WPDC technique was tested using the Phishing URL dataset from the Kaggle repository. The experimental findings confirm the better performance of the ODAE-WPDC model with maximum accuracy of 99.28%.

Keywords: cybersecurity; internet of things; cloud computing; computational models; deep learning; metaheuristics; phishing detection; website phishing

1. Introduction

Cybercrime can be defined as crime that targets networks or computers. Computer crimes are covered by a wide range of potentially criminal actions. Phishing is regarded as most frequently employed attack over social networks. With these assaults, the phisher endeavors to obtain personal data from the user to be utilized dishonestly toward users [1,2]. In the current digital business scenario, many corporations are making use of the ever-evolving changes of cyberspace, owing to the development of the internet day by day, particularly because of the impacts of COVID-19 which has pushed every person to highly utilize internet in every field. As the largest computer network [3], the internet is a serious platform for the success of business and its growth, as most marketable trades are held online [4]. In spite of the ease linked with online transactions from businesses as well as users, there occurs an online menace called phishing. Phishing indulges in making a well-designed website (WS) that imitates prevailing authentic commercial WSs for deceiving users and illegally acquiring their login credentials and documents, which alleviates phishers in obtaining accessibility to the legitimate financial data of users [5]. Inappropriately, the phishing impact was fatal because legal users who were affected were prone to find theft and data breaches and do not have a faith in electronic banking and online trade. Phishing commonly appears through an email which is sent to users, from trustworthy resources, which urges them in adjusting their login credentials by following or clicking a hyperlink in these emails [6].

Phishing is symbolically the same as fishing in water bodies; however, rather than catching fish, invaders attempt to obtain the confidential information of users. Phishing WSs seem to be same as the corresponding legal WSs for alluring great numbers of internet users. The current advancements in the detection of phishing have resulted in the progress of several novel techniques on the basis of visual similarity [7]. In recent decades, the usage of deep learning (DL), computational technique, and machine learning (ML) have grown exponentially in evolving solutions for several fields, particularly education, medicine, finance, and cybersecurity. Whereas such applications of ML methods have proven advantageous in several domains, they also have several disadvantages, such as adversarial attacks, a lack of benchmark datasets, the cost of architecture, imbalanced datasets, and the inability to learn from small datasets. Conversely, innovative techniques, namely DL, generative adversarial networks, one-shot learning, and continuous learning, were applied successfully for sorting several responsibilities in such domains. Thus, it becomes important to implement such novel techniques in life-critical missions and measure the success of less conventional techniques utilized in such domains [8].

This study presents an optimal deep autoencoder network based website phishing detection and classification (ODAE-WPDC) model. The proposed ODAE-WPDC model applies input data pre-processing at the initial stage to get rid of missing values in the dataset. Then, feature extraction and artificial algae algorithm (AAA) based feature selection (FS) are utilized. The DAE model with the received features carries out the classification process, and the parameter tuning of DAE technique is performed using the invasive weed optimization (IWO) algorithm to accomplish enhanced performance. The IWO is a derivative-free real parameter optimization technique that mimics the ecological behavior of colonizing weeds. The performance validation of the ODAE-WPDC methodology was tested utilizing benchmark Kaggle repository. In short, the paper's contributions can be summarized as follows.

- Propose an intelligent model using metaheuristic and deep learning model to identify phishing websites via feature selection and classification processes;
- Employ AAA based feature subset selection process to reduce curse of dimensionality;
- Apply IWO with DAE classifier and the hyperparameter tuning process using the IWO algorithm helps in achieving enhanced performance;
- Validate the performance of the proposed model on the Phishing URL dataset from the Kaggle repository.

2. Related Works

Numerous works related to cybersecurity-based solutions are available in the literature [9,10]. The authors in [11] concentrate on implementing a DL structure for detecting phishing WSs. This work initially designs two kinds of features for web phishing, such as original and interaction features. The detection method dependent upon DBN is then projected. In [12], it can be projected a manner for detecting malicious URL addresses with accuracy, utilizing CNNs. In contrast to the preceding mechanism, whereas URL or traffic statistics or web contents are analyzed, it can be analyzed only the URL text. Therefore, this technique is faster and detects zero-day attacks. Do et al. [13] establish the model of phishing and DL from the context of cybersecurity. Afterward, classifications of phishing detection and DL techniques are offered for classifying the recent works into several types. Then, taking the presented classification as baseline, this research widely analyzes the recent DL approaches and examines their benefits and drawbacks.

The authors in [14] examine a novel technique for identifying phishing WSs utilizing hyperlinks accessible from the source code of HTML webpage from the equivalent WS. This feature is utilized for training the supervised DNN approach with Adam optimizing to differentiate fraudulent WSs from genuine WSs. The presented DL approach with Adam optimizer utilizes a listwise method for classifying phishing as well as genuine WSs. Odeh et al. [15] propose the recent methods for phishing WS recognition utilizing the ML approaches. The popularly studied methods are concentrated on classical ML approaches. Ada Boosting, SVM, RF, and NB are the powerful ML approaches studied in the works. This review work also recognizes DL-based approaches with optimum efficiency to detect phishing WSs related to the conventional ML approaches. Makkar and Kumar [16] examine a cognitive spammer structure that eliminates spam pages if the search engines compute the webpage rank score. The structure identifies web spam with the assistance of the LSTM network by training the link features. In [17], a real-time anti-phishing model that utilizes seven distinct classifier approaches and NLP based features is presented. The model has the subsequent differentiating property in other studies in analyses: language independence, utilization of massive size of legitimate and phishing datasets, real-time implementation, recognition of novel WSs, independence in third-party service, and utilization of feature-rich classifications.

Lee et al. [18] propose an effective phishing page detection model by the use of multiple models, where every model is trained by the insertion of (controlled) noises in a subset of arbitrarily elected features from entire set of features. Ghaleb et al. [19] introduce a 2-stage ensemble learning approach with the integration of random forest (RF) based pre-classification and multilayer perceptron (MLP) based decision making. The trained MLP classification model substitutes the majority voting method of the three trained RF models to make decisions. Kondracki et al. [20] present the initial examination of the man-in-the-middle (MITM) phishing toolkit. With the detailed investigation of the toolkit, the implicit network level characteristics are identified, which can be employed for the detection process. In addition, an ML-based classification model is derived to find the existence of toolkits for online communication purposes. Noah et al. [21] introduce an anti-phishing model named PhisherCop, which is based on the stochastic gradient descent (SGD) and a support vector classifier (SVC) model. The authors in [22] introduce the Crawlphish model to automatically detect and categorize client-side cloaking utilized by recognized phishing websites. The authors also present a taxonomy of eight distinct kinds of evasion over three high-level classes.

ML-based phishing website detection utilizes ML models for the detection of manually extracted phishing website URL features. The efficacy of the recognition process can be enhanced by this approach. It necessitates experts in the extraction of URL features manually, designing a training set for phishing website detection, and, lastly, utilizing supervised learning approaches for phishing website detection. To resolve the manual feature extraction process, the DL models are found to be useful. At the same time, the choice of proper DL model is a difficult process. In particular, when phishers alter the attacking strategies for leveraging the system susceptibilities and the users' unawareness, the selection of the proper model can result in unpredicted outcomes, resulting in a waste of effort and eventually affecting the model's accuracy and efficiency. On the other hand, the fine-tuning procedure of DL models is another challenging problem that needs to be resolved. Motivated to solve this problem, in this work, the IWO algorithm is applied to fine tune the DAE parameters to accomplish maximum detection accuracy.

3. The Proposed Model

In this study, a novel ODAE-WPDC model is introduced for the recognition and classification of WS phishing to achieve cybersecurity. At the primary stage, the proposed ODAE-WPDC model applies input data pre-processing at the initial stage to get rid of missing values in the dataset. This is followed by feature extraction, and the AAA based FS process is utilized. Finally, the IWO with DAE model is applied for the classification process. Figure 1 depicts the block diagram of the ODAE-WPDC approach.

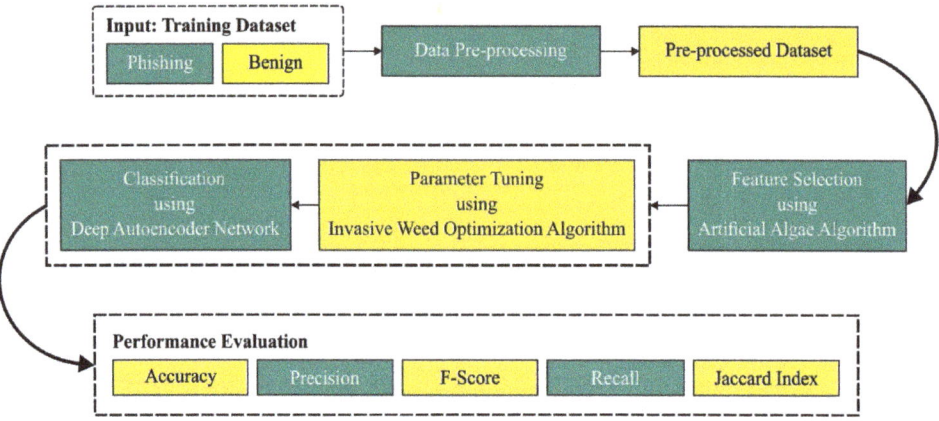

Figure 1. Block diagram of ODAE-WPDC approach.

3.1. Data Pre-Processing

This is the initial processing of data for preparing them for initial processing or further examination. It removes the feature which has missing values or null values. The significant features compared with phishing WS URLs are removed with this phase. At this point, features such as URL length, abnormal URL, statistical report, and so on, are extracted for phishing URL recognition.

3.2. Design of AAA Based FS Technique

Once the raw data are pre-processed and features are extracted, the AAA-FS model is utilized to choose feature subsets. In 2015, Uymaz et al. [23] presented AAA, a bio-inspired metaheuristic optimized technique to overcome real-time and continuous optimization issues. It is a stimulation for the search activity of microalgae. Every individual is regarded as an artificial algal community (AAC) from the population-based technique; also, every AAC resembles a solution from the problem space. The life cycle encompasses mitotic reproduction, altering the dominant species, and environmental adaptation. The adaptation stage, the reproduction or evolutionary stage, and the helical movement phase are the three stages of AAA. The evolutionary/reproduction stage is exploited for replenishing the community cell by resurrecting algae by mitotic division when they have enough light and nutrients in the environment. Algae perform a movement named helical motion. The algae population exists in liquid atmosphere and congregates nearer to the liquid surface wherever there is a sufficient light source. The algae cell uses their flagellum (organelle) for helical motion [24]. Figure 2 depicts the flowchart of AAA and explained in Algorithm 1.

Algorithm 1: Pseudocode of AAA

Initialization: Generate N population of algae colonies
Determine fitness $f(x_i), i = 1, 2, \ldots, N, D$
where x_i = algae colony, N = number of algae colonies, and that the D = problem dimensionality
while termination condition is unsatisfied do
for $i = 1$ to n do
while energy of ith colony not done do
Employ helical movement stage
end while
end for
Employ evolutionary/reproduction stage
Employ adaptation stage
end while

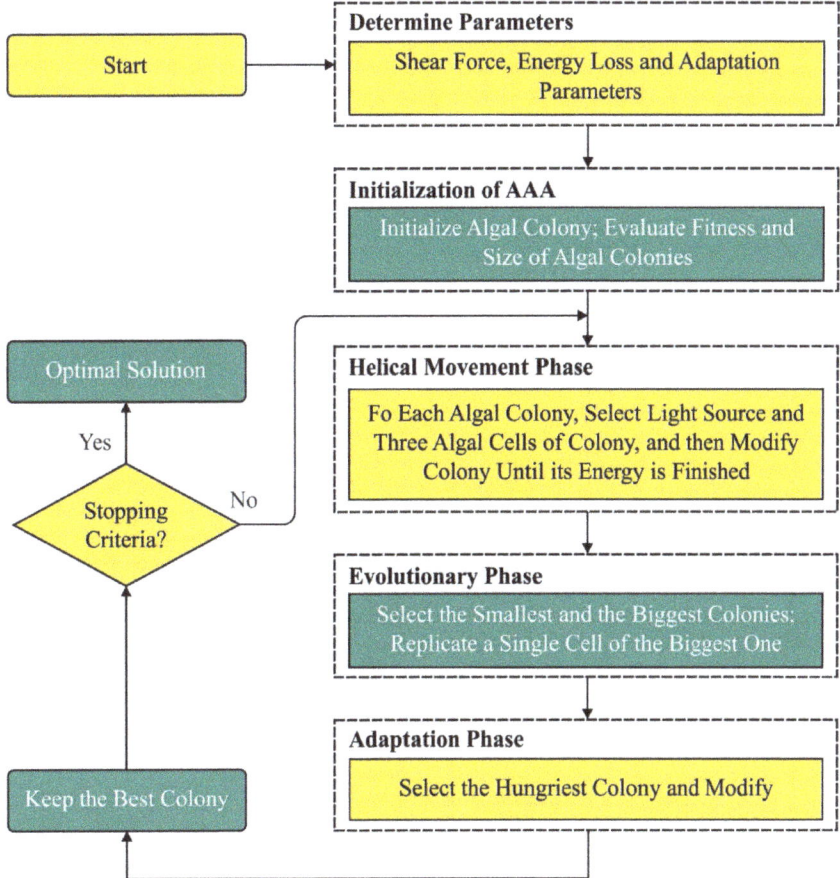

Figure 2. Flowchart of AAA.

The fitness function (FF) utilized in the presented AAA-FS system was planned to contain a balance between the amount of chosen features from all the solutions (minimal) and the classifier accuracy (maximal) reached by utilizing these chosen features; Equation (1) demonstrates the FF for evaluating the solution.

$$\text{Fitness} = \alpha \gamma_R(D) + \beta \frac{|R|}{|C|} \tag{1}$$

whereas $\gamma_R(D)$ implies the classifier error rate of provided classier (the K-nearest neighbor (KNN) technique is utilized). $|R|$ refers to the cardinality of the chosen subset and $|C|$ signifies the entire amount of features from the dataset. α, and β are two parameters equivalent to the significance of classifier quality and subset length. $\in [1, 0]$ and $\beta = 1 - \alpha$.

3.3. Process Involved in DAE Classification

When the features are selected, they can be fed into the DAE classification approach. An SAE is also known as DAE, which is the original deep network that comprises AE using several hidden layers and generates sensitive power [25]. For the classifier issue, the softmax classification is widely selected by the resultant layer. Next, the recreation of input instances with lesser error is a popular method. The trained set is provided by

$$(X, Y) = \left\{ \left(x^{(n)}, y^{(n)} \right) \middle| n = 1, 2, \ldots, N \right\} \tag{2}$$

In Equation (2), $y^{(n)}$ indicates a sample trademark $x^{(n)}$. The number of instances is represented as N. For each instance of trainable dataset $x^{(n)}$, the code encoded using $h^{(n)} = f\left(x^{(n)}\right)$ later decodes $h^{(n)}$ for reconstructing with $x?^{(n)} = g\left(h^{(n)}\right)$, and f and g are the encoder and decoder variables. This is resolved by diminishing errors among the inputs and reconstructions.

$$h^{(n)} = s\left(Wx^{(n)} + b \right) \tag{3}$$

$$x?^{(n)} = s\left(Wh^{(n)} + b? \right) \tag{4}$$

The sigmoid function is represented as $s(\cdot)$, a trained dataset using energy utilization as follows:

$$(\theta) = \frac{1}{N} \sum_{n=1}^{N} \frac{1}{2} \left\| x^{(n)} - x?^{(n)} \right\|_2^2 \tag{5}$$

Parameter absence in s and θ from linear conversion. The standard auto-counter is fundamental for the model of DAE that encodes $x^{(n)}$ to hidden notation $h^{(n1)}$ that is provided to the following input port of DAE. The recurrence of the process of the consequential layer for $l = 1, \ldots, L$, where L characterizes the number of hidden layers from DAE. The resultant layer is involved in the topmost hidden layer for monitoring the trained procedure. All the layers produce the best outcomes because of training the design parameter. Fine-tuning is commonly utilized from NN as a global optimization technique; hence, it enhances the DAE accuracy. The deviation of true labels from output values is decreased by the fine-tuning process. The representation of the square error cost depends on ideal samples stated in the following:

$$J\left(W, b; x^{(n)}, y^{(n)} \right) = \frac{1}{2} \left\| y^{(n)} - y?^{(n)} \right\|_2^2 \tag{6}$$

The energy function $J(W, b)$ forces the results to be nearer to the true label throughout the whole preparation and determines the procedure of fine-tuning.

$$J(W, b) = \frac{1}{N} \sum_{n=1}^{N} J\left(W, b; x^{(n)}, y^{(n)} \right) \tag{7}$$

From the equation, $(W, b) = \left\{ \left(W^{(l)}, b^{(l)} \right) | 1 = 1, 2, \ldots, L \right\}$ are encoder constraints of the whole layer. The initialization of the parameter is the initial phase of the DL technique, thus minimizes the constraint updating through energy function with a stochastic technique to complete the DAE tuning.

3.4. Hyperparameter Optimization

At the final stage, the IWO algorithm assists in attaining maximum outcome by the use of the IWO-based hyperparameter tuning process. The IWO algorithm is a bio-simulated mathematical optimization technique that mimics the natural behaviors of weeds [26]. IWO has lots of benefits, namely very strong robustness, simplicity of structure, and requiring fewer parameters; it is utilized for solving linear, nonlinear, general, and multidimensional optimization problems. It is assumed to be effective in converging to the most suitable solution using fundamental characteristics, namely growth, seeding, and competition in a weed colony.

Initial population: Firstly, the population is distributed in a random fashion through the D-dimension solution space, as weeds are created at random.

Reproduction: The number of seeds generated by all the weeds is estimated based on fitness. Every seed has a probability of reproducing; also, the reproduction rate ranges from higher to lesser depends upon an optimal-to-worse-fit seed. Then, the seed develops into a wild plant able to generate new units, and it is formulated as follows:

$$ot_n = \frac{f - f_{worst}}{f_{best} - f_{worst}} (S_{max} - S_{min}) + S_{min} \qquad (8)$$

In Equation (8), f denotes the fitness of the weed. f_{worst} and f_{best} indicate the worse and optimal fitness of the present population, correspondingly. S_{min} and S_{max} refer to the lesser and higher counts of seeds.

Spatial distribution: The seed generated is distributed in a random fashion through the D-dimension search space, usually an arbitrary number taking a mean corresponding to zero with a variance. By scattering the seeds arbitrarily, it can be guaranteed that they are nearer to the parental plant. However, the standard deviation (SD) (σ) would decrease from a primary value (σ_{init}) to last value (σ_{final}). Then, it equated to the following.

$$\sigma_{cur} = \frac{(iter_{max} - iter)^n}{(iter_{max})^n} \left(\sigma_{init} - \sigma_{final} \right) + \sigma_{final} \qquad (9)$$

In Equation (9), $iter_{max}$ denotes the maximal iteration count, σ_{cur} denotes the SD at present step, σ_{init} signifies the 1st SD, σ_{final} represents the final SD, and n indicates the modulation index.

Competitive exclusion: Here, the weed number in a colony exceeds the maximal population count with rapid reproductions. Next, the created seed is permitted for propagating to search spaces. Next, lower fitness weeds are detached for attaining the maximal population allowable from the colony. This process is continued till the maximal iteration or ending condition is accomplished. The weeds using the optimum fitness are preferred as the most suitable solution as illustrate in Algorithm 2.

Algorithm 2: Pseudocode of IWO technique

Begin {
Initializing population of weeds, set parameters;
Current_iteration = l;
While (Current_iteration< Max_iteration) do
{
Estimate an optimum and worse fitness from the populations
Estimate the SD std depends on iteration
For all the weeds w from the population W
{
Calculate the amount of seeds for w depending on their fitness
Choose the seeds in the possible solution nearby the parent weed w from a neighborhood with standard distribution containing mean = 0 and SD = std;
Increase seeds created to population W
If (| W | >Max_SizePopulation)
{
Sorting the population w based on its fitness
W = SelectBetter (weed, seed, Max_SizePopulation)
} End if
} End for
Current_iteration = Current_iteration+ 1;
} End while
} End

The IWO system develops a FF for achieving maximal classifier efficacy. It solves a positive integer for defining the best performance of candidate results.

$$\text{fitness}(x_i) = \text{Classifier Error Rate}(x_i) = \frac{\text{number of misclassified samples}}{\text{Total number of samples}} * 100 \quad (10)$$

4. Results and Discussion

The experimental validation of the ODAE-WPDC model is tested using a dataset from the Kaggle repository [27]. The dataset holds 4898 samples under a legitimate class and 6157 samples under a phishing class as depicted in Table 1. The results are examined in terms of distinct measures, such as accuracy, precision, recall, F-score, and Jaccard index. For effective detection performance, the values of these measures should be high.

Table 1. Dataset details.

Class Name	No. of URLs
Legitimate	4898
Phishing	6157
Total Number of URL's	11,055

Figure 3 illustrates the confusion matrices produced by the ODAE-WPDC model under distinct folds. On fold-1, the ODAE-WPDC model recognizes 4816 samples under the legitimate class and 6066 samples under the phishing class. On fold-3, the ODAE-WPDC approach recognizes 4839 samples under the legitimate class and 6128 samples under the phishing class. Additionally, on fold-4, the ODAE-WPDC system recognizes 4833 samples under the legitimate class and 6131 samples under the phishing class. At last, on fold-5, the ODAE-WPDC methodology recognizes 4846 samples under the legitimate class and 6129 samples under the phishing class.

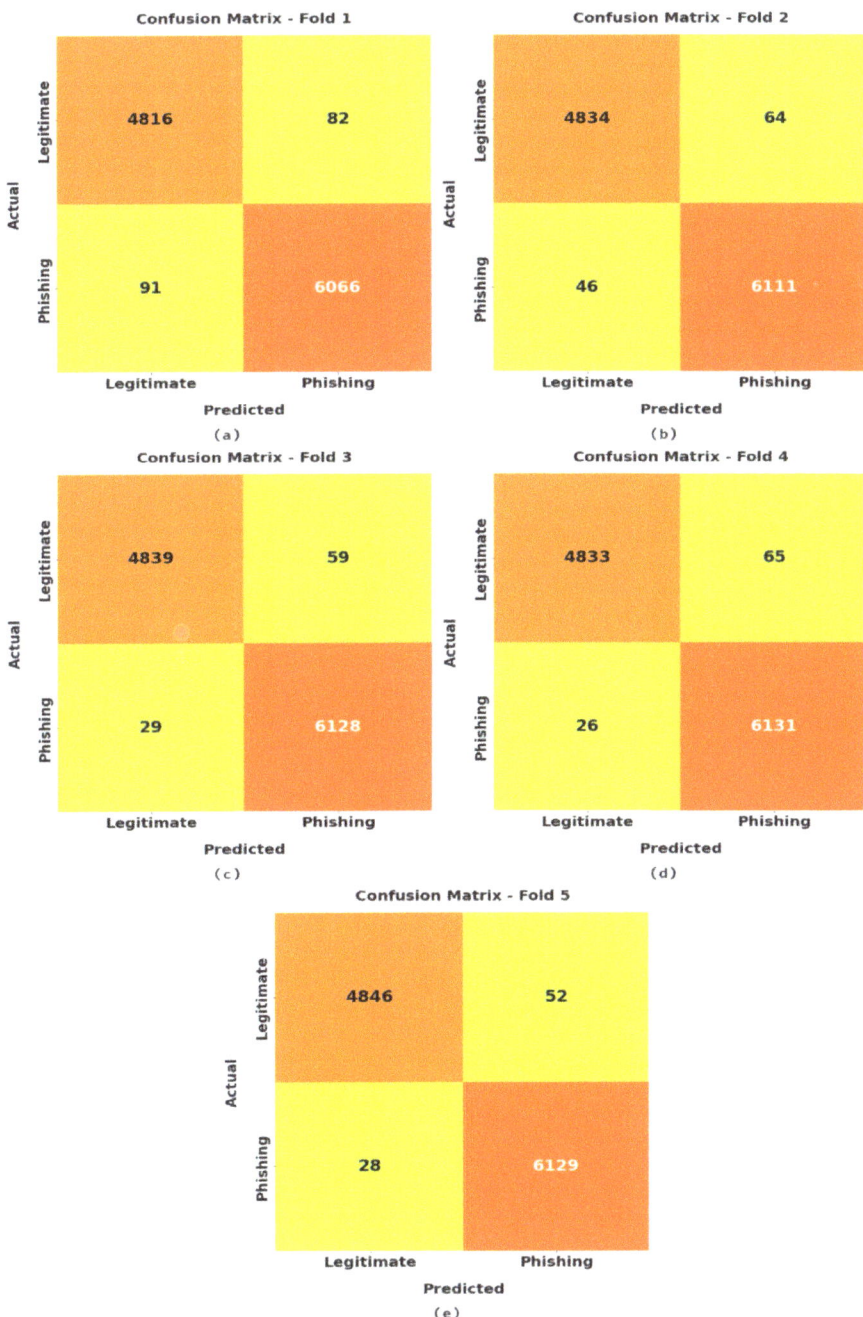

Figure 3. Confusion matrices of ODAE-WPDC approach: (**a**) Fold-1, (**b**) Fold-2, (**c**) Fold-3, (**d**) Fold-4, and (**e**) Fold-5.

Table 2 and Figure 4 illustrate a brief classification result of the ODAE-WPDC approach under varying folds. The experimental outcomes indicate that the ODAE-WPDC model has resulted in maximum performance under all folds. For sample, with fold-1, the ODAE-WPDC model offers an average $accu_y$ of 98.44%, $prec_n$ of 98.41%, $reca_l$ of 98.42%, F_{score} of 98.41%, and J_{index} of 96.88%. Simultaneously, with fold-2, the ODAE-WPDC approach has an accessible average $accu_y$ of 99%, $prec_n$ of 99.01%, $reca_l$ of 98.97%, F_{score} of 98.99%, and J_{index} of 98%. Concurrently, with fold-3, the ODAE-WPDC method has an obtainable average $accu_y$ of 99.20%, $prec_n$ of 99.23%, $reca_l$ of 99.16%, F_{score} of 99.19%, and J_{index} of 98.40%. Along with that, with fold-4, the ODAE-WPDC system presents an average $accu_y$ of 99.18%, $prec_n$ of 99.21%, $reca_l$ of 99.13%, F_{score} of 99.17%, and J_{index} of 98.34%. At last, with fold-5, the ODAE-WPDC approach has an obtainable average $accu_y$ of 99.28%, $prec_n$ of 99.29%, $reca_l$ of 99.24%, F_{score} of 99.27%, and J_{index} of 98.54%.

Table 2. Result analysis of ODAE-WPDC approach with various measures and folds.

Class Labels	Accuracy	Precision	Recall	F-Score	Jaccard Index
Fold 1					
legitimate	98.44	98.15	98.33	98.24	96.53
phishing	98.44	98.67	98.52	98.59	97.23
Average	**98.44**	**98.41**	**98.42**	**98.41**	**96.88**
Fold 2					
legitimate	99.00	99.06	98.69	98.88	97.78
phishing	99.00	98.96	99.25	99.11	98.23
Average	**99.00**	**99.01**	**98.97**	**98.99**	**98.00**
Fold 3					
legitimate	99.20	99.40	98.80	99.10	98.21
phishing	99.20	99.05	99.53	99.29	98.58
Average	**99.20**	**99.23**	**99.16**	**99.19**	**98.40**
Fold 4					
legitimate	99.18	99.46	98.67	99.07	98.15
phishing	99.18	98.95	99.58	99.26	98.54
Average	**99.18**	**99.21**	**99.13**	**99.17**	**98.34**
Fold 5					
legitimate	99.28	99.43	98.94	99.18	98.38
phishing	99.28	99.16	99.55	99.35	98.71
Average	**99.28**	**99.29**	**99.24**	**99.27**	**98.54**

Figure 5 provides an average $accu_y$ inspection of the ODAE-WPDC methodology under distinct folds. The figure implies that the ODAE-WPDC model has gained effectual outcomes under every fold. For instance, with fold-1, the ODAE-WPDC model has obtained an average $accu_y$ of 98.44%. Additionally, with fold-2, the ODAE-WPDC approach has reached an average $accu_y$ of 99%. With fold-3, the ODAE-WPDC system has attained an average $accu_y$ of 99.20%. In addition, with fold-4, the ODAE-WPDC approach has obtained an average $accu_y$ of 99.18%. At last, with fold-5, the ODAE-WPDC methodology has gained an average $accu_y$ of 99.28%.

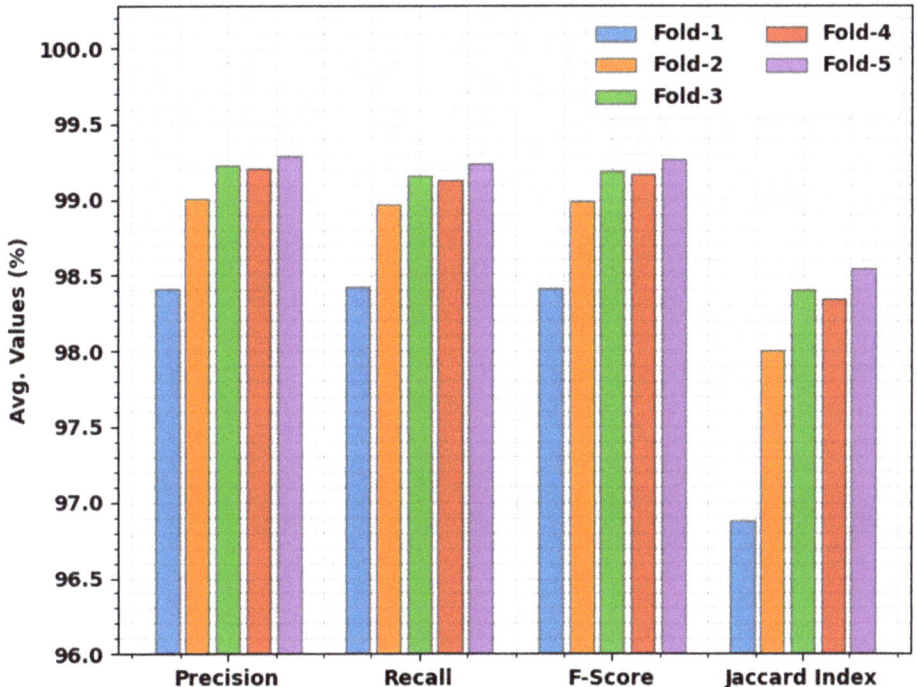

Figure 4. Average analysis of ODAE-WPDC approach with various measures and folds.

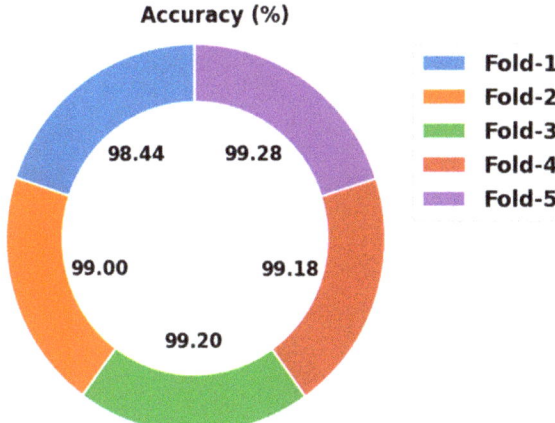

Figure 5. Average accuracy analysis of ODAE-WPDC approach with distinct folds.

The training accuracy (TA) and validation accuracy (VA) attained by the ODAE-WPDC system on test dataset is demonstrated in Figure 6. The experimental outcomes imply that the ODAE-WPDC algorithm has gained maximal values of TA and VA. Specifically, the VA seems to be higher than TA.

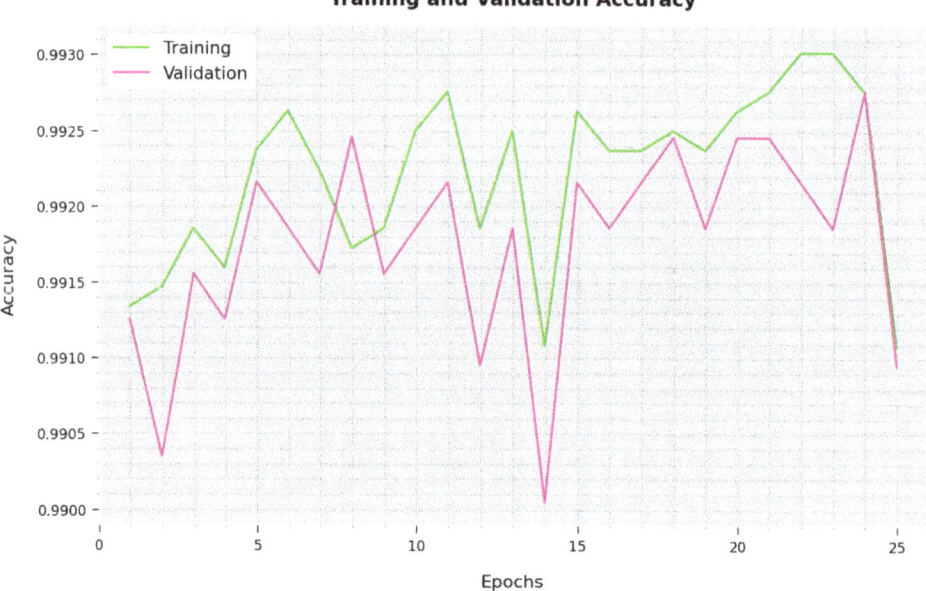

Figure 6. TA and VA analysis of ODAE-WPDC approach.

The training loss (TL) and validation loss (VL) achieved by the ODAE-WPDC approach on test dataset are established in Figure 7. The experimental outcomes infer that the ODAE-WPDC system has accomplished the least values of TL and VL. Specifically, the VL seems to be lower than TL.

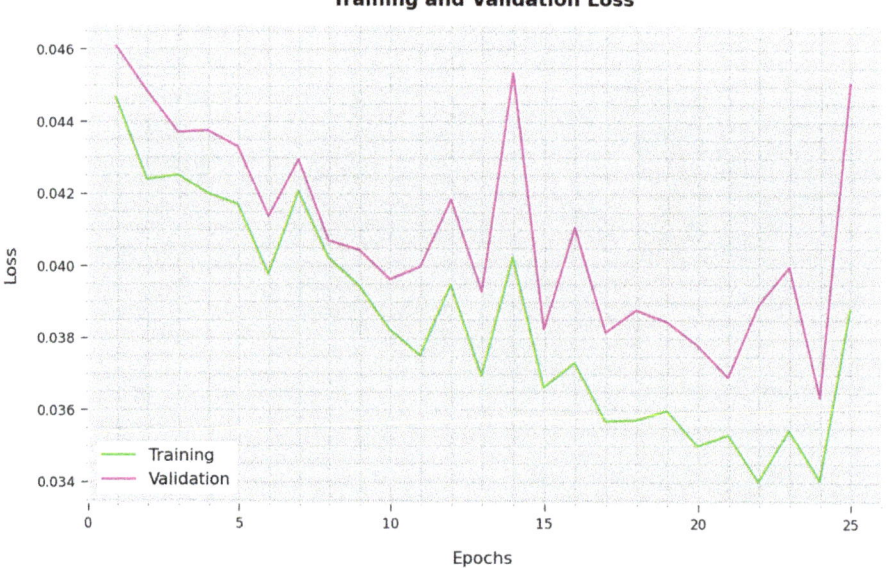

Figure 7. TL and VL analysis of ODAE-WPDC approach.

Finally, a detailed comparative study of the algorithm with other algorithms on WS phishing detection is given in Table 3 [28,29]. The experimental findings state that the ODAE-WPDC methodology has gained maximal performance over the other models.

Table 3. Comparative analysis of ODAE-WPDC approach with recent algorithms.

Methods	Accuracy	Precision	Recall	F-Score
ODAE-WPDC	99.28	99.29	99.24	99.27
DL-SGD	94.64	94.97	95.17	94.50
DL-RMSProp	92.84	93.77	95.34	95.52
DL-Adam	94.69	94.87	95.93	95.27
SI-BBA	94.93	94.59	94.84	94.78
PDGAN	94.12	94.96	94.02	92.21
NIOSELM	93.40	94.65	94.66	90.86
MLP-SL	87.80	88.75	87.41	74.75
SVM-SL	83.37	87.22	88.54	75.21

Figure 8 illustrates a comparative $prec_n$ and $reca_l$ inspection of the ODAE-WPDC system with recent models. The figure implies that the ODAE-WPDC approach has resulted in enhanced performance in terms of $prec_n$ and $reca_l$. With regard to $prec_n$, the ODAE-WPDC system has obtained improved $prec_n$ of 99.29%, whereas the DL-SGD, DL-RMSProp, DL-Adam, SI-BBA, PDGAN, and NIOSELM models have gained $prec_n$ of 94.97%, 93.77%, 94.87%, 94.59%, 94.96%, and 94.65%, respectively. In addition, in terms of $reca_l$, the ODAE-WPDC model has obtained higher $reca_l$ of 99.24% whereas the DL-SGD, DL-RMSProp, DL-Adam, SI-BBA, PDGAN, and NIOSELM methods have achieved $reca_l$ of 95.17%, 95.34%, 95.93%, 94.84%, 94.02%, and 94.66%, correspondingly.

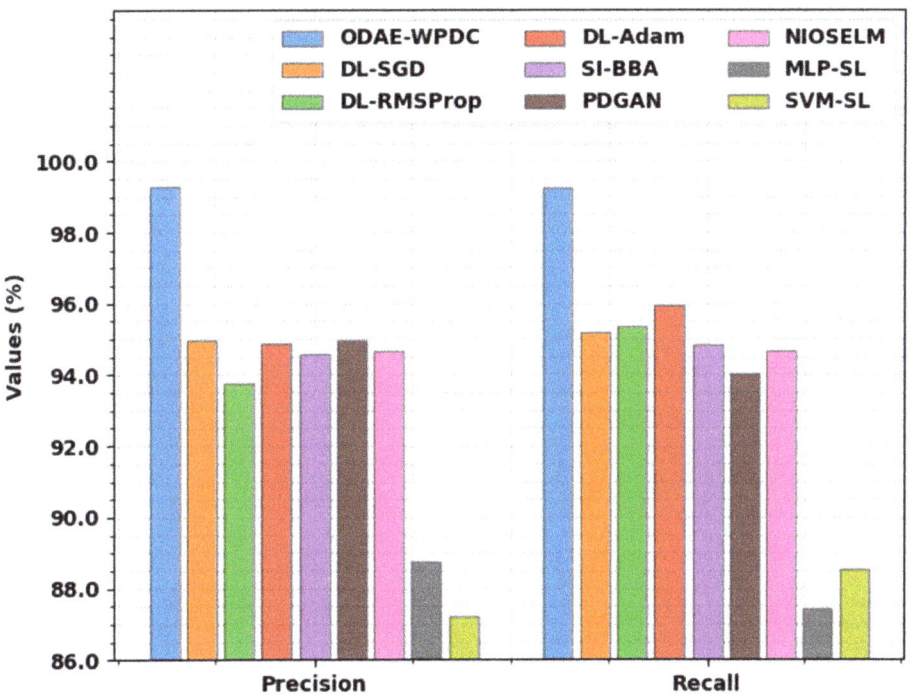

Figure 8. $Prec_n$ and $reca_l$ analysis of ODAE-WPDC approach with existing methodologies.

Figure 9 showcases a comparative $accu_y$ and F_{score} examination of the ODAE-WPDC methodology with recent techniques. The figure exposes that the ODAE-WPDC system has resulted in enhanced performance with regard to $accu_y$ and F_{score}. Interms of $accu_y$, the ODAE-WPDC system has obtained enhanced $accu_y$ of 99.28%, whereas the DL-SGD, DL-RMSProp, DL-Adam, SI-BBA, PDGAN, and NIOSELM algorithms have reached $accu_y$ of 94.64%, 92.84%, 94.69%, 94.93%, 94.12%, and 93.40%, correspondingly. With regard to F_{score}, the ODAE-WPDC system has obtained higher F_{score} of 99.27%, whereas the DL-SGD, DL-RMSProp, DL-Adam, SI-BBA, PDGAN, and NIOSELM systems have reached F_{score} of 94.50%, 95.52%, 95.27%, 94.78%, 92.21%, and 90.86%, correspondingly.

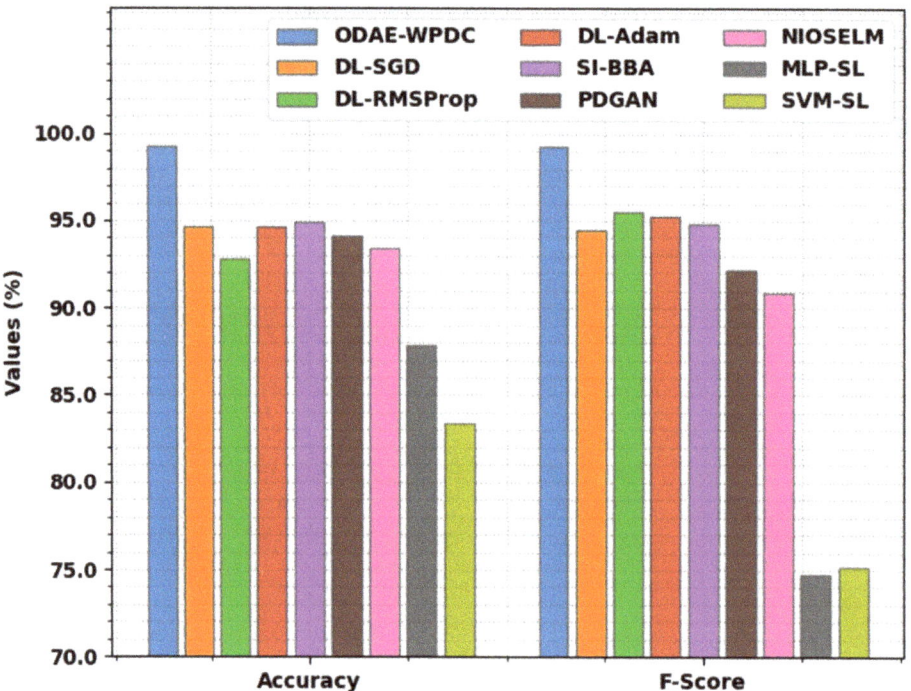

Figure 9. $Accu_y$ and F_{score} analysis of ODAE-WPDC approach with existing methodologies.

From the detailed results and discussion, it is clear that the ODAE-WPDC model has shown effectual phishing WS detection and classification performance.

5. Conclusions

In this study, a novel ODAE-WPDC model was introduced for the recognition and classification of WS phishing to accomplish cybersecurity. At the primary stage, the proposed ODAE-WPDC model applies input data pre-processing at the initial stage to get rid of missing values in the dataset. This is followed by feature extraction, and the AAA based FS process is utilized. Finally, the IWO with the DAE model is applied for the classification process, where the IWO algorithm assists in attaining maximum outcome. The performance validation of the ODAE-WPDC model is tested utilizing the benchmark Kaggle repository. The experimental findings confirm the better performance of the ODAE-WPDC model over recent DL models. Thus, the presented ODAE-WPDC model can be utilized for security in the digital era. In future, the presented ODAE-WPDC model can be extended to the design of a weighted ensemble voting process.

6. Limitations and Future Scope

In future, we would like to verify the performance of the proposed model on other datasets and experiments with more novel features and their influence. A major drawback of our model is that it cannot identify whether the URL is active or not; therefore, it is essential to verify whether the URL is active or not before detection for ensuring the detection performance. At the same time, the computational complexity of the proposed model can be analyzed in future. Additionally, few attackers utilize URLs that are not impersonations of other websites, and such URLs will not be identified. In addition, the robust nature of the proposed model can be tested against adversarial attacks which are commonly utilized by malicious parties. In the future, we plan to exploit novel models for automatic extraction of other features to detect phishing sites, such as web code features, web text features, and web icon features.

Author Contributions: Conceptualization, H.A.; Investigation, S.S.A. and M.M.; Methodology, H.A. and S.S.A.; Project administration, M.A.D.; Resources, F.S.A.; Software, F.S.A., I.A.-T. and M.M.; Supervision, I.A.-T.; Validation, K.A.A. and A.S.A.A.; Writing—original draft, H.A., K.A.A. and A.S.A.A.; Writing—review & editing, K.A.A., A.S.A.A. and M.A.D. All authors have read and agreed to the published version of the manuscript.

Funding: The authors extend their appreciation to the Deanship of Scientific Research at King Khalid University for funding this work through Large Groups Project under grant number (61/43). Princess Nourah bint Abdulrahman University Researchers Supporting Project number (PNURSP2022R319), Princess Nourah bint Abdulrahman University, Riyadh, Saudi Arabia. The authors would like to thank the Deanship of Scientific Research at Umm Al-Qura University for supporting this work by Grant Code: (22UQU4210118DSR09).

Institutional Review Board Statement: Not applicable.

Informed Consent Statement: Not applicable.

Data Availability Statement: Data sharing not applicable to this article as no datasets were generated during the current study.

Conflicts of Interest: The authors declare that they have no conflict of interest. The manuscript was written with contributions of all authors. All authors have approved the final version of the manuscript.

Ethics Approval: This article does not contain any studies with human participants performed by any of the authors.

References

1. Shahrivari, V.; Darabi, M.M.; Izadi, M. Phishing Detection Using Machine Learning Techniques. *arXiv* **2020**, arXiv:2009.11116.
2. Al-Qarafi, A.; Alrowais, F.; Alotaibi, S.S.; Nemri, N.; Al-Wesabi, F.N.; Al Duhayyim, M.; Marzouk, R.; Othman, M.; Al-Shabi, M. Optimal Machine Learning Based Privacy Preserving Blockchain Assisted Internet of Things with Smart Cities Environment. *Appl. Sci.* **2022**, *12*, 5893. [CrossRef]
3. Crawford, M.; Khoshgoftaar, T.M.; Prusa, J.D.; Richter, A.N.; Al Najada, H. Survey of review spam detection using machine learning techniques. *J. Big Data* **2015**, *2*, 23. [CrossRef]
4. Nugraha, A.F.; Tama, D.A.; Istiqomah, D.A.; Ramadhani, S.T.A.; Kusuma, B.N.; Windarni, V.A. Feature Selection Technique for improving classification performance in the web-phishing detection process. *Conf. Ser.* **2022**, *4*, 25–31. [CrossRef]
5. Varshney, G.; Misra, M.; Atrey, P.K. A survey and classification of web phishing detection schemes. *Secur. Commun. Netw.* **2016**, *9*, 6266–6284. [CrossRef]
6. Adebowale, M.A.; Lwin, K.T.; Hossain, M.A. Intelligent phishing detection scheme using deep learning algorithms. *J. Enterp. Inf. Manag.* **2020**. [CrossRef]
7. Jain, A.K.; Gupta, B.B. A machine learning based approach for phishing detection using hyperlinks information. *J. Ambient Intell. Humaniz. Comput.* **2019**, *10*, 2015–2028. [CrossRef]
8. Alam, T.M.; Shaukat, K.; Hameed, I.A.; Khan, W.A.; Sarwar, M.U.; Iqbal, F.; Luo, S. A novel framework for prognostic factors identification of malignant mesothelioma through association rule mining. *Biomed. Signal Process. Control.* **2021**, *68*, 102726. [CrossRef]
9. Shaukat, K.; Luo, S.; Varadharajan, V.; Hameed, I.A.; Chen, S.; Liu, D.; Li, J. Performance comparison and current challenges of using machine learning techniques in cybersecurity. *Energies* **2020**, *13*, 2509. [CrossRef]

10. Shaukat, K.; Luo, S.; Varadharajan, V.; Hameed, I.A.; Xu, M. A survey on machine learning techniques for cyber security in the last decade. *IEEE Access* **2020**, *8*, 222310–222354. [CrossRef]
11. Yi, P.; Guan, Y.; Zou, F.; Yao, Y.; Wang, W.; Zhu, T. Web phishing detection using a deep learning framework. *Wirel. Commun. Mob. Comput.* **2018**, *2018*, 4678746. [CrossRef]
12. Wei, W.; Ke, Q.; Nowak, J.; Korytkowski, M.; Scherer, R.; Woźniak, M. Accurate and fast URL phishing detector: A convolutional neural network approach. *Comput. Netw.* **2020**, *178*, 107275. [CrossRef]
13. Do, N.Q.; Selamat, A.; Krejcar, O.; Herrera-Viedma, E.; Fujita, H. Deep Learning for Phishing Detection: Taxonomy, Current Challenges and Future Directions. *IEEE Access* **2022**. [CrossRef]
14. Lakshmi, L.; Reddy, M.P.; Santhaiah, C.; Reddy, U.J. Smart phishing detection in web pages using supervised deep learning classification and optimization technique adam. *Wirel. Pers. Commun.* **2021**, *118*, 3549–3564. [CrossRef]
15. Odeh, A.; Keshta, I.; Abdelfattah, E. Machine learningtechniquesfor detection of website phishing: A review for promises and challenges. In Proceedings of the 2021 IEEE 11th Annual Computing and Communication Workshop and Conference (CCWC), Las Vegas, NV, USA, 27–30 January 2021; pp. 0813–0818.
16. Makkar, A.; Kumar, N. An efficient deep learning-based scheme for web spam detection in IoT environment. *Future Gener. Comput. Syst.* **2020**, *108*, 467–487. [CrossRef]
17. Sahingoz, O.K.; Buber, E.; Demir, O.; Diri, B. Machine learning based phishing detection from URLs. *Expert Syst. Appl.* **2019**, *117*, 345–357. [CrossRef]
18. Lee, J.; Ye, P.; Liu, R.; Divakaran, D.M.; Chan, M.C. Building robust phishing detection system: An empirical analysis. *NDSS MADWeb* 2020. [CrossRef]
19. Ghaleb, F.A.; Alsaedi, M.; Saeed, F.; Ahmad, J.; Alasli, M. Cyber Threat Intelligence-Based Malicious URL Detection Model Using Ensemble Learning. *Sensors* **2022**, *22*, 3373.
20. Kondracki, B.; Azad, B.A.; Starov, O.; Nikiforakis, N. Catching Transparent Phish: Analyzing and Detecting MITM Phishing Toolkits. In Proceedings of the 2021 ACM SIGSAC Conference on Computer and Communications Security 2021, Virtual Event, Korea, 15–19 November 2021; pp. 36–50.
21. Noah, N.; Tayachew, A.; Ryan, S.; Das, S. Poster: PhisherCop-An Automated Tool Using ML Classifiers for Phishing Detection. In Proceedings of the 43rd IEEE Symposium on Security and Privacy (IEEE S&P 2022), San Francisco, CA, USA, 23–26 May 2022.
22. Zhang, P.; Oest, A.; Cho, H.; Sun, Z.; Johnson, R.C.; Wardman, B.; Sarker, S.; Kapravelos, A.; Bao, T.; Wang, R.; et al. Crawlphish: Large-scale analysis of client-side cloaking techniques in phishing. In Proceedings of the 2021 IEEE Symposium on Security and Privacy (SP), San Francisco, CA, USA, 24–27 May 2021; pp. 1109–1124.
23. Uymaz, S.A.; Tezel, G.; Yel, E. Artificial algae algorithm (AAA) for nonlinear global optimization. *Appl. Soft Comput.* **2015**, *31*, 153–171. [CrossRef]
24. Kocer, H.G.; Uymaz, S.A. A Modified Artificial Algae Algorithm For Large Scale Global Optimization Problems. *Int. J. Intell. Syst. Appl. Eng.* **2018**, *6*, 306–310. [CrossRef]
25. Raja, P.S. Brain tumor classification using a hybrid deep autoencoder with Bayesian fuzzy clustering-based segmentation approach. *Biocybern. Biomed. Eng.* **2020**, *40*, 440–453. [CrossRef]
26. Srinivas, S.T.P. Application of improved invasive weed optimization technique for optimally setting directional overcurrent relays in power systems. *Appl. Soft Comput.* **2019**, *79*, 1–13.
27. Available online: https://www.kaggle.com/akashkr/phishing-url-eda-and-modelling/data (accessed on 12 March 2022).
28. Rendall, K.; Nisioti, A.; Mylonas, A. Towards a multi-layered phishing detection. *Sensors* **2020**, *20*, 4540. [CrossRef] [PubMed]
29. Kumar, P.P.; Jaya, T.; Rajendran, V. SI-BBA–A novel phishing website detection based on Swarm intelligence with deep learning. *Mater. Today Proc.* **2021**, *in press*.

Article

Factors Affecting Cybersecurity Awareness among University Students

Mohammed A. Alqahtani

Department of Computer Information Systems, College of Computer Science and Information Technology, Imam Abdulrahman Bin Faisal University, P.O. Box 1982, Dammam 31441, Saudi Arabia; maqhtani@iau.edu.sa; Tel.: +966-50-584-8693

Abstract: One of the essential stages in increasing cyber security is implementing an effective security awareness program. This work studies the present level of security knowledge among Imam Abdulrahman Bin Faisal University college students. A module was created to assist the students in becoming more informed. The main contribution of this work is an assessment of cybersecurity awareness among the university students based on three essential aspects: password security, browser security, and social media. Numerous questions were designed and sent to them to evaluate their awareness. The current survey received as many as 450 responses with their answers. Various statistical analyses were applied to the responses, including the validity and reliability test, feasibility test of a variable, correlation test, multicollinearity test, multiple regression, and heteroskedasticity test, carried out using SPSS. Furthermore, a multiple linear regression model and coefficient of determination, a hypothesis test, ANOVA test, and a partial test using ANOVA were also carried out. The hypothesis investigated here concerns password security, browser security, and social media. The results of partial hypothesis testing using a t-test showed that the password security variable significantly affects cybersecurity awareness (p-value = 0.0001). The regression coefficient of the password security variable in the multiple linear regression model was found to have a beta value of 0.147. In addition, the browser security variable significantly affects awareness, with a p-value = 0.0001. The regression coefficient of the password security variable had a beta value of 0.188. The social media activities variable significantly affects cybersecurity awareness (p-value = 0.0001). The regression coefficient of the social media activities variable had a beta value of 0.241. Based on the research conducted, it is concluded that knowledge of password security, browser security, and social media activities significantly influences cybersecurity awareness in students. Overall, students have realized the importance of cybersecurity awareness.

Keywords: cybersecurity; password security; browser security; social media; ANOVA; SPSS

Citation: Alqahtani, M.A. Factors Affecting Cybersecurity Awareness among University Students. *Appl. Sci.* 2022, 12, 2589. https://doi.org/10.3390/app12052589

Academic Editor: Suhuai Luo

Received: 14 January 2022
Accepted: 24 February 2022
Published: 2 March 2022

Publisher's Note: MDPI stays neutral with regard to jurisdictional claims in published maps and institutional affiliations.

Copyright: © 2022 by the author. Licensee MDPI, Basel, Switzerland. This article is an open access article distributed under the terms and conditions of the Creative Commons Attribution (CC BY) license (https://creativecommons.org/licenses/by/4.0/).

1. Introduction

The rapid advancement of contemporary technology has altered our life, particularly the methods of communication utilized to provide information and interact with people. Everywhere in the world, several networking techniques have been developed. In response, both the social and commercial spheres have begun to offer additional services and embrace new technologies to give customers data access anywhere at any time and from any place. The primary motivation for automation operations and innovation is to help the diverse variety of customers, fast-expanding due to increased Internet usage [1].

As a result, the number of hackers and organized cybercrime gangs has skyrocketed. These cybercriminals have been exploring new ways to carry out cyber-attacks. The primary motivation for cyber criminals seems to be the personal benefit gained by acquiring sensitive information and retaining it for blackmail. Hackers may also benefit by supplying private information to competition on the dark web, making cyberspace insecure and presenting significant threats to businesses and customers. As a result, cyber security breaches have become a severe danger to world security and the economy, compromising essential infrastructure and wreaking havoc on company performance, resulting in significant cognitive property loss [2].

Cyber security should be emphasized throughout a business, not only in IT [3,4]. The global trend in cyber security issues is primarily due to the fact that most personnel do not adequately adhere to the specific security regulations and instructions supplied in the workplace. People represent a significant security vulnerability that exposes organizational assets to external and internal attackers; they are the weakest link [5,6]. The human factor is the most common way for hackers to get unauthorized access to vital systems in a protected environment [7,8]. As a result, implementing proactive cyber security measures is essential, particularly in developed nations where the Internet is a fundamental part of everyone's life, such as Saudi Arabia. During 2007–2009, the ratio of Internet users improved significantly, rising from 43 percent to 51 percent. By 2018, the rate of Internet users was around 19% [9–13].

The Kingdom of Saudi Arabia has expanded its investment in boosting its security infrastructure, according to the Telecommunications Act of June 2001. Therefore, it is vital to strengthen and manage the telecommunications industry [14]. It was for this purpose that the Communications and Information Technology Commission (CITC) was established to supervise Internet regulation and network traffic. In addition, the Computer Emergency Response Team (CERT) was established in 2006 to provide organizations with the knowledge and skills needed to identify and prevent cyber-attacks through teaching and training activities [14]. As a result of the incorporation of cyber security in Saudi Vision 2030, the Kingdom's standing in the sphere of technological advancement has rapidly increased in industrialized nations [15].

Cyber security awareness has received insufficient attention given the fast rise in cyber dangers and cybercrime in the Kingdom. The importance of security has not been examined among college students [16]. Since hacking attacks of data systems in schools and colleges are becoming more widespread, students must understand the implications and problems of cyber security and cybercrime. There is an urgent need to design a comprehensive training program to raise awareness of the consequences of personal information loss, which may undermine student confidence and institutional credibility [17–20].

It is the most basic and widely used safeguarding system. The first stage in obtaining safe access is to provide the user's login and passcode. The main issue with passcodes is that we can forget them. As a result, we frequently search for ways to remember them, such as writing them in a notebook, using toolkits to organize and save passcodes (passcode managers or passcode keepers), or by using "Cookies", which keep the user ID and passcode (hashed) to access the website. Another disadvantage of this method is that passcodes could be stolen or decrypted [21–23].

Increased Web Browser Attack—The services supplied by developing technologies are often delivered through web pages. Web browsers are undoubtedly the most widely adopted apps, allowing consumers to undertake a wide range of tasks that attach them to an outside world. As a result, Internet browsers are becoming an immensely crucial tool for millions of Internet users nowadays. Unfortunately, like every piece of software, Internet browsers have a variety of flaws [24,25]. The hackers use such defects to gain control of the user's computer, hack the customer's data, delete files and use the stolen machine to target other systems. According to an Osterman Research report [26], 11 million virus variants had been detected by 2008, with 90 percent of these viruses originating from covert downloads from prominent and often credible locations. If Internet browser consumers do not identify a rogue website, they risk disclosing personal details to a potentially hazardous party. Our survey focuses on active security indicators since active security measures are directly tied to automatic hacking identification in Internet browsers.

Social media are electronic connections (such as social networking websites and microblogging platforms) wherein people build online groups to exchange information, thoughts, or private messages. Privacy is defined as "independence from unapproved access" and the capacity to govern one's data since only those whom the possessor desires to have access to them are permitted to use them. This encompasses both authorities with respect to what material is visible on social media and who may see it. Social media use is widespread across general culture and on school campuses. The growing reputation of social media websites has given rise to a new range of concerns and problems that now confront us in the twenty-first century. Since digital networks are their primary modes of communication, modern college youth are at a higher risk of image injury or loss of money than previous generations. As a result, we conducted an experimental evaluation of students' cyber security understanding and activities, concentrating on the most frequent security vulnerabilities facing the overall ecosystem. Some of the key contributions are listed below:

- A cybersecurity awareness assessment was carried out with the college students of Imam Abdulrahman Bin Faisal University based on a few key issues, such as password security, browser security, and social media;
- An investigation was conducted to analyze the students' level of knowledge about security concerns, especially cybercrime;
- Statistical analysis was performed and, based on numerous tests, the results were estimated;
- The data was collected through the survey questionnaires and, based on the responses, SPSS and ANOVA tools were utilized to make the analysis.

The remainder of this paper is organized as follows: Section 2 contains a literature review, Section 3 discusses the research methodology, Section 4 presents the results which were subject to many tests, and Section 5 consists of a discussion of the results, after which the paper is concluded.

2. Literature Review

This section highlights previous findings undertaken to measure individual cyber security awareness levels. It should be noted, however, that only a few studies have aimed to determine the level of cyber security awareness among students and the associated significant challenges.

2.1. Cybersecurity Awareness

Cyber security awareness and training programs might be an element of national security and they should be well-structured to provide people with a basic grasp of cyber security. Al-Janabi and Al-Shourbaji [27] studied Middle Eastern security awareness, concentrating on school environments and examining cyber security within teaching faculties, among researchers and students. The authors revealed that participants in the Middle East do not have a basic understanding of the importance of cyber security. As a result, all users and administrators should be given safety awareness and training as part of an overall safety management strategy. Ahmed et al. [28] investigated cyber security recognition in the Bangladeshi population and evaluated the acquired data using Pearson's chi-squared test [29]. According to these findings, governments fail to offer the necessary guidelines and awareness initiatives. As a result, most individuals are uninformed about cybercrime and cyber security risks.

Most academic organizations' business strategies do not incorporate active cyber security awareness and training initiatives. Slusky and Partow-Navid [30] examined the results of security testing for a group of pupils at California State University, Los Angeles, USA, College of Business and Economics. They discovered that the main issue with cyber security awareness is not a lack of essential knowledge, as one might think; instead, it is the methods pupils use when coping with these issues in real-world situations. The results were meant to aid the institution in developing its curriculum, which included extra information security training.

2.2. Students' Knowledge

Alotaibi et al. [31] investigated the level of cyber security knowledge among college students. Their investigation revealed that cyber security awareness in Saudi university students is poor since most students were unaware of their data protection. Correspondingly, Senthilkumar and Easwaramoorthy [32] studied university students in Tamil Nadu's key towns to examine their attentiveness to cyber security. They concentrated on particular cyber security risks, such as malware-infected websites, phishing, and the theft of personal information. According to their findings, students' awareness of cyber security and related threat problems was above average, with 70% of respondents having a basic understanding of cyber security dangers. As a result, the authors proposed that security awareness and training programs be launched at a higher level to guarantee that learners can protect their data from cyber-attacks.

Moallem [33] investigated students' opinions regarding cyber security in California's Silicon Valley. Since learners' behavior is variable, the author assessed the cyber security level in the largest and most influential technology environment. Even when they were aware that their actions were being seen and tracked, college students were unaware that their data was not safely transported across university systems. As a result, institutions should offer training regularly to influence students' behavior and increase their awareness of the basics of cyber security and cyber threats [34]. In addition, Moallem [35] discussed the level of security awareness and theft mindfulness. Fraudsters may not always utilize the same cyber-attacks, according to the author.

Instead, they switch between phishing scams, network traffic, and other methods of deceit. As a result, it is vital to develop a plan to raise cyber security awareness and secure critical data. Zwilling et al. [36] investigated the relationship between cyber security awareness, comprehension, and activity with protection product users in Turkey, Israel, Poland, and Slovenia. The findings showed that although familiar users possessed adequate cyber security awareness, it was seldom used in practice. Preliminary research results at Nigerian institutions revealed that students possessed basic cyber security knowledge but were unsure how to secure their information [37]. Al said et al. [38] aimed to measure end-user awareness of phishing attempts, emphasizing understanding and reactions to cyber security risks. Several writers have demonstrated experimentally that consumers with limited information may be readily duped [39–41].

2.3. Password Security

As a result of the increasing number of passcodes to recall, users either choose simple but default passcodes [42] or reprocess their possibly strong passcode [43–45], occasionally with slight adjustments or merely by pursuing predetermined building activities [46]. According to one survey, 80% of users retained their existing passcodes wherever feasible whereas 16% changed them to one of the passcodes they had been using on some other website, while 4% used passcodes that were more or less fresh [47]. One of the most severe security issues caused by passcode repetition arises in the context of data theft. Consumers are warned that when a website they use is hacked by the European Union's General Data Protection Regulation (GDPR), they are strongly advised to change their passcodes. Even if the user accomplishes this, however, other identities secured with the same credentials are also vulnerable. It has been claimed that about eight billion records were released in different data thefts in the first nine months of 2019 alone [48], possibly opening the gates to many more companies, some of which are vital for the user or the community. According to an American study of users of various backgrounds and ages [49], consumers have a skewed knowledge of safety features. According to the findings of this study, respondents overvalued the safety enhancement provided by adding digits to their passcodes while underestimating the reliability of employing keyboard rhythms and frequent terms. In a poll conducted by [50], individuals not only overvalued the enhanced safety of attaching characters or numbers at the end of passcodes but often reused passcodes or portions of passcodes. Another prevalent occurrence is the incorporation of private details into user-chosen passcodes.

In research by [51], which examined over 20 million chunks of information from Chinese users, it was discovered that experts used passcodes with a standard size of 8–11 characters, whereas pupils used shorter passcodes. In terms of passcode protection, they found that more than half of consumers had passcodes that merely consisted of numbers and less than a third contained a mix of special typescripts. The research also indicated that more than 12 percent of corporate users utilize their birthdays and cell phone numbers in their passcodes, while 11.5 percent use their username and e-mail to generate their passcodes. Another study of Chinese passcodes [52] found that the usage of Chinese characters, alone or in conjunction with dates and numerals, accounted for 26% of the whole, suggesting that the use of English alphabets is prevalent. It was also noted that genuine Chinese character logins were created using only two to four Chinese characters.

2.4. Social Media

"Users' comprehension of dangers and how to defend themselves against computer hackers is consequently crucial in modern existence", writes [31]. As per a Pew Research Centre [53] study, 69 percent of US people use Facebook and 73 percent use YouTube. Instagram, Pinterest, Snapchat, LinkedIn, Twitter, Reddit, and WhatsApp have much smaller percentages of users. Eighty percent of people aged 18–24 use at least one social networking site. Specifically, 94% use YouTube, 81% use Facebook, 78% use Snapchat, 71% use Instagram, and 45% use Twitter. In Richardson's [54] (2017) study, 90 percent of respondents used Facebook and Snapchat, while 70 percent used Instagram. Most users check their profiles many times every day [53] (Pew Research Center, 2019). Knight-McCord [55] (2016) researched which social networking sites were most popular among students. They administered a survey to 363 pupils online and in person. Previous research discovered that Instagram was the most popular site, with Snapchat and Facebook second. LinkedIn and Pinterest, on the other hand, were less popular. According to Sharma, Jain, and Tiwari [56], 84 percent of students believe that posting personal information on social networking sites (SNS) is harmful. Moallem [33] (2018) researched cyber security knowledge among students at two California State universities in Silicon Valley.

3. Materials and Methods

A survey approach was utilized to meet the study's goals and collect qualitative data on the degree of cyber security awareness among Imam Abdulrahman Bin Faisal University students. The study was carried out online to ensure that a mixed group of male and female pupils' responses were collected quickly and responsibly. There were 20 items in the survey covering all aspects of cyber security, including five demographic items.

The questions in the Internet use section were designed to elicit information about students' online behavior. The questions about the usage of security technologies were designed to assess current security practices in IAU University students. The browser security component was designed to evaluate students' comprehension of the security of the browsers they often use. Finally, the networking sites and cyber security knowledge portions examined students' understanding of the risks of utilizing various social networking platforms and how to respond to a cybercrime occurrence. As a result, we investigated the students' cyber security awareness, abilities, behavior and attitudes, and self-perceptions. These questions were distributed to undergraduate and post-graduate students, and a total of 450 responses were received. These responses were again categorized according to the hypothesis and analysis. The following are the categories of questions: Questions based on password, browser, and social media activities. The responses to these questions were multiple-choice answers, with the following choices: Strongly Agree, Agree, Neutral, Disagree, Strongly Disagree.

The following are the questions drafted:

Q1. Passwords are made up of 12 letters and a combination of letters, digits, or signs.

Q2. Change password periodically.
Q3. Use previously used passwords whenever needed to create a password.
Q4. Use a single secure passcode for all web pages and logins.
Q5. It is inconvenient to have a different long and solid passcode for every webpage and account.
Q6. I do not mind sharing my passwords with my friends.

The questions related to browser security are as follows:

Q7. The web browser should be updated regularly.
Q8. Avoid installing extensions from third-party websites.
Q9. Examine the web browser's privacy controls and parameters regularly.
Q10. Examine browsing history for any unusual activity.

The questions related to social media activities are as follows:

Q11. It is OK to publish private photographs on social networking sites.
Q12. Accepting invitations from outsiders seems OK.
Q13. There is no concern with openly posting one's present location on social networking sites.
Q14. No problem with adding all personal information to social media.
Q15. Learn how to submit any danger or questionable conduct on social networks.

The passcode is an essential security element that protects data and information while allowing access to authenticated systems. A passcode should be at least 12 characters, including letters and numerals, capital and lowercase letters, and at least one symbol or unique character [43]. Given this, we investigated the students' understanding of the fundamental concepts of password security and how they handle their passwords.

4. Results

4.1. Demographic Data

Demographic data in this research is in the form of respondent data: gender, age, education level, computer skills, and how often respondents make online purchases. The distribution of demographic data can be seen in Table 1.

Table 1. Distribution of research respondent demographic data (n = 450).

Variable	Category	Number	Percentage (%)
Gender	Male	238	52.8%
	Female	212	47.2%
Age	<20	178	39.5%
	20–35	240	53.3%
	36–49	28	6.2%
	50–65	4	1%
Education	Diploma	16	3.6%
	Bachelor's Degree	417	92.6%
	Master's Degree	10	2.2%
	PhD	7	1.6%
Computer Skill	Beginner	67	14.9%
	Intermediate	237	52.7%
	Advance	146	32.4%
Purchase Online	Rarely	132	30%
	Frequently	318	70%

In Table 1, it can be seen that the number of female respondents (52.8%) is greater than that of male respondents. Most of the respondents were aged 20–35 years (53.3%), followed by respondents aged less than 20 years (39.5%). A large number of respondents were in this age group because the main target of this research is students, the level of education attained by most of the students in this study being a bachelor's degree (92.6%). Based on computer skills, most respondents have skills in using computers at an intermediate level (52.7%), followed by respondents who are proficient in using computers (32.4%). In the field of online purchasing, it can be seen that most of the respondents often purchase online (70%).

4.2. Description of the Independent Variable (X) Used

4.2.1. Password Security (X_1)

A password is a secret set of characters or words used to authenticate access to digital systems and computer systems. A password is one of the most critical factors in protecting data and information, but it is also hazardous because it is vulnerable to attack [55]. In good computer security practice, passwords must be between 8 (eight) and 24 (twenty-four) characters long and include at least one uppercase letter, one number, and one unique character [57]. These are usually formed from frequently used words, although this is not recommended as they are easier to guess or decipher.

From the information in Table 2, it is known that as many as 32% of students agree and 29% even strongly agree that one ought to use a strong password. However, most students (41%) disagree that passwords should be changed periodically; most students (39%) use their old passwords to create new passwords. Most students (30%) are also more likely to use one password for all websites/accounts and consider using long passwords very inconvenient. However, students are not willing to tell or share their passwords with friends. Based on these results, students still lack awareness of password security.

Table 2. The questions about the password security variable.

Question	Totally Disagree	Disagree	Neutral	Agree	Totally Agree
Passwords are made up of 12 letters and a combination of letters, digits, or signs.	4%	17%	18%	32%	29%
Change password periodically.	18%	41%	20%	14%	7%
Use previously used passwords whenever needed to create a password.	10%	18%	17%	39%	16%
Use a single secure passcode for all web pages and logins.	10%	23%	19%	30%	18%
It is inconvenient to have a different long and solid passcode for every webpage and account.	10%	11%	13%	34%	32%
I do not mind sharing my passwords with my friends.	54%	23%	12%	8%	4%

4.2.2. Browser Security (X_2)

Browser Security is essential for securing user data and information. The browser is considered to be the main door in conducting online activities, so the browser is the main target for hackers or cyber thieves to access sensitive information [58]. Keeping up-to-date with the latest version is one of the most effective ways to help secure your browser or another system.

From the results in Table 3, it is known that as many as 40% of students agree and 39% even strongly agree that the web browser must be updated regularly. As many as 38% of students strongly agree that installing extensions from third-party websites should be avoided. Most of the students (35%) agreed that the security settings and configurations of the web browser should be checked periodically, and as many as 36% of students studied browser history to find any suspicious activity. Based on these results, it is shown that students have a good level of awareness of browser security.

4.2.3. Social Media Activities (X_3)

In the era of increasingly advanced use of technology, surfing on social media has become a part of our daily life. People can access information in various fields, share their daily activities, and have non-face-to-face interactions through social media.

Table 3. The questions about the browser security variable.

Question	Totally Disagree	Disagree	Neutral	Agree	Totally Agree
The web browser should be updated regularly.	1%	5%	15%	40%	39%
Avoid installing extensions from third-party websites	2%	8%	18%	34%	38%
Examine the web browser's privacy controls and parameters regularly.	4%	12%	22%	35%	27%
Examine the browsing history for any unusual activity.	6%	11%	20%	36%	27%

From the results in Table 4, it can be seen that most students disagree (25%) or strongly disagree (23%) to upload personal photos on social media. Meanwhile, most students are neutral about accepting friendships from strangers on social media. However, some students strongly disagreed that one ought to share one's current social media location and disagreed that one ought to add all one's personal information on one's social media pages. As many as 68% of students already know how to report suspicious activity on social media.

Table 4. The questions about the social media activities variable.

Question	Totally Disagree	Disagree	Neutral	Agree	Totally Agree
It is OK to publish private photographs on social networking sites.	23%	25%	25%	21%	6%
Accepting invitations from outsiders seems OK	21%	26%	28%	21%	4%
There is no concern with openly posting one's present location on social networking sites.	49%	28%	12%	8%	3%
No problem with adding all personal information to social media.	33%	22%	22%	18%	5%
Learn how to submit any danger or questionable conduct on social networks.	4%	14%	14%	37%	31%

Figure 1 shows the most used social media by people around the world. For example, it can be seen that Facebook is the most used social media application with almost 2700 million or 2.7 billion active users every month in 2021.

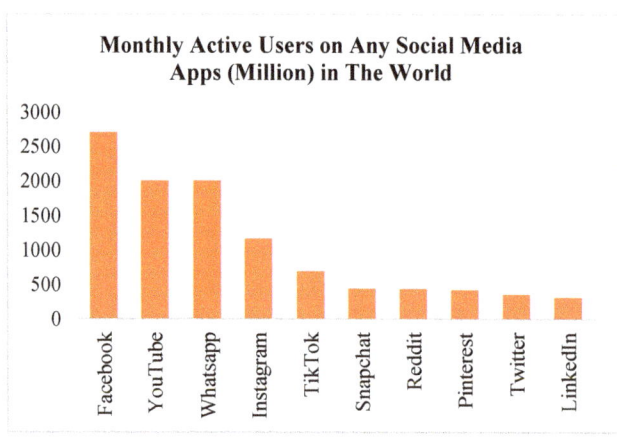

Figure 1. The most used social media in the world.

4.2.4. Data Analysis

Validity and Reliability Test

The validity test [57–59] results for each item from 450 respondents in this study are presented in Table 5.

Table 5. Validity test results.

Variable	Question Item	r-Value	r-Table
Password Security (X_1)	Q1	0.334	
	Q2	0.183	
	Q3	0.509	
	Q4	0.596	
	Q5	0.481	
	Q6	0.513	
Browser Security (X_2)	Q1	0.552	
	Q2	0.605	
	Q3	0.826	0.092
	Q4	0.791	
Social Media Activities (X_3)	Q1	0.683	
	Q2	0.692	
	Q3	0.717	
	Q4	0.740	
	Q5	0.298	
Cybersecurity Awareness (Y)	Q1	0.590	
	Q2	0.657	
	Q3	0.339	
	Q4	0.598	

Table 5 shows the results of testing the validity of each item from the 450 respondents studied. The results of the validity test show that all questions about the independent variables, namely, password security (X_1), browser security (X_2), social media activities (X_3), and also the dependent variable, namely, cybersecurity awareness (Y), have a correlation value (r-value) > r table (0.092). This indicates that each question is valid. So, it can be concluded that all questions used in this study are suitable for further research. After obtaining the results on the validity, the reliability test was carried out to determine the reliability of each statement presented in Table 6.

Table 6. Reliability Test Results.

Cronbach's Alpha	Number of Items	Description
0.596	19	Reliable enough

Table 6 shows the reliability testing results, namely, the Cronbach's Alpha value of 0.596. Cronbach's Alpha value is between 0.5–0.6. This indicates that every statement used in the variable is reliable enough, with the result that all statement items used in this study are suitable for further research.

Feasibility Test of a Variable

This stage tested the correlation between variables using Bartlett's test and the Kaiser–Meyer–Olkin (KMO) test. This test is carried out to assess the feasibility of a variable analyzed using factor analysis [60].

Table 7 shows that the significance value of Bartlett's test of sphericity is 0.000, the p-value (0.000) < α (0.05), which means that there is a correlation between variables. Furthermore, it can be seen that if the KMO value is 0.783, the KMO value is between the values 0.5–1, which means that the variables are homogeneous. Both tests have been met so that the variables can be predicted and further analysis can be carried out.

Table 7. KMO and Bartlett's Test.

Kaiser–Meyer–Olkin Measure of Sampling Adequacy		0.783
Bartlett's Test of Sphericity	Approximate Chi-Square	1795.927
	Df	171
	Sig	0.000

Correlation Test

A Correlation test [61] is a process to test the independent and dependent variables to determine the level of closeness of the relationship between two variables.

Table 8 shows the correlation component matrix containing the correlation values between the variables used in the study. The main focus of this test is to determine the relationship level between each independent variable—password security (X_1), browser security (X_2), and social media activities (X_3)—and cybersecurity awareness (Y). To make it easier to interpret the strength of the relationship between the two variables, the authors provide the following criteria (Sarwono, 2006).

Table 8. Correlation component matrix.

Variable	Password Security	Browser Security	Social Media Activities	Level of Awareness
Password Security	1			
Browser Security	0.023	1		
Social Media Activities	0.298	−0.074	1	
Level of Awareness	0.277	0.184	0.366	1

Based on Table 8, Password Security is positively related to cybersecurity awareness (r = 0.277). However, the correlation value is between 0.25–0.5, indicating a moderate level of relationship between password security and cybersecurity awareness. Browser Security is positively related to cybersecurity awareness (r = 0.184). The correlation value is between 0–0.25, indicating a low relationship between browser security and cybersecurity awareness. Social media activities positively relate to cybersecurity awareness (r = 0.366). The correlation value is between 0.25–0.5, indicating a moderate relationship between social media activities and cybersecurity awareness Table 9.

Table 9. Guidelines for providing an interpretation of correlation coefficients.

Correlation Value (r)	Interpretation
0	No correlation
>0–0.25	Low Correlation
>0.25–0.5	Moderate Correlation
>0.5–0.75	High Correlation
>0.75–0.99	Very High Correlation
1	Perfect Correlation

4.2.5. Multiple Tests

Assumptions Test

The residuals are assumed to be generally distributed in multivariate normality–multiple regression. However, no multiple regression presupposes that the independent variables are not substantially connected. The variance inflation factor (VIF) values are used to test this assumption [62].

Normality Test

The normality assumption is related to the residual distributions. This is considered customarily distributed, and the regression line is fitted to the data so that the mean of the residuals is zero.

The normality test [63] results using the normal p-plot with 450 respondents can be seen in Figure 2. The normal p-plot shows that all data points are spread around the line. This indicates that the data has met the assumption of normality.

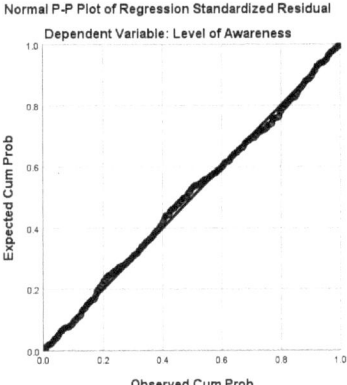

Figure 2. Normality test.

Multicollinearity Test

The results of the multicollinearity test using the VIF (variance inflation factor) value can be seen in Table 10.

Table 10. Multicollinearity Test.

Variable	VIF Value
Password Security (X_1)	1.100
Browser Security (X_2)	1.008
Social Media Activities (Y)	1.105

The VIF value in Table 10 shows that the VIF value of the three variables is less than 10 (VIF < 10), so it can be concluded that all the independent variables used in this study do not experience multicollinearity.

Heteroskedasticity Test

This study detects the occurrence of heteroskedasticity [64] by looking at the pattern of data points on the scatter-plot graph. Figure 3 shows that the observation points spread randomly and do not form a design or line. The plot also indicates whether the data distribution is around the zero point. This suggests that the regression model is free from heteroskedasticity problems, and the heteroskedasticity assumption has been fulfilled.

Multiple Linear Regression Model and Coefficient of Determination (R^2)

All classical assumption tests have been fulfilled; the next step is to build multiple linear regression model equations. The regression model equation that is produced can be used to analyze the effect of password security, browser security, and social media activities on cybersecurity awareness. The regression coefficient values are shown in Table 11.

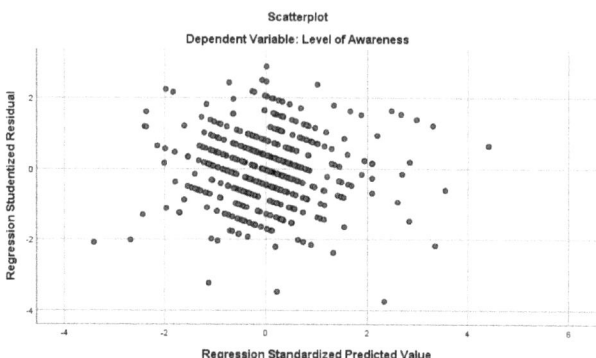

Figure 3. Heteroskedasticity Test.

Table 11. Multiple linear regression coefficient.

Variable	Regression Coefficient (β)
Intercept	4.301
Password Security (X_1)	0.147
Browser Security (X_2)	0.188
Media Social Activities (X_3)	0.241

The multiple linear regression model formed based on the regression coefficients in Table 11 is as follows:

$$\text{Cybersecurity Awareness} = 4.301 + (0.147)\, X_1 + (0.188)\, X_2 + (0.241)\, X_3$$

The regression coefficient value above can be explained such that if the level of student knowledge of password security increases by 1%, then the level of cybersecurity awareness will increase by 14.7%. Likewise, if the level of student knowledge of browser security rises by 1%, then cybersecurity awareness will increase by 18.8%. Finally, if student knowledge of social media activities increases by 1%, then cybersecurity awareness will increase by 24.1%.

The coefficient of determination is the value used to measure how much the ability of the independent variable included in the model can explain the variation of the dependent variable. Based on Table 12, the coefficient of determination (R^2) is 0.206, meaning that password security, browser security, and social media activities contribute to the influence of cybersecurity awareness by 20.6%, while the residual value of 79.4% (100% − 20.6%) indicates that other factors that affect cybersecurity awareness are not included in the model.

Table 12. Correlation Coefficient and Determination.

Model	R	R^2	Adjusted R^2
Regression	0.454	0.206	0.201

4.2.6. Hypothesis Test

ANOVA Test (F-Test)

The following is an F-test to see whether the independent variable has a simultaneous effect on the dependent variable [65]. The hypothesis in this test is as follows:

Hypothesis 0.

1: *Password Security (X_1), Browser Security (X_2), and Social Media Activities (X_3) together are not significantly related to Cybersecurity Awareness (Y).*

2: *Password Security (X_1), Browser Security (X_2), and Social Media Activities (X_3) together are significantly related to Cybersecurity Awareness (Y).*

Table 13 shows the results of the p-value (0.000) < 0.05, so it can be concluded that Password Security (X_1), Browser Security (X_2), and Social Media Activities (X_3) together have a significant effect on Cybersecurity Awareness (Y).

Table 13. F-test Results.

Model	F	Sig (p-Value)
Regression	38.666	0.000

Partial Test (t-Test)

A partial test [66] using the t-test is used to determine the significant effect of each independent variable on the dependent variable. The hypothesis in the partial test is as follows:

Hypothesis 1.

1: Password Security (X_1) is not significantly related to Cybersecurity Awareness (Y).
2: Password Security (X_1) is significantly related to Cybersecurity Awareness (Y).

Hypothesis 2.

1: Browser Security (X_2) is not significantly related to Cybersecurity Awareness (Y).
2: Browser Security is (X_2) is significantly related to Cybersecurity Awareness (Y).

Hypothesis 3.

1: Social Media Activities (X_3) is not significantly related to the Cybersecurity Awareness (Y).
2: Social Media Activities (X_3) is significantly related to Cybersecurity Awareness (Y).

Table 14 shows the results of partial hypothesis testing (t-test). Based on these results, the conclusions are:

(1) The Password Security variable (X_1) has a p-value (0.0001) < (0.05), so it can be concluded that Password Security (X_1) has a significant effect on Cybersecurity Awareness (Y).
(2) The Browser Security variable (X_2) has a p-value (0.0001) < (0.05), so it can be concluded that Browser Security (X_2) has a significant effect on Cybersecurity Awareness (Y).
(3) The Social Media Activities (X_3) variable has a p-value (0.0001) < (0.05), so it can be concluded that Social Media Activities (X_3) have a significant effect on Cybersecurity Awareness (Y).

Table 14. Results of t-test.

Variable	t-Value	Sig (p-Value)
Password Security (X_1)	3.931	0.0001
Browser Security (X_2)	4.839	0.0001
Social Media Activities (X_3)	7.428	0.0001

5. Discussion

The results of partial hypothesis testing using the t-test (Table 14) show that the password security variable significantly affects cybersecurity awareness (p-value = 0.0001). The regression coefficient of the password security variable in the multiple linear regression model (Table 11) shows the beta value of 0.147. Therefore, it can be concluded that password security has a positive and significant effect on cybersecurity awareness. The positive impact shows that using passwords will increase cybersecurity awareness by 14.7%. The browser security variable significantly affects cybersecurity awareness (p-value = 0.0001). The regression coefficient of the password security variable shows a beta value of 0.188. Therefore, it can be concluded that browser security has a positive and significant effect on cybersecurity awareness. The positive impact shows that knowledge of browser security will increase cybersecurity awareness by 18.8%. The social media activities variable significantly impacts cybersecurity awareness (p-value = 0.0001). The regression coefficient of the social media activities variable shows a beta value of 0.241. Therefore, it can be concluded that social media activities positively and significantly affect cybersecurity awareness. The positive effect shows that using social media will increase cybersecurity awareness by 24.1%.

The results of simultaneous hypothesis testing using the F-test (Table 13) show that password security, browser security, and social media activities have simultaneously significant effects on cybersecurity awareness (p-value < 0.05). The magnitude of the influence of the two variables can be seen based on the value of the coefficient of determination (R^2) obtained in this study, which is 0.206, indicating that password security, browser security, and social media activities contribute to the influence of cybersecurity awareness by 20.6%. Meanwhile, the residual value of 79.4% indicates that other factors that affect cybersecurity awareness are not included in the model. It should be emphasized that not all models with a low R^2 are bad models. According to [67] (2019), regression models with R^2 values below 50% can be accepted in several fields, such as the social field and the study of human behavior. Suppose the value of R^2 is low but the independent variable has a significant effect. In that case, the model can still provide conclusions about the relationship of the independent variable to the dependent variable.

The p-value (p-value < 0.05) indicates that the respondents in this study already have an awareness of cybersecurity awareness, but it is still low; this is because they do not take more or actual actions to implement cybersecurity in their daily life ($R^2 = 0.206$). Several reasons were thought to affect the results, probably because most respondents in this study (53%) were women. According to (Alotaibi et al., 2017), men have a higher awareness of cybersecurity than women. The research that supports the results of this study is research conducted by Alharbi and Tassaddiq (2021) among students at Majmaah University, Saudi Arabia, which included 60% male respondents and stated that students at Majmaah University already have a high level of awareness of cybersecurity awareness. It is proven by the high R^2 value reaching 55% ($R^2 = 0.55$) and the variables used, such as security tools, browser safety, social networking, and other cybersecurity knowledge, have a positive effect (p-value < 0.05).

Based on the three variables used, the password security variable has the lowest coefficient value ($\beta = 0.147$), implying that students still lack awareness of password security. It can be seen that most students (41%) disagree that passwords must be changed periodically; most students (30%) are more likely to use 1 password for all websites/accounts and think that using long passwords is very inconvenient. According to [68], users may have difficulty in remembering a long and complex password. Yildirim (2019) [69] said that instead of requiring users to follow strict password policy rules, motivating and directing them to create solid, easy-to-remember passwords seem to be a more efficient and helpful way. Users can also use strong passwords only if the system or account requires a high level of security [70].

6. Conclusions

Based on the research conducted, it can be concluded that knowledge of password security, browser security, and social media activities significantly influence cybersecurity awareness in students. Overall, students have realized the importance of cybersecurity awareness. However, in practice, students' levels of cybersecurity awareness are still lacking, especially when it comes to password security. Students usually do not pay much attention to using good and correct passwords to protect their accounts or websites. Based on the research results explained in the previous chapter, the summary is obtained as follows: Password Security variable (X_1) has a significant and positive effect on Cybersecurity Awareness (p-value = 0.0001, = 0.143). This shows that a good knowledge about password security could increase awareness because passwords are the main means of accessing and maintaining accounts or other systems. The knowledge about student password security in this study is still deficient. Students usually do not pay much attention to using good and correct passwords to protect their accounts or websites. Browser Security variable (X_2) has a significant and positive effect on Cybersecurity Awareness (p-value = 0.0001, = 0.188).

This shows that good knowledge about browser security can increase awareness. The level of knowledge about student browser security in this study is good; it can be seen from the number of students who always update their browsers regularly and tend to pay attention to the security of the browsers they use. The Social Media Activities (X_3) variable has a significant and positive effect on Cybersecurity Awareness (p-value = 0.0001, = 0.241). This shows that proper and correct social media activities can increase awareness. The activity of using social media by students in this study was good and can be seen from the number of students who prefer to keep their personal information from being too widely spread through social media. The students also know how to report suspicious threats on social media. Password Security (X_1), Browser Security (X_2), and Social Media Activities (X_3) variables simultaneously have a significant effect on Cybersecurity Awareness (p-value = 0.000), with a correlation coefficient of 20.6% ($R2 = 0.206$). This shows that the independent variable used can explain the level of cybersecurity awareness of 20.6%. All the SPSS analysis tables are listed in the Appendix A.

7. Limitations of the Work

Based on these results, several things can be done to increase cybersecurity awareness in students by means of socialization and campaigns related to cybersecurity. It should be noted that this research still has several limitations, such as the level of question reliability, which is still not decent, and limited use of the independent variables. This research, also, did not always represent another more comprehensive cybersecurity topic. In future research, it is recommended to add more variables that might affect cybersecurity awareness.

8. Comparative Analysis

There are several works in the literature wherein a similar methodology is applied to assess student's awareness for cybersecurity, as discussed in the literature review section. The following are the works sharing this perspective: Senthilkumar and Easwaramoorthy [32] studied university students in Tamil Nadu's key towns to examine their attentiveness to cyber security. They concentrated on particular cyber security risks, such as malware-infected websites, phishing, and the theft of personal information. According to their findings, students' awareness of cyber security and related threat problems was above average, with 70% of respondents having a basic understanding of cyber security dangers. Another work conducted by Moallem [33] investigated students' opinions regarding cyber security in California's Silicon Valley.

Similarly, Knight-McCord [53] (2016) researched which social networking sites were most popular with students. They administered a survey to 363 pupils online and in person. Previous research discovered that Instagram was the most popular site, followed by Snapchat and Facebook. LinkedIn and Pinterest, on the other hand, were less popular. According to Sharma, Jain, and Tiwari [54], 84 percent of students believe that posting personal information on social networking sites (SNS) is harmful. Finally, Moallem [33] (2018) researched cyber security knowledge in students at two California State universities in Silicon Valley.

Funding: This research received no external funding.

Institutional Review Board Statement: Not applicable for studies not involving humans or animals.

Informed Consent Statement: Not applicable.

Data Availability Statement: The data used in this study is based on the survey for the questions distributed among the students of the university.

Acknowledgments: The author would like to thank the Dean of College of Computer Science and Information Technology, Imam Abdulrahman Bin Faisal University.

Conflicts of Interest: The author declares no conflict of interest.

Appendix A

1. Validity Test

Correlations

		Q8	Q9	Q10	Q11	Q12	Q13	Password Security
Q8	Pearson Correlation	1	.309**	−.204**	.074	−.210**	−.034	.334**
	Sig. (2-tailed)		.000	.000	.117	.000	.474	.000
	N	450	450	450	450	450	450	450
Q9	Pearson Correlation	.309**	1	−.377**	−.159**	−.244**	.050	.183**
	Sig. (2-tailed)	.000		.000	.001	.000	.292	.000
	N	450	450	450	450	450	450	450
Q10	Pearson Correlation	−.204**	−.377**	1	.352**	.352**	.153**	.509**
	Sig. (2-tailed)	.000	.000		.000	.000	.001	.000
	N	450	450	450	450	450	450	450
Q11	Pearson Correlation	.074	−.159**	.352**	1	.140**	.103*	.596**
	Sig. (2-tailed)	.117	.001	.000		.003	.029	.000
	N	450	450	450	450	450	450	450
Q12	Pearson Correlation	−.210**	−.244**	.352**	.140**	1	.128**	.481**
	Sig. (2-tailed)	.000	.000	.000	.003		.007	.000
	N	450	450	450	450	450	450	450
Q13	Pearson Correlation	−.034	.050	.153**	.103*	.128**	1	.513**
	Sig. (2-tailed)	.474	.292	.001	.029	.007		.000
	N	450	450	450	450	450	450	450
Password Security	Pearson Correlation	.334**	.183**	.509**	.596**	.481**	.513**	1
	Sig. (2-tailed)	.000	.000	.000	.000	.000	.000	
	N	450	450	450	450	450	450	450

**. Correlation is significant at the 0.01 level (2-tailed).
*. Correlation is significant at the 0.05 level (2-tailed).

Correlations

		Q14	Q15	Q16	Q17	Browser Security
Q14	Pearson Correlation	1	.127**	.313**	.218**	.552**
	Sig. (2-tailed)		.007	.000	.000	.000
	N	450	450	450	450	450
Q15	Pearson Correlation	.127**	1	.297**	.266**	.605**
	Sig. (2-tailed)	.007		.000	.000	.000
	N	450	450	450	450	450
Q16	Pearson Correlation	.313**	.297**	1	.641**	.826**
	Sig. (2-tailed)	.000	.000		.000	.000
	N	450	450	450	450	450
Q17	Pearson Correlation	.218**	.266**	.641**	1	.791**
	Sig. (2-tailed)	.000	.000	.000		.000
	N	450	450	450	450	450
Browser Security	Pearson Correlation	.552**	.605**	.826**	.791**	1
	Sig. (2-tailed)	.000	.000	.000	.000	
	N	450	450	450	450	450

**. Correlation is significant at the 0.01 level (2-tailed).

Correlations

		Q18	Q19	Q20	Q21	Q22	Social Media Activities
Q18	Pearson Correlation	1	.376**	.318**	.387**	.023	.683**
	Sig. (2-tailed)		.000	.000	.000	.632	.000
	N	450	450	450	450	450	450
Q19	Pearson Correlation	.376**	1	.429**	.390**	-.017	.692**
	Sig. (2-tailed)	.000		.000	.000	.724	.000
	N	450	450	450	450	450	450
Q20	Pearson Correlation	.318**	.429**	1	.551**	-.015	.717**
	Sig. (2-tailed)	.000	.000		.000	.751	.000
	N	450	450	450	450	450	450
Q21	Pearson Correlation	.387**	.390**	.551**	1	-.043	.740**
	Sig. (2-tailed)	.000	.000	.000		.364	.000
	N	450	450	450	450	450	450
Q22	Pearson Correlation	.023	-.017	-.015	-.043	1	.298**
	Sig. (2-tailed)	.632	.724	.751	.364		.000
	N	450	450	450	450	450	450
Social Media Activities	Pearson Correlation	.683**	.692**	.717**	.740**	.298**	1
	Sig. (2-tailed)	.000	.000	.000	.000	.000	
	N	450	450	450	450	450	450

**. Correlation is significant at the 0.01 level (2-tailed).

2. Reliability Test

Reliability Statistics

Cronbach's Alpha	N of Items
.596	19

3. Feasibility test of a variable

KMO and Bartlett's Test

Kaiser-Meyer-Olkin Measure of Sampling Adequacy.		.783
Bartlett's Test of Sphericity	Approx. Chi-Square	1795.927
	df	171
	Sig.	.000

4. Correlation Test

Correlations

		Password Security	Browser Security	Social Media Activities
Password Security	Pearson Correlation	1	.023	.298**
	Sig. (2-tailed)		.634	.000
	N	450	450	450
Browser Security	Pearson Correlation	.023	1	-.074
	Sig. (2-tailed)	.634		.116
	N	450	450	450
Social Media Activities	Pearson Correlation	.298**	-.074	1
	Sig. (2-tailed)	.000	.116	
	N	450	450	450

**. Correlation is significant at the 0.01 level (2-tailed).

5. Multicollinearity Test

Coefficients[a]

Model		Unstandardized Coefficients		Standardized Coefficients	t	Sig.	Collinearity Statistics	
		B	Std. Error	Beta			Tolerance	VIF
1	(Constant)	4.301	.922		4.663	.000		
	Password Security	.147	.037	.174	3.931	.000	.909	1.100
	Browser Security	.188	.039	.205	4.839	.000	.992	1.008
	Social Media Activities	.241	.032	.329	7.428	.000	.905	1.105

a. Dependent Variable: Level of Awareness

6. Regression

Coefficients[a]

Model		Unstandardized Coefficients		Standardized Coefficients	t	Sig.	Collinearity Statistics	
		B	Std. Error	Beta			Tolerance	VIF
1	(Constant)	4.301	.922		4.663	.000		
	Password Security	.147	.037	.174	3.931	.000	.909	1.100
	Browser Security	.188	.039	.205	4.839	.000	.992	1.008
	Social Media Activities	.241	.032	.329	7.428	.000	.905	1.105

a. Dependent Variable: Level of Awareness

7. R^2

Model Summary[b]

Model	R	R Square	Adjusted R Square	Std. Error of the Estimate
1	.454[a]	.206	.201	2.411

a. Predictors: (Constant), Social Media Activities, Browser Security, Password Security

b. Dependent Variable: Level of Awareness

8. ANOVA Test (F-Test)

ANOVA[a]

Model		Sum of Squares	df	Mean Square	F	Sig.
1	Regression	674.349	3	224.783	38.666	.000[b]
	Residual	2592.771	446	5.813		
	Total	3267.120	449			

a. Dependent Variable: Level of Awareness

b. Predictors: (Constant), Social Media Activities, Browser Security, Password Security

9. *t*-Test

Model		Unstandardized Coefficients		Standardized Coefficients	t	Sig.	Collinearity Statistics	
		B	Std. Error	Beta			Tolerance	VIF
1	(Constant)	4.301	.922		4.663	.000		
	Password Security	.147	.037	.174	3.931	.000	.909	1.100
	Browser Security	.188	.039	.205	4.839	.000	.992	1.008
	Social Media Activities	.241	.032	.329	7.428	.000	.905	1.105

a. Dependent Variable: Level of Awareness

References

1. Gamreklidze, E. Cyber security in developing countries, a digital divide issue: The case of Georgia. *J. Int. Commun.* **2014**, *20*, 200–217. [CrossRef]
2. Garg, A.; Curtis, J.; Halper, H. Quantifying the financial impact of IT security breaches. *Inf. Manag. Comput. Secur.* **2003**, *11*, 74–83. [CrossRef]
3. Green, J.S. *Cyber Security: An Introduction for Non-Technical Managers*, 1st ed.; Routledge: London, UK, 2016; pp. 1–264.
4. Shaukat, K.; Luo, S.; Varadharajan, V.; Hameed, I.A.; Xu, M. A Survey on Machine Learning Techniques for Cyber Security in the Last Decade. *IEEE Access* **2020**, *8*, 222310–222354. [CrossRef]
5. Whitman, M.E.; Mattord, H.J. *Principles of Information Security*; Receiv. US Pat. Pers. Identif. device. 2005; Cengage Learning: Boston, MA, USA, 2011; p. 1.
6. Shaukat, K.; Luo, S.; Chen, S.; Liu, D. Cyber Threat Detection Using Machine Learning Techniques: A Performance Evaluation Perspective. In Proceedings of the 2020 International Conference on Cyber Warfare and Security (ICCWS), Albany, NY, USA, 17–18 March 2022.
7. Willard, N.E. *Cyber-Safe Kids, Cyber-Savvy Teens: Helping Young People Learn to Use the Internet Safely and Responsibly*; John Wiley & Sons: Hoboken, NJ, USA, 2007.
8. Simsim, M.T. Internet usage and user preferences in Saudi Arabia. *J. King Saud Univ.-Eng. Sci.* **2011**, *23*, 101–107. [CrossRef]
9. Internet Usage in the Kingdom of Saudi Arabia. Available online: www.citc.gov.sa/en/reportsandstudies/studies/Pages/Computer-and-Internet-Usage-in-KSA-Study.aspx (accessed on 20 February 2021).
10. Aboul Enein, S. Cybersecurity Challenges in the Middle East. Available online: https://www.gcsp.ch/publications/cybersecurity-challenges-middle-east (accessed on 30 April 2021).
11. Sait, S.M.; Al-Tawil, K.M.; Ali, S.; Hussain, A. *Use and effect of Internet in Saudi Arabia*; KFUPM: Dhahran, Saudi Arabia, 2003.
12. Katz, F.H. The Effect of a University Information Security Survey on Instruction Methods in Information Security. In Proceedings of the 2nd Annual Conference on Information Security Curriculum Development, New York, NY, USA, 23–24 September 2005.
13. Alshankity, Z.; Alshawi, A. Gender differences in internet usage among faculty members: The case of Saudi Arabia. In Proceedings of the 2008 Conference on Human System Interactions, Krakow, Poland, 25–27 May 2008.
14. Hathaway, M.; Spidalieri, F.; Alsowailm, F. *Kingdom of Saudi Arabia Cyber Readiness at a Glance*; Potomac Institute for Policy Studies: Arlington, VA, USA, 2017.
15. Nurunnabi, M. Transformation from an Oil-based Economy to a Knowledge-based Economy in Saudi Arabia: The Direction of Saudi Vision 2030. *J. Knowl. Econ.* **2017**, *8*, 536–564. [CrossRef]
16. ALArifi, A.; Tootell, H.; Hyland, P. Information Security Awareness in Saudi Arabia. In Proceedings of the CONF-IRM 2012, Vienna, Austria, 21–23 May 2012.
17. Aloul, F.A. The Need for Effective Information Security Awareness. *J. Adv. Inf. Technol.* **2012**, *3*, 176–183. [CrossRef]
18. Boneh, D.; Lynn, B.; Shacham, H. Short Signatures from the Weil Pairing. In Proceedings of the International Conference on the Theory and Application of Cryptology and Information Security, Gold Coast, QLD, Australia, 9–13 December 2001.
19. Liu, X.; Zhang, Y.; Wang, B.; Yan, J. Mona: Secure Multi-Owner Data Sharing for Dynamic Groups in the Cloud. *IEEE Trans. Parallel Distrib. Syst.* **2013**, *24*, 1182–1191. [CrossRef]
20. Kamara, S.; Lauter, K. Cryptographic Cloud Storage. In Proceedings of the International Conference on Financial Cryptography and Data Security, Tenerife, Spain, 25–28 January 2010.
21. Pfleeger, C.P.; Pfleeger, S.L.R. *Security in Computing*, 4th ed.; Prentice Hall: Hoboken, NJ, USA, 2006.
22. Egan, M.; Mather, T. *The Executive Guide to Information Security: Threats, Challenges, and Solutions*, 1st ed.; Addison-Wesley Professional: Boston, MA, USA, 2004.
23. Stolfo, S.J.; Bellovin, S.M.; Hershkop, S.; Keromytis, A.D.; Sinclair, S.; Smith, S.W. *Insider Attack and Cyber Security: Beyond the Hacker*, 1st ed.; Springer: Boston, MA, USA, 2008.
24. Soghoian, C. A Remote Vulnerability in Firefox Extensions. Available online: http://paranoia.dubfire.net/2007/05/remote-vulnerability-in-firefox.html (accessed on 12 June 2013).

25. Reis, C.; Barth, A.; Pizano, C. Browser Security: Lessons from Google Chrome: Google Chrome developers focused on three key problems to shield the browser from attacks. *Queue* **2009**, *7*, 3–8. [CrossRef]
26. Osterman Research. Available online: http://www.ostermanresearch.com/ (accessed on 15 June 2013).
27. Al_Janabi, S.; Al-Shourbaji, I. A Study of Cyber Security Awareness in Educational Environment in the Middle East. *J. Inf. Knowl. Manag.* **2016**, *15*, 1650007. [CrossRef]
28. Ahmed, N.; Kulsum, U.; Bin Azad, I.; Momtaz, A.S.Z.; Haque, M.E.; Rahman, M.S. Cybersecurity awareness survey: An analysis from Bangladesh perspective. In Proceedings of the 2017 IEEE Region 10 Humanitarian Technology Conference (R10-HTC), Dhaka, Bangladesh, 21–23 December 2017.
29. Plackett, R.L. Karl Pearson and the Chi-Squared Test. *Int. Stat. Rev. Int. Stat.* **1983**, *51*, 59–72. [CrossRef]
30. Slusky, L.; Partow-Navid, P. Students Information Security Practices and Awareness. *J. Inf. Priv. Secur.* **2012**, *8*, 3–26. [CrossRef]
31. Alotaibi, F.; Furnell, S.; Stengel, I.; Papadaki, M. A survey of cyber-security awareness in Saudi Arabia. In Proceedings of the 2016 11th International Conference for Internet Technology and Secured Transactions (ICITST), Barcelona, Spain, 5–7 December 2016.
32. Senthilkumar, K.; Easwaramoorthy, S. A Survey on Cyber Security awareness among college students in Tamil Nadu. In Proceedings of the IOP Conference Series: Materials Science and Engineering, Vellore, India, 2–3 May 2017.
33. Moallem, A. Cyber Security Awareness among College Students. In Proceeding of the International Conference on Applied Human Factors and Ergonomics, Orlando, FL, USA, 21–25 July 2018.
34. Taha, N.; Dahabiyeh, L. College students information security awareness: A comparison between smartphones and computers. *Educ. Inf. Technol.* **2021**, *26*, 1721–1736. [CrossRef]
35. Moallem, A. *Cybersecurity Awareness among Students and Faculty*; CRC Press: Boca Raton, FL, USA, 2019.
36. Zwilling, M.; Klien, G.; Lesjak, D.; Wiechetek, Ł.; Cetin, F.; Basim, H.N. Cyber Security Awareness, Knowledge and Behavior: A Comparative Study. *J. Comput. Inf. Syst.* **2020**, *62*, 82–97. [CrossRef]
37. Garba, A.; Sirat, M.B.; Hajar, S.; Dauda, I.B. Cyber Security Awareness among University Students: A Case Study. *J. Crit. Rev.* **2020**, *7*, 16. [CrossRef]
38. Aljeaid, D.; Alzhrani, A.; Alrougi, M.; Almalki, O. Assessment of End-User Susceptibility to Cybersecurity Threats in Saudi Arabia by Simulating Phishing Attacks. *Information* **2020**, *11*, 547. [CrossRef]
39. Al-Khater, W.A.; Al-Ma'Adeed, S.; Ahmed, A.A.; Sadiq, A.S.; Khan, M.K. Comprehensive Review of Cybercrime Detection Techniques. *IEEE Access* **2020**, *8*, 137293–137311. [CrossRef]
40. Garba, A.A.; Siraj, M.M.; Othman, S.H.; Musa, M.A. A Study on Cybersecurity Awareness among Students in Yobe State University, Nigeria: A Quantitative Approach. *Int. J. Emerg. Technol.* **2020**, *11*, 41–49.
41. Shaukat, K.; Suhuai, L.; Vijay, V.; Hameed, I.A.; Shan, C.; Dongxi, L.; Jiaming, L. Performance comparison and current challenges of using machine learning techniques in cybersecurity. *Energies* **2020**, *13*, 2509. [CrossRef]
42. Florencio, D.; Herley, C. A Large-Scale Study of Web Password Habits. In Proceedings of the 16th International Conference on World Wide Web, Banff, AB, Canada, 8–12 May 2007.
43. Stobert, E.; Biddle, R. The Password Life Cycle: User Behaviour in Managing Passwords. In Proceedings of the 10th Symposium on Usable Privacy and Security, MP, Canada, 9–11 July 2014.
44. Wash, R.; Rader, E.; Berman, R.; Wellmer, Z. Understanding Password Choices: How Frequently Entered Passwords Are Re-Used across Websites. In Proceedings of the Twelfth Symposium on Usable Privacy and Security, Denver, CO, USA, 22–24 July 2016.
45. Shaukat, K.; Rubab, A.; Shehzadi, I.; Iqbal, R. A socio-technological analysis of cyber crime and cyber security in Pakistan. *Transylv. Rev.* **2017**, *1*, 84.
46. Haque, S.T.; Wright, M.; Scielzo, S. Hierarchy of users' web passwords: Perceptions, practices and susceptibilities. *Int. J. Human-Comput. Stud.* **2014**, *72*, 860–874. [CrossRef]
47. Bang, Y.; Lee, D.-J.; Bae, Y.-S.; Ahn, J.-H. Improving information security management: An analysis of ID–password usage and a new login vulnerability measure. *Int. J. Inf. Manag.* **2012**, *32*, 409–418. [CrossRef]
48. 2020 Data Breaches. Available online: https://www.identityforce.com/blog/2020-data-breaches (accessed on 2 September 2021).
49. Ur, B.; Bees, J.; Segreti, S.M.; Bauer, L.; Christin, N.; Cranor, L.F. Do Users' Perceptions of Password Security Match Reality? In Proceedings of the 2016 CHI Conference on Human Factors in Computing Systems, San Jose, CA, USA, 7–12 May 2016.
50. Ur, B.; Fumiko, N.; Jonathan, B.; Segreti, S.M.; Richard, S.; Lujo, B.; Nicolas, C.; Cranor, L.F. I Added '!'at the End to Make It Secure': Observing Password Creation in the Lab. In Proceedings of the Eleventh Symposium on Usable Privacy and Security, Ottowa, ON, Canada, 22–24 July 2015.
51. Liu, Z.; Hong, Y.; Pi, D. A Large-Scale Study of Web Password Habits of Chinese Network Users. *J. Softw.* **2014**, *9*, 293–297. [CrossRef]
52. Han, G.; Yu, Y.; Li, X.; Chen, K.; Li, H. Characterizing the semantics of passwords: The role of Pinyin for Chinese Netizens. *Comput. Stand. Interfaces* **2017**, *54*, 20–28. [CrossRef]
53. Pew Research Center. Social Networking Fact Sheet. 2019. Available online: https://www.pewinternet.org/2018/03/01/social-media-use-in-2018/ (accessed on 2 September 2021).
54. Richardson, C. Student Perceptions of the Impact of Social Media on College Student Engagement. Available online: https://scholarcommons.sc.edu/etd/4417/ (accessed on 2 September 2021).
55. Knight-McCord, J.; Cleary, D.; Grant, N.; Herron, A.; Lacey, T.; Livingston, T.; Emanuel, R. What social media sites do college students use most. *J. Undergrad. Ethn. Minor. Psychol.* **2016**, *2*, 21–26.

56. Sharma, B.K.; Jain, M.; Tiwari, D. Students perception towards social media—With special reference to Management Students of Bhopal Madhya Pradesh. *Int. J. Eng. Appl. Sci.* **2015**, *2*, 30–34.
57. Shay, R.; Komanduri, S.; Patrick, G.; Kelley, P.; Giovanni, L.; Mazurek, M.L.; Lujo, B.; Nicolas, C.; Lorrie, F.C. Encountering Stronger Password Requirements: User Attitudes and Behaviors. In Proceedings of the Sixth Symposium on Usable Privacy and Security, Redmond, WA, USA, 14–16 July 2010.
58. Carstens, D.S.; McCauley-Bell, P.R.; Malone, L.C.; DeMara, R.F. Evaluation of the human impact of password authentication practices on information security. *Inf. Sci. J.* **2004**, *7*, 1–19.
59. Heale, R.; Twycross, A. Validity and reliability in quantitative studies. *Évid. Based Nurs.* **2015**, *18*, 66–67. [CrossRef]
60. Koepp, G.A.; Snedden, B.J.; Flynn, L.; Puccinelli, D.; Huntsman, B.; Levine, J.A. Feasibility Analysis of Standing Desks for Sixth Graders. *ICAN Infant, Child, Adolesc. Nutr.* **2012**, *4*, 89–92. [CrossRef]
61. Piaw, C.Y. *Mastering Research Statistics*; Malaysia; McGraw Hill Education: New York, NY, USA, 2013.
62. Finch, H. Comparison of the Performance of Nonparametric and Parametric MANOVA Test Statistics when Assumptions Are Violated. *Methodology* **2005**, *1*, 27–38. [CrossRef]
63. Shapiro, S.S.; Francia, R.S. An approximate analysis of variance test for normality. *J. Am. Stat. Assoc.* **1972**, *67*, 215–216. [CrossRef]
64. Schwert, G.W.; Paul, J.S. Heteroskedasticity in stock returns. *J. Financ.* **1990**, *45*, 1129–1155. [CrossRef]
65. Wilcox, R.R.; Ventura, L.C.; Karen, L.T. New monte carlo results on the robustness of the anova f, w and f statistics. *Commun. Stat. Simul. Comput.* **1986**, *15*, 933–943. [CrossRef]
66. Kierepka, E.M.; Latch, E.K. Performance of partial statistics in individual-based landscape genetics. *Mol. Ecol. Resour.* **2014**, *15*, 512–525. [CrossRef] [PubMed]
67. Frost, J. *Regression Analysis: An Intuitive Guide for Using and Interpreting Linear Models*; Statisics by Jim Publishing: State College, PA, USA, 2019.
68. Keith, M.; Shao, B.; Steinbart, P.J. The usability of passphrases for authentication: An empirical field study. *Int. J. Human-Comput. Stud.* **2007**, *65*, 17–28. [CrossRef]
69. Yıldırım, M.; Mackie, I. Encouraging users to improve password security and memorability. *Int. J. Inf. Secur.* **2019**, *18*, 741–759. [CrossRef]
70. Florêncio, D.; Herley, C.; Van Oorschot, P.C. Password Portfolios and the Finite-Effort User: Sustainably Managing Large Numbers of Accounts. In Proceedings of the 23rd USENIX Security Symposium, San Diego, CA, USA, 20–22 August 2014.

Article

Secure Healthcare Record Sharing Mechanism with Blockchain

Ghulam Qadar Butt [1], Toqeer Ali Sayed [2], Rabia Riaz [1], Sanam Shahla Rizvi [3] and Anand Paul [4,*]

[1] Department of CS&IT, University of Azad Jammu and Kashmir, Muzaffarabad 13100, Pakistan; ghulamqadir90@gmail.com (G.Q.B.); rabia.riaz@ajku.edu.pk (R.R.)
[2] Faculty of Computer and Information Systems, Islamic University of Madinah, Madinah 42351, Saudi Arabia; toqeer@iu.edu.sa
[3] Raptor Interactive (Pty) Ltd., Eco Boulevard, Witch Hazel Ave, Gauteng 0157, South Africa; sanam.shahla@raptorinteractive.com
[4] School of Computer Science and Engineering, Kyungpook National University, Daegu 37224, Korea
* Correspondence: paul.editor@gmail.com

Abstract: The transfer of information is a demanding issue, particularly due to the presence of a large number of eavesdroppers on communication channels. Sharing medical service records between different clinical jobs is a basic and testing research topic. The particular characteristics of blockchains have attracted a large amount of attention and resulted in revolutionary changes to various business applications, including medical care. A blockchain is based on a distributed ledger, which tends to improve cyber security. A number of proposals have been made with respect to the sharing of basic medical records using a blockchain without needing earlier information or the trust of patients. Specialist service providers and insurance agencies are not secure against data breaches. The safe sharing of clinical records between different countries, to ensure an incorporated and universal medical service, is also a significant issue for patients who travel. The medical data of patients normally reside on different healthcare units around the world, thus raising many concerns. Firstly, a patient's history of treatment by different physicians is not accessible to the doctor in a single location. Secondly, it is very difficult to secure widespread data residing in different locations. This study proposed record sharing in a chain-like structure, in which every record is globally connected to the others, based on a blockchain under the suggestions and recommendations of the HL7 standards. This study focused on making medical data available, especially of patients who travel in different countries, for a specific period of time after validating the required authentication. Authorization and authentication are performed on the Shibboleth identity management system with the involvement of patient in the sanction process, thereby revealing the patient data for the specific period of time. The proposed approach improves the performance with respect to other record sharing systems, e.g., it reduces the time to read, write, delete, and revoke a record by a noticeable margin. The proposed system takes around three seconds to upload and 7.5 s to download 250 Mb of data, which can contain up to sixteen documents, over a stable network connection. The system has a latency of 413.76 ms when retrieving 100 records, compared to 447.9 and 459.3 ms in previous systems. Thus, the proposed system improved the performance and ensured seclusion by using a blockchain.

Keywords: blockchain; cyber-security; medical services; cyber-attacks; data communication; distributed ledger; identity management; RAFT; HL7; electronic health record; Hyperledger Composer

1. Introduction

There are numerous methods of data communication, each having specific advantages and disadvantages, for which security and privacy are an important concern. In the case of medical data availability, the trust required to provide information, transparency, and access control are important factors, because malicious individuals such as hackers are constantly improving their techniques, with a focus on identifying loopholes in the data transmission process.

Health is the basis of a happy life, and humans are now the beneficiaries of technical advances in the clinical industry [1]. An electronic health record (EHR) is the computerization of a patient's medical history, e.g., test reports and doctor prescriptions. The EHR enables the digital sharing of data with medical officers in any global location. Creating an EHR over the internet ensures that patient information is instantly available to any hospital around the world, when needed, regardless of the hospital that created it. Many EHR systems exist around the world, each with its own specifications. Sharing of information between different EHR systems requires mutual co-ordination, which is achieved through the use of standards [2]. An EHR system must both meet communication standards and be suitable for data models for inter-EHR system communications.

The Internet of Things (IoT) has embraced the blockchain to enhance its security, privacy, and monitoring [3,4]. Many IoT platforms use a blockchain as a distributed ledger to save their data. A number of blockchain architectures exist because each blockchain network needs to follow an architecture to perform transactions in the network. Similarly, platforms exist that use the IoT, blockchains, and the cloud collectively [3]. The research undertaken to date has led to the ecosystem shown in Figure 1. The IoT is shown as a platform in the first layer of the ecosystem.

The blockchain has addressed a number of complications in healthcare; for example, the secure transfer of information between different entities [5], efficiency enhancement due to low-cost transactions, and the restriction of access to information to the individuals concerned [6]. Many blockchain platforms are used in healthcare, and choosing an appropriate platform is a subject of debate within the industry [7–9]. The ecosystem in Figure 1 shows the latest electronic health record sharing mechanisms in its application layer. Trusted authorities are the backbone of the digital economy, and verify the legitimacy of the receiver in a transaction. The inclusion of a third party increases the risk of data being misused, compromised, and hacked [10]. The blockchain address this issue via the use of a distributed ledger and consensus [11,12]. The blockchain has a promising future in the modern world, in which many activities are undertaken online, especially in regard to businesses and commerce [13].

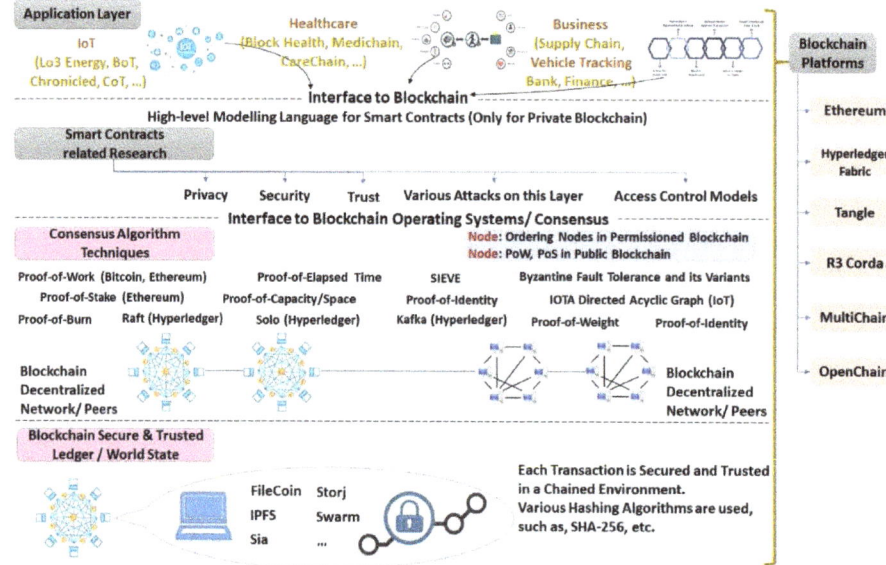

Figure 1. Working of the blockchain (by same author [14]).

The current research provides, first, a complete design of a framework that integrates global healthcare record systems. This solution is helpful for patients who travel regularly to other countries and, in the case of an emergency, are unable to provide their health history from their home healthcare system. Second, a prototype implementation of a health system is provided over a blockchain and remotely retrieves the records of a remote patient. Third, a general performance analysis was performed over the permissioned blockchain. The transaction analysis shown in the Results and Evaluations Section clearly shows the advantages of this study compared to other similar systems.

The proposal presented in this study enhances the security of the communication of patient data with the use of a blockchain, and lowers the burden on systems via the use of identity management. According to our findings, no previous study has used Shibboleth identity management with a blockchain for the transfer of health-related information to create a global system with proper implementation. In this study, the RAFT algorithm, Hyperledger Fabric, and identity management were used to create a low-burden system for medical record sharing. The results clearly show the dominance of the proposed system with respect to the current EHR systems.

2. Background

The world of Information Technology (IT) has revolutionized methods of dealing with data in various sectors. In particular, healthcare services have become more approachable, flexible, and efficient. An EHR can efficiently keep and transfer the medical documents of a patient, and be used to maintain a detailed patient history. However, the diversity of file formats used by various EHR systems results in issues relating to interoperability, scattering, and security. This study introduces a blockchain to resolve these issues.

2.1. Blockchain

A blockchain is a chain of blocks, often called a distributed ledger, without any ownership. The idea was presented initially by Satoshi Nakamoto in the creation of a cryptocurrency. A blockchain appears as a distributed ledger and has no sovereignty; that is, no individual or organization can dictate the interchange and access of information [15]. The term "distributed ledger" means that data is stored at multiple locations, and is not maintained or owned by a single entity. Thus, any change in the network is replicated on every node in the system, as if every node has the original document [16]. The same ledger is distributed to all nodes, so it is almost impossible to make malicious changes. The ledger stores information in the form of blocks, each of which has header and data sections. The data section stores the transactions, whereas the header sections contain the block metadata. Every header contains hashes of the current and previous blocks.

2.1.1. Types of Blockchain

Blockchains can be divided into two main categories, private and public, with are characterized by huge difference depending on need of the technology. Private blockchains control access and do not allow the general public to have unauthorized access to the network. A node must be authorized by all other nodes before it is provided access [17], but any transaction in the network is visible to all of the authorized nodes of the network. Private blockchains do not have a proof of work or mining, which is in contrast to the operation of a public blockchain. Hyperledger Fabric and Quorum are examples of private blockchains [18].

A public blockchain is open to all, and each node can read and utilize the blockchain to perform any transaction without a central register. In public blockchains, it is optional for each node in the network to validate a modification. Ethereum is an example of an open-source public blockchain. Ethereum uses the Solidity language to create its smart contracts [19], which was created by the Ethereum community. Bitcoin is a cryptocurrency based on a public blockchain, which takes much longer to complete a transaction compared to a private blockchain. According to the official information about the Bitcoin cryptocurrency, it may take up to ten minutes for a transaction to complete [20].

Another type of blockchain exists that combine the benefits of both public and private blockchain properties. Known as the Consortium blockchain, a group of individuals control the network while maintaining the efficiency and privacy of the blockchain.

2.1.2. Blockchain Working

The working of a blockchain can be understood using the scenario in Figure 2, in which a node of the network wants to enter a record in the blockchain network. This request is broadcast to the network, validated by a defined algorithm of the network, and permanently added to the network. This new record becomes unmodifiable after verification of the block [21].

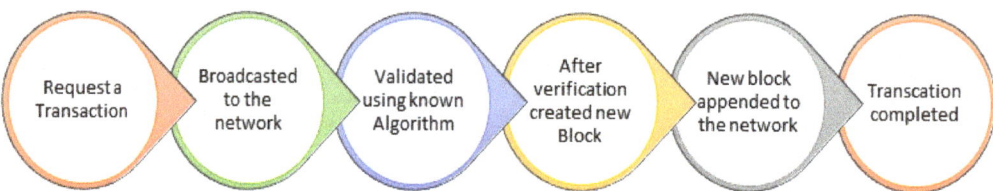

Figure 2. Working of a blockchain.

2.2. Communication

Communication is the process of transferring information from one place to another [22]. Every communication must consist of a sender, a message, and a receiver. The sender and receiver can be a person or a computerized device, whereas the message can be text, audio, video, voice, or other formats. Accuracy, effectiveness, security, and unambiguity are the main concerns of all communication, and are sometimes hard to achieve. In the case of modern communication, where the sender and receiver can be in different locations around the world, the main concern is ensuring that information is transferred correctly to the receiver, without others listening to the communication during the process.

Significant technological improvements have been made, especially in the field of communication, allowing a receiver to receive information from the sender in seconds. At the same time, threats to communication have also increased. Modern communication requires the inclusion of a form of encryption to minimize the chances of hacking during the communication process [23]. Figure 3 shows the complete communication process. The center of all communication is the message to be transferred, and efforts are made to maintain its integrity. Different forms of security protocols are followed to achieve the security and integrity of the communication, depending on the type of message and the medium through which it will be transferred.

In the system under study, patients, health personal, and service providers are considered users; all of these roles have different levels of authorization. Patients may wish to share their clinical information with other doctors, laboratories, insurance companies, or research centers. Health personal are requesters of the service, e.g., a doctor asking a patient for their previous medical data. Service providers manage the client's data, and are also known as administrators.

Communication Menaces

There are numerous ways a communication can be compromised, and all three components of communication (sender, receiver, and message) can be victims of an attack by hackers. Some common attacks and their possible solutions are described in [24]. Session hijacking aims to attain unauthorized access to any communication [25], and is also referred to as a man in the middle attack (MIMA). In session hijacking, the hijacker pretends to be the legitimate sender or receiver while bypassing the actual legitimate connection. This type of attack is used to steal information, to listen to conversations, and for spying. Session hijacking can be performed by sniffing the network, using a brute force attack (BFA), or using cross-site scripting (XSS) [26]. Session hijacking can be minimized in a network by using a secure socket shell (SSH), https (the secure mode of a website), or a complex session ID [27].

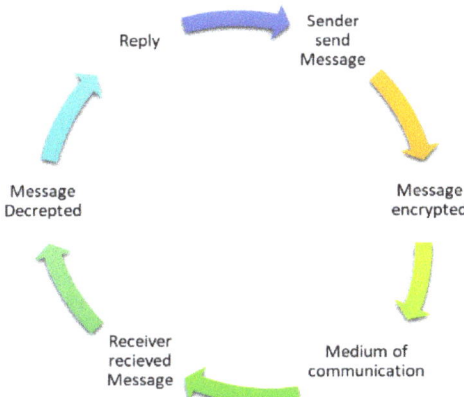

Figure 3. Secure communication process.

Bots (originating from "robot") are software applications over the Internet working on automated tasks. A combination of bots can form a botnet, which can propagate and organize itself to compromise the system of communication. The bots have the ability to install worms that can harm the system by replicating themselves, and also install backdoors that can bypass the authentication and encryption in the system [28]. Bots also cause a denial of service (DoS), and its advanced form, a distributed denial of service (DDoS), which can take a network or system artificially offline. Such challenges and their remedies are discussed in [29]. In probing DNS caches, the IP address of the system accessing the network is checked in a local DNS server, and only IP addressed present in the local DNS server are allowed [30]. Malware (from "malicious software") is a computer program created with the intention of damaging a system or network. There are numerous types of malware, which are intended to have different behaviors; a list is provided in [31]. Data acquisition malware takes data from the victim; honeypots and spam-traps are existing examples. Anti-virus programs can detect data acquisition malware. Behavior monitoring malware aims to monitor changes in the system state and sends the collected data to the attacker, which can be utilized for malicious purposes. These types of malware are identified by updated antivirus software. Account harvesting malware takes users' credentials from a database, search engine, webpage, or any online system, using a computer program. These attacks can be reduced by using a strong password policy, using different passwords for different systems or websites, and by locking accounts after a certain number of failed attempts. The authors in [32] created a penetration testing methodology to secure networks from these attacks.

A Trojan horse is a social engineering method that deceives a user about its true intention, and installs a backdoor that remotely controls the victim's computer, to alter or delete the victim's data [33]. A Trojan horse attack can be avoided by taking extra care when browsing the Internet [34], e.g., use only trusted software, never open mail from unknown senders, do not surf untrusted sites, install authorized antivirus software, and use a firewall to protect against unknown attackers. Packet sniffing targets the transmission medium; all of the communication packets between two participants of a network are captured and analyzed using specialized software. This type of attack can be countered by using a trusted medium of communication, never allowing unauthorized persons near the server, and only permitting trusted computers to access the network. Port scanning regularly scans a system's ports to identify an open port for malicious purposes [35]. An open, compromised port can be catastrophic for any system, and can allow a hacker to access the system's data. This attack can be avoided by disabling the port scanning of the system. A Byzantine attack compromises mobile networks, and involves the hacking of one of the devices on the network due to the leakage of information or credentials, which allows that device to act as a legitimate device. This type of attack is very difficult to identify, but can be minimized by continuous monitoring of the behavior of every device on the network and blocking devices that act abnormally [36]. The threats to a network can be detected using specialized software [37], and incorporating techniques to detect malware, spyware, and other undesired applications on the network.

2.3. Health Level Seven (HL7)

Standards are commonly needed, and HL7 is a well-known organization that creates standards. The exchange of clinical data is only possible between EHR systems if the systems are built on common standards during development; an example is the identification of the mandatory fields of patient information or tests. The global use of HL7 in clinical environments has streamlined the healthcare practice. According to its official website, HL7 has more than 1600 members in more than 50 countries, including corporate members, stakeholders, medicine companies, drug vendors, and suppliers

Health care is also a major initiative of some of the biggest global industries. In recent years, the health care industry has improved significantly, further advanced by inventions in the IoT. However, the communication of IoT and medical data is contentious issue. Although electronic health record (EHR) systems are able to manage the global needs of health-related industries, the security of medical data is a matter of concern. A lightweight and efficient mechanism is needed in the EHR system for the secure transfer of medical data on the basis of standards. This study follows the standards of HL7, one of the leading organizations in the creation of standards in the medical field, to create a robust, expandable, and reliable system for medical data communication.

2.4. Hyperledger Fabric

IBM's Hyperledger Fabric is a primary private blockchain platform for creating and maintaining distributed systems using modular consensus to follow a customized trust model. Fabric applications are written in general purpose languages including Java, Go, and node.js, whereas the smart contract is written in a domain-specific language. Hyperledger Fabric provides greater flexibility and an entirely different blockchain design that deals efficiently with the exhaustion of resources, attacks, and non-determinism [38]. Hyperledger Fabric is written in the Go language, which consists of endorsers, committers, a ledger, a database, and gossip. Endorsers are the peers in favor of transaction or chaincode execution. Committers are the peers that validate the proper configuration and verify the transaction according to the endorsement policy. The ledger consists of a transaction manger and a block store, to verify other transactions and to update the ledger. Gossip checks for ledger failures and maintains the correctness and efficiency of the whole system [39].

Hyperledger Fabric has two main components i.e., chaincode and the endorsement policy. Chaincode is a smart contract that lies at the heart of all the applications in Fabric and runs in the execution phase. It runs separately from Fabric code in a separate container called a Docker container. It stores data in CouchDB through a key-value that can be 'get' or 'put' to read or write transactions in the database. The endorsement policy runs validation and behaves as a protocol of the transaction validation, and cannot be altered by any non-trusted application. An endorsement policy enables chaincode to select the endorser of a transaction. Transactions are initiated by the clients using a chaincode function, who then digitally sign it and send it to the channel. All the peers check the authenticity, structure, and authorization of newly created transactions, via a number of checks that must be verified by the peers. If the peers verify all of the checks, the transaction is executed and the response value is stored in the key-value store.

All endorsements sent by the peers are gathered by the client and matched with the endorsement policy requirements. After gathering the required endorsements, resources are provided in the case of a read request. In the case of a write request, then all of the endorsements are collected and forwarded to an ordering service for the addition of the transaction. The ordering service sends all of the transactions, with their endorsement, to all peers on the same channel, where each channel contains all of the nodes communicating with each other and sharing information with each other over a blockchain network. The peers on the channel verify each of the transactions according to the endorsement fulfillment policy, which contains the smart contract agreement between all the stakeholders. On successful verification, the block is added to the ledger, but all of the endorsing peers have to commit the transaction.

2.5. Consensus Algorithm for Decentralized Trust Management

In the consensus algorithm, all of the nodes of the blockchain network reach an agreement regarding the latest state of the ledger. This consensus stabilizes the blockchain network and maintains the trust of the peers on the distributed network. There are different types of consensus algorithms, some of which are described here.

2.5.1. Proof-of-Work

This is the most famous consensus algorithm, and was initially used by Bitcoin, in which the miner has to solve a complex mathematical puzzle, thus requiring huge computing power. Among all of the peers, the peer that solves the puzzle first can mine a new block in the network.

2.5.2. Byzantine Fault Tolerant (BFT)

BFT introduced voting into the consensus, in which every node has to vote and must come to an agreement about the network's current condition. All the nodes in the network collectively define the blockchain ledger, which is divided into clusters on each node using Kafka. Maximum nodes in the network must participate in the process of voting for a decision in order to minimize the errors in the network. The most important benefit of using this algorithm in a network is that it maintains the network integrity, and will not crash, even if all nodes are not included in the voting process.

2.5.3. Proof-of-Stake

This is a simple algorithm based on the stake a node has in the form of Bitcoin. In contrast to proof-of-work, it does not require high processing power and can be mined with the minimum resources. The node can mine the block according to the percentage of Bitcoin it has, e.g., if a node has 5% of the Bitcoin, then it can mine 5% of the proof-of-stake blocks. Proof-of-stake provides maximum security against network attacks.

2.5.4. Proof-of-Capacity

Proof-of-capacity is the best alternative to proof-of-work and proof-of-stake. In proof-of-capacity, rather than using data centers for mining or the utilization of Bitcoins, free hard disk space is used in the consensus. The node with the maximum free hard disk space has a high probability of being chosen to mine the next block and to win a reward in the shape of a block.

2.5.5. Paxos

The Paxos algorithm is used to reach a consensus in a group of distributed computers. A node or group of nodes choses a value from a number of available choices, and sends it to the network as a broadcast. A consensus is reached when a majority of the nodes agrees on a chosen value. In the case of disagreement, an automated process terminates the consensus. Paxos is efficient in term of resource utilization as it will terminate the consensus instead of being endlessly blocked.

2.5.6. RAFT

RAFT is commonly used due its fault-tolerant nature, simplicity, and efficiency in distributed systems. In RAFT, the network is divided into three types of nodes: leader, candidates, and followers. In this algorithm, every new node must be added to the leader, which is also responsible for maintaining the log in the network, and the algorithm clones it in the network. In the case of a transaction, the leader broadcasts the write request to the followers and verifies its response. On confirmation from all of the nodes, the new transaction is added. A candidate is a node who wants to become a leader, and the leader is chosen on the basis of the votes of the followers. The candidate having the maximum number of followers will become the leader and the previous leader becomes a follower because it lost its majority. Figure 4 explains the complete process of the algorithm.

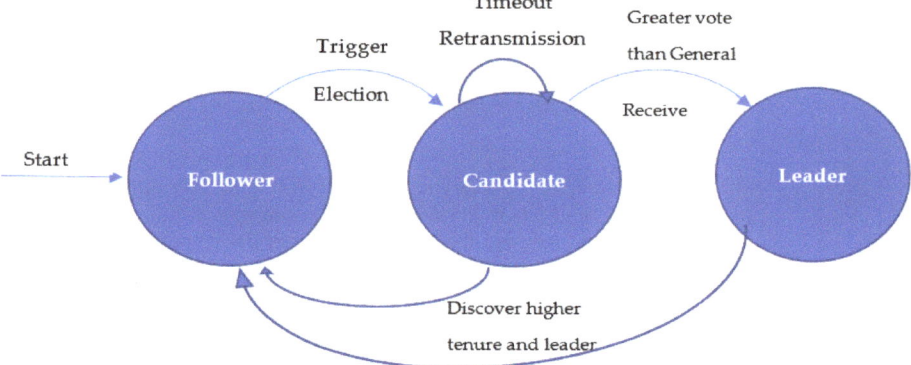

Figure 4. Working of the RAFT consensus.

2.6. Identity Management

Identity management is the task of creating and maintaining user identities. This task recognizes the individuals in a company, network, or country, and controls their access to the assets [40]. Most companies use identity management to lower the burden of data storage because it is not economical to save the record of a user who visited the company only once. An identity provider also enables the option of single sign-on (SSO) for users who want to access the system only once. The current study uses Shibboleth identity management because it is easy to configure and is free to use for study purposes.

Shibboleth is an open-source, multinational, federated identity management architecture [41]. The main concerns of identity management relate to the identity provider (IdP), service provider (SP), and the communication between them [42]. Shibboleth identity management uses Security Assertion Markup Language (SAML) for information transmission between the IdP and SP. Shibboleth identity management also permits the SP to manage their shared users' profile data. It also supports local single sign-on (SSO) and organizational level SSO, for inter-individual and inter-organizational communication, respectively. Users must follow the required procedure to receive the service from Shibboleth identity management. First, the user asks the SP for the service. This request is then forwarded to the IdP by the SP, and the IdP asks for user authentication. The IdP validates the response from the user. After validation, the IdP asks the SP to include the request of the user and provide the user with the service that it demanded [43].

3. Related Work

A blockchain solution for healthcare record sharing, based on Hyperledger Caliper, was proposed in [44]. Another study [45] focused on encryption schemes for sharing of records using a blockchain over cloud services; confusion and anonymity techniques were proposed for encryption of data in the presented model. A Bayesian model for monitoring activities was used in [46], which are then stored on a blockchain network without any consensus algorithm; here, the scheme merely focuses on creating a smart home and collecting data from different modules. Another paper on medical data communication with a blockchain for a cloud-based network mainly discusses security and encryption techniques [47]. A blockchain network based on Hyperledger Caliper intended for small businesses was proposed in [48]. The most recent related work is presented in [49], but this study is limited only to creating a data bank of the medical records and securing it using blockchain technology. Another blockchain-based solution for heath record sharing was proposed in [50]; however, it lacks encryption techniques and the cloud-based structure is not fit for some organizations.

An interesting study regarding the topic of discussion was presented in [51]; however, due to the use of mutable storage, the response time was slower than that of the proposed scheme. The research in [52] summarized some of the main studies related to blockchain and health, and also drew a comparison between these systems. However, it did not provide an implementation of their findings, and only compared the existing systems at the current time. Another system created under the blockchain umbrella was presented in [53]. This is an efficient system based on Hyperledger Fabric; although it has some similarities with our system, the study was not related to healthcare, and its results were inferior to those of the system presented in the current study. Ref. [54] presents a state-of-the-art network for sharing information, with the inclusion of identity management; however, this study is difficult to implement due to the much higher production cost. Another significant study in the field of secure transfer of information in health is presented in [55]. In this research, the authors propose a new model for information interchange between IoT devices using a blockchain network and the efficiency of a 5G network. Although the study showed promise, it is currently only a proposal and no implementation plan has yet been designed. A blockchain technology for communication in health applications due to the privacy and security provided by the blockchain was proposed in [56]. The study also proposes the use of cloud technology with Fabric, but the study does not provide an idea of how to implement it in the real world. All the studies presented above are either just proposals and are not yet implemented, or have lower efficiency than the system under study, due to the different limitations discussed above. Some also have a higher cost, are difficult to implement, or use cloud technology with the blockchain.

4. Proposed Solution

A blockchain is a distributed ledger with built-in security and privacy features, and can be used in communication by storing messages in chains of blocks for transmission, thus reducing many of the attacks that may occur during the secure communication. Applications related to financial transactions and users' personal data require strict access control. An audit is also required of who accessed the data, the time at which they accessed it, and the length of time for which they had access. All of these issues can be resolved using a blockchain's built-in feature; that is, once a transaction is confirmed in the blockchain, it is almost impossible to modify it in verifiable way [57]. The peer-to-peer nature of a blockchain makes it highly fault tolerant, because each node has the same copy as that of the other nodes, and it is difficult to alter all of these copies. In a system attack, the intruder is unable to change anything meaningful, and can be easily identified due to the log management of the blockchain.

A consensus is also required from all the participating nodes in order to perform a transaction or communication in a network. The use of the consensus reduces the effects of DoS or DDoS attacks, and makes it difficult to add malware to the blockchain network. Cryptography is also a built-in feature of blockchain, because every transaction in a network is communicated or stored in the form of a hash [58]. Each blockchain network uses a specialized hashing algorithm that is very difficult to crack. Thus, if an eavesdropper listens to a communication or has access to a transaction through packet sniffing, they cannot make use of it because it cannot be decrypted [59]. A blockchain network is not located at a single location, nor is it owned. This decentralized nature of a blockchain makes it resistant to port scanning attacks and also prevents the network from being destroyed. Due to the decentralized nature of a blockchain, the system availability is much higher than that of traditional systems. All of these features were the inspiration for the use of a blockchain in this study.

4.1. System Architecture of Proposed Model

The system under study uses an innovative architecture for medical data communications with the use of a blockchain, as shown in Figure 5. The suggested design consists of a service provider in a home station, a Shibboleth identity provider, and a blockchain ledger. The service provider must be registered in the home station, and provides the information to remote stations when required. The home station properly investigates the information, and only provides the information after verifying the role and authentication level of the medical person demanding the information. The home station prohibits access to the information if the request is not appropriate to the level of the role asking for the information.

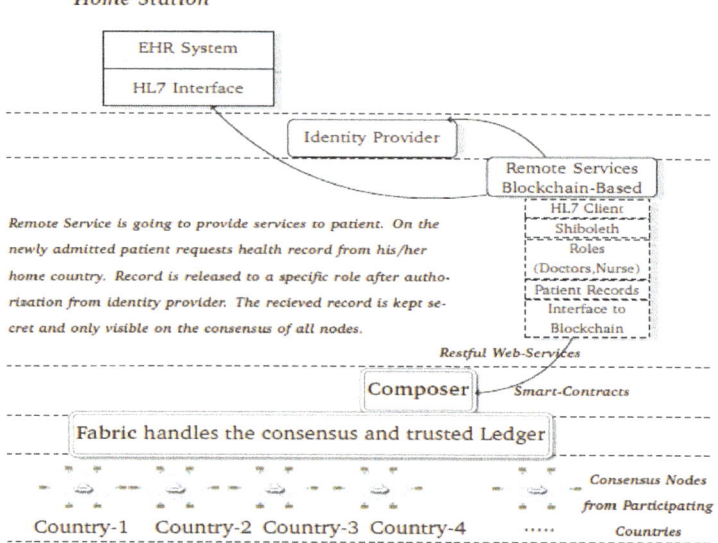

Figure 5. Proposed architecture.

In this study, Shibboleth federated identity management was included as the service provider due to its open-source nature and its adaptability in the domain. Using Shibboleth, each medical person is given a unique id and is authorized according to their role. Depending on their role, it is decided whether the healthcare personal should be given SSO or complete login credentials for that role, and for how long these credentials remain active for the particular medical person.

The blockchain maintains all records using CouchDB, according to the standards provided by HL7, thus ensuring the interoperability between different systems. This study used a permission blockchain, so no proof-of-work concept is required; rather, consensus is achieved using an automated procedure to maintain the efficiency of the system. A well-known Hyperledger algorithm, RAFT, was used as the consensus algorithm. RAFT is a fault-tolerant and easily understandable consensus algorithm that enables clients to create distributed systems as a single system. Randomized election, log replication, fault tolerance, and ease of use are the distinguishing properties that motivated the use of RAFT in this study.

4.2. Working Procedure

The client must by registered on the home station (HS) to be eligible to receive the services of the system. Algorithm 1 shows the working procedure for the registration of a client on the HS, in the case in which a patient traveled to a remote station (RS) and required their medical history from their home station. The client needs to open the interface provided by the identity provider corresponding to the HS through a web application, arranged by the patient's own country. Due to the security and sensitivity of healthcare data, the HS does not deliver sensitive information to a non-approved user; however, the HS asks the login credentials to be entered; the system then follows the procedure for authentication as shown in Algorithm 2. It first checks if the client has blockchain network access, and then asks for the client's login credentials. After a successful login, all of the relevant IdPs are displayed, which are authenticated by the HS.

Algorithm 1: Create_Contract: Algorithm that create a smart contract in blockchain network

---

Input: BlockchainAddress Ba, Timestamp Ts, HomeStation Hs, Client Ct, Terms&Conditions Tc
Output: Bool
1:     if Ct exist then
2:         return false
3:     else if Ct agrees on Tc then
4:         mapping Ct to Ba
5:         add it to ledger of Hs with Ts
6:         return true

A blockchain intermediary node is used to save the transactions on the blockchain network. The correspondence between the remote station and the home station is transmitted through this node, which is also associated with the blockchain through Hyperledger Composer. Figure 6 shows the complete working process in a sequence diagram. The Shibboleth identity provider provides the complete list of IdPs for their roles. This is also provided to all of the registered home stations, and these IDs are shared through a signed XML document for security purposes. The HS diverts the solicitations to the Shibboleth for approval of the mentioned job. The web application demands credentials, which are given by the respective IdP, and the HS requires the IdPs to be approved, regardless of their actions or their designation. All of the authentication and security are maintained by the IdP, and the service provider then diverts the resources to the HS, in addition to the approval tokens delivered by the IdP.

Algorithm 2: Access_Request: Algorithm shows how a client access its data on network

---

Input: BlockchainAddress Ba, Client Ct, Credentials Cd
Output: Bool
1:     if Ct is not Ba then
2:         throw;
3:     end
4:     if Cd $\geq$ Approved then
5:         return true
6:     else
7:         return false

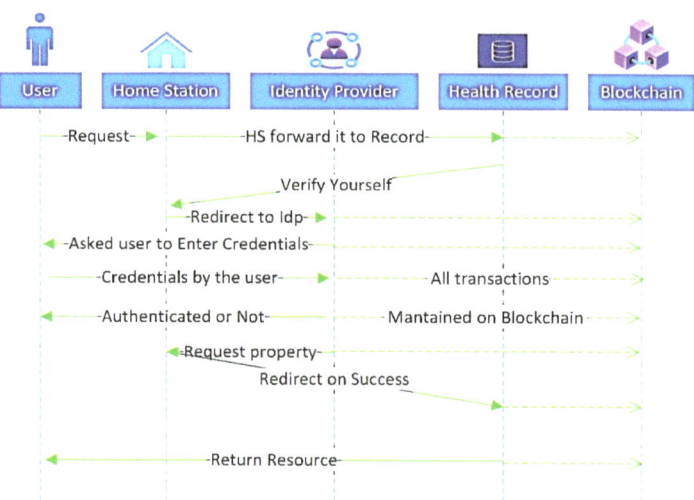

Figure 6. Proposed system's sequence diagram.

The HS approves the metadata, utilizing the protocols related to the security of the system, and delivers the clinical data in normalized form. The proposed design is based on the HL7 standards, which are presently used in numerous countries, because very little effort is required for their integration into the system. The proposed strategy safeguards the privacy of the entities utilizing the clinical data. It also recognizes the privilege of the patient to acquire the information about these elements, and makes it feasible and scalable for the HS. The distributed deployment and modular architecture lower the deployment burden for all parties involved in the process, and results in a steady change to the new system.

Algorithm 3 shows how patients and health personnel access the network. The access given to the user (patients) depends on their registration on the network, whereas the heath personnel access is subject to the person's role and the time required to access a document. Creating transactions in the network is restricted only to the specific authorized health personnel, and each access to the network by authorized personnel is stored, such as in a log book in the blockchain.

4.3. Implementation

This study was built on three basic modules, namely, the blockchain, Shibboleth, and HL7. The user identity, such as a CNIC or passport number, is required by the client to fetch his home station information to create a URL to communicate with the HL7 server. Net-HL7 was used in this study, with the help of a PHP parser through the PEAR extension. Figure 7 shows the code snippet of the interaction with the HL7 server.

When the client requests patient records from the remote HL7 server, the client connected with the network is redirected to the second module, Shibboleth, for authentication, and the Shibboleth module receives authentication from HL7 client. This blockchain network records all of the transactions during the process. The network communication work using the Apache shibd daemon and its source is located at httpd.conf(/etc/apache2/httpd.conf) on Apache, which redirects each web request to the mod shib. The communication between IdP and shibd uses Security Assertion Markup Language (SAML), and SSL is also implied to ensure security. During the execution, the service provider trusts the authentication of IdP and creates an authentication assertion as a response of authenticity. The Federated Identity Authentication (FIA) system is used by the Shibboleth for the consensus. When a remote station wants to access the information from the home station using HL7 standards, the FIA registers the remote station with a unique id. Figure 8 shows SAML snippets when a remote station wants to access the information from the home station

Algorithm 3: Blockchain Network Access and Registration

1. **Procedure:** BlockchainNetworkAccessRegistration
2. **Requirements from Health Personnel for Patient Data Access**: 1. Personnel Role Pr,
    2. Required Time Rt, Credentials for the Blockchain Network access CrBN
3. Patient Pt, ViewNetwork Vn, HealthPersonnel Hp, CreateTransactions Ct,
4. BroadcastToNetwrok BtN, AskForAuthorization AFA, Terms and Conditions Tc, Smart
5. Contract SC, BlockchainNetwork BN, PatientUniqueId PuId,
6. If Pt registered then {
7.   Vn ();
8.   If Hp authorized Pt data then {
9.   Vn ();
10.   If Hp authorized to Ct then {
11.   Ct (); BtN ();
12.   }
13.   }
14.   Else { AFA ();
15.   If Hp AFA then {
16.   If (Pr, Rt ==true) {return CrBN;}
17.   }
18. }
19. Else {
20.   If Patient agrees on Tc then {
21.   Create SC ();
22.   BtN ();
23.   If BN approves then {Return PuId;}
24.   Else {Request denied}
25.   }
26. }

```php
<? php
require_once " Net/HL7/Segment.php";
require_once " Net/HL7/Message.php";
require_once " Net/HL7/Connect.php";
    $memo = new Net_HL7_Message();
    $memo -> addSegment(new Net_HL7_Segments_MSH());
    $seg = new Net_HL7_Segment ("PID");
    $seg -> setField(3, "XXX");
    $memo -> addSegment( $seg );
    echo "Trying to connect";
    $socket = new Net_Socket ();
    $success = $socket -> connect (" https://user-id.home-station");
    if( $success instanceof PEAR_Error ){
        echo "Error:{ $success -> getMessage()}";
        exit (-1);
    }
    $conn=new Net_HL7_Connection ( $socket );
    echo "Sending message\n".$memo ->toString(true);
    $response = $conn -> send( $memo );
    if ($response ){
        echo "Received answer \n".$response->toString( true );
    }
    $conn -> close ();
?>
```

Figure 7. Interaction with HL7 server.

    The complete implementation process of this study is shown in Figure 9. Hyperledger Composer uses a business application model (BNA) for data manipulation, in which every response received or dispatch is registered against the unique id of each user. In this study, the BNA append-only mode was used to document all of the transactions on the blockchain.

The authorized persons from each organization can view this ledger via an interface, and the ledger can also be used to track or audit any transaction.

```
 1  <saml:AttributeStatement>
 2      <saml:Attribute Name="portal_id">
 3          <saml:AttributeValue xsi:type="xs:anyType">
 4              060D00000000SHZ
 5          </saml:AttributeValue>
 6      </saml:Attribute>
 7      <saml:Attribute Name="organization_id">
 8          <saml:AttributeValue xsi:type="xs:anyType">
 9              00DD0000000F7P5
10          </saml:AttributeValue>
11      </saml:Attribute>
12  </saml:AttributeStatement>
```

Figure 8. SAML code for information access.

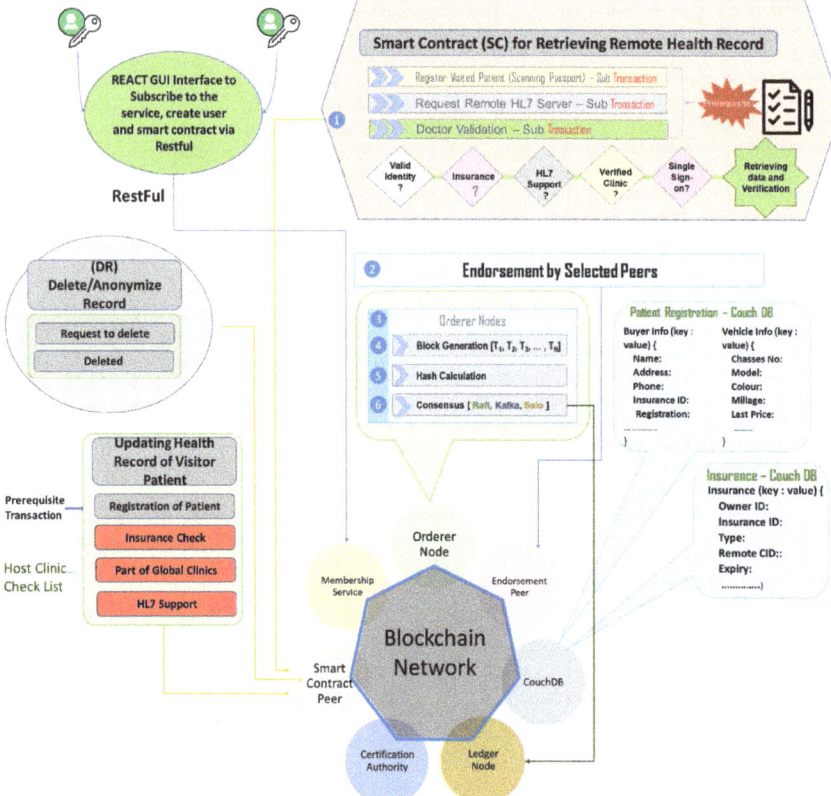

Figure 9. Complete implementation diagram.

5. Results and Evaluations

All of the results obtained below were generated using the system specification shown in Table 1.

Table 1. Specification of the environment.

Specification	Value
CPU	Dell server (intel 3.4 quad-core i7)
Memory	32 GB
Network Bandwidth	4 Mb CIR
Concurrent blockchain nodes	20

The use of the blockchain in the communication process protects the medical data by encrypting it using asymmetric cryptography. It also improves the efficiency in terms of the total cost of the system for storage and document access. The comparison of this study with other EHR systems shows that the document access and retrieval time is faster in the proposed approach compared to that in the other systems. Table 2 summarizes the comparison between the system under study and other existing systems. The data in Table 2 clearly indicate the superiority of the system under study with respect to the existing alternatives ([50,51,60,61]). The alternative approaches are either centralized or semi-centralized. This is in contrast to the system under study, which is based on a decentralized network, thus making it durable and coherent in terms of availability and access.

Table 2. Comparison between existing frameworks and the proposed system.

Schemes	[60]	[50]	[61]	[51]	Proposed System
Source Data	Yes	Yes	Yes	Yes	Yes
Data Storage Type	PACS	Cloud Server	Dedicated	Mutable P2P	Immutable Storage
Tamper Proof	No	Yes	Yes	Yes	Yes
Encryption Type	Not Mentioned	Not Mentioned	Symmetric	Asymmetric	Asymmetric
Database Sharing	PACS	Blockchain	Blockchain	Blockchain	Blockchain
Smart Contract	No	Yes	No	No	Yes
Attack Resilience	No	No	No	No	Yes
Database Type	Centralized	Centralized	Centralized	Semi-Centralized	De-Centralized

The storage type used by [51] is a mutable peer-to-peer storage network with manual entry by the health personal, and [60] uses picture archiving and communication systems (PACS). As a result of their respective approaches, both of these systems are vulnerable to data attacks by hackers, and to anomalies created due to the duplication of data. The proposed system is superior due to its use of an immutable blockchain technology and hashes to store data, which removes the probability of data duplication. The proposed system provides users full command of their information with greater security, clarity, and integrity. Due to the use of a blockchain, the proposed system's transactions are not prone to deletion and information can be easily recovered in the case of a node failure. Encryption and decryption on all the comparative systems are performed manually, which can cause data issues. In contrast, the proposed system utilizes the advantages of the built-in features of the blockchain technology for encryption and decryption. Protection of documents after decryption is also an issue, which is resolved in this system with the use of digital signatures.

The proposed system also provides a great deal of resilience against cyber-attacks, thus improving the overall security of the system. This resilience is not provided by any of the comparative approaches. The proposed system is based on encryption and each transaction is encrypted prior to transfer. Due to the use of asymmetric encryption and immutable storage, the proposed system is secure and transaction alteration is almost impossible due to the presence of the distributed ledger, which protects it from alterations. Due to the fault tolerance of RAFT, the consensus algorithm used in this study, the system is robust and reduces the downtime of the network.

Appl. Sci. **2022**, *12*, 2307

5.1. Performance Analysis

The performance of the blockchain network can be measured by analyzing the running time with the variation in the number of orderers and peers. The running time is short for a small network with few orderers and peers. Table 3 shows the running time with a different number of orderers and peers in Hyperledger Fabric. The results are based on the average of thirty different running times, using the same number of orderers and peers in a network. The results were gathered by ensuring that the overhead of other applications does not alter the performance of the block in the network; this was achieved by using Hyperledger Fabric to create the block in the permissioned blockchain network. Figures 10 and 11, respectively, show the time taken to upload and download the medical documents using the proposed system.

Table 3. Performance analysis of block creation.

Peers	Orderers	Running Time
3	1	3.8 s
3	2	3.9 s
5	1	4.7 s
5	2	4.7 s
7	1	5.2 s
7	2	5.3 s

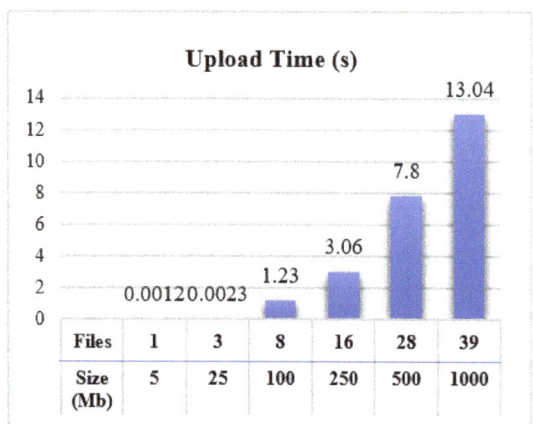

Figure 10. Uploading performance in seconds.

The variation in the graph shows a gradual increase in the time required for uploading and downloading documents (i.e., a receipt, body scan, prescription, X-ray, etc.). In the proposed system, the system takes around three seconds to upload 250 Mb of data, which can contain up to sixteen documents, over a stable network connection with reasonable bandwidth.

The uploading time increases with the increase in the file size, and it takes 7.8 s to upload a file of 500 Mb. All these results were gathered using a virtual machine with the Ubuntu 16.4 operating system, with no other application software installed except the recommended software for the proposed system. The downloading time also shows a gradual increase. As shown in Figure 11, it takes almost three and a half seconds to download a file of 100 Mb, and 26.34 s to download a file of 1000 Mb, over a stable internet connection with reasonable bandwidth.

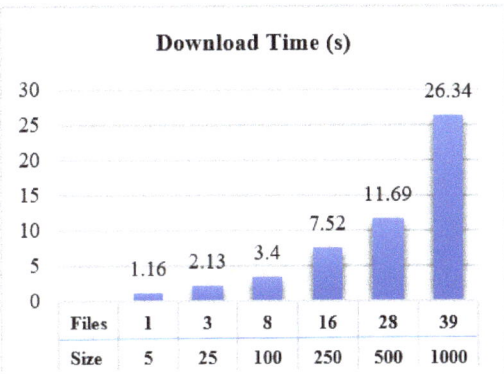

Figure 11. Downloading performance in seconds.

The time required to execute the different policies (read, write, update, delete, and revoke) can be used to analyze system performance. Figure 12 shows comparative analysis of the respective policies introduced in [51,61,62] with the system under study; each comparison is for the execution time of each policy. The experimental results clearly show that the proposed system is superior for almost every type of policy used.

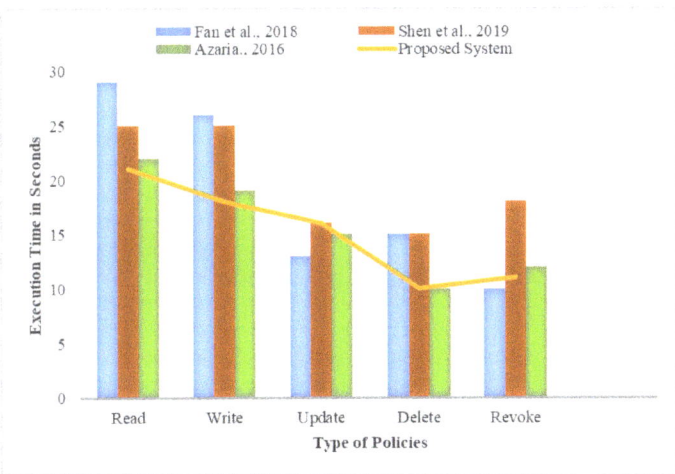

Figure 12. Comparison of policies with respect to execution time.

5.2. Latency Analysis

The delay between the action of a user and the response from the system is known as the latency or the trip time of a data packet. Latency analysis can also be used for performance evaluation; a lower latency means that the system is more responsive and efficient. Figure 13 shows the comparison of the latency of the proposed system with that of [53,54].

5.3. Limitations

As in all systems, benefits are achieved in combination with limitations. In the proposed system, it is difficult to connect current EHR systems that are not created according to the HL7 standards. Furthermore, all of the systems around the world, and every client/patient, must be registered to the network in order to attain the benefits of the network.

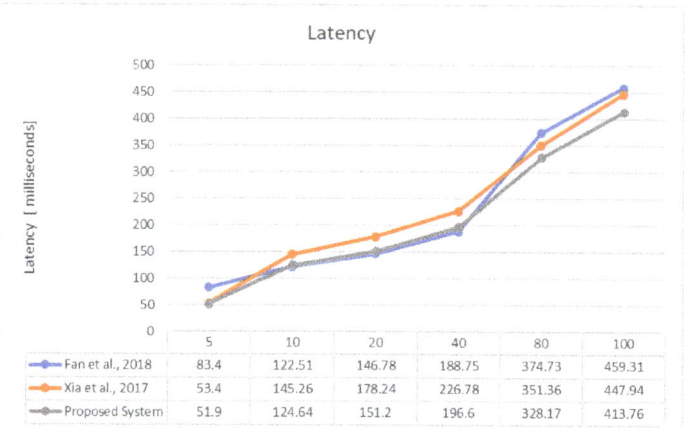

Figure 13. Comparison of the delay against the number of requests.

6. Conclusions and Future Work

Although many systems for online record sharing exist, including medical data sharing, most of these are designed either for a specific location, region, or institute, such as a hospital, or do not meet the expected security levels. Most global communications systems are centralized. However, with the advent of the blockchain in cryptocurrency, many fields are attracted toward the idea of decentralization and the benefits provided by customized changes. Blockchain technology has advanced the information technology industry. In this study, a revolutionary blockchain technology was proposed for use in the medical communication field, and a global health record exchange system that is not dependent on the location of the user was created for the transfer of medical data. Using blockchain technology and the Shibboleth federated identity management system, the proposed system performs authentication of the users and the person requiring users' information, under the guidance and support of Health Level Seven standards. The proposed system ensures that a patient is able to provide their medical information to any healthcare worker around the world, without any risk of the data being leaked or hacked.

The system provides appropriate security for all of the stakeholders present in the consensus, and stores each copy of their transaction or data in their home station network. The data shared with the remote country or location is temporary and deleted after a certain period of time or according to the user's requirement; however, every record is maintained in the ledger of the network to maintain the integrity of the data. Blockchain technology is currently penetrating almost every field and shows promise for future applications. However, in this study, it is only used to enable secure data communication in healthcare. In the future, this work can be expanded to add other medical aspects, such as doctors' prescriptions, pharmacy transactions, and vendors' purchases and sales. These additional topics require further research.

Author Contributions: Conceptualization, T.A.S.; Formal analysis, G.Q.B.; Funding acquisition, A.P.; Investigation, G.Q.B.; Methodology, T.A.S.; Project administration, R.R.; Resources, R.R. and S.S.R.; Software, G.Q.B.; Supervision, R.R.; Validation, T.A.S.; Visualization, G.Q.B.; Writing—original draft, G.Q.B. and T.A.S.; Writing—review & editing, R.R., S.S.R. and A.P. All authors have read and agreed to the published version of the manuscript.

Funding: This research work was supported by the National Research Foundation of Korea (NRF) grants funded by the Korean government under reference number (2020R1A2C1012196).

Institutional Review Board Statement: Not applicable.

Informed Consent Statement: Not applicable.

Data Availability Statement: Not applicable.

Acknowledgments: Special acknowledgement to Junaid Gul for his help and guidance during the research work. We would like to thank HED AJK for the utilization of their servers for testing. We would like to acknowledge the Deanship of research, Islamic University of Madinah for their support in all aspects of completing this research.

Conflicts of Interest: The authors declare no conflict of interest.

References

1. Collins, F.S. Exceptional Opportunities in Medical Science: A View from the National Institutes of Health. *JAMA* **2015**, *313*, 131–132. [CrossRef] [PubMed]
2. Fernández-Alemán, J.L.; Señor, I.C.; Lozoya, P.Á.O.; Toval, A. Security and privacy in electronic health records: A systematic literature review. *J. Biomed. Inform.* **2013**, *46*, 541–562. [CrossRef] [PubMed]
3. Khushi, M.; Shaukat, K.; Alam, T.M.; Hameed, I.A.; Uddin, S.; Luo, S.; Yang, X.; Reyes, M.C. A comparative performance analysis of data resampling methods on imbalance medical data. *IEEE Access* **2021**, *9*, 109960–109975. [CrossRef]
4. Christidis, K.; Devetsikiotis, M. Blockchains and smart contracts for the Internet of Things. *IEEE Access* **2016**, *4*, 2292–2303. [CrossRef]
5. Transaction, C.P. *Blockchain: Opportunities for Health Care*; Technical Report; Deloitte Touche Tohmatsu Ltd.: London, UK, 2018; Volume 1.
6. Ali, T. Z notation formalization of blockchain healthcare document sharing based on crbac. *J. Inf. Commun. Technol. Robot. Appl.* **2018**, *9*, 16–29.
7. TierIon. TierIon: Technology and Products that Reduce the Cost and Complexity of Trust. 2018. Available online: https://tierion.com/ (accessed on 18 September 2018).
8. GEMOS. The Blockchain Operating System. 2018. Available online: https://enterprise.gem.co/ (accessed on 18 September 2018).
9. Brannan, B. Healthcoin-Blockchain-Enabled Platform for Diabetes Prevention. Available online: https://medium.com/blockchain-healthcare-review/healthcoin-blockchain-enabled-platform-for-diabetes-prevention-b3448b34cf36 (accessed on 21 August 2018).
10. Haidar, F.; Kaiser, A.; Lonc, B.; Urien, P.; Denis, R. C-its use cases: Study, extension and classification methodology. In Proceedings of the 2018 IEEE 87th Vehicular Technology Conference (VTC Spring), Porto, Portugal, 3–6 June 2018.
11. Xu, Y.; Li, Q.; Min, X.; Cui, L.; Xiao, Z.; Kong, L. E-commerce blockchain consensus mechanism for supporting high-throughput and real-time transaction. In Proceedings of the International Conference on Collaborative Computing: Networking, Applications and Worksharing, Beijing, China, 10–11 November 2016; pp. 490–496.
12. Li, K.; Li, H.; Hou, H.; Li, K.; Chen, Y. Proof of vote: A high performance consensus protocol based on vote mechanism & consortium blockchain. In Proceedings of the 2017 IEEE 19th International Conference on High Performance Computing and Communications; IEEE 15th International Conference on Smart City; IEEE 3rd International Conference on Data Science and Systems, Bangkok, Thailand, 18–20 December 2017.
13. Nasir, A.; Shaukat, K.; Khan, K.I.; Hameed, I.A.; Alam, T.M.; Luo, S. What is Core and What Future Holds for Blockchain Technologies and Cryptocurrencies: A Bibliometric Analysis. *IEEE Access* **2020**, *9*, 989–1004. [CrossRef]
14. Syed, T.A.; Alzahrani, A.; Jan, S.; Siddiqui, M.S.; Nadeem, A.; Alghamdi, T. A comparative analysis of blockchain architecture and its applications: Problems and recommendations. *IEEE Access* **2019**, *7*, 176838–176869. [CrossRef]
15. Nakamoto Michael, J.; Cohn AL, A.N.; Butcher, J.R. Blockchain technology. *Journal* **2018**, *1*, 35–45.
16. Nakamoto, S. Bitcoin: A peer-to-peer electronic cash system. *Econometrica* **2019**, 1–48.
17. Yaga, D.; Mell, P.; Roby, N.; Scarfone, K. *NISTIR 8202 Blockchain Technology Overview*; National Institute of Standards and Technology, US Department of Commerce: Washington, DC, USA, 2018.
18. Vukolić, M. Rethinking permissioned blockchains. In Proceedings of the ACM Workshop on Blockchain, Cryptocurrencies and Contracts, Abu Dhabi, United Arab Emirates, 2 April 2017; pp. 3–7.
19. Yu, H.; Sun, H.; Wu, D.; Kuo, T.T. Comparison of Smart Contract blockchains for Healthcare Applications. In *AMIA Annual Symposium Proceedings*; American Medical Informatics Association: Bethesda, MD, USA, 2019; Volume 2019, p. 1266.
20. AlTaei, M.; Al Barghuthi, N.B.; Mahmoud, Q.H.; Al Barghuthi, S.; Said, H. Blockchain for UAE Organizations: Insights from CIOs with opportunities and challenges. In Proceedings of the 2018 International Conference on Innovations in Information Technology (IIT), Al Ain, United Arab Emirates, 18–19 November 2018; pp. 157–162.
21. Niranjanamurthy, M.; Nithya, B.N.; Jagannatha, S. Analysis of blockchain technology: Pros, Cons and SWOT. *Clust. Comput.* **2019**, *22*, 14743–14757. [CrossRef]
22. Luhmann, N. What is communication? *Commun. Theory* **1992**, *2*, 251–259. [CrossRef]
23. Planer, R.J.; Godfrey-Smith, P. Communication and representation understood as sender–receiver coordination. *Mind Lang.* **2020**, *36*, 750–770. [CrossRef]
24. Shaukat, K.; Luo, S.; Varadharajan, V.; Hameed, I.A.; Chen, S.; Liu, D.; Li, J. Performance comparison and current challenges of using machine learning techniques in cybersecurity. *Energies* **2020**, *13*, 2509. [CrossRef]
25. Baitha, A.K.; Vinod, S. Session Hijacking and Prevention Technique. *Int. J. Eng. Technol.* **2018**, *7*, 193–198. [CrossRef]

26. Jain, V.; Sahu, D.R.; Tomar, D.S. Session Hijacking: Threat Analysis and Countermeasures. In Proceedings of the International Conference on Futuristic Trends in Computational Analysis and Knowledge Management, Greater Noida, India, 25–27 February 2015.
27. Burgers, W.; Verdult, R.; Eekelen, M.V. *Prevent Session Hijacking by Binding the Session to the Cryptographic Network Credentials*; Nordic Conference on Secure IT Systems; Springer: Berlin/Heidelberg, Germany, 2013.
28. Liu, J.; Xiao, Y.; Ghaboosi, K.; Deng, H.; Zhang, J. Botnet: Classification, attacks, detection, tracing, and preventive measures. *EURASIP J. Wirel. Commun. Netw.* **2009**, *2009*, 692654. [CrossRef]
29. Shaukat, K.; Alam, T.M.; Hameed, I.A.; Khan, W.A.; Abbas, N.; Luo, S. A Review on Security Challenges in Internet of Things (IoT). In Proceedings of the 2021 26th International Conference on Automation and Computing (ICAC), Portsmouth, UK, 2–4 September 2021; pp. 1–6.
30. Grangeia, L. *Dns Cache Snooping*; Technical Report; Securi Team—Beyond Security: Cupertino, CA, USA, 2004.
31. Rieck, K.; Holz, T.; Willems, C.; Düssel, P.; Laskov, P. Learning and classification of malware behavior. In Proceedings of the International Conference on Detection of Intrusions and Malware, and Vulnerability Assessment, Paris, France, 10–11 July 2008; pp. 108–125.
32. Shaukat, K.; Faisal, A.; Masood, R.; Usman, A.; Shaukat, U. Security quality assurance through penetration testing. In Proceedings of the 2016 19th International Multi-Topic Conference (INMIC), Islamabad, Pakistan, 5–6 December 2016; pp. 1–6.
33. Zhang, X. *The Diagnosis and Prevention of Computer Virus*; China Environmental Science Press: Beijing, China, 2008.
34. Zhu, Z. Study on Computer Trojan Horse Virus and Its Prevention. *Int. J. Eng. Appl. Sci.* **2015**, *2*, 257840.
35. Uma, M.; Padmavathi, G. A Survey on Various Cyber Attacks and their Classification. *IJ Netw. Secur.* **2013**, *15*, 390–396.
36. Awerbuch, B.; Curtmola, R.; Holmer, D.; Nita-Rotaru, C.; Rubens, H. *Mitigating Byzantine Attacks in Ad HocWireless Networks*; Technical Report Version; Department of Computer Science, Johns Hopkins University: Baltimore, MD, USA, 2004.
37. Shaukat, K.; Luo, S.; Chen, S.; Liu, D. Cyber Threat Detection Using Machine Learning Techniques: A Performance Evaluation Perspective. In Proceedings of the 2020 International Conference on Cyber Warfare and Security (ICCWS), Islamabad, Pakistan, 20–21 October 2020; pp. 1–6.
38. Androulaki, E.; Barger, V.; Bortnikov, C.; Cachin, K.; Christidis, A.; De Caro, D.; Enyeart, C.; Ferris, G.; Laventman, Y.; Manevich, S.; et al. Hyperledger fabric: A distributed operating system for permissioned blockchains. In Proceedings of the Thirteenth EuroSys Conference, EuroSys'18, Porto, Portugal, 23–26 April 2018; pp. 30:1–30:15.
39. Karp, R.; Schindelhauer, C.; Shenker, S.; Vocking, B. Randomized rumor spreading. In Proceedings of the Symposium on Foundations of Computer Science (FOCS), Redondo Beach, CA, USA, 12–14 November 2000; pp. 565–574.
40. Kumar, V.; Bhardwaj, A. Identity Management Systems. *Int. J. Strateg. Decis. Sci.* **2018**, *9*, 63–78. [CrossRef]
41. Needleman, M. The Shibboleth Authentication/Authorization System. *Ser. Rev.* **2004**, *30*, 252–253. [CrossRef]
42. Dudczak, A.; Helinski, M.; Mazurek, C.; Mielnicki, M.; Werla, M. Extending the Shibboleth identity management model with a networked user profile. In Proceedings of the 2008 1st International Conference on Information Technology, Gdansk, Poland, 18–21 May 2008. [CrossRef]
43. Birrell, E.; Schneider, F.B. Federated identity management systems: A privacy-based characterization. *IEEE Secur. Priv.* **2013**, *11*, 36–48. [CrossRef]
44. Tanwar, S.; Parekh, K.; Evans, R. Blockchain-based electronic healthcare record system for healthcare 4.0 applications. *J. Inf. Secur. Appl.* **2020**, *50*, 102407. [CrossRef]
45. Chen, Y.; Meng, L.; Zhou, H.; Xue, G. A Blockchain-Based Medical Data Sharing Mechanism with Attribute-Based Access Control and Privacy Protection. *Wirel. Commun. Mob. Comput.* **2021**, *2021*, 6685762. [CrossRef]
46. Khezr, S.; Benlamri, R.; Yassine, A. Blockchain-based Model for Sharing Activities of Daily Living in Healthcare Applications. In Proceedings of the 2020 IEEE International Conference on Dependable, Autonomic and Secure Computing, International Conference on Pervasive Intelligence and Computing, International Conference on Cloud and Big Data Computing, Intl Conf on Cyber Science and Technology Congress (DASC/PiCom/CBDCom/CyberSciTech), Calgary, AB, Canada, 17–22 August 2020; pp. 627–633.
47. Tan, L.; Yu, K.; Shi, N.; Yang, C.; Wei, W.; Lu, H. Towards secure and privacy-preserving data sharing for COVID-19 medical records: A blockchain-empowered approach. *IEEE Trans. Netw. Sci. Eng.* **2021**, *9*, 271–281. [CrossRef]
48. Zaabar, B.; Cheikhrouhou, O.; Jamil, F.; Ammi, M.; Abid, M. HealthBlock: A secure blockchain-based healthcare data management system. *Comput. Netw.* **2021**, *200*, 108500. [CrossRef]
49. Lee, J.S.; Chew, C.J.; Liu, J.Y.; Chen, Y.C.; Tsai, K.Y. Medical blockchain: Data sharing and privacy preserving of EHR based on smart contract. *J. Inf. Secur. Appl.* **2022**, *65*, 103117. [CrossRef]
50. Xia, Q.I.; Sifah, E.B.; Asamoah, K.O.; Gao, J.; Du, X.; Guizani, M. MeDShare: Trust-less medical data sharing among cloud service providers via blockchain. *IEEE Access* **2017**, *5*, 14757–14767. [CrossRef]
51. Shen, B.; Guo, J.; Yang, Y. MedChain: Efficient healthcare data sharing via blockchain. *Appl. Sci.* **2019**, *9*, 1207. [CrossRef]
52. Prokofieva, M.; Miah, S.J. Blockchain in healthcare. *Australas. J. Inf. Syst.* **2019**, *23*. [CrossRef]
53. Syed, T.A.; Siddique, M.S.; Nadeem, A.; Alzahrani, A.; Jan, S.; Khattak MA, K. A novel blockchain-based framework for vehicle life cycle tracking: An end-to-end solution. *IEEE Access* **2020**, *8*, 111042–111063. [CrossRef]
54. Choudhury, O.; Fairoza, N.; Sylla, I.; Das, A. A blockchain framework for managing and monitoring data in multi-site clinical trials. *arXiv* **2019**, arXiv:1902.03975.

55. Srinivasu, P.N.; Bhoi, A.K.; Nayak, S.R.; Bhutta, M.R.; Woźniak, M. Blockchain Technology for Secured Healthcare Data Communication among the Non-Terminal Nodes in IoT Architecture in 5G Network. *Electronics* **2021**, *10*, 1437. [CrossRef]
56. Clim, A.; Zota, R.D.; Constantinescu, R. Data exchanges based on blockchain in m-Health applications. *Procedia Comput. Sci.* **2019**, *160*, 281–288. [CrossRef]
57. Wood, G. Ethereum: A secure decentralised generalised transaction ledger. *Ethereum Proj. Yellow Paper* **2014**, *151*, 1–32.
58. Schneier, B.; Kelsey, J. Cryptographic Support for Secure Logs on Untrusted Machines. In Proceedings of the USENIX Security Symposium, San Antonio, TX, USA, 26–29 January 1998.
59. Schneier, B.; Kelsey, J. Secure audit logs to support computer forensics. *ACM Trans. Inf. Syst. Secur.* **1999**, *2*, 159–176. [CrossRef]
60. Langer, S.G.; Tellis, W.; Carr, C.; Daly, M.; Erickson, B.J.; Mendelson, D.; Moore, S.; Perry, J.; Shastri, K.; Warnock, M.; et al. The RSNA Image Sharing Network. *J. Digit. Imaging* **2014**, *28*, 53–61. [CrossRef] [PubMed]
61. Fan, K.; Wang, S.; Ren, Y.; Li, H.; Yang, Y. Medblock: Efficient and secure medical data sharing via blockchain. *J. Med. Syst.* **2018**, *42*, 1–11. [CrossRef] [PubMed]
62. Azaria, A.; Ekblaw, A.; Vieira, T.; Lippman, A. Medrec: Using blockchain for medical data access and permission management. In Proceedings of the 2016 2nd International Conference on Open and Big Data (OBD), Vienna, Austria, 22–24 August 2016; pp. 25–30.

Article

Detecting Small Anatomical Structures in 3D Knee MRI Segmentation by Fully Convolutional Networks

Mengtao Sun [1], Li Lu [1], Ibrahim A. Hameed [1,*], Carl Petter Skaar Kulseng [2] and Kjell-Inge Gjesdal [2]

1. Department of ICT and Natural Sciences, Faculty of Information Technology and Electrical Engineering, Norwegian University of Science and Technology, 6009 Ålesund, Norway; mengtao.sun@ntnu.no (M.S.); lulinw2018@gmail.com (L.L.)
2. Sunnmøre MR-Klinikk, 6010 Ålesund, Norway; carlkulseng@gmail.com (C.P.S.K.); k.i.gjesdal@medisin.uio.no (K.-I.G.)
*   Correspondence: ibib@ntnu.no; Tel.: +47-41315695

Citation: Sun, M.; Lu, L.; Hameed, I.A.; Kulseng, C.P.S.; Gjesdal, K.-I. Detecting Small Anatomical Structures in 3D Knee MRI Segmentation by Fully Convolutional Networks. Appl. Sci. 2022, 12, 283. https://doi.org/10.3390/app12010283

Academic Editors: Manuel Armada and Fabio La Foresta

Received: 20 September 2021
Accepted: 27 December 2021
Published: 28 December 2021

Publisher's Note: MDPI stays neutral with regard to jurisdictional claims in published maps and institutional affiliations.

Copyright: © 2021 by the authors. Licensee MDPI, Basel, Switzerland. This article is an open access article distributed under the terms and conditions of the Creative Commons Attribution (CC BY) license (https://creativecommons.org/licenses/by/4.0/).

Abstract: Accurately identifying the pixels of small organs or lesions from magnetic resonance imaging (MRI) has a critical impact on clinical diagnosis. U-net is the most well-known and commonly used neural network for image segmentation. However, the small anatomical structures in medical images cannot be well recognised by U-net. This paper explores the performance of the U-net architectures in knee MRI segmentation to find a relative structure that can obtain high accuracies for both small and large anatomical structures. To maximise the utilities of U-net architecture, we apply three types of components, residual blocks, squeeze-and-excitation (SE) blocks, and dense blocks, to construct four variants of U-net, namely U-net variants. Among these variants, our experiments show that SE blocks can improve the segmentation accuracies of small labels. We adopt DeepLabv3plus architecture for 3D medical image segmentation by equipping SE blocks based on this discovery. The experimental results show that U-net with SE block achieves higher accuracy in parts of small anatomical structures. In contrast, DeepLabv3plus with SE block performs better on the average dice coefficient of small and large labels.

Keywords: medical image segmentation; convolutional neural networks; SE block; U-net; DeepLabV3plus

1. Introduction

Knee osteoarthritis is the most common musculoskeletal disease in the world [1]. Lesions commonly induce structural changes within the small articular cartilage [2]. MRI (magnetic resonance imaging) technologies provide the means to characterise structural alterations in different joint tissues affected by osteoarthritis. Patients who undergo knee MRI for presumed musculoskeletal disease can also have unexpected vascular findings or pathology in the imaged field. [3]. In general, osteoarthritis is categorised by the progressive degradation of joint tissues with various abnormalities [4] and has been a severe issue in recent years. However, some small anatomical structures around the joint are hardly detected. For example, the veins and ligaments can show critical early alarms in musculoskeletal lesions [5]. This study will explore the performance of small structure segmentation in knee MRI by using deep learning.

The accurate segmentation of structures is helpful in clinical workflows in multiple domains such as diagnostic intervention and treatment planning. However, manual segmentation of anatomical structures is often time-consuming, labour-intensive, and prone to errors; therefore, it has prompted studies on automated segmentation [6]. The knee joint is one of the most important joints in the human body and is frequently injured in sports and other accidents. Automated knee segmentation can assist orthopaedists in examining and treating various kinds of knee lesions. Deep convolutional neural networks (CNNs) have been used for medical image segmentation since the rapid development of deep learning techniques in recent decades. They have improved the segmentation accuracy, and decreased the time and manual labour.

The definition of semantic segmentation is that each pixel or voxel of an image is marked with a specific label. A well-performed model can accurately classify each pixel or voxel. Traditionally, global features or structural features are beneficial for classification. They can be acquired through stacked convolutions with strides and various pooling operations, but the spatial information can be lost gradually during this process. Fully convolution networks (FCNs) [7] solved this problem, to some extent, by using three techniques: (1) replacing fully connected layers with convolutions to output images instead of probabilities; (2) using deconvolution to implement upsampling to reconstruct the output image; and (3) using skip connections to fuse information from layers with different strides to improve segmentation details.

Medical image segmentation requires higher accuracy than natural image segmentation and requires neural networks to adjust the architecture to yield more precise segmentation. U-net [8] was developed based on FCN. It uses a symmetrical encoder–decoder architecture and has succeeded in medical image segmentation [9,10]. In U-net, the encoder is a downsampling path that extracts features from input images through the combination of convolutions. The decoder uses upsampling operations instead of pooling, many stacked deconvolutions, and skip connections to combine the features with those in the encoder. These components enable the network to exploit multi-scale context information to obtain high-accuracy segmentation results.

Most medical images are 3D, such as MRI and CT (computed tomography) [11]. 3D medical image segmentation is computationally expensive; therefore, systems are commonly trained patch-wise. When patch-wise training is adopted, the receptive field is reduced initially, which will hinder the ability to capture global features and larger context. To address this problem, we adopt networks that can gain the same receptive field with fewer parameters and enable us to use a larger patch size to feed the network. DeepLab series [12–15] is designed for 2D image segmentation with high accuracy and detailed segmentation maps. DeepLabv1 [12] introduces atrous convolution and fully connected conditional random fields (CRF) to solve the problems brought by reduced resolution. DeepLabv2 [13] proposes atrous spatial pyramid pooling (ASPP), which uses multiple parallel atrous convolution layers with different sampling rates. DeepLabv3 [14] discusses four types of FCNs and improved ASPP. DeepLabv3plus [15] improves ASPP with atrous depthwise separable convolution to get the same receptive field with fewer parameters than standard convolutions. It uses an asymmetrical encoder–decoder architecture. The encoder is comprised of improved Xception and ASPP. The decoder uses bilinear upsampling concatenated with the corresponding low-level features from the network backbone.

Medical datasets are usually imbalanced, which will reduce the performance of machine learning models [16–18]. For the annotated MRI knee images used in this work, there are multiple classes where the frequencies of voxels of each class are extraordinarily different. For example, the size of bone is much larger than blood vessel (see Section 4). When the networks with fewer parameters are selected, their representation capacity may not be sufficient to maintain the required details to obtain accurate segmentation results for small objects/organs. However, patch-wise training cannot be avoided if complicated networks are chosen, damaging captured structural features that are beneficial for the segmentation of larger structures. For example, bones will be carelessly separated into different patches, making it difficult for the model to learn their structural features. Therefore, structural features need to be better extracted to assist the segmentation. We need to consider the results between the required segmentation details of both small and large structures and the computational cost.

This paper proposes different U-net variants to check the performance between diverse knee anatomical structures. Inspired by DeepLabv3plus, we further develop DeepLabv3plus with ASPP (atrous spatial pyramid pooling). We test the effectiveness of DeepLabv3plus variants to balance the capability of global feature extraction and required resolution. As a result, DeepLabv3plus variants perform better than U-net variants in terms of the average dice coefficient of all structures. The main contributions include:

(1) We propose four types of 3D U-net variants aimed at small anatomical structure segmentation in MRI images. We found that SE block performs well in small anatomical detection;
(2) Based on the success of SE block in U-net variants, we apply the DeepLabv3plus with SE block and transfer the 2D DeepLabv3plus into a 3D version for anatomical segmentation of real MRI images;
(3) In experiments, we improve the results from the small anatomical structure segmentation on the knee MRI images provided by Sunnmøre MR-Klinikk. Based on the experiments, it is concluded that DeepLabv3plus variants could achieve relatively high segmentation accuracy of small structures without decreasing accuracy for large structures.

The rest of this paper is organised as follows: Section 2 introduces the related works on image segmentation. Section 3 describes our applied neural networks, U-net and the recent version of DeepLab. Section 4 discuss the experimental results on the MRI dataset. The conclusions are described in Section 5.

2. Related Works

Machine learning techniques are widely applied in recent medical applications, such as disease detection [19,20] and medical robots [21]. However, typical data-driven models perform differently under diverse requirements [22–24]. For medical image segmentation, researchers proposed dozens of neural networks with encoder–decoder architectures, such as SegNet [25], RefineNet [26], and DecovNet [27]. The architectures mainly consisted of an encoder, a decoder, and fusion techniques. The encoder is responsible for extracting features from input images, where the dimension of feature maps is reduced. It can be seen as a classification neural network without fully connected layers. For example, SegNet uses VGG16 [28] in the encoder, DeepLabv3plus uses improved Xception [29] as a part of its encoder. In the decoder, the spatial dimension of feature maps is recovered through various upsampling operations, which is the opposite of the encoder. The third important part is the fusion technique, which can utilise multi-scale features from the encoder to recover the spatial resolution in the decoder. For example, U-net uses skip connection to fuse the features in the encoder with the features in the decoder.

The fusion of features in different scales is beneficial in improving the accuracy of semantic segmentation. DeepLabv3 [14] discussed four types of FCNs to capture multi-scale context, including image pyramid, encoder–decoder, context module (e.g., using atrous convolution as an approach), and spatial pyramid pooling. The first one is usually applied during the inference stage [30]. For the other three approaches, DeepLabv3plus takes advantage of them to propose a network that employs the architecture of encoder–decoder with atrous separable convolution.

ASPP (atrous spatial pyramid pooling) is one of the most important techniques used in the DeepLab series. It was proposed in DeepLabv2 [13] and developed based on spatial pyramid pooling, which was proposed by [31] to capture the context of images in different strides. DeepLabv2 employs a combination of spatial pyramid pooling with atrous convolution and named it ASPP, which is computationally efficient compared with the original method. DeepLabv3 improves ASPP by adding 1×1 convolution in the first layer and global average pooling in the last layer. In addition, DeepLabv3plus exploits atrous depthwise separable convolution to replace atrous convolution, which reduces the number of parameters to implement ASPP again. DeepLabv3plus is designed for 2D natural image segmentation. In this work, we modified the ASPP technique to 3D image segmentation.

3D image segmentation is very computationally expensive, and therefore related techniques that can make it more efficient are highly appreciated. Due to limited computing resources, volumetric inputs are usually cut into patches to feed them into 3D networks, enabling the use of a large input image size to feed the networks if the network can be simplified. Other methods to decrease the computing resource are involved. For example, a 3D volume image is comprised of 2D slices, so researchers such as [32] attempted to use 2D networks to segment 2D slices and then fuse the results into a 3D volume image again. However, there are spatial information losses that have an adverse influence on volume image segmentation results. In addition, there are multiple labels in our datasets, including large structures and small structures. FocusNet [33] proposes a method that uses different networks to segment large structures and small structures, fusing the results to form the final segmentation and achieve high segmentation accuracy.

Researchers have proposed several MRI segmentation models aimed at various tissues for knee joint treatment. Reference [34] applied using U-net for capturing the complex morphology and texture of thigh muscle and adipose tissue. The results showed a good clinical effect compared with contralateral knees without knee pain and comparable effect size to manual segmentation. However, muscle and adipose tissue are large structures that can be more easily perceived. The authors did not research any other small issues that may lead to potential lesions. Reference [35] performed conditional Generative Adversarial Networks (cGANs) as a robust and potentially improved method for semantic segmentation than U-Net. Their works showed better results. However, they only consider three types of anatomical structures. The target objects are still apparent in MRI segmentation. Moreover, the attainment of cGANs is generally harder than U-net because the model requires more hyperparameters, and more training attempts were involved in adversary. Reference [36] analysed how 2D U-net functioned on cartilage and meniscus segmentation of knee MR imaging data for morphology and relaxometry compared with manual segmentation. They found that U-Net demonstrates efficacy and precision in quickly generating accurate segmentations that can be used to monitor and diagnose osteoarthritis. However, their model only considers cartilage and meniscus, and their experiments did not achieve 3D modelling. To our knowledge, it is very difficult to detect many small targets simultaneously in one model, and there is no existing research performing many small target segmentation in the knee joint MRI dataset.

As per the biomedical aspect, especially MRI segmentation, researchers focus on improving the segmentation accuracy of an anatomical structure. Awan et al. proposed ResNet-14 CNN, which achieves higher performance on knee ligament segments [37]. Simantiris et al. utilised a Dilated CNN to construct a cardiac MRI segmentation network that has produced the most satisfactory evaluation on dice coefficient [38]. Coupé et al. introduced AssemblyNet, a large ensemble CNN network for whole-brain MRI segmentation [39]. Their networks defeated the U-Net baseline, which is also one of our baseline models. However, although these models generally give better performance on testing images, they may ignore recognising specific small anatomical structures. We also found that CNN-based models have played a significant role in, and positively influenced, real-world medical applications [37–40].

This paper takes advantage of the above-mentioned encoder–decoder architecture to build improved networks, i.e., U-net variants and DeepLabv3plus variants. They showed a greater capability in experiments to segment small structures without losing the accuracy of large structures.

3. Methods

To explore the segmentation performances of different encoder–decoder architectures on our datasets, we developed two types of networks, i.e., U-net variants and DeepLabv3plus variants. Their architectures are shown in Figure 1.

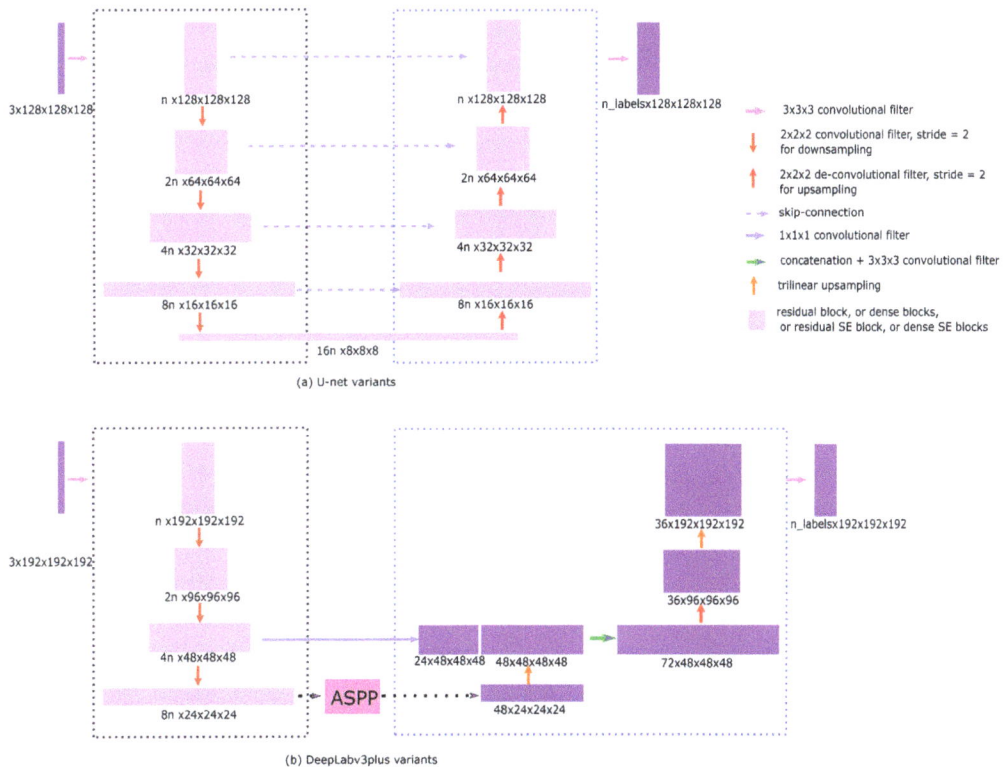

Figure 1. Architectures of U-net variants and DeepLabv3plus variants.

3.1. U-Net Variants

Figure 1a shows the architecture of U-net variants (n = 24), where n is the number of channels. The downsampling path on the left (encoder) extracts features using convolutions from the input images. The upsampling path on the right (decoder) uses deconvolutions to reconstruct the details for the final segmentation results. The skip connections are used to fuse features of different layers obtained in the downsampling path with those in the upsampling path to improve segmentation accuracy.

To maximise the performance of U-net architecture, we used SE blocks with residual and dense structures to construct four types of blocks, namely residual blocks, residual SE blocks, dense blocks, and dense SE blocks. Their structures are shown in Figure 2. SE blocks can be conveniently added in a residual structure and a non-residual structure. For residual structures with SE blocks, several convolution blocks are stacked first. Then, we use SE blocks to strengthen essential features. SE blocks are introduced by Squeeze-and-Excitation Networks (SENet) [11,41]. It improves a prediction accuracy through modelling the correlations between channels and adaptively strengthening important features.

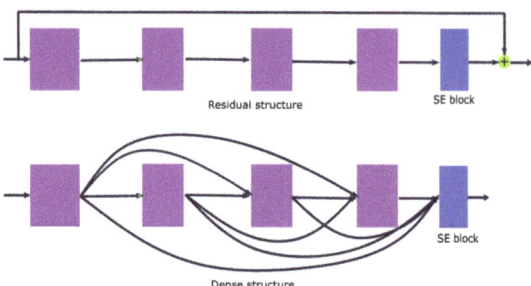

Figure 2. Residual structure and dense structure.

A dense convolutional network (DenseNet) [42] considers that the residual connections combining the input with the output of stacked convolutions by summation impede the information flow in the network. Then, a different connectivity pattern was proposed: concatenation rather than summation. The structure is also shown in Figure 2, where four-layer dense blocks precede SE block.

Each layer takes all preceding feature maps as the input to reuse these features to take advantage of features gained in different layers to exploit the network's potential. For dense structures, we added SE block in a non-residual block (i.e., dense block). Thus, four types of blocks are formed, including residual blocks, residual SE blocks, dense blocks, and dense SE blocks. For the blocks in the encoder path and the decoder path, we fill them using these four types of blocks, respectively, to form four U-net variants.

3.2. DeepLabv3plus Variants

DeepLabv3plus is designed for 2D natural image semantic segmentation. The advanced components used in it provide us with an alternative method to extract features from the images. For example, ASPP with depthwise separable convolution enables us to capture the multi-scale features of images with fewer parameters. If we modify them according to the features of 3D medical images and use them in the network, it assists in the reduction of the required computing power and improves the segmentation results and overall performance.

The encoder of DeepLabv3plus comprises improved Xception and ASPP. However, the features in medical images are not as complicated as in natural images. It is not necessary to use such complex networks to recognise the pattern in the dataset. In addition, 3D volume image segmentation is computationally expensive, and adopting too deep networks might waste computing resources. Here, we used a similar network to U-net variants to replace Xception as the primary network in the encoder, as shown in Figure 1. Four types of blocks can be used here as well. ASPP reduced the number of filters and obtained a larger receptive field. In addition, three layers of downsampling are employed in DeepLabv3plus variants instead of four layers in the U-net variants, and half reduces the numbers of channels in each layer, so n = 12 in Figure 1. The last layer of the encoder is removed, and ASPP is added at the bottom of the encoder in the same way as it is in DeepLabv3plus.

ASPP is a powerful tool that enables us to capture multi-scale information on images and obtain larger receptive fields with fewer parameters and hence more efficient performance and more accurate segmentation results. The implementation details are shown in Figure 3, where we employ a $1 \times 1 \times 1$ convolution to get the first feature map. A $1 \times 1 \times 1$ convolution can select the important features from the input and is frequently used to reduce the dimension of feature maps (i.e., depth). Then, $3 \times 3 \times 3$ atrous depthwise separable convolutions, with dilatation rates of 4, 8, and 12, are used to get the following three feature maps. Different rates could effectively capture multi-scale information. Finally, global average pooling is applied to obtain the last feature map. We concatenate these five feature maps and use a 1 × 1 × 1 convolution to choose the important features from them and reduce the number of channels (i.e., depth). To be concatenated, these five output feature maps must have the same dimensions.

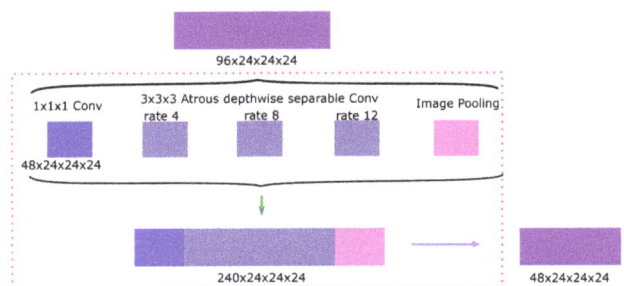

Figure 3. Structure of ASPP.

Atrous depthwise separable convolution is used to obtain the three feature maps in the middle. The calculation process is explained as follows. Each input channel is convolved with the convolution filter first, and then use 1 × 1 × 1 convolution to choose feature maps from different channels. For the first step, we set the stride s to 1, the padding number p to same as the dilation rate r, and apply the 3 × 3 × 3 convolution filter (k = 3) for each channel. As a result, the width of output feature maps, can be calculated by:

$$W_{out} = 1/s * (w_{in} + 2p - r(k-1) - 1) + 1 = w_{in} \quad (1)$$

The height and depth can be obtained in the same way. For atrous convolution, the voxels can be calculated according to the equation:

$$y(i, j, k) = \sum_{d=0}^{2} \sum_{h=0}^{2} \sum_{w=0}^{2} x(i + w*r, j + h*r, k + d*r) * W(w, h, d) \quad (2)$$

After this process, the size of feature maps remains unchanged (C_in, D, H, W). Then, we use 1 × 1 × 1 convolution to choose the features from different channels, and the size of the feature maps is changed to (C_out, D, H, W).

For depthwise separable convolution, the number of parameters used in the process above is:

$$3 \times 3 \times 3 \times chan_{in} + 1 \times 1 \times 1 \times chan_{in} \times chan_{out} = 27 \times chan_{in} + chan_{in} \times chan_{out} \quad (3)$$

If we use standard convolution, the number of parameters should be:

$$3 \times 3 \times 3 \times chan_{in} \times chan_{out} = 27 \times chan_{in} \times chan_{out} \quad (4)$$

Thus, it reduces the number of parameters when the number of channels used in the network is large.

The decoder part in DeepLabv3plus uses bilinear interpolation for 2D images, and the factor of upsampling is 4. For our DeepLabv3plus variants, we utilise trilinear interpolation to implement upsampling instead of deconvolution used in U-net architecture, which reduces the number of parameters again. However, we use 2 as the upsampling factor, because medical image segmentation requires higher accuracy than natural image segmentation. Trilinear interpolation is beneficial for saving computing resources, but it damages the representative capacity of the decoder compared with deconvolution. We add one deconvolution upsampling block between the trilinear interpolation operations to introduce more flexibility in the upsampling path. To take advantage of the features extracted by the encoder, we also concatenate the features obtained before ASPP in the encoder with the first trilinear interpolation feature map. The result is used as the input of the $3 \times 3 \times 3$ deconvolution block.

3.3. Loss Functions

Small object/organ segmentation is always a challenge in semantic segmentation. In our case, the smallest structure takes up less than 0.01% of the whole volume of the MRI images. Dice loss was introduced by V-net [43]. It was developed based on the Dice coefficient to address the problem that the learning process is trapped in the local minimum when the predictions are strongly biased towards the background. We also use weighted dice loss as the loss function. Weighted dice loss uses weighting to adjust the importance of different categories in training. This is commonly used to address the imbalance problem in samples by adding weight on the category whose proportion is small. It is calculated according to the equation:

$$\text{Loss} = 1 - \frac{1}{n} \times \sum_{i=1}^{n}(w_i \times \frac{2 \times \sum_{j=1}^{m} t_{ij}p_{ij} + \text{smooth}}{\sum_{j=1}^{m}(t_{ij}+p_{ij}) + \text{smooth}}) \qquad (5)$$

where n is the number of classes, w_i is the weight of class i, m is the number of voxels of class i, t_{ij} is the j-th voxel of class i using one-hot encoding in the truth, and p_{ij} is the corresponding voxel in the prediction. To set the weights, we use the percentages of classes in the dataset.

The performances of the networks in this paper are evaluated by dice coefficients for each class. To compare the predicted segmentation and the ground truth for each class, the percentage of class y predicted as class x was calculated according to:

$$P_{(x,y)} = \frac{n_{(x,y)}}{n_y} \qquad (6)$$

where $n_{(x,y)}$ is the number of voxels predicted as class x but annotated as class y in the ground truth, n_y is the number of voxels annotated as class y in the ground truth. It is the recall rate for class x when x = y. Notably, it is not a confusion matrix. We call it a performance matrix for short in this paper. The data in the diagonal line are the recall rate for each class. They should be 1 if all voxels are segmented correctly. The data in the diagonal line will be precise if it replaces the denominator of (6) as the number of voxels predicted as class y.

3.4. Hyperparameter

The original size of the images is $400 \times 400 \times 400$. We conduct the experiments of the four U-net variants on the dataset. The time of a single training epoch of U-net with residual blocks on the dataset of resolution $400 \times 400 \times 400$ is about 7 h. Because of the constraints on GPU memory, we set the patch size to $128 \times 128 \times 128$ and the batch size to 1. We found that the training with a larger patch size and a smaller batch size performs better than the training with a smaller patch size and larger batch size.

DeepLabv3plus variants utilise several techniques to reduce the number of parameters, enabling us to use a larger patch size to feed the networks. The patch size used for training DeepLabv3plus variants has increased from $128 \times 128 \times 128$ to $192 \times 192 \times 192$. Although we increase the patch size, the model parameters are still lower than U-Net, and the training time of an epoch for DeepLabv3plus variants is less than 10 min.

The MR images were obtained from 20 volunteers: 18 volunteers provide the training dataset and 2 volunteers provide the testing dataset. Each volunteer provides 30 images; the total number of images was 600, that is 90% (540 images) for training and 10% (60 images) for testing. The main hyperparameters of U-Net and DeepLabv3plus are displayed in Figure 1. We directly concatenate the results together when we receive all the outputs from patches.

All the networks are trained on GPU GeForce RTX 2080 Ti, with a GPU memory of 11 GB GDDR6 and by using an Adam optimiser. The initial learning rate is set to 0.01 for training with dice loss and is set to 0.001 for training with weighted dice loss. The learning rates were set to be reduced by a factor of 0.5 after two epochs if the validation loss is not decreasing. The training was stopped when the loss on the validation dataset had not decreased for at least three epochs.

4. Experiments and Results

The knee MRI images provided by Sunnmøre MR-Klinikk used in our experiments were manually annotated. The final dataset used to compare the architecture of U-net variants and DeepLabv3plus variants contains 13 labels. Figure 4 shows the extraordinary imbalance of the labels on the final dataset. The background accounts for 60.43% on average in all samples. The largest label is AD (adipose tissue), accounting for 19.17%, while the smallest is ACL (anterior cruciate ligament), accounting for 0.03%. Table 1 shows the abbreviations and values of classes (structures) in performance matrices. The red classes in Table 1 are the small organs in terms of the statistics of Figure 4.

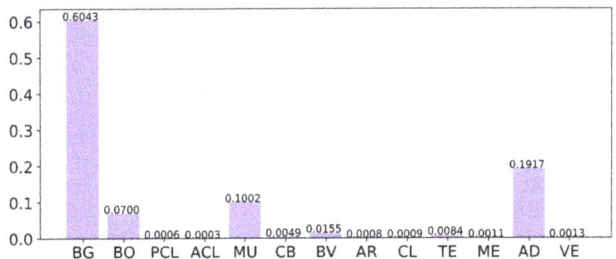

Figure 4. Frequencies of voxels for each class.

Table 1. Abbreviations and values of classes.

Classes	Abbreviations	Index
Background	BG	0
Bone	BO	1
Posterior cruciate ligament	PCL	2
Anterior cruciate ligament	ACL	3
Muscle	MU	4
Cortical bone	CB	5
Blood vessel (popliteal artery/vein++)	BV	6
Artery	AR	7
Collateral ligament	CL	8
Tendons	TE	9
Menisci	ME	10
Adipose tissue (fat)	AD	11
Veins	VE	12

The dataset contains annotated knee MRI images from 20 volunteers. For each knee image, three weighted volumes, including T1 (longitudinal relaxation time), PD (proton density), and FS (fat-saturation) are provided. Different weighted volumes provide different contrasts for different tissues. For example, T1-weighted images provide high contrast for fat, but low contrast for water. FS pulse sequences can improve the detection of musculoskeletal lesions. The sizes of these images is $400 \times 400 \times 400$. We cut each image into patches to feed them into the networks and use a large selection of them for training and the remaining for validation. (An example MRI can be found in Section 4.3).

4.1. Results on U-Net Variants

The performances of U-net variants are shown in Table 2.

Table 2. Performances of U-net variants.

Class	Dice Loss			Weighted Dice Loss		
	U-Net	U-Net + Res	U-Net + Res	U-Net + Res + SE	U-Net + Dense	U-Net + Dense + SE
BG	0.94	0.987	0.992	0.989	0.990	0.990
BO	0.95	0.917	0.831	0.938	0.932	0.948
PCL	0	0.002	0.153	0.347	0.338	0.228
ACL	0	0	0.083	0.096	0.084	0.041
MU	0.95	0.927	0.944	0.956	0.928	0.939
CB	0	0.567	0.500	0.457	0.495	0.515
BV	0	0.556	0.622	0.603	0.555	0.648
AR	0	0.057	0.198	0.270	0.152	0.194
CL	0	0.041	0.470	0.248	0.237	0.370
TE	0	0.726	0.701	0.723	0.641	0.726
ME	0	0.191	0.133	0.126	0.139	0.107
AD	0.92	0.919	0.876	0.919	0.904	0.925
VE	0	0	0.396	0.491	0.305	0.528
Avg-All organs	0.289	0.453	0.531	0.551	0.515	0.551
Avg-Small organs	0	0.238	0.362	0.373	0.327	0.373

For U-net and U-net + residual blocks [43] with dice loss, large structures bone (BO), muscle (MU), and adipose tissue (AD) are segmented correctly, but most of the small structures are missing (see Table 2). The main reason for this is the extremely imbalanced classes in the dataset.

To increase the importance of small structures, weighted dice loss is adopted. We set the weights according to the proportions of the classes in the dataset. From Table 2, we can see that the results for small structures are improved, but the accuracy of BO is decreased. One possible reason is that when patch-wise training is used, they are unavoidably cut into several parts for the bones since they account for a large proportion of the image and their positions are in the middle. It is difficult for the neural network to distinguish its pattern because the special structure of bones is scattered into different patches. To improve the network's performance, SE blocks are added, the results of small structures are improved compared with that of no SE blocks. Moreover, the accuracy of BO has a little increasement.

In conclusion, by using SE-based methods, U-Net + Res + SE or U-Net + Dense + SE, it can be pointed out that with the help of SE block, average evaluations are apparently increased. During our training, another valuable observation is that the bones are segmented more completely than those on the smaller patch size. The main reason is that a larger patch size is beneficial for the networks to capture the global features. When a larger patch size is used, more parts of bones will be in the same patch. As a result, it can be segmented more correctly.

4.2. Results with DeepLabv3plus Variants

Because it is confirmed that SE structure can improve the performance of the networks, we further train the networks with SE blocks for both residual structure and dense structure in DeepLabv3plus. As is shown in Table 3, two variants are trained first, including one in which the basic network uses residual block and one in which the basic network uses dense block. We found that adding SE block can improve the two DeepLabv3plus baselines without SE block. As shown in Table 3 and Figure 5, we also find that DeepLabv3plus variants can segment the structures better than U-net variants.

Table 3. Performances of DeepLabv3plus-based model.

Class	U-Net + Res	Deeplab + Dense	Deeplab + Res	Deeplab + Dense + SE	Deeplab + Res + SE
BG	0.987	0.977	0.984	0.986	0.983
BO	0.917	0.809	0.797	0.958	0.936
PCL	0.002	0.703	0.800	0.752	0.522
ACL	0	0.345	0.457	0.462	0.504
MU	0.927	0.926	0.950	0.969	0.976
CB	0.567	0.639	0.701	0.825	0.861
BV	0.556	0.553	0.627	0.813	0.781
AR	0.057	0.534	0.422	0.622	0.671
CL	0.041	0.449	0.536	0.681	0.589
TE	0.726	0.519	0.609	0.685	0.745
ME	0.191	0.706	0.794	0.844	0.819
AD	0.919	0.798	0.799	0.927	0.91
VE	0	0.227	0.344	0.290	0.265
Avg-All organs	0.453	0.629	0.678	0.755	0.735
Avg-Small organs	0.238	0.519	0.588	0.663	0.639

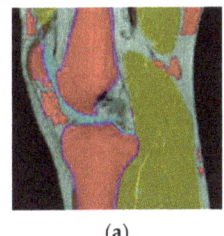
(a)

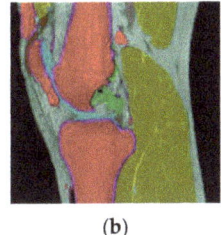
(b)

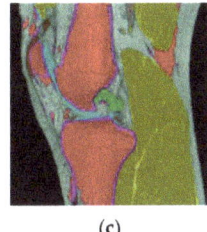
(c)

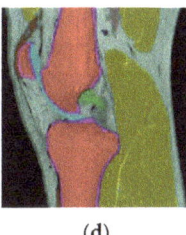
(d)

Figure 5. A case study of segmentation experiments. (**a**): U-Net + Res with dice loss. (**b**): Deeplab + Dense + SE with dice loss. (**c**): Deeplab + Res + SE with dice loss. (**d**): Ground truth.

Where (a) shows the segmentation of the results of U-Net + Res with dice loss, (b) and (c) show the results of DeepLabv3plus variants with dice loss. We can see that, for example, the green part (PCL) in the middle is not segmented correctly in (a), but it is segmented in (b) and (c). The results are shown in Table 2. With dice loss, the accuracies of small anatomical segments are quite acceptable compared with the results on U-Net + Res. One reason could be that advanced components, such as ASPP, are used to obtain a larger receptive field without losing too much resolution. Generally speaking, Deeplab + Dense + SE performs better than Deeplab + Res + SE. Deeplab + Dense + SE has higher average accuracies on small structures, especially in PCL, BV, and CL. Deeplab + Res + SE has slightly higher accuracies on ACL, MU, and CB.

Figure 6b shows the performance matrix of Deeplab + Dense + SE, where we can see it achieved relatively high accuracies on all anatomical segments compared with U-Net + Res (as it is shown in Figure 6a). For U-Net + Res with dice loss, small structures, including PCL(2), ACL(3), AR(7), and CL(8) were missing, and predicted as other structures such as BG(0), CB(5), and BV(6). An example of the segmentation result of Residual SE Deeplab with dice loss is shown in Figure 5c, where we can see that there is a small part of AD(11) predicted as BO(1), similar to the results of Dense SE Deeplab with dice loss. A possible reason could be that patch-wise training that negatively influences the capture ability of structural features of bones. However, this problem has already been solved largely in DeepLabv3plus variants.

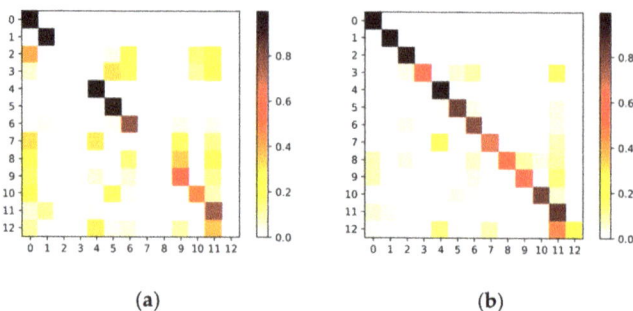

Figure 6. (a) Performance matrix of U-Net-based model; (b) performance matrix of DeepLabv3plus-based model.

4.3. Discussion

We trained U-net and U-Net + Res with dice loss as the preliminary model. Then, we proposed new varieties to discover the small and low-resourced pixels in the MRI dataset, i.e., the structures with SE block. The proposed varieties showed a satisfactory performance on small organ segmentation.

For U-Net + Res trained with dice loss, from Table 3 we can see that some small anatomical structures such as PCL and ACL are not segmented correctly. For the U-net variant with residual SE blocks trained with weighted dice loss, the performances on the small structures are improved.

The main question is that the neural networks have a smaller field of view on the resolution $400 \times 400 \times 400$, although the patch sizes used on the two datasets are the same. The patch-wise training can be seen as reducing the receptive field of the images at the beginning. For the downsampling dataset, the view was reduced to $(128/400)^3 \approx 0.033$. The locations of anatomical structures are in the centre of the image and will be separated into different patches; therefore, the difficulty of recognising their patterns increases.

Tables 2 and 3 show the comparison of U-net variants and DeepLabv3plus variants. DeepLabv3plus variants enable us to segment all structures and achieve relatively higher average accuracy with dice loss. However, U-net variants cannot segment the small structures correctly, leading to lower average accuracy. Generally speaking, DeepLabv3plus variants perform better than U-net variants in terms of average dice coefficient on all labels with dice loss.

DeepLabv3plus-based models are overall better than U-net-based models. Compared with natural images, the MR image semantics are relatively simple, and the pattern is relatively fixed; both high-level and low-level semantic features appear to be very important. To utilise the features, U-Net applied skip connection and U-shaped structure to combine the high-level and low-level features. However, this network becomes too complex, leading to more parameters in the model. Because it is tricky to obtain medical imaging data, many studies only provide data for less than 100 cases. Therefore, the model we designed should not be too large. Too many parameters can easily lead to overfitting.

In U-net, the receptive field of pixels on the feature map depends on convolution and pooling operations. The receptive field of ordinary convolution can only increase two pixels at a time step, and the progress is too slow. The increase of the receptive field of the traditional convolutional network is generally done by pooling operation. The pooling operation will increase the receptive field while reducing the image's resolution, thus losing some information. Moreover, the upsampling of the pooled image will make it impossible to restore a lot of detailed information, limiting segmentation accuracy.

To address the problem, DeepLabv3plus utilises a new atrous convolution. It was performed in the ASPP structure (see Figure 3), which simultaneously satisfies:

1. Connecting high- and low- MRI features together;
2. Significantly reducing model parameters, and thus alleviating overfitting and shortening training time.

As a result, in our experiments, DeepLabv3plus variants achieve the best performance on average accuracy. However, the performance could be improved further by adopting more advanced components. These components should be able to obtain a larger receptive field with fewer parameters and have the ability to reserve details during the process.

5. Conclusions

This work attempted to use annotated knee MRI images by Sunnmøre MR-Klinikk to explore two types of encoder–decoder architecture FCNs, including U-net and DeepLabv3plus. Based on FCN, some neural network variants are proposed, which uses U-net as the basic network, ASPP to capture the multi-scale feature of images, and atrous depthwise separable convolutions to reduce the number of parameters in the encoder. The decoder utilises trilinear interpolation without parameters to implement upsampling instead of deconvolution. This architecture enables us to use a larger patch size and achieves relatively high segmentation accuracies on small structures without the sacrifice of accuracies on large structures. In addition, the training time is significantly reduced from hours to minutes on one epoch.

For U-net architecture, we use four types of blocks, including residual blocks, residual SE blocks, dense blocks, and dense SE blocks, to replace the standard convolution blocks in the original network. The experiments show that the segmentation accuracies of small structures are improved with SE structures. For DeepLabv3plus variants, SE structures also help improve the small structure detection and, compared with U-Net, they require fewer parameters, run faster, and perform better in terms of average accuracy. In conclusion, DeepLabv3plus networks with SE block better capture structural features in MRI segmentation.

Author Contributions: Conceptualization, M.S. and L.L.; methodology, M.S. and L.L.; software, L.L.; validation, M.S.; formal analysis, M.S.; investigation, M.S.; resources, C.P.S.K. and K.-I.G.; data curation, C.P.S.K. and K.-I.G.; writing—original draft preparation, M.S. and L.L.; writing—review and editing, M.S. and I.A.H.; visualization, L.L.; supervision, I.A.H.; project administration, I.A.H.; funding acquisition, I.A.H. All authors have read and agreed to the published version of the manuscript.

Funding: This research was funded by Norwegian University of Science and Technology.

Institutional Review Board Statement: Not applicable.

Informed Consent Statement: Not applicable.

Data Availability Statement: No new data were created or analyzed in this study. Data sharing is not applicable to this article.

Conflicts of Interest: The authors declare no conflict of interest.

References

1. Panfilov, E.; Tiulpin, A.; Klein, S.; Nieminen, M.T.; Saarakkala, S. Improving robustness of deep learning based knee mri segmentation: Mixup and adversarial domain adaptation. In Proceedings of the IEEE/CVF International Conference on Computer Vision Workshops, Seoul, Korea, 27–28 October 2019; pp. 450–459.
2. Nieminen, M.T.; Casula, V.; Nevalainen, M.T.; Saarakkala, S. Osteoarthritis year in review 2018: Imaging. *Osteoarthr. Cartil.* **2019**, *27*, 401–411. [CrossRef] [PubMed]
3. Gaetke-Udager, K.; Fessell, D.P.; Liu, P.S.; Morag, Y.; Brigido, M.K.; Yablon, C.; Jacobson, J. Knee MRI: Vascular pathology. *Am. J. Roentgenol.* **2015**, *205*, 142–149. [CrossRef] [PubMed]
4. Castañeda, S.; Roman-Blas, J.A.; Largo, R.; Herrero-Beaumont, G. Subchondral bone as a key target for osteoarthritis treatment. *Biochem. Pharmacol.* **2012**, *83*, 315–323. [CrossRef] [PubMed]
5. More, S.; Singla, J.; Abugabah, A.; AlZubi, A.A. Machine Learning Techniques for Quantification of Knee Segmentation from MRI. *Complexity* **2020**, *2020*, 6613191. [CrossRef]

6. Isensee, F.; Jaeger, P.F.; Kohl, S.A.; Petersen, J.; Maier-Hein, K.H. nnU-Net: A self-configuring method for deep learning-based biomedical image segmentation. *Nat. Methods* **2021**, *18*, 203–211. [CrossRef]
7. Li, Y.; Zhao, H.; Qi, X.; Wang, L.; Li, Z.; Sun, J.; Jia, J. Fully Convolutional Networks for Panoptic Segmentation. In Proceedings of the IEEE/CVF Conference on Computer Vision and Pattern Recognition, Nashville, TN, USA, 20–25 June 2021; pp. 214–223.
8. Calisto, M.B.; Lai-Yuen, S.K. AdaEn-Net: An ensemble of adaptive 2D–3D Fully Convolutional Networks for medical image segmentation. *Neural Netw.* **2020**, *126*, 76–94. [CrossRef] [PubMed]
9. Luo, X.; Zeng, W.; Fan, W.; Zheng, S.; Chen, J.; Liu, R.; Liu, Z.; Chen, Y. Towards cascaded V-Net for automatic accurate kidney segmentation from abdominal CT images. In Proceedings of the Medical Imaging 2021: Image Processing, Online, 15–19 February 2021; Volume 11596, p. 1159619.
10. Zhao, W.; Jiang, D.; Queralta, J.P.; Westerlund, T. MSS U-Net: 3D segmentation of kidneys and tumors from CT images with a multi-scale supervised U-Net. *Inform. Med. Unlocked* **2020**, *19*, 100357. [CrossRef]
11. Zeng, G.; Yang, X.; Li, J.; Yu, L.; Heng, P.A.; Zheng, G. September. 3D U-net with multi-level deep supervision: Fully automatic segmentation of proximal femur in 3D MR images. In Proceedings of the International Workshop on Machine Learning in Medical Imaging, Quebec City, QC, Canada, 10 September 2017; Springer: Cham, Switzerland; pp. 274–282.
12. Zhang, S.; Ma, Z.; Zhang, G.; Lei, T.; Zhang, R.; Cui, Y. Semantic image segmentation with deep convolutional neural networks and quick shift. *Symmetry* **2020**, *12*, 427. [CrossRef]
13. Chen, L.C.; Papandreou, G.; Kokkinos, I.; Murphy, K.; Yuille, A.L. Deeplab: Semantic image segmentation with deep convolutional nets, atrous convolution, and fully connected crfs. *IEEE Trans. Pattern Anal. Mach. Intell.* **2017**, *40*, 834–848. [CrossRef]
14. Chen, L.C.; Papandreou, G.; Schroff, F.; Adam, H. Rethinking atrous convolution for semantic image segmentation. *arXiv Preprint* **2017**, arXiv:1706.05587.
15. Chen, L.C.; Zhu, Y.; Papandreou, G.; Schroff, F.; Adam, H. Encoder-decoder with atrous separable convolution for semantic image segmentation. In Proceedings of the European Conference on Computer Vision, Munich, Germany, 8–14 September 2018; pp. 801–818.
16. Alam, T.M.; Shaukat, K.; Mahboob, H.; Sarwar, M.U.; Iqbal, F.; Nasir, A.; Hameed, I.A.; Luo, S. A Machine Learning Approach for Identification of Malignant Mesothelioma Etiological Factors in an Imbalanced Dataset. *Comput. J.* **2021**. [CrossRef]
17. Khushi, M.; Shaukat, K.; Alam, T.M.; Hameed, I.A.; Uddin, S.; Luo, S.; Yang, X.; Reyes, M.C. A comparative performance analysis of data resampling methods on imbalance medical data. *IEEE Access* **2021**, *9*, 109960–109975. [CrossRef]
18. Yang, X.; Khushi, M.; Shaukat, K. Biomarker CA125 Feature Engineering and Class Imbalance Learning Improves Ovarian Cancer Prediction. In Proceedings of the 2020 IEEE Asia-Pacific Conference on Computer Science and Data Engineering (CSDE), Gold Coast, Australia, 16–18 December 2020; pp. 1–6.
19. Latif, M.Z.; Shaukat, K.; Luo, S.; Hameed, I.A.; Iqbal, F.; Alam, T.M. Risk factors identification of malignant mesothelioma: A data mining based approach. In Proceedings of the 2020 International Conference on Electrical, Communication, and Computer Engineering (ICECCE), Istanbul, Turkey, 12–13 June 2020; pp. 1–6.
20. Alam, T.M.; Shaukat, K.; Hameed, I.A.; Khan, W.A.; Sarwar, M.U.; Iqbal, F.; Luo, S. A novel framework for prognostic factors identification of malignant mesothelioma through association rule mining. *Biomed. Signal Processing Control.* **2021**, *68*, 102726. [CrossRef]
21. Shaukat, K.; Iqbal, F.; Alam, T.M.; Aujla, G.K.; Devnath, L.; Khan, A.G.; Iqbal, R.; Shahzadi, I.; Rubab, A. The impact of artificial intelligence and robotics on the future employment opportunities. *Trends Comput. Sci. Inf. Technol.* **2020**, *5*, 050–054.
22. Shaukat, K.; Luo, S.; Varadharajan, V.; Hameed, I.A.; Xu, M. A survey on machine learning techniques for cyber security in the last decade. *IEEE Access* **2020**, *8*, 222310–222354. [CrossRef]
23. Shaukat, K.; Luo, S.; Varadharajan, V.; Hameed, I.A.; Chen, S.; Liu, D.; Li, J. Performance comparison and current challenges of using machine learning techniques in cybersecurity. *Energies* **2020**, *13*, 2509. [CrossRef]
24. Shaukat, K.; Luo, S.; Chen, S.; Liu, D. Cyber Threat Detection Using Machine Learning Techniques: A Performance Evaluation Perspective. In Proceedings of the 2020 International Conference on Cyber Warfare and Security (ICCWS), Islamabad, Pakistan, 20–21 October 2020; pp. 1–6.
25. Badrinarayanan, V.; Kendall, A.; Cipolla, R. Segnet: A deep convolutional encoder-decoder architecture for image segmentation. *IEEE Trans. Pattern Anal. Mach. Intell.* **2017**, *39*, 2481–2495. [CrossRef] [PubMed]
26. Lin, G.; Milan, A.; Shen, C.; Reid, I. Refinenet: Multi-path refinement networks for high-resolution semantic segmentation. In Proceedings of the IEEE conference on Computer Vision and Pattern Recognition, Honolulu, HI, USA, 21–26 July 2017; pp. 1925–1934.
27. Noh, H.; Hong, S.; Han, B. Learning deconvolution network for semantic segmentation. In Proceedings of the IEEE International Conference on Computer Vision, Santiago, Chile, 7–13 December 2015; pp. 1520–1528.
28. Simonyan, K.; Zisserman, A. Very deep convolutional networks for large-scale image recognition. In Proceedings of the International Conference on Learning Representations, San Diego, CA, USA, 7–9 May 2015; pp. 1–14.
29. POLAT, Ö. Detection of Covid-19 from Chest CT Images using Xception Architecture: A Deep Transfer Learning based Approach. *Sak. Univ. J. Sci.* **2021**, *25*, 813–823. [CrossRef]
30. Xu, Y.; Gong, M.; Chen, J.; Chen, Z.; Batmanghelich, K. 3D-BoxSup: Positive-Unlabeled Learning of Brain Tumor Segmentation Networks from 3D Bounding Boxes. *Front. Neurosci.* **2020**, *14*, 350. [CrossRef] [PubMed]

31. Peng, C.; Ma, J. Semantic segmentation using stride spatial pyramid pooling and dual attention decoder. *Pattern Recognit.* **2020**, *107*, 107498. [CrossRef]
32. Song, Y.; Yu, Z.; Zhou, T.; Teoh, J.Y.C.; Lei, B.; Choi, K.S.; Qin, J. Learning 3d features with 2d cnns via surface projection for ct volume segmentation. In Proceedings of the International Conference on Medical Image Computing and Computer-Assisted Intervention, Lima, Peru, 4–8 October 2020; pp. 176–186.
33. Kaul, C.; Manandhar, S.; Pears, N. Focusnet: An Attention-Based Fully Convolutional Network for Medical Image Segmentation. In Proceedings of the 2019 IEEE 16th International Symposium on Biomedical Imaging (ISBI 2019), Venice, Italy, 8–11 April 2019; pp. 455–458.
34. Kemnitz, J.; Baumgartner, C.F.; Eckstein, F.; Chaudhari, A.; Ruhdorfer, A.; Wirth, W.; Eder, S.K.; Konukoglu, E. Clinical evaluation of fully automated thigh muscle and adipose tissue segmentation using a U-Net deep learning architecture in context of osteoarthritic knee pain. *Magn. Reson. Mater. Phys. Biol. Med.* **2020**, *33*, 483–493. [CrossRef] [PubMed]
35. Kessler, D.A.; MacKay, J.W.; Crowe, V.A.; Henson, F.M.; Graves, M.J.; Gilbert, F.J.; Kaggie, J.D. The optimisation of deep neural networks for segmenting multiple knee joint tissues from MRIs. *Comput. Med. Imaging Graph.* **2020**, *86*, 101793. [CrossRef]
36. Norman, B.; Pedoia, V.; Majumdar, S. Use of 2D U-Net convolutional neural networks for automated cartilage and meniscus segmentation of knee MR imaging data to determine relaxometry and morphometry. *Radiology* **2018**, *288*, 177–185. [CrossRef] [PubMed]
37. Javed Awan, M.; Mohd Rahim, M.S.; Salim, N.; Mohammed, M.A.; Garcia-Zapirain, B.; Abdulkareem, K.H. Efficient detection of knee anterior cruciate ligament from magnetic resonance imaging using deep learning approach. *Diagnostics* **2021**, *11*, 105. [CrossRef] [PubMed]
38. Simantiris, G.; Tziritas, G. Cardiac mri segmentation with a dilated cnn incorporating domain-specific constraints. *IEEE J. Sel. Top. Signal Process.* **2020**, *14*, 1235–1243. [CrossRef]
39. Coupé, P.; Mansencal, B.; Clément, M.; Giraud, R.; de Senneville, B.D.; Ta, V.-T.; Lepetit, V.; Manjon, J.V. AssemblyNet: A large ensemble of CNNs for 3D whole brain MRI segmentation. *NeuroImage* **2020**, *219*, 117026. [CrossRef] [PubMed]
40. Mohammed, M.A.; Abdulkareem, K.H.; Mostafa, S.A.; Ghani, M.K.A.; Maashi, M.S.; Garcia-Zapirain, B.; Oleagordia, I.; AlHakami, H.; Al-Dhief, F.T. Voice pathology detection and classification using convolutional neural network model. *Appl. Sci.* **2020**, *10*, 3723. [CrossRef]
41. Hu, J.; Shen, L.; Sun, G. Squeeze-and-excitation networks. In Proceedings of the IEEE Conference on Computer Vision and Pattern Recognition, Salt Lake City, UT, USA, 18–23 June 2018; pp. 7132–7141.
42. Huang, G.; Liu, Z.; Van Der Maaten, L.; Weinberger, K.Q. Densely connected convolutional networks. In Proceedings of the IEEE Conference on Computer Vision and Pattern Recognition, Honolulu, HI, USA, 21–26 July 2017; pp. 4700–4708.
43. Milletari, F.; Navab, N.; Ahmadi, S. V-Net: Fully Convolutional Neural Networks for Volumetric Medical Image Segmentation. In Proceedings of the 2016 Fourth International Conference on 3D Vision (3DV), Stanford, CA, USA, 25–28 October 2016; pp. 565–571.

Article

Columns Occurrences Graph to Improve Column Prediction in Deep Learning Nlidb

Shanza Abbas [1], Muhammad Umair Khan [1], Scott Uk-Jin Lee [1,*] and Asad Abbas [2]

[1] Department of Computer Science and Engineering, Hanyang University, Ansan 15588, Korea; shanza92@hanyang.ac.kr (S.A.); mumairkhan@hanyang.ac.kr (M.U.K.)
[2] Faculty of Information Technology, University of Central Punjab, Lahore 54000, Pakistan; asadabbas.grw@ucp.edu.pk
* Correspondence: scottlee@hanynag.ac.kr

Citation: Abbas, S.; Khan, M.U.; Lee, S.U.-J.; Abbas, A. Columns Occurrences Graph to Improve Column Prediction in Deep Learning Nlidb. *Appl. Sci.* **2021**, *11*, 12116. https://doi.org/10.3390/app112412116

Academic Editors: Kamran Shaukat and Suhuai Luo

Received: 10 November 2021
Accepted: 7 December 2021
Published: 20 December 2021

Publisher's Note: MDPI stays neutral with regard to jurisdictional claims in published maps and institutional affiliations.

Copyright: © 2021 by the authors. Licensee MDPI, Basel, Switzerland. This article is an open access article distributed under the terms and conditions of the Creative Commons Attribution (CC BY) license (https://creativecommons.org/licenses/by/4.0/).

Abstract: Natural language interfaces to databases (NLIDB) has been a research topic for a decade. Significant data collections are available in the form of databases. To utilize them for research purposes, a system that can translate a natural language query into a structured one can make a huge difference. Efforts toward such systems have been made with pipelining methods for more than a decade. Natural language processing techniques integrated with data science methods are researched as pipelining NLIDB systems. With significant advancements in machine learning and natural language processing, NLIDB with deep learning has emerged as a new research trend in this area. Deep learning has shown potential for rapid growth and improvement in text-to-SQL tasks. In deep learning NLIDB, closing the semantic gap in predicting users' intended columns has arisen as one of the critical and fundamental problems in this research field. Contributions toward this issue have consisted of preprocessed feature inputs and encoding schema elements afore of and more impactful to the targeted model. Various significant work contributed towards this problem notwithstanding, this has been shown to be one of the critical issues for the task of developing NLIDB. Working towards closing the semantic gap between user intention and predicted columns, we present an approach for deep learning text-to-SQL tasks that includes previous columns' occurrences scores as an additional input feature. Overall exact match accuracy can also be improved by emphasizing the improvement of columns' prediction accuracy, which depends significantly on column prediction itself. For this purpose, we extract the query fragments from previous queries' data and obtain the columns' occurrences and co-occurrences scores. Column occurrences and co-occurrences scores are processed as input features for the encoder–decoder-based text to the SQL model. These scores contribute, as a factor, the probability of having already used columns and tables together in the query history. We experimented with our approach on the currently popular text-to-SQL dataset Spider. Spider is a complex data set containing multiple databases. This dataset includes query–question pairs along with schema information. We compared our exact match accuracy performance with a base model using their test and training data splits. It outperformed the base model's accuracy, and accuracy was further boosted in experiments with the pretrained language model BERT.

Keywords: deep learning; text-to-SQL; natural language processing; database; machine learning; machine translation

1. Introduction

Recently, enormous databases have come to contain substantial knowledge about an organization because of the digital storage of data. These vast data repositories can contribute to research in data analysis and finding trends and patterns therein, according to any particular research goal. Increasingly, data repositories concerning medical health, movies and employee data require direct access by users according to their questions and queries. Traditionally, users have needed to learn structured query languages such as SQL to get precise results from relational databases. All experts of a particular domain, for example, medicine, do not necessarily know structured query languages, limiting the access of organizational knowledge to a limited number of users. Therefore, existing data storage is not being utilized to its maximum potential.

Compulsory knowledge of structured query language for comprehensive access to all aspects of data has become a hurdle. Translating natural language questions into structured query language would provide maximum user access to relational databases. Asking questions in English-language text provides constraint-free access to databases, liberating the user from careful selection and click-based interfaces. Solving text-to-SQL tasks can expose the whole relational database for users to utilize and analyze according to their needs and choices. Seeking a solution for this issue leads us toward the field of natural language processing. However, natural language processing techniques, alone, cannot solve this problem, as the database, itself, is a critical part of the stated problem in this context, leading us to data-science methods as well.

Combining natural language processing and data science methods may yield the solution to building a natural language interface for databases. Thus, translating natural language queries into structured-language queries is a struggling area for merging natural language processing and data science. The goal is to translate natural language queries into SQL that can be executed on a system to access its data for all kinds of users. Translating natural language questions into programmed language has been a long-standing problem [1,2]. In this work, we have focused on a natural language interface to databases by the generation of executable SQL queries. Figure 1 elaborates the text-to-SQL task briefly.

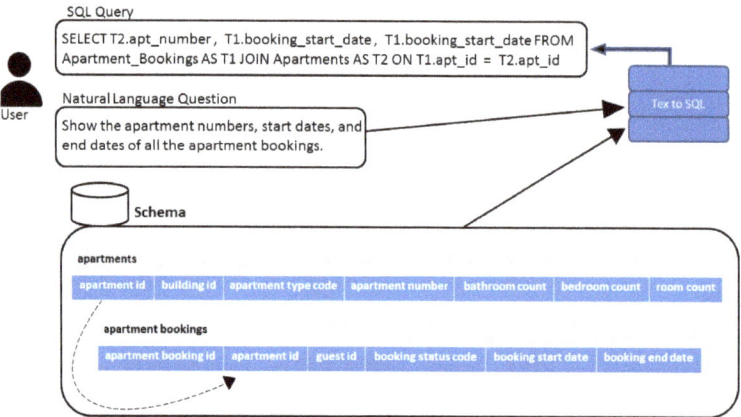

Figure 1. text-to-SQL task.

Deep learning has been an emerging tool in various research areas like communication, machine translation, and networking. Deep learning methods have arrived at competitive performances, compared with the traditional techniques, in a short time. They have been shown to be a potential tool for growth, even for mature fields with a higher bar of entry for new approaches, such as communication [3,4]. Deep learning has exhibited its problem-solving potential and growth in mobile traffic classification, as well. Though port information is not critical when working with deep learning traffic classifiers, mobile classifiers using deep learning methods can identify the application sources from which information is coming. Feature representations of direct-input data from training can be a potential path for improving traffic classifiers [5].

Deep learning has also shown promising results in the area of encrypted mobile traffic classification. However, deep learning, here, has some limitations because it is less mature in this area than are traditional methods, besides which, its black-box nature allows the least human intervention but contributes to resolving some of the complex matters in improving performance [6,7]. Deep learning has recently been adopted for text-to-SQL tasks; keeping in mind deep learning's success stories in neighbouring research areas, deep learning shows potential for rapid improvement in this task as well.

The initial work in adapting deep learning to text-to-SQL tasks was primarily based on neural network sequence-to-sequence learning [8], adopting copying and attention mechanisms and the sequence-to-sequence RNN model to improve translation accuracy. These approaches improved the basic framework and their contributions were pioneering in NLIDB systems with deep learning concepts.

Recent work in the text-to-SQL research area mainly focuses on improving two significant aspects, syntactic accuracy and semantic accuracy. Semantic accuracy is to interpret the user's intention correctly and map it to a given database schema. The semantic gap between mapping user's preferences from natural language query into schema nomenclature is also known as a mismatch [9,10] or lexical problem [11,12]. Often, exact column names are not mentioned in the text query. Instead, one of the synonyms of column names are mentioned, or the intended column's value is mentioned. This scenario makes mapping the intended column to the actual column name in the database vague. Figure 2 elaborates the issue more precisely with an example. The natural language question in Figure 2 does not have the exact intended column name in the SQL query, which makes the column prediction vague in the given example.

Natural Language Question:
    What is the average number of rooms of studio apartments?
SQL Query:
    SELECT avg(room_count) FROM Apartments WHERE apt_type_code = "Studio"

Figure 2. Example of no column mention in NL Question.

Bridging the gap between user intentions and data can improve column predictions and, ultimately, impact overall accuracy [13]. Primarily, this issue of semantic gap occurs during the keyword mapping component of the whole process. Keyword mapping is part of the text-to-SQL translation process in which words from a natural language query are mapped to column names and values from the database schema. Formulating a query with the user's intended columns and values from the database is the fundamental semantic issue of this task.

This semantic issue has been an intricate part of the text-to-SQL task because NLIDB systems are intended for everyday users who do not necessarily have explicit knowledge of database schemas. Therefore, they cannot specify the schema items in their natural language questions precisely. Finding a pattern within previous user queries and extracting co-occurrences between columns and between columns and tables would resolve the issue of mapping the intended schema elements as closely as possible to the user's choice in a structured query. The calculated pattern of previous query histories can provide a concept of typical users' preferences regarding the database and columns in question. Therefore, in this work, we have focused on filling the semantic gap between database schemas and users' intentions with the help of patterns established from previous query data. In this work, we have captured such patterns in a co-occurrences graph of various columns. The graph is explained in detail in Section 4.1. Co-occurrences graph scores can be utilized in two main steps; (1) capturing the occurrences and co-occurrences of columns and tables in previous query data; and (2) integrating that data as feature input and other input vectors in a deep learning NLIDB model.

A similarity measure has been described to capture scores from the column co-occurrences graph effectively. We have performed experiments with a text-to-SQL task on the Spider dataset. The Spider dataset and its difficulty categorization and criteria are explained in Section 5. Our experiments show that our approach improves exact match accuracy. We have compared our results with a base model of SyntaxSQLNet and two other contributions that have implemented preprocessing on input feature vectors and integrated with SyntaxSQLNet [14–16]. We show that our work improved accuracy up to 10% in an experiment with BERT embedding. The rest of the paper is constructed as shown in Figure 3 below. Table 1 in the following contains all the acronyms used in the article.

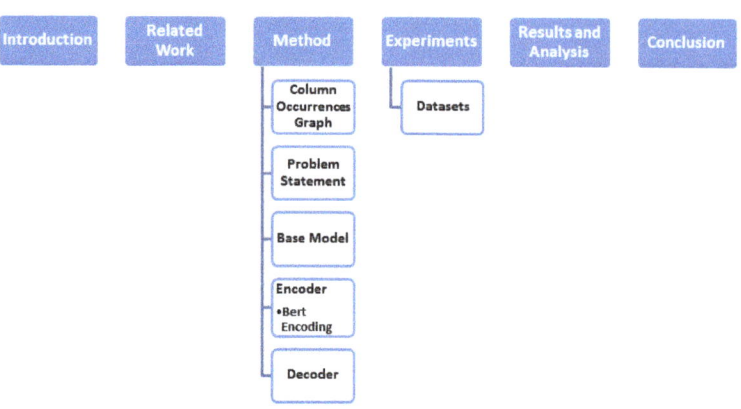

Figure 3. Paper Structure.

Table 1. Acronyms used in the paper.

Acronyms	Expansions
NLIDB	natural language interface to database
NL	natural language
NLP	natural language processing
DB	database
DL	deep learning
BERT	bidirectional encoder representations from transformation
GloVe embeddings	global vectors representation
SQL	structured query language

2. Background Study

2.1. Word Embedding

Word embedding is a vector representation of words learned in an architecture similar to neural networks. Similar words have similar and so closer representations in a predefined vector space. This vector representation is learned from a predefined, fixed-size library. The three most common techniques used for word embedding are an embedding layer, Word2Vec and GloVe. Word2Vec is a statistical technique for capturing the local meaning and context of a stand-alone text corpus [17,18].

On the other hand, gloVe extends the Word2Vec technique, combining its local context capturing and global matrix-factorization statistics. It uses statistics from the entire corpus of text to build a matrix of word co-occurrence. GloVe performs relatively better than Word2Vec.

2.2. Encoder–Decoder Structure

Encoder–decoder architectures for machine translation have been emerging since [19,20] used all the models based on an encoder that encoded a variable-length text sentence into a fixed-length vector. The decoder decoded the variable-length text from the same fixed-length vector to generate the targeted output translation. In the context of a text-to-SQL task, the LSTM encoder converts variable-length text sentences into a hidden state of the encoder, which is a fixed-length vector. RNN layers are then stacked upon each other to build the final form of the encoder. These RNN layers structures contribute to capturing the context of the words and temporal dependencies in the sequence. The last step of the RNN acts as the hidden state from the encoder that is passed to the decoder [21]; this context vector encapsulates the whole meaning and the context of the sequence for the decoder to translate.

The decoder is the other half of the structure, which receives the hidden state from the encoder, encapsulating all the possible information of the sequence [19]. The decoder is another LSTM consisting of the stack of RNN layers along with the prediction layer. It converts the hidden state vector into an SQL query based on the information stored in the hidden state vector. The encoder–decoder architecture consists of two LSTMs that allow the variable-length input-output.

2.3. Attention Mechanism

The encoder–decoder architecture does not perform very well when sentences sequence grow longer [19] because of a built-in behavior of LSTM by which it can only remember that which that it has just seen. This makes it difficult for the encoder LSTM to encapsulate all the required information in one context vector, especially for longer sentences. The attention mechanism proposed by the [22] deals with these issues by structuring a method to embed all the words of a sequence in the context vector. For this purpose, they calculated a weighted sum of the hidden states to form a final hidden-state vector. The following equation has been proposed to calculate such weights:

$$C_i = \sum_{j=1}^{T_x} \alpha_{ij} h_j \tag{1}$$

3. Related Work

An NLIDB (natural language interface to database) system aims to cover the language hurdle between users and database systems. With NLIDB systems, non-technical users can also interact with the system without a knowledge of structured query languages. Therefore, NLIDB systems provide friendlier and greater access to relational databases for a broader range of users. Users query an NLIDB system in plain- or natural language text. The natural language question is then translated into a structured query language (SQL) query to be executed by the database engine and provide the user-intended results. Work by [1] is one of the early contributions to NLIDB [1], in which they presented an NLIDB task with brief examples describing problem statements and emphasized the importance of separating the linguistic task from the database information in their NLIDB task. To this end, syntax tree-based and semantic-based systems have been in the leading position, alongside intermediate representations of text and SQL languages. Until this point, the format of text query had been fixed, such as with fixed-syntax queries and menu-based systems, to limit associated semantic problems.

Subsequently, Ref. [2] proposed a method based on knowledge representation to separate the exact match tokens of natural language questions in the context to database elements. Moving further along the NLIDB research timeline, Ref. [23] introduced the tree kernels concept in NLIDB systems. They integrated tree kernels to rank candidate queries. Further work in this area has belonged to two categories; pipeline-method NLIDBs [24] and neural-network NLIDBs. Deep learning is used most in research on neural-network NLIDBs. Deep learning NLIDBs can be categorized further into sequence-to-sequence learning [8] and sequence-to-set learning. For our work, we have adopted sequence-to-set learning.

Sequence-to-set learning for text-to-SQL tasks was initially proposed to solve the 'order matters' issue [25]. The reward is calculated based on the whole ground-truth sequence compared to the gold-standard query for sequence-to-sequence structures. Sequence-to-set learning has been a fundamental approach for much work in NLIDB systems, in parallel with sequence-to-sequence learning, as the order of the columns does not matter in the context of execution results [8]. Later, however, in the timeline of NLIDB systems, semantic accuracy became one of the significant issues in processing text-to-SQL tasks, as it has a substantial contribution in overall accuracy. Researchers have attempted to resolve this issue in various ways, such as with slot-filling approaches [26–28], which separate the syntactic and semantic issues by dealing with the former via building syntax grammatically before predicting the schema elements to populate slots. This allowed models to focus more on the semantic issue while predicting columns and tables. Then, Ref. [12] proposed global reasoning by a gating GCN to encode the DB schema for improving the prediction of its elements. Schema linking is another way to tackle mismatch issues, and was recently used in IRNet [10,29].

IRNet was extended to a sequence-based approach by [8]. They incorporated schema linking and intermediate representation into the baseline method. Schema linking, in IRNet, is done by simple string matching to identify the columns and tables mentioned in the question, labelling them with the column's information type. Although IRNet improved upon the baseline method, it is still not clear how schema linking impacts performance [10]. They separated the schema-linking task from the overall text-to-SQL task to analyze the impact of schema linking, showing that separating the schema entities from the questions and using placeholders instead allows the model to focus more on the syntactic component and improve overall query accuracy. Therefore, it is impactful on overall accuracy, but schema linking is not a perfect solution for semantic issues in text-to-SQL tasks. Additionally, using table content in the process has also improved prediction accuracy [30]. Despite this accuracy improvement, table contents may not be available in all cases, due to confidentiality. "Human in the loop" is another method of improving the output, in the context of capturing the user's intention, by taking feedback from them and revising it accordingly. DialSQL performs post-processing over the output of a prediction model. They take users' feedback in the form of multiple-choice questions. Various options related to defined error categories are provided for the user to select from. Then, taking the user's input into account, they improve the predicted query according to the user's provided information. This process requires the user to be trained and to explain the defined user categories beforehand. Ref. [31] advanced the "human in the loop" method by collecting user feedback in natural language and improving the interface's usability, as compared with DialSQL. With a "human in the loop", recruiting experts who know the database schema well enough to point to semantic errors is an additional effort compared with the other approaches. Both of these methods perform post-processing over generated output queries.

Various research contributions have proposed the preprocessing of input features to map DB schema elements to the user's question. Such work, by [14], implemented data anonymization over the DB schema and text queries before encoding the input features. Data anonymization consists of identifying the DB elements in the question via probability scores. Placeholders then replace the identified DB elements for the training phase. After anonymizing the text question from the DB elements, many training examples become similar and thus can share in the training process. Column/cell binding is the final step in generating probability distributions for the DB elements. The authors integrated this preprocessed anonymized data with an existing model, SyntaxSqlNet, for their experiments.

Another example of preprocessing feature vectors to impact a learning model is shown by [16]. They used column value polarities, generated beforehand, and integrated them with SyntaxSQLNet to better predict data elements. In the present work, we have followed a similar pattern of extending the baseline model by adding a preprocessed-input feature, i.e., column occurrences scores. Our contribution is unique in that we have utilized the data from previous queries to find patterns of users' intentions regarding the columns required of their questions. After a co-occurrences score is calculated it is integrated with SyntaxSQLNet as an additional feature vector. We have made the required changes to the

4. Methods

4.1. Column Occurrences Graph

First, we introduce the column occurrences graph. Following the idea of [32], the column occurrences graph is built from the query log or, in the Spider dataset case, from the previous SQL queries of a particular database in the training data. Example of such set of queries is shown in Figure 4. Figure 5 shows the columns occurrence frequency in the set of queries. Figure 6 shows the columns occurrences graph, where nodes represent the frequency of individal column occurrence and edges represent the co-occurrences of the comuns. The intuition of this graph is to capture the user's intention for clearer column prediction. Primarily in cases when the exact column name is not mentioned in the text question, prediction of one column can assist in predicting the other columns as well. Our method is an extended version of [32], in that we compute occurrences and co-occurrences of columns specifically, explicitly excluding the "from" part of queries to avoid noise and repetition. Instead, tables are concatenated with their column names, column types and relations, following the encoding method of [27]. Graph G contains edges, e, representing the column occurrences and vertices, v, representing co-occurrences of the involved schema elements in a particular database's query sets to capture this intuition. Following the idea of [32], the Dice similarity coefficient is used to reflect columns co-occurrences as follows:

$$Dice_{(C_1,C_2)} = \frac{2 \times n_e(C_1,C_2)}{n_v(C_1) + n_v(C_2)} \quad (2)$$

C_1 and C_2 are pairs of columns at a given time, and n_v and n_c are co-occurrences and occurrences of the respective column elements. Finally, the accumulate Dice coefficient for all column pairs is calculated with the following equation.

$$Score_{COG}(\phi) = [\prod_{(C_1,C_2)\in \phi T^2} Dice_{(C_1,C_2)}]^{\frac{1}{|\phi|}} \quad (3)$$

```
17x- SELECT apt_number, bedroom_count FROM Apartments
3x-SELECT max(room_count), max(bedroom_count) FROM Apartments WHERE T2.apt_type_code ="Flat"
4x-SELECT T2.apt_number, T1.booking_start_date FROM Apartment_Bookings AS T1 JOIN Apartments AS
     T2 ON T1.apt_id = T2.apt_id and T2.apt_type_code = "Flat"
```

Figure 4. Example of a set of queries.

21x: Apartments:apt_number	3x: Apartments:room_count
3x: Apartments:bedroom_count	3x: Apartments:building_id ?op ?var
4x: Apartment_Bookings:booking_start_date	4x: Apartments:apt_type_code ?op ?var

Figure 5. Columns Occurrences.

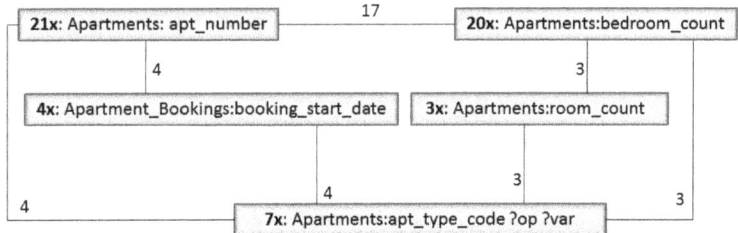

Figure 6. Column Occurrences Graph.

This section elaborates on our work and its implications for the issue of minimizing the ambiguities in the column prediction phase of the text-to-SQL task. First of all, we describe a problem statement for the semantic component of the text-to-SQL task. After that, the workings and components of the base model are explained to understand our extended work. The rest of the section addresses the implications of the column occurrences score in this work.

4.2. Problem Statement

Given a natural language text query Q and database schema primarily consisting of column names concatenated with table names and type information, labelled COL, our goal is to improve column prediction accuracy and ultimately enhance the model's overall accuracy. Utilizing previously used queries in a particular database can minimize the gap between the predicted columns and the user's intended output columns. Given that precalculated column-occurrences graph score, COG, along with Q and COL, PVALCOL is generated, ultimately generating the corresponding SQL, is the final goal. Text queries or natural language questions are treated as series of tokens to feed into the encoder–decoder model.

4.3. Base Model

Our base model, SyntaxSQLNet [27], is an encoder–decoder grammar-based slot-filling approach. The encoder encodes columns, the natural language question and history tokens as inputs, applying an attention mechanism to embed the most relevant question tokens in a columnular context. The weighted sum is calculated to bring the hidden state of the question token to the columns' attention. Decoders of the model predict the SQL syntax via a grammar to call modules based on history tokens. For semantic slot filling, the model has nine separate modules consisting of independent and respective biLSTM decoders. The column-predicting module is one of these nine modules and is trained separately.

$$P_{COL}^{num} = p(W_1^{num} H_{Q/COL}^{num}{}^T + W_2^{num} H_{HS/COL}^{num}{}^T) \quad (4)$$

The equation above reflects the column module's intuition. It is formulated in two parts; finding the total number of columns in the query, followed by the prediction of the column's values. The first equation computes the number of columns in the query, where $H_{Q/COL}$ is the hidden state of the question-to-column word embedding and $H_{HS/COL}$ represents the hidden state of the history of the last decoded element to the columns' attention mechanism. W_1 and W_2 are trainable parameters. Softmax was used for the probability distribution.

$$P_{COL}^{val} = p(W_1^{val} H_{Q/COL}^{val}{}^T + W_2^{val} H_{HS/COL}^{val}{}^T + W_3^{val} H_{COL}{}^T) \quad (5)$$

4.4. Encoder

The word embedding of question tokens, the schema, and history tokens is obtained from a pretrained GloVe [18] embedding. The current decoding history is further encoded with a biLSTM, denoted by HS [27]. We adopted the idea from [33] for schema encoding to capture self-attention of the schema elements. Schema encoding starts from obtaining the embedded column names, whererafter table names are embedded, as are column types. These initial embeddings are concatenated together. Self-attention is used between columns to capture the internal structure of the schema more effectively, where table names are also integrated. In the self-attention layer, another layer of biLSTM is applied to connect them and denoted as H_{COL}. The table schema encoding process is portrayed in Figure 7.

Following [27], after tokenization and GloVe embedding, the natural language question is encoded with biLSTM. To effectively capture the meaning and context of natural language questions fully with respect to the available column and tables in the database schema, an attention mechanism layer is applied, with the outputs of the hidden state of the question tokens' biLSTMs and the columns' biLSTMs, generating the $H_{Q/COL}$. Figure 8 shows the NL question tokens encoding process.

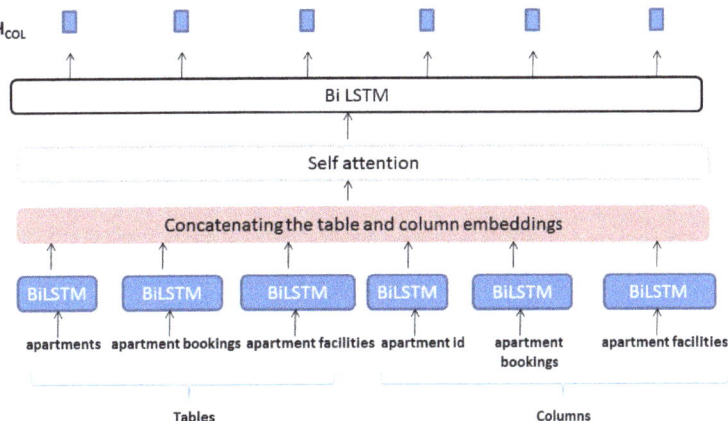

Figure 7. Table Schema Encoder.

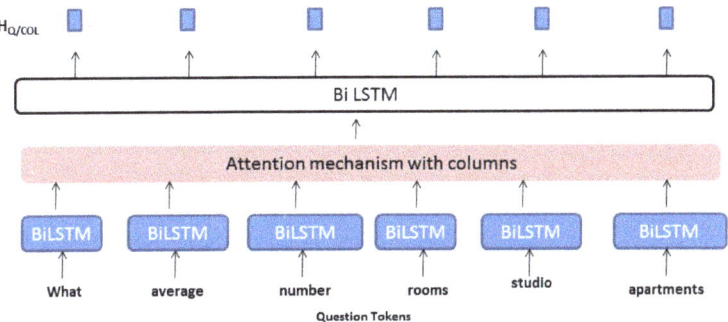

Figure 8. Question Encoder.

Columns occurrences scores have a graphical structure, with nodes as columns and edges as their co-occurrences. The embedded column names and occurrence scores are integrated. Along with other input features, column occurrence scores are also embedded via GloVe embedding, and then a biLSTM is applied. The hidden-state input of this biLSTM is further processed with the columns' hidden states to implement an attention mechanism between the question embedding and column occurrences embedding to find the relevant pairs of co-occurrences and their scores, denoted by $H_{COG/Q}$.

4.5. BERT Embedding of Input Features

Another option is to encode the input features using a pretrained BERT model. Question tokens and schema elements are fed into one sequence with a separator token. That sequence of input tokens is then provided to the BERT model. The final hidden state of the BERT is used as embedded input for the decoder. Previously, BERT has been shown to improve the overall accuracy of many models. We conducted one experiment with BERT, as well, to exhibit its compatibility.

4.6. Decoder

The decoder used in SyntaxSQLNet [27] is a recursively activating, sketch-based sequence-to-set approach. Nine separate decoder modules for each task are trained independently from each other. Grammar is used to structure the syntax of a query and the calling of modules for each prediction. The decoder history path is encoded as part of the input to decide the next module with which to predict the next token. The sequence-to-set approach is used to avoid the 'order matters' problem caused in sequence-to-sequence approached [8], as identified by [27]. For example, "select id, name" is equivalent to "select name, id"; however, in the traditional sequence-to-sequence approach, the model penalizes these over even correct queries if the order of the sets is changed. The attention mechanism in [27] is generalized for all embeddings, as follows:

$$H_{\frac{1}{2}} = softmax(H_1 W H_2^T) H_1 \qquad (6)$$

where W is a trainable parameter and H_1 and H_2 are the last hidden states of the biLSTM. Softmax was used for the calculation of probability distribution. The output of each module is computed in a sketch mode, independently of each other and whenever required, according to the syntax grammar [27].

The column module first computes the number of columns and then the values of the columns of the whole query altogether. We extended the column module by adding column occurrences scores as an input feature and using self-attention between columns instead of simple column embeddings, as follows:

$$P_{COL}^{val} = p(W_1^{val} H_{Q/COL}^{val\,T} + W_2^{val} H_{HS/COL}^{val\,T} + W_3^{val} H_{COL}^{T} + W_4^{val} H_{COL/Q}^{val\,T}) \qquad (7)$$

Here, W_1, W_2, W_3 and W_4 are trainable weights. Similarly, other modules are called according to the decoding history path and syntax grammar. For further details of the whole decoder and other modules, we refer the reader to the [25].

5. Experiments

This model was implemented in PyTorch [34]. Input questions and columns were tokenized using the Stanford toolkit [35] to process the sentence. A GloVe word-embedding vector was fed the one-hot vector output from the Stanford toolkit. A pretrained GloVe word-embedding model was used for all input features, such as columns, text questions, history tokens and COSs (column occurrence scores). All the word embeddings, here, were fixed-length vectors. Fixed-length vectors from the word-embedding model were then used as the input for the biLSTM model in the encoder. The dimension of the layers was 124, and the dropout rate was 0.2. An Adam optimizer was used to train the model.

Datasets

Despite the discussed works' successes, generalizing to new datasets was not an important factor in their models. Most of these models were built on traditional datasets, such as GeoQuery and ATIS. The task definitions of these datasets were comparatively simple and insufficient for practical use. The maximum complexity of these datasets was 500 SQL labels, which we expanded by paraphrasing approximately ten questions for each structured query. The test and training sets of queries contained overlapping queries, reducing the task's complexity. Another dataset used in this field is WikiSQL. It includes separate databases for training and testing purposes. Despite being a comparatively complex dataset, in terms of its larger size and multiple databases, it nonetheless has more straightforward queries. Such simple questions are inadequate to addressing the practical issues in semantic parsing. Yu et al. (2018b) have recently developed a complex dataset called the Spider dataset to cope with these issues. The Spider dataset contains around 6000 complex queries, along with 200 databases and multiple tables. This dataset defines the task of text-to-SQL with more complexity and can train cross-domain models.

Spider is the latest large-scale human-annotated dataset for text-to-SQL tasks [36]. It consists of 146 databases, along with their schemas, and 8659 query and question pairs. It has a training split of 752 queries and 1659 questions from previously established datasets, such as Scholar [37], IMDB & Yelp [38], GeoQuery [39], Restaurants [40], and Academic [41].

We used the Spider dataset primarily to evaluate our model with exact match accuracy. We used a split of query–question pairs of 130 for training, 36 for development, and 40 for the test, with a random distribution. Evaluation was performed according to the Spider evaluation script [36]. Beyond exact match accuracy, there are options for execution accuracy and logical form accuracy, as well. We chose exact match accuracy because execution accuracy can give false positives in some scenarios, wherein outputs may be similar, despite the schema columns from which they need to select being different [36]. Logical form accuracy could be more beneficial for syntactic improvement-oriented work. As this work focuses on the prediction of user-intended columns, exact match accuracy better represents our desired performance improvement.

This cross-domain and multitable dataset also introduced difficulty levels for model evaluation. Difficulty criteria contain a set of rules. The presence of particular rules decides the difficulty of the query from among easy, medium, hard and extra hard [36]. Figure 9 below shows the examples of easy, medium, complex and extra-hard queries.

Easy:
SELECT avg(room_count) FROM Apartments WHERE apt_type_code = "Studio"

Medium:
SELECT T1.booking_start_date FROM Apartment_Bookings AS T1 JOIN Apartments AS T2 ON T1.apt_id = T2.apt_id WHERE T2.apt_type_code = "Duplex"

Hard:
SELECT max(T2.bathroom_count), max(T2.bedroom_count) FROM Apartment_Bookings AS T1 JOIN Apartments AS T2 ON T1.apt_id = T2.apt_id WHERE T1.booking_status_code ="Provisional" and T2.apartment_type_code= "Studio"

Extra Hard:
SELECT T2.apt_number FROM Apartment_Bookings AS T1 JOIN Apartments AS T2 ON T1.apt_id = T2.apt_id WHERE T1.booking_status_code = "Confirmed" INTERSECT SELECT T2.apt_number FROM Apartment_Bookings AS T1 JOIN Apartments AS T2 ON T1.apt_id = T2.apt_id WHERE T1.booking_status_code = " Confirmed"

Figure 9. Query Difficulty Examples.

Easy queries can contain only one keyword among "where", "join", "like", "having", "or", "limit", "order by" and "group by". Medium queries may contain two of these keywords. Queries categorized as "easy" do not have more than one entry in a select column, such as a "where" condition, aggregate function, or "order by" clause. Medium queries can have any two such clauses with more than one entry. Hard queries are those having at least three clauses with more than one entry, as shown in the example. The hard query in Figure 7 has two aggregate functions, two select column entries and two "where" conditions. Hard queries also contain two keywords (where, join, or, limit, order by, group by). All queries that do not fall within these three categorize are extra hard.

6. Results and Analysis

Although our decoder is similar to the base model SyntaxsqlNet, our columns occurrences score, in the encoder, allows the model to include user intentions regarding column prediction from the database. In addition, overall accuracy increased with our model's greater focus on column prediction. Our model achieved a prominent increase in exact match accuracy. Table 2 shows the experimental results in the form of exact match accuracy compared with the base model and two other methods from [14,16]. Our model's performance was higher than the base model in terms of exact match accuracy. Efforts by [14,16] are similar to our work in preprocessing the input features to impact overall model performance. Our integration of column occurrences scores outperformed the other two models, contributing to "understanding accurate intention regarding column prediction from the natural language questions". Column prediction by column occurrences score enhanced the overall accuracy and outperformed the previous similar works [16] by, at our model's highest accuracy, 9.7%. Work by [16] extended the SyntaxSQLNet model by integrating the column value polarities as a feature vector [14], wherein they anonymized their input utterances to conceal lexical problems, minimizing semantic issues before data encoding. Column occurrences score and the self-attention mechanism between columns also contributed to the improved results.

We also experimented, on our model as well as the base model, with a pretrained language model, BERT. It improved the exact match accuracy even better for both models. Table 3 shows the partial matching accuracy, in terms of F1 scores, for "select", "where", "group by", "order by" and "keywords" separately. As shown in the table, accuracy improvement was less in the "group by", "order by" and "keywords" than the "select" and "where" clauses. The reason behind this is that group-by and order-by data are less represented in the training data. Therefore, there was less margin for improvement. Besides this observation, our overall exact match improvement shows our approach's potential for further work improvements in this area.

Table 2. Exact Match Accuracy Comparison.

Method	Easy	Medium	Hard	Extra Hard	All
SyntaxSQLNET	43.3%	22.8%	22.3%	4.2%	25.3%
DAE [14]	45.2%	30.5%	25.7%	7.9%	29.8%
SyntaxSQLNET + BERT	56.1%	31.7%	29.5%	8.9%	33.7%
Adjective-Noun Phrasing Knowledge [16]	67.5%	48.2%	41.7%	14.7%	45.4%
SyntaxSQLNet + COS (Ours)	84.2%	59.9%	59.5%	18.6%	55.1%
Ours + BERT	97.6%	70.2%	67.7%	24.8%	64.8%

Table 3. Clause-Wise F1 score accuracy.

Method	Select	Where	Group by	Order by	Keywords
SyntaxSQLNET	62.4%	34.1%	34.9%	56.8%	85.9%
DAE	59.8%	40.1%	38.4%	57.6%	91.2%
SyntaxSQLNET + BERT	71.0%	47.7%	38.5%	61.2%	89.3%
Adjective-Noun Phrasing Knowledge	70.1%	44.8%	63.2%	67.8%	76.8%
SyntaxSQLNet + COS (Ours)	71.5%	50.2%	65.0%	68.5%	77.9%
Ours + BERT	80.2%	61.9%	77.4%	80.0%	86.2%

7. Conclusions

In the field of NLIDB, bridging the gap between user-intended columns in a NL query and the predicted columns in the SQL query has been an ongoing issue. To resolve this semantic issue, various methods have been proposed, including preprocessing the data before its entrance to the model to reduce the semantic complexity. We have proposed an approach to include column occurrences scores extracted from previously executed user queries. We extended the base SyntaxSQLNet approach to emphasize column prediction accuracy with the help of a column occurrences scores graph. Column occurrences scores, in a previously executed queries database, shows the commonly used columns of that database by users with respect to the other columns, bridging the gap between predicted SQL query and user intended columns for a particular query. Our experiment shows that bridging the column-prediction and user-intention gap has the potential to enhance the overall accuracy of NLIDB systems. We extended the column module in SyntaxSQLNet, adjusting its encoder–decoder accordingly. We predicted the columns that were nearest to the user's intentions by adding column occurrences scores as an additional input feature to the model. This study shows that predicting user-intended columns can enhance overall accuracy.

Author Contributions: S.A. formulated the theoratical formalism and investigation. M.U.K. and A.A. contributed to the development and experimenting. S.U.-J.L. supervised the process and contributed with the funding aquisition. All authors discussed and analyzed the results and formulated the final menuscript. All authors have read and agreed to the published version of the manuscript.

Funding: This research received no external funding.

Informed Consent Statement: Not applicable.

Data Availability Statement: The data that support the findings of this study are openly available at github: https://yale-lily.github.io/spider, Reference number [36].

Conflicts of Interest: All authors declare that they have no conflict of interest.

References

1. Androutsopoulos, I.; Ritchie, G.D.; Thanisch, P. Natural Language Interfaces to Databases—An Introduction. *Nat. Lang. Eng.* **1995**, *1*, 29–81. [CrossRef]
2. Popescu, A.-M.; Etzioni, O.; Kautz, H. Towards a theory of natural language interfaces to databases. In Proceedings of the 8th International Conference on Intelligent User Interfaces, Miami, FL, USA, 12–15 January 2003; pp. 149–157.
3. Alam, T.M.; Mushtaq, M.; Shaukat, K.; Hameed, I.A.; Sarwar, M.U.; Luo, S. A Novel Method for Performance Measurement of Public Educational Institutions Using Machine Learning Models. *Appl. Sci.* **2021**, *11*, 9296. [CrossRef]
4. O'Shea, T.; Hoydis, J. An Introduction to Deep Learning for the Physical Layer. *IEEE Trans. Cogn. Commun. Netw.* **2017**, *3*, 563–575. [CrossRef]
5. Aceto, G.; Ciuonzo, D.; Montieri, A.; Pescapé, A. Mobile Encrypted Traffic Classification Using Deep Learning: Experimental Evaluation, Lessons Learned, and Challenges. *IEEE Trans. Netw. Serv. Manag.* **2019**, *16*, 445–458. [CrossRef]
6. Alam, T.M.; Shaukat, K.; Mahboob, H.; Sarwar, M.U.; Iqbal, F.; Nasir, A.; Luo, S. A Machine Learning Approach for Identification of Malignant Mesothelioma Etiological Factors in an Imbalanced Dataset. *Comput. J.* **2021**. [CrossRef]
7. Aceto, G.; Ciuonzo, D.; Montieri, A.; Pescapé, A. Toward effective mobile encrypted traffic classification through deep learning. *Neurocomputing* **2020**, *409*, 306–315. [CrossRef]
8. Zhong, V.; Xiong, C.; Socher, R. Seq2sql: Generating structured queries from natural language using reinforcement learning. *arXiv* **2017**, arXiv:1709.00103.
9. Naseem, U.; Khushi, M.; Khan, S.K.; Shaukat, K.; Moni, M.A. A comparative analysis of active learning for biomedical text mining. *Appl. Syst. Innov.* **2021**, *4*, 23. [CrossRef]
10. Guo, J.; Zhan, Z.; Gao, Y.; Xiao, Y.; Lou, J.G.; Liu, T.; Zhang, D. Towards complex text-to-sql in cross-domain database with intermediate representation. *arXiv* **2019**, arXiv:1905.08205.
11. Latif, M.Z.; Shaukat, K.; Luo, S.; Hameed, I.A.; Iqbal, F.; Alam, T.M. Risk factors identification of malignant mesothelioma: A data mining based approach. In Proceedings of the 2020 International Conference on Electrical, Communication, and Computer Engineering (ICECCE), Istanbul, Turkey, 12–13 June 2020; pp. 1–6.
12. Bogin, B.; Gardner, M.; Berant, J. Global reasoning over database structures for text-to-sql parsing. *arXiv* **2019**, arXiv:1908.11214.
13. Shaukat, K.; Luo, S.; Varadharajan, V.; Hameed, I.A.; Xu, M. A survey on machine learning techniques for cyber security in the last decade. *IEEE Access* **2020**, *8*, 222310–222354. [CrossRef]
14. Dong, Z.; Sun, S.; Liu, H.; Lou, J.G.; Zhang, D. Data-anonymous encoding for text-to-SQL generation. In Proceedings of the 2019 Conference on Empirical Methods in Natural Language Processing and 9th International Joint Conference on Natural Language Processing, Hong Kong, China, 3–7 November 2019; pp. 5405–5414.
15. Javed, U.; Shaukat, K.; Hameed, I.A.; Iqbal, F.; Alam, T.M.; Luo, S. A review of content-based and context-based recommendation systems. *Int. J. Emerg. Technol. Learn.* **2021**, *16*, 274–306. [CrossRef]
16. Liu, H.; Fang, L.; Liu, Q.; Chen, B.; Lou, J.G.; Li, Z. Leveraging adjective-noun phrasing knowledge for comparison relation prediction in text-to-sql. In Proceedings of the 2019 Conference on Empirical Methods in Natural Language Processing and 9th International Joint Conference on Natural Language Processing, Hong Kong, China, 3–7 November 2019; pp. 3515–3520.
17. Khushi, M.; Shaukat, K.; Alam, T.M.; Hameed, I.A.; Uddin, S.; Luo, S.; Reyes, M.C. A comparative performance analysis of data resampling methods on imbalance medical data. *IEEE Access* **2021**, *9*, 109960–109975. [CrossRef]
18. Pennington, J.; Socher, R.; Manning, C.D. Glove: Global vectors for word representation. In Proceedings of the EMNLP 2014: Conference on Empirical Methods in Natural Language Processing, Doha, Qatar, 25–29 October 2014; pp. 1532–1543.

19. Cho, K.; Merriënboer, B.V.; Gulcehre, C.; Bahdanau, D.; Bougares, F.; Schwenk, H.; Bengio, Y. Learning phrase representations using RNN encoder-decoder for statistical machine translation. *arXiv* **2014**, arXiv:1406.1078.
20. Sutskever, I.; Vinyals, O.; Le, Q.V. Sequence to sequence learning with neural networks. In Proceedings of the Advances in Neural Information Processing Systems, Montreal, QC, Canada, 8–13 December 2014; pp. 3104–3112.
21. Cho, K.; Merriënboer, B.V.; Bahdanau, D.; Bengio, Y. On the properties of neural machine translation: Encoder-decoder approaches. *arXiv* **2014**, arXiv:1409.1259.
22. Bahdanau, D.; Cho, K.; Bengio, Y. Neural machine translation by jointly learning to align and translate. *arXiv* **2014**, arXiv:1409.0473.
23. Giordani, A.; Moschitti, A. Translating Questions to SQL Queries with Generative Parsers Discriminatively Reranked. 2012. Available online: https://aclanthology.org/C12-2040.pdf (accessed on 10 November 2021).
24. Saha, D.; Floratou, A.; Sankaranarayanan, K.; Minhas, U.F.; Mittal, A.R.; Özcan, F. ATHENA: An ontology-driven system for natural language querying over relational data stores. *Proc. VLDB Endow.* **2016**, *9*, 1209–1220. [CrossRef]
25. Xu, X.; Liu, C.; Song, D. Sqlnet: Generating structured queries from natural language without reinforcement learning. *arXiv* **2017**, arXiv:1711.04436.
26. Lee, D. Clause-wise and recursive decoding for complex and cross-domain text-to-SQL generation. *arXiv* **2019**, arXiv:1904.08835.
27. Yu, T.; Yasunaga, M.; Yang, K.; Zhang, R.; Wang, D.; Li, Z.; Radev, D. Syntaxsqlnet: Syntax tree networks for complex and cross-domaintext-to-sql task. *arXiv* **2018**, arXiv:1810.05237.
28. Lin, K.; Bogin, B.; Neumann, M.; Berant, J.; Gardner, M. Grammar-based neural text-to-sql generation. *arXiv* **2019**, arXiv:1905.13326.
29. Lei, W.; Wang, W.; Ma, Z.; Gan, T.; Lu, W.; Kan, M.Y.; Chua, T.S. Re-Examining the Role of Schema Linking in Text-to-SQL. 2020. Available online: https://aclanthology.org/2020.emnlp-main.564.pdf (accessed on 10 November 2021).
30. Chen, Y.; Guo, X.; Wang, C.; Qiu, J.; Qi, G.; Wang, M.; Li, H. Leveraging Table Content for Zero-shot Text-to-SQL with Meta-Learning. In Proceedings of the AAAI Conference on Artificial Intelligence, Online, 2–9 February 2021; Volume 35, pp. 3992–4000.
31. Elgohary, A.; Hosseini, S.; Awadallah, A.H. Speak to your parser: Interactive text-to-SQL with natural language feedback. *arXiv* **2020**, arXiv:2005.02539.
32. Baik, C.; Jagadish, H.V.; Li, Y. Bridging the semantic gap with SQL query logs in natural language interfaces to databases. In Proceedings of the IEEE 35th International Conference on Data Engineering (ICDE), Macao, China, 8–11 April 2019; pp. 374–385.
33. Zhang, R.; Yu, T.; Er, H.Y.; Shim, S.; Xue, E.; Lin, X.V.; Radev, D. Editing-based SQL query generation for cross-domain context-dependent questions. *arXiv* **2019**, arXiv:1909.00786.
34. Paszke, A.; Gross, S.; Chintala, S.; Chanan, G.; Yang, E.; DeVito, Z.; Lin, Z.; Desmaison, A.; Antiga, L.; Lerer, A. Automatic differentiation in pytorch. In Proceedings of the 31st Conference on Neural Information Processing Systems (NIPS 2017), Long Beach, CA, USA, 4–9 December 2017.
35. Manning, C.D.; Surdeanu, M.; Bauer, J.; Finkel, J.R.; Bethard, S.; McClosky, D. The Stanford CoreNLP natural language processing toolkit. In Proceedings of the 52nd Annual Meeting of the Association for Computational Linguistics (ACL 2014), Baltimore, MD, USA, 23–24 June 2014; pp. 55–60.
36. Yu, T.; Zhang, R.; Yang, K.; Yasunaga, M.; Wang, D.; Li, Z.; Radev, D. Spider: A large-scale human-labeled dataset for complex and cross-domain semantic parsing and text-to-sql task. *arXiv* **2018**, arXiv:1809.08887.
37. Iyer, S.; Konstas, I.; Cheung, A.; Krishnamurthy, J.; Zettlemoyer, L. Learning a neural semantic parser from user feedback. *arXiv* **2017**, arXiv:1704.08760.
38. Yaghmazadeh, N.; Wang, Y.; Dillig, I.; Dillig, T. SQLizer: Query synthesis from natural language. In Proceedings of the ACM on Programming Languages, Paris, France, 15–21 January 2017; pp. 1–26.
39. Zelle, J.M.; Mooney, R.J. Learning to parse database queries using inductive logic programming. In Proceedings of the National Conference on Artificial Intelligence, Portland, OH, USA, 4–8 August 1996; pp. 1050–1055.
40. Tang, L.R.; Mooney, R.J. Using multiple clause constructors in inductive logic programming for semantic parsing. In *European Conference on Machine Learning*; Springer: Berlin/Heidelberg, Germany, 2001; pp. 466–477.
41. Li, F.; Jagadish, H.V. Constructing an interactive natural language interface for relational databases. *Proc. VLDB Endow.* **2014**, *8*, 73–84. [CrossRef]

Article

Predicting Academic Performance Using an Efficient Model Based on Fusion of Classifiers

Ansar Siddique [1,*], Asiya Jan [2], Fiaz Majeed [2], Adel Ibrahim Qahmash [3], Noorulhasan Naveed Quadri [4] and Mohammad Osman Abdul Wahab [5]

1. Department of Software Engineering, University of Gujrat, Gujrat 50700, Pakistan
2. Department of Information Technology, University of Gujrat, Gujrat 50700, Pakistan; 19025956-003@uog.edu.pk (A.J.); fiaz.majeed@uog.edu.pk (F.M.)
3. College of Education, King Khalid University, Abha 61413, Saudi Arabia; aqahmash@kku.edu.sa
4. College of Computer Science, King Khalid University, Abha 61413, Saudi Arabia; qnaveed@kku.edu.sa
5. Department of English, Faculty of Languages and Translation, King Khalid University, Abha 61413, Saudi Arabia; moothman@kku.edu.sa
* Correspondence: dr.ansarsiddique@uog.edu.pk

Citation: Siddique, A.; Jan, A.; Majeed, F.; Qahmash, A.I.; Quadri, N.N.; Wahab, M.O.A. Predicting Academic Performance Using an Efficient Model Based on Fusion of Classifiers. *Appl. Sci.* **2021**, *11*, 11845. https://doi.org/10.3390/app112411845

Academic Editors: Kamran Shaukat, Suhuai Luo and Federico Divina

Received: 21 October 2021
Accepted: 9 December 2021
Published: 13 December 2021

Publisher's Note: MDPI stays neutral with regard to jurisdictional claims in published maps and institutional affiliations.

Copyright: © 2021 by the authors. Licensee MDPI, Basel, Switzerland. This article is an open access article distributed under the terms and conditions of the Creative Commons Attribution (CC BY) license (https://creativecommons.org/licenses/by/4.0/).

Abstract: In the past few years, educational data mining (EDM) has attracted the attention of researchers to enhance the quality of education. Predicting student academic performance is crucial to improving the value of education. Some research studies have been conducted which mainly focused on prediction of students' performance at higher education. However, research related to performance prediction at the secondary level is scarce, whereas the secondary level tends to be a benchmark to describe students' learning progress at further educational levels. Students' failure or poor grades at lower secondary negatively impact them at the higher secondary level. Therefore, early prediction of performance is vital to keep students on a progressive track. This research intended to determine the critical factors that affect the performance of students at the secondary level and to build an efficient classification model through the fusion of single and ensemble-based classifiers for the prediction of academic performance. Firstly, three single classifiers including a Multilayer Perceptron (MLP), J48, and PART were observed along with three well-established ensemble algorithms encompassing Bagging (BAG), MultiBoost (MB), and Voting (VT) independently. To further enhance the performance of the abovementioned classifiers, nine other models were developed by the fusion of single and ensemble-based classifiers. The evaluation results showed that MultiBoost with MLP outperformed the others by achieving 98.7% accuracy, 98.6% precision, recall, and F-score. The study implies that the proposed model could be useful in identifying the academic performance of secondary level students at an early stage to improve the learning outcomes.

Keywords: educational data mining; supervised learning; secondary education; academic performance

1. Introduction

Educational data mining (EDM) is a growing area of research that is being used to explore educational data for different academic purposes. The main application of EDM is the prediction of students' academic performance [1,2]. In data mining, the analysis and interpretation of student academic performance are regarded as suitable analysis, evaluation, and assessment tools [3]. In the present era of a knowledge economy, the students are the key element for the socio-economic growth of any country, so keeping their performance on track is essential. Data mining (DM) methods are applied to learn hidden knowledge and patterns which assist administrators and academicians in decision making regarding the delivery of instructions. DM techniques have applications in numerous areas including retail business, the health sector, marketing, banking, bioinformatics, counter-terrorism, and many others are also using it to enhance productivity and efficiency [4].

Education plays a vital role in the development of any nation. The education in Pakistan has improved in the past few years; it is further striving to enhance academic performance to produce a well-educated and competitive workforce to meet the requirements of the market [5]. The academic performance of high school students is a critical concern for parents, teachers, the education department, and the government. The performance of students at the secondary level is highly influenced by their demographic, schooling, social background, family background, and psychological factors [6]. Individuals vary from one another in terms of these factors, and hence their academic performance differs accordingly [5]. It is therefore important to predict students' academic performance, taking into account the aforementioned parameters.

The performance of secondary level students in science subjects is expected to be high in order to provide quality entrants at a higher level of education, which is key to prosperity and the knowledge economy [7]. Therefore, the lower secondary level is very crucial for students aiming for science as a major subject, because it is a baseline for setting their academic goals. Ninth-grade students need to consider grades as imperative at the lower secondary level as they act as a stepping-stone in subsequent educational levels. Academic performance can be enhanced by identifying weak areas concerning academics and personal traits. To achieve this, the design of a prediction system is indispensable to estimation of students' academic progress at an early stage before they in board examination. Such prediction may be beneficial in multiple ways. For example, it can help in reinforcing students to improve their performance in their weak areas. Secondly, it may assist in the selection of subjects where students can perform better. Thirdly, it can be useful in deciding on career goals. Finally, it can assist in awarding accurate grades to students based on their previous performance in COVID-19-like situations where administering examinations is impossible. Therefore, a prediction system should be in place to predict the performance of ninth-grade students at an early stage of the academic year to keep them on track and enable them to perform better in board examinations. The basic objective is to minimize the dropout and failure ratios of students at the lower secondary level. Additionally, the selection of subjects in grade nine is considered important in students' academic growth and professional advancement. To support education in a traditional setting, numerous systems such as massive open online courses (MOOCS), intelligent tutoring systems (ITS) and web-based educational systems have been designed but there is a dearth of systems to predict students' academic progress [8]. As per our knowledge, in Pakistan, there is no prediction system available to measure students' progress at the lower secondary level.

It has been described that data mining approaches analyze an organization's historical data and figure out the required pattern or information that is otherwise impossible [9]. In DM, both classification and regression are used to build predictive models. The classification techniques are used on pre-classified data to characterize the unclassified data [10]. The classification can be performed using different learning schemes such as decision trees (ID3, REP Tree and C4.5, etc.), logistic regression (LogitBoost), backtracking (MLP), and probability (Naïve Bayes, Bayes Network). These algorithms are known as single classifiers which have some limitations for the accuracy of the model. It is therefore important to improve the performance of single classifiers. To achieve such a goal, the ensemble method has been introduced which combines different classifiers into a single unit. However, in the ensemble structure, many areas must be explored to increase the accuracy of prediction models. A research study has been conducted to discover other algorithms of learning schemes in different ensemble methods which can help in predicting students' academic performance with greater accuracy [11]. This research intends to propose a classification model developed by fusion of single-based classifiers and ensemble-based classifiers to predict the academic performance of secondary-level students based on their academic and personal traits.

The prediction of students' grades from their academic data along with other features is a useful application in EDM; it is therefore becoming a suitable source of information that can be utilized in multiple ways to improve the quality of education. The major contributions of this research study towards EDM include (a) the identification of the personal traits of secondary school students. (b) Development of a dataset by gathering data from four different secondary schools located in three different cities. The academic data were collected through a student information system and data related to personal characteristics and socioeconomic conditions was gathered using online and physical surveys. (c) Building of a model which analyzes students' academic and personal data and predicts their academic progress with higher accuracy and precision.

The rest of the paper is organized as follows: Section 2 presents a literature review that highlights the findings of prior research studies in order to identify the set of the most common factors affecting students' academic performance. Secondly, it determines the most frequently used data mining techniques in previous research. Section 4 presents the research methodology, and the section is about data collection and data preprocessing. In Section 5, the conclusion and future prospects of this research study have been presented.

2. Literature Review

EDM is burgeoning due to the massive growth of educational resources, the internet, and the usage of online tools to impart education [12]. Consistent research efforts are being made to improve the quality of educational tools. This section provides an overview of the factors that may affect students' academic progress and technologies that are helpful in making predictions regarding students' academic progress. A systematic review has been conducted to determine factors that affect student performance through information mining procedures [13]. The study handled numerous subjects, one of which was to recognize the significant characteristics which can be utilized in anticipating student performance. The results indicated that the internal assessments and aggregate evaluation points are the most incessant qualities utilized for predicting academic performance. Additionally, other significant properties were identified including personal and inner appraisal, previous record, extra-curricular activities, and social attributes. The decision tree and neural networks were found as the most regularly utilized information-digging strategies [14].

Another research study [15] considered the cumulative grade point average as a prominent factor for measuring student performances in each semester. Additionally, the study also interprets normal class tests and assignments, previous academic failure, and study duration as the appreciable factors for predicting student performances. In [16] author stated that academic attainments are somehow linked with students' extracurricular activities and presented the presence of the student in a class as the strongest predictor for academic performance.

The study [17] found that family attributes and academic attributes were the deciding factors for prediction. The cumulative grade point average of students and their external and internal assessments marks were also the most frequently used attributes by the researchers. Another research [18] also showed the performance prediction of fourth-year undergrad students using pre-university marks and considering marks obtained in courses of the second year. They only considered grades for performance prediction and ignored the family and socio-economic attributes of the students.

A comprehensive analysis of supervised machine learning techniques was conducted and applied to predict students' performance in the examination. They considered different factors including demographics and social interest to predict students' expected score in the final term as well as students at risk [19].

A survey study was conducted using a sample of 1500 United State students to identify the impact of the COVID-19 pandemic on higher education. It has been revealed through analysis and a classification model that the shocks related to health and economics brought about by COVID-19 varied by socioeconomic factors [20]. Another study gathered students' pre-university marks, first and second-year marks through a large-sized sample and applied a predictive model on it to envisage students' CGPA at the final semester [21].

Table 1 shows the set of attributes used at the secondary level to predict students' academic performance.

Table 1. Student attributes used for predicting performances.

Student Attributes	Possible Values Used in All Research Papers While Implementing the DM Algorithm
Academic Attributes	Internal and external assessment, lab marks, sessional marks, attendance, Cumulative Grade Point Average (CGPA), semester marks, grade, seminar performance, assignment, attendance, schools marks, previous academic marks, etc.
Personal Attributes	Age, gender, height, weight, Emotional Intelligence (EI), student interest, level of motivation, communication, sports person, hobbies and ethnicity, etc.
Family Attributes	Qualification, occupation, income, status, support, siblings, responsibilities, etc.
Social Attributes	Number of friends, social networking, girls'/boys' friends, movies, travel outings, friends' parties, etc.
School Attributes	Teaching medium, accommodation, infrastructure, water and toilet facilities, transportation system, class size, school reputation, school status, class size, school type, teaching methodology, etc.

Another research study [22] proposed a predictive investigation framework to gauge the satisfaction level of university students regarding an online summer program. The students were given a questionnaire, consisting of questions related to socioeconomic, demographics, and some other indicators. Regression and ANOVA analysis were applied in that prediction model to interpret learners' interaction. Data mining approaches are being widely used by academic analysts to assess the effectiveness of education by processing and interpreting the huge volumes of data [23]. For the timely completion of students' degree requirements, their future performance was predicted based on their academic record. A novel machine learning method was used to predict the students' performance in a degree program [24]. A brief overview of multiple machine learning techniques along with comparison of time complexity of models was presented. The work shows the current limitations and challenges of machine learning techniques [25].

It has been shown that composite methods are vital for improving single classifiers and accuracy of predictive models. Bagging, Boosting and stacking, etc. are different types of ensemble methods that use a blend of models to improve composite models. Among them, bagging is utilized for classification and prediction purposes. The study handled the imbalance dataset with a SMOTTEEN technique with ensemble classifiers to produce high results. Since every model comprises some limitations, so the ultimate purpose of ensemble methods was to join the strength of single different models with the aim to achieve higher accuracy [26].

Another research presented two prediction models for estimating the student performance in final examinations. A K-Nearest Neighbor algorithm and support vector machine algorithm were used as a prediction technique to estimate the students' performance in final examinations on the basis of their demographic, class and social attributes [27].

In the field of EDM, researchers made efforts to study different kinds of attributes and properties that influence students' learning and performance results [28].

There are so many data mining approaches, but some mining approaches are being considered more effective. Such as machine learning-based ensemble methods also known as composite methods which are being considered as a vital approach to strengthening single classifiers. This approach leverages the power of multiple models to attain improved prediction accuracy than any of the individual models could achieve independently [29].

3. Research Methodology

This section describes the research methodology in detail. The implementation of the data mining approach is completely described in this section. The Waikato Environment for Knowledge Analysis (WEKA) [30] was used to perform data mining tasks. The research methodology consists of different phases and experiments conducted during this research. The pictorial representation of research methodology is given in Figure 1.

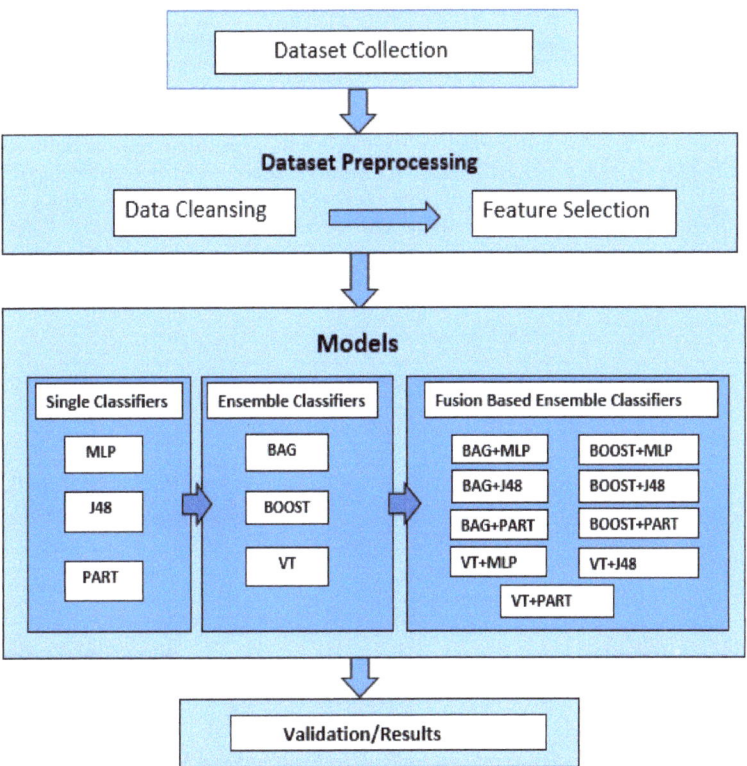

Figure 1. Proposed methodology.

The data collection was based on attributes suggested by researchers as the most rational attributes to predict academic performance at secondary level of education. The dataset was collected using an online and physical survey from four different schools based on students' academic, demographic, social, and family attributes. A dataset comprising 1227 records was collected that is currently available online at Kaggle. It includes 21 attributes in total of four different types including demographics, family, social, and academic. A total of 16 attributes remained after a feature selection process. The outcome is categorized into seven classes of grades including A+, A, B+, B, C, D and F. This section demonstrates the detailed description of selected attributes. Table 2 provides a brief description of every attribute that was used in this study.

The first step in data pre-processing is data cleansing, which is used to remove all the irrelevant attributes. The dataset consists of 1227 records in total. After detecting the missing values from different features, some records were removed from the dataset. The removal of records does not lead a model towards biasness, if dataset is used for training as a whole for each algorithm instead of subset of the dataset [31,32]. To reduce the computational complexity while implementing the mining techniques, missing values were also removed. The second step in data preprocessing is feature selection which is used to reduce dimensionality in feature space and obtain better classification results [26] because training on high-dimensional data leads to overfitting of the model. The subset of original features have been picked up through feature selection method which leads to the removal of redundant and obsolete characteristics without losing any important information [26]. This study applied filter-based methods using information gain-based selection to evaluate crucial features which may help in developing good performance models. Filter-based feature selection is a ranking method, used to rank the attributes according to their rank values by overlooking the remaining ones and then through application to the learning ones. In a rank-based method, values were given to each attribute according to their ranks in building a good model. Information gain is a filter-based feature ranking technique that is based on the information theory where information is provided about the target class attribute given the value of the dependent class attribute [33]. Out of 21 features, 16 were selected based on the rank that is close in its relationship with the final predicted outcome and gives better results. The foremost motive of the proposed model is to predict the students' performances under the classes such as A+, A, B+, B, C, D, and F, where nominal and numeric data are converted into ordinal values with the help of the discretization technique. The class distribution is shown in Table 2.

Table 2. Dataset description and possible values.

S. No	Attributes	Description
1	GE	Gender (Male, Female)
2	HA	Home Address Urban, Rural)
3	PCA	Parent Cohabitation Status (Living together, Apart)
4	QFR	Quality of family Relationship (Very Good, Good, Not Good)
5	MJ	Mother Job (Yes, No)
6	FJ	Father Job (Yes, No)
7	ME	Mother Education (None, Elementary, Secondary, Higher)
8	FE	Father Education (None, Elementary, Secondary, Higher)
9	FS	Family Size (Less than 3, Greater or equal to 3)
10	GF	Going out with friends (Yes, No)
11	PF	Past Failures (Yes, No)
12	NS	Attended Nursery School (Yes, No)
13	HE	Want to take Higher Education (Yes, No)
14	R	Relationship (Yes, No)
15	IA	Internet access at home (Yes, No)
16	ECA	Extra-Curricular Activities (Yes, No)
17	DST	Daily Study Time (<2 h, 2 to 5 h, 5 to 10 h, >10 h)
18	HST	Home to school Travel Time (<15 min, 15 to 30 min, 30 min to 1 h, >1 h)
19	EG	8th Class Grades (A+, A, B+, B, C, D)
20	NG1	9th Class First Term Grades (A+, A, B+, B, C, D, F)
21	NG2	9th Class Final Term Grades (A+, A, B+, B, C, D, F)

The research methodology is mainly premised on ensemble methods including bagging, boosting, and stacking, which is a different kind of ensemble method which uses a blend of models [29]. Among these methods, bagging, boosting, and stacking can be utilized for classification and prediction. Each model has some strengths and limitations, so the ultimate objective of ensemble methods is to complement the models, in order to achieve higher prediction accuracy. The bagging method is used to sort the tuples randomly into different bags while developing a model. The process is known as bootstrap aggregation. All models in bagging are built in parallel and, for the overall decision, an average is taken from all models, which lowers the variance in the model. It has been shown that bagging achieves the highest efficiency relative to the other methods [34,35].

Bootstrap improves on bagging. It is developed sequentially by assigning weights to the tuples classified incorrectly by previous classifiers and thus receive more attention from the next classifier. The weighted average is finally taken to build the final decision. The boosting algorithms are highly capable, take weak and low-performing models, and convert them into robust models. The boosting classifier methods include AdaBoost, GradientBoost and MultiBoost, etc. [36].

The effectiveness of the boosting method has been examined and it was found that the method is an efficient and effective strategy for classification and prediction [37,38].

Random forest is also an ensemble method which is an improved version of bagging, and it is used for classification and regression. In the training phase, it creates multiple decision trees and produces the mode of classes as well as generating a mean prediction of an individual in regression problems. It also performs random sampling on features with the help of feature engineering. It builds prediction models based on the aggregation of decision trees [39]. Another ensemble method is voting, which combines the output predictions from multiple models. This technique is used to enhance the performance of models in comparison to any single classifier model. The technique is mainly used for regression and classification problems. In the classification method, the prediction from multiple models of each label is aggregated and the majority vote label is predicted, which may be considered as a meta-model. The method of combining the decision of different algorithms requires stacking algorithms. The most common way to develop the training dataset for the meta-model is through k-fold cross-validation of the base models, where the out-of-fold predictions are used as a premise for the training dataset for the meta-model. After training, a meta-model from different models is assembled and is trained on the resultant of component models. Thus the heterogeneous ensemble model is created using this approach as the component model comprises diverse algorithms [37–39].

The importance of different ensemble techniques such as bagging, boosting, and voting classifiers can be viewed through various recent studies where hybridization of ensemble classifiers with base classifiers is a current research trend. Livieris et al. proposed a prediction model which was based on Bagging and Boosting and created two strategies to successfully combine the predictions of weight-constrained neural networks (WCNNs) [40]. Similarly, another study has explored bagging, boosting, and voting classifiers for the automated classification of news articles, in particular concerning identification of fake content from real content. They highlighted that the novel aspect of their research is the use of various ensemble methods including bagging, boosting, and voting classifiers to investigate their performance over multiple datasets [41]. Yang et al. proposed a two-layer ensemble approach to enhance the performance of the software defect prediction process. In the inner layer, they have combined decision tree and bagging to form a random forest model. In the outer layer, they used random under-sampling to train various random forest models and applied staking to ensemble them once again [42].

3.1. Phase 1: Classification Using Base Classifier

Several classification learning schemes are being used for classification and prediction, such as decision trees (REP Tree, C4.5, CART, and J48, etc.), probability (Naïve Bayes and Bayes Networks, etc.), backtracking (ANN like MLP, etc.), logistic regression (Logistic Boost, etc.), and so many other schemes are highly embraced. Any of them used independently are referred to as a single base classifier.

Previous research studies revealed that, among other classification learning schemes, the Multilayer perceptron, J48, and PART are the most efficient and frequently used classifiers for performance prediction. The performance of such classifiers was studied regarding training time, efficiency, and accuracy of prediction. It has been found that J48 took less training time for each data instance than the MLP classifier. The MLP, PART, and J48 showed higher accuracy for both large and small size data sets. Moreover, it has also been examined that the PART algorithm provided better accuracy in every case with and without noise [38].

3.1.1. Multilayer Perceptron Classifier

A multilayer perceptron (MLP) is a feed-in class to the artificial neural network. It utilizes back-propagation for training, referred to as a supervised learning technique. MLP consists of an input layer, a hidden layer, and an output layer. Each node is known as a neuron excluding the input nodes and uses a non-linear ReLu activation function [43]. This non-linear activation along with its multiple layers distinguishes it the from linear perceptron. The ReLu activation function is simple and efficient, as it has been empirically observed that training a network with this function tended to converge quickly and reliably in comparison to other activation functions. Furthermore, it also helps in detecting data that cannot be separated linearly [43].

3.1.2. J48 Classifier

The J48 algorithm was developed by Ross Quinlan to classify different datasets and applications to enhance the results of classification. J48 is used to generate decision trees that are based on C4.5 algorithms. Every aspect of data is divided into small subsets based on a decision tree. It employs greedy search and top-down search by all branches to build a decision tree for modeling of the classification process [44]. This decision tree can estimate the missing attributes and deal with certain distinctive and varying features. Furthermore, it can be used to examine the data continuously [45,46].

3.1.3. PART Classifier

The developed version of the ripper algorithm and C4.5 is a partial decision tree algorithm that does not require global optimization to produce appropriate rules for classification [38]. It helps in building a partial decision tree on different sets of instances and produces rules for decision trees [47]. PART is an algorithm that uses a divide-and-conquer mechanism to build a partial C4.5 decision tree in each iteration, i.e., it generates a PART decision list, and makes the best leaf into a rule [44].

3.2. Phase 2: Building Model by Ensemble Methods

Ensemble methods are an influential and efficient development in data mining and machine learning. The philosophy of ensemble classification is based on the decision of a group of experts instead of a single expert. This research uses three main techniques including Bagging (BAG), Boosting (BST), and voting (VT) as these techniques are highly recommended by previous research in order to attain high accuracy and low errors in prediction [46]. Basically, ensemble methods are classified as homogenous and heterogeneous ensemble methods. Homogenous ensemble methods apply a single algorithm on various training datasets to construct multiple classifiers such as bagging and boosting. Conversely, different algorithms are used to manipulate training datasets to make various models in heterogeneous ensemble models including voting and stacking [48].

3.2.1. Bagging

Bagging, or bootstrap aggregation, is an efficient ensemble technique used for classification. The bagging technique takes a sample of data randomly, puts them into different sample-sized bags, and then trains them on a classifier. It is mostly used as an ensemble method to reduce variance in data, randomize the design process, and finally create an ensemble from them [49]. It has also been observed that bagging provides high efficiency [34]. In this research study, the bagging technique samples the data erratically into different sample-sized bags and trains them on random forest, a basic classifier for bagging, and aggregates their specific forecasts into a final prediction [50].

3.2.2. Boosting

Boosting is another robust algorithm of ensemble learning that creates a strong learner from weak learners. It generates many weak learners with the help of a decision tree and combines them to form a strong learner. It helps in reducing errors during prediction and makes a model less biased. The effectiveness of the boosting method has been examined and it was concluded that it is an efficient and effective strategy for classification and prediction [38]. The boosting technique used in this research is MultiBoostAB (MB), as it is an extension of the AdaBoost technique to form decision committees but with a lower error rate in comparison to AdaBoost [51,52].

3.2.3. Voting

Voting is also known for its heterogeneous nature where classifiers comprise different algorithms which are used to predict the final outcome. It creates two or more models and each of them make their predictions [36]. It is based on an aggregating network that is used to determine the weights' mean. It is a model that combines the result of multiple classifiers on basis of weights [53]. There are three types of voting including majority voting, unanimous voting, and plurality voting. The majority voting reflects more than 50% votes for the final decision; in unanimous voting, all classifiers develop an agreement for final decisions, whereas polarity voting considers the majority of votes to decide the final outcome. In this research, majority voting was used to combine classifiers because it provides better results in terms of accuracy, as indicated by prior research [53,54]. Moreover, three different algorithms including Naive Bayes, IBk, and ZeroR were used in this study for voting.

3.3. Phase 3: Building Model by Hybrid Ensemble Methods

This phase includes the building, training and testing of hybrid ensemble-based models by hybridizing them with base classifiers. The fusion of base classifiers with ensemble models enhances the generalization and prediction capability of ensemble models. The hybrid models of machine learning, build accurate and efficient machine learning models and feed their output to each other [55].

These models include BAG + J48, BAG + MLP, BAG + PART followed by BST + J48, BST + MLP, BST + PART. The last hybrid ensemble-based models were VT + J48, VT + MLP, VT + PART.

3.4. Phase 4: Performance Comparison Analysis

To determine the performance of an algorithm, evaluation metrics were used. The performance validation of models was generated through 10-fold cross-validation. The k-fold cross-validation procedure divides a limited dataset into k non-overlapping folds. Each of the k folds are allowed to be used as a held back test set whilst all other folds are collectively utilized as a training dataset. A total of k models are fit and evaluated on the k holdout test sets and report the mean performance. The evaluation in this study was conducted using a 10-fold cross-validation technique. The technique divided the whole dataset into 10 subsets of equal size; out of 10 subsets, 9 were used for training and the 1 remaining was used for testing. The process was iterated ten times; the final result was estimated as the average error rate on test examples [55].

The evaluation metrics include accuracy, precision, recall, and F-score, which were used to examine the performance of each predictive model. Such predictive models were figured out based on True-Positive (TP), False-Positive (FP), True-Negative (TN), and False-Positive (FP).

4. Experiments and Evaluation

WEKA was used to evaluate the proposed classification model and to make comparisons. In this study, different experiments were conducted sequentially to assess students' performance. The comparison was made through various single base classifiers, ensemble-based classifiers, and fusion ensemble classifiers. The time complexity of each algorithm is also represented in terms of Big O notation which plays an important role in finding the efficiency of algorithms [25]. Additionally, a comparative analysis has been performed to discover performance improvements in different models. The experiments detected the efficient model in predicting student academic performance at the secondary level. To acquire precise results during evaluation, 10-fold cross-validation was used.

4.1. Experiments with Base Classifiers and Ensemble Base Classifiers

The three base classifiers including MLP, J48, and PART were applied after the data preprocessing stage. The evaluation results showed that among these three base classifiers, MLP outperformed the other classifiers, achieving greater accuracy (i.e., 88.52) as shown in Figure 2. The figure has two parts; in the first part, the bar chart presents the performance of classifiers in terms of accuracy, precision, recall, and F-score. The second part presents the performance of classifiers in tabular form through the same measures. The MLP classifier also performed better in terms of other measures such as precision, recall, and F-score. The time complexity of the MLP classifier is O(emnk), which is a composition of interconnected neurons, whereas J48 and PART have a time complexity of O(mn2), which works on the If and Then rule until the predicted class has not been obtained.

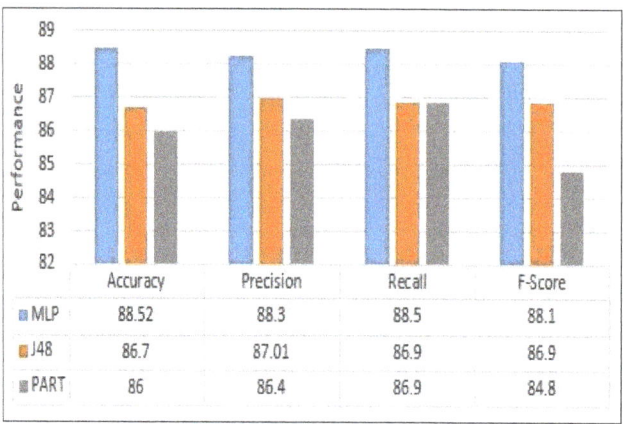

Figure 2. Single-based classifiers.

Furthermore, three different ensemble classifiers including bagging, multiboost, and voting were built. Among these three ensemble classifiers, multiboost outperformed the other classifiers, achieving higher accuracy (i.e., 95.7) as shown in Figure 3. The figure comprises two parts; in the first part, the bar chart shows the performance of classifiers in terms of accuracy, precision, recall, and F-score. The second part indicates the performance of classifiers in tabular form through the same measures. The classifier also performed better in terms of other measures such as precision, recall, and F-score. The time complexity of bagging is (O(klogn), where k is the number of bags.

4.2. Experiments with Fusion Ensemble-Based Models

The aim of this phase was to develop hybridization of ensemble classifiers with single-based classifiers. This experiment evaluated nine fused ensemble models including fusion of BAGGING (BAG) with MLP, PART, and J48, MultiBoost fusion with MLP, PART, and J48 as well as Voting (VT) fusion with MLP, PART, and J48. The results of these models are shown in Figures 4–6.

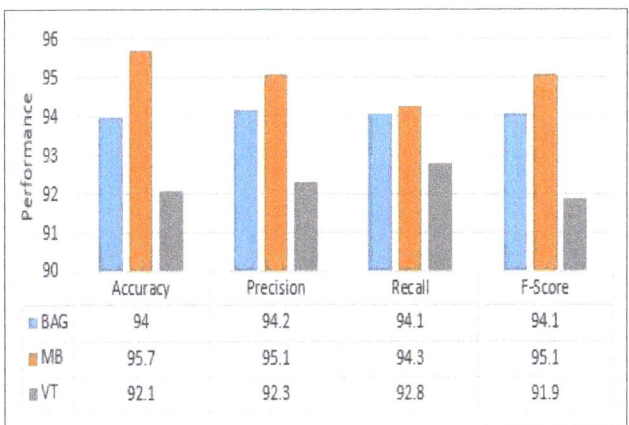

Figure 3. Ensemble-based classifiers.

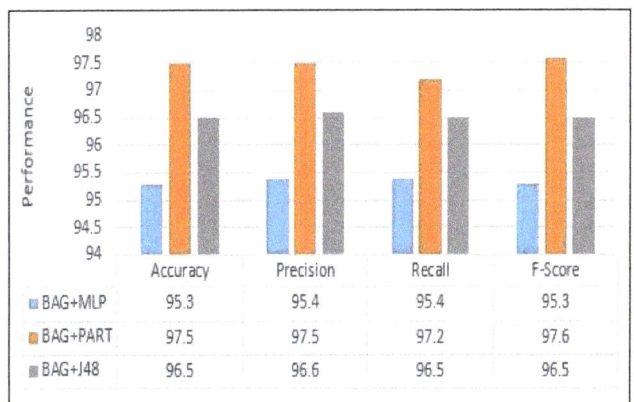

Figure 4. Bagging with single-based classifiers.

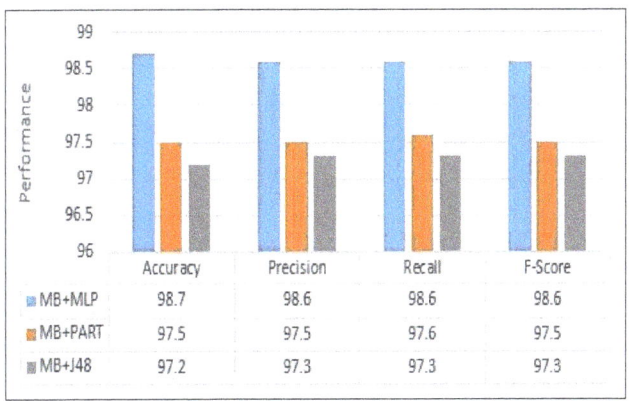

Figure 5. MultiBoostAB with single-based classifiers.

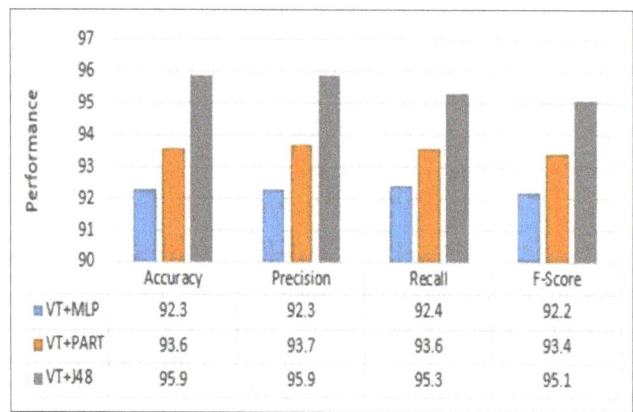

Figure 6. Voting with single-based classifiers.

The evaluation results related to BAG fusion with PART showed the highest accuracy (i.e., 97.50%). The model also performed very well with respect to precision, F-score and recall, as shown in Figure 4. The experiment results related to MB fusion with MLP achieved the highest accuracy (i.e., 98.7), as shown in Figure 5. This model has achieved good performance with regard to precision, recall, and F-score. The results related to the fusion of VT with different single classifiers showed that VT + J48 achieved greater accuracy (i.e., 95.9%), as shown in Figure 6. This model also showed better performance in terms of precision, recall, and F-score. Each of Figures 4–6 consist of two parts; in the first part, the bar chart presents the performance of classifiers in terms of accuracy, precision, recall, and F-score. The second part shows the performance of classifiers in tabular form through the same measures.

4.3. Comparative Analysis of Applied Techniques

A comparative analysis was performed to analyze the performance of different classifiers evaluated during this study. To analyze the performance, the comparison of the evaluation results of single classifiers, ensemble-based classifiers, and fusion-based ensemble models is presented in this section. First, this section presents the comparison between single-based models and ensemble-based models. Secondly, a comparison is performed between fusion ensemble-based models.

The experimental results shown in Figure 7 depict that all of the ensemble-based models outperformed concerning all measures including accuracy, recall, precision, and F-score in comparison with single-based classifiers. Figure 7 shows the performance of models through bar charts and numeric terms.

The purpose of this experiment was to identify the high-performing fusion model by comparing fusion-based models. The results showed that fusion-based models improve the precision and accuracy of the student prediction model.

Figure 8 presents the performance of classifiers using a bar chart and table of numeric terms. The results shown in the above figure indicate that MB and MLP performed very well in terms of all measures. The fusion model MB + MLP achieved 98.7 accuracy and 98.6% precision, recall, and F-score which is higher than those for all other fusion models. The rest of the fusion models also showed relatively good performance. Overall, the results showed that fusion-based models improve the accuracy and precision of student predictions in comparison to single- and ensemble-based models. For effective communication, it is to be considered that the false positive rate, also known as the rate of sensitivity, should be nearly zero. The sensitivity rate for the MB + MLP model can be seen very close to zero, which strengthens the performance of the model.

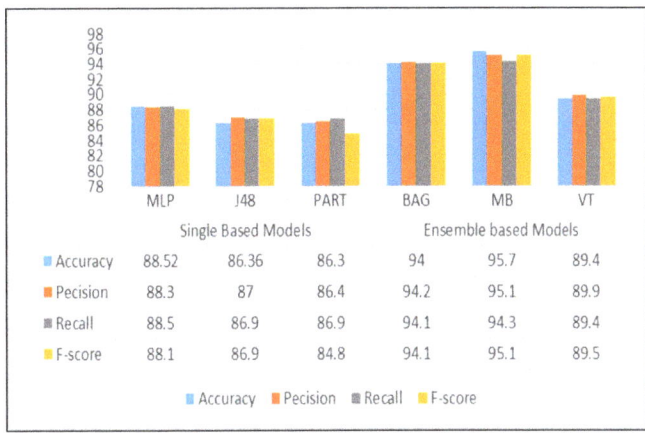

Figure 7. Comparison of single and ensemble-based classifiers.

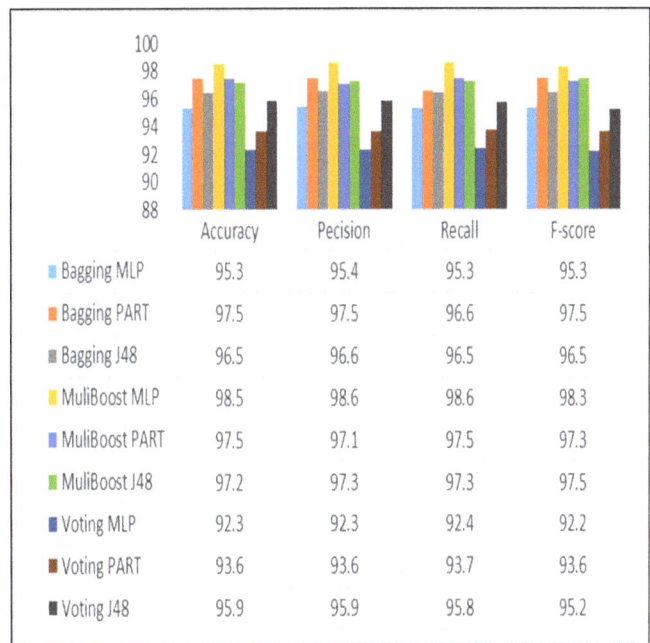

Figure 8. Comparison of fusion-based ensemble classifiers.

The F-measure of fusion-based MultiBoostAB and MLP has produced an average of 0.987 score that is a very significant result. It gives an average weight of the true positive as 0.988 and false positive rate as 0.004, as shown in Table 3.

As an average, the overall accuracy rate of the proposed model is evaluated as 98.7%. It shows that fusion-based ensemble models provide better precise outcomes, while classifying instances is very helpful in the evaluation of students' performance.

Table 3. Result obtained for MB + MLP.

Correctly Classified Instances		1185			98.7 %
Incorrectly Classified Instances		15			1.24 %
TP Rate	FP Rate	Precision	Recall	F-Measure	Class
0.997	0.008	0.976	0.997	0.986	A+
0.996	0.001	0.996	0.996	0.996	B
0.983	0.001	0.994	0.983	0.988	B+
0.994	0.007	0.983	0.994	0.989	A
0.969	0.000	1.000	0.969	0.984	C
0.909	0.000	1.000	0.909	0.952	F
0.943	0.000	1.000	0.988	0.971	D
		Weighted Average			
0.988	0.004	0.988	0.986	0.987	

Figure 9 below shows the fusion-based ensemble model of ninth-class grade division based on the performance of MB + MLP and the class column represents the final performance prediction grades of the ninth class. In machine learning, sensitivity or recall is termed as the true positive rate and is used to measure the percentages of actual positives, which are identified correctly. The sensitivity rate should be nearer to one in order to obtain the true positive values.

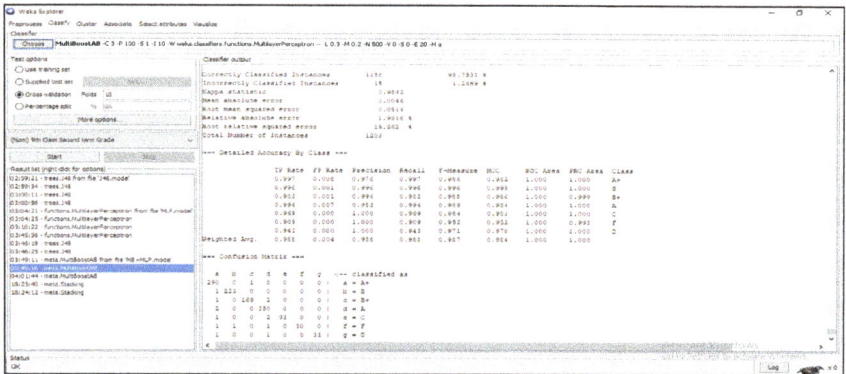

Figure 9. Fusion-based ensemble models (MB + MLP) result.

As shown in the above figure, the A+ grade has a true positive value of 290, whereas the false negative and false positive values are 7 and 1. The A grade has a true positive value of 350 with 8 false negative and positive values. Similarly, the values including 169, 223, 93, 33 and 30 are the true positive values of grades B+, B, C, D, and F.

The false-positive ratio (FPR) is the proportion of incorrectly classified negative instances. It has been discovered that a good model should have a false positive rate nearer to 0.0, which indicates less incorrectly classified negative instances.

A confusion matrix is a technique in which the performance of a classifier is summarized. From the confusion matrix, it was derived that, amongst the students from the dataset, 24.1% students secure an A+ grade, 18.5% students achieve a B grade, 14.0%, 29.1%, 7.7%, 2.4% and 2.7% students secure B+, A, C, F, D grades, respectively. This distribution obtains more insight from the model analysis.

Statistical hypothesis testing is used to make a claim related to the distribution of data or whether a set of results vary from one another. The null hypothesis is essential in interpreting the results and ensuring the strength of the claim of model performance by some statistical analysis. An Analysis of Variance test (ANOVA) is used in this study where statistical hypothesis testing is performed by estimating the p-value which is used to interpret the results of a test to either reject or fail to reject the null hypothesis. The p-value is selected as 0.05 for this study. The activity is conducted by comparing the p-value to the pre-chosen threshold value called alpha.

If the p-value < alpha, the null hypothesis would be rejected or we would fail to reject the null hypothesis in the p-value > alpha case.

The issue is addressed as whether the single and ensemble-based classifiers' performances are similar to fusion-based ensemble classifiers or not. The performances are evaluated by the four performance evaluation metrics (accuracy, precision, recall and F-measure) with the use of a collected dataset.

After testing, it was revealed that the four performance evaluation metrics are relatively higher for fusion-based ensemble classifiers models. By using the one-way ANOVA test, the p-value turned out to be 0.045 for single-based classifiers and 0.002 for ensemble-based classifiers, which is less than the significance value of alpha. Hence, the null hypothesis was rejected and the claim about the efficiency of the fusion-based ensemble model was strengthened.

4.4. Comparison of Applied Approach with Existing Approaches

Numerous research studies in EDM have been conducted using multiple classifiers to predict the performance of students. Sakri et al. have recently proposed an ensemble model to identify at-risk students and advise them to regulate their learning. They hybridized four single classifiers with four ensemble algorithms including bagging, random subspace, multilayer perceptron, and random forest. The evaluation results showed that the ensemble model achieved 91.70% accuracy, 86.1%, and the F-score was 87.3% [26]. Another study identified at-risk students, predicting their learning performance through their learning behavior based on their logging data history. They used Logistic Regression along with Random Forest, Multilayer Perceptron, and Gaussian Naive Bayes. The results showed that Random Forest surpasses the baseline Logistic Regression and other models with 89% accuracy, 89% precision, 88% recall, and 88% F1 score [56]. Emmanuel et al. introduced a model to predict students' success based on their daily activities. They hybridized different single classifiers with bagging, boosting, and random forest. The experiment results showed that the model achieved 96.9% accuracy [57]. Another recent study predicted students' intermediate results based on their academic characteristics. The evaluation results indicated that the model attained 96.64% accuracy [58]. A model has been suggested to estimate the institutional performance based on key performance indicators using data mining techniques. The results showed that the artificial neural networks performed better in achieving accuracy (i.e., 82.9%) in comparison to other machine learning models employed in the study [59]. The student performance in a learning management system based on behavioral features was predicted by applying ensemble methods including bagging, boosting, and random forest to augment the performance of classifiers. An accuracy of 91.5% was achieved through the application of ensemble methods to the classifiers to enhance academic performance [60]. Ragab et al. introduced a data mining-based forecast model to determine students' accomplishments. The data mining techniques used to evaluate students' performance include a decision tree, logistic regression, a naïve Bayes tree, an artificial neural network, a support vector machine, and a k-nearest neighbor. To improve the productivity of these classifiers, they used ensemble methods such as bagging, boosting, random forest, and voting. The results showed that the decision tree algorithm accuracy increased with bagging from 90.4% to 91.4%. Similarly, recall results were increased from 0.904 to 0.914, and precision results were also improved from 0.905 to 0.914 [61]. Another study undertook the task of student performance prediction by extracting features from an e-learning system. The proposed model comprises five traditional machine learning algorithms which were complemented by four well-established ensemble techniques including bagging, boosting, stacking, and voting. The F1 score measured by the NB model by the integration of boosting and GBT with AdaBoost were 0.71% and 0.75%, respectively [62]. Adejo et al.'s research focused on the prediction of students' performance using data mining techniques along with the support of ensemble methods. They also proposed novel hybrid classifiers to gain accurate predictions of student performance. The results showed that the hybrid model outperformed the other classifiers in terms of accuracy (i.e., 81.67) precision (i.e., 79.62), recall (i.e., 75.86), and F-score (i.e., 77.69) in comparison to base classifiers and ensemble techniques applied in the same research [54].

The fusion ensemble-based approach introduced in this research study to improve academic performance attained the highest accuracy (i.e.,98.7%) precision (i.e., 98.6%) recall (i.e., 98.6%) and F-score (i.e., 98.6) in comparison to state-of-the-art ensemble approaches proposed in EDM. Thus, the result acquired in this study demonstrates the reliability of the proposed predictive model. The performance of our approach represents improvements in terms of all measures relative to existing approaches which emphasize that the fusion of ensemble techniques can improve the fraction of prediction.

5. Limitations

This study is limited to predicting the performance of students studying in a physical learning environment and lacks envisagement of the performance of students in online learning. The data set should be extended to evaluate the performance of students in both physical and virtual educational settings. The proposed system is deficient in suggesting apposite learning streams to the students based on their learning performance to pursue further educational goals. Another limitation of this study is that the factors are identified only concerning a specific educational level rather than providing a framework of factors for all educational levels including elementary, secondary, higher secondary, and tertiary.

6. Conclusions and Future Work

Numerous DM techniques have been implemented in academia as a standard procedure for interpreting the bulk of students' data and then mining them into one meaningful datum and knowledge to support decision-making processes. An early performance prediction would be beneficial for at-risk students, facing difficulty in attaining good grades in the class. To support such students in their learning to improve their progress, it is important to periodically predict their performance so they can be supported. A robust fusion-based ensemble model was developed considering students' demographic, family, social and academic attributes to make predictions. The model is highly useful in assessing students at early stages. After building many models involving single, ensemble, and fusion-based ensemble classifiers, MultiBoostAB ensemble classifier with MLP base appears as the best model to predict students' performance at the lower secondary level.

A logical extension of this research would be the building of a meta-analysis system on a larger dataset for future study which can be considered as a decision support method based on the model that will achieve the highest efficiency and effectiveness.

Furthermore, the study can be enhanced by the use of hybrid feature selection methods to help predict student performances, so each feature becomes more optimal and significant in terms of student performance prediction. The advanced ensemble-based machine learning algorithm, in particular extreme gradient boosting, could also be used in this domain.

Author Contributions: Conceptualization, A.S.; Data curation, A.J. and A.S.; Formal analysis, A.J. and M.O.A.W.; Funding acquisition, N.N.Q.; Investigation, A.J.; Methodology, F.M.; Project administration, N.N.Q. and M.O.A.W.; Resources, A.I.Q., N.N.Q. and M.O.A.W.; Software, A.J.; Supervision, A.S. and F.M.; Validation, F.M. and A.I.Q.; Visualization, A.I.Q.; Writing—original draft, A.S.; Writing—review & editing, A.S. and F.M. All authors have read and agreed to the published version of the manuscript.

Funding: The authors extend their appreciation to the Deanship of Scientific Research at King Khalid University for funding and support for this work under Research under grant number R.G.P.1/184/42.

Institutional Review Board Statement: Not applicable.

Informed Consent Statement: Not applicable.

Data Availability Statement: The current study dataset is publicly available online (https://www.kaggle.com/asiyajan001.student-performance-perdiction, accessed on 8 December 2021) for research purposes.

Acknowledgments: Authors thankfully acknowledge all those who contributed this work scientifically, administratively, financially and academically during the whole research process.

Conflicts of Interest: The authors declare that they have no conflict of interest to report regarding the present study.

References

1. Kamran, S.; Nawaz, I.; Aslam, S.; Zaheer, S.; Shaukat, U. Student's performance in the context of data mining. In Proceedings of the 2016 19th International Multi-Topic Conference (INMIC), Islamabad, Pakistan, 5–6 December 2016; pp. 1–8.
2. Kamran, S.; Nawaz, I.; Aslam, S.; Zaheer, S.; Shaukat, U. *Student's Performance: A Data Mining Perspective*; LAP Lambert Academic Publishing: Koln, Germany, 2017.
3. Iqbal, M.S.; Luo, B. Prediction of educational institution using predictive analytic techniques. *Educ. Inf. Technol.* **2018**, *24*, 1469–1483. [CrossRef]
4. Kaur, A.; Umesh, N.; Singh, B. Machine Learning Approach to Predict Student Academic Performance. 2018. Available online: www.ijraset.com734 (accessed on 16 July 2021).
5. Aslam, M.; Malik, R.; Rawal, S.; Rose, P.; Vignoles, A. Do government schools improve learning for poor students? Evidence from rural Pakistan. *Oxf. Rev. Educ.* **2019**, *45*, 802–824. [CrossRef]
6. Abid, A.; Kallel, I.; Blanco, I.; Benayed, M. Selecting relevant educational attributes for predicting students' academic performance. In *Intelligent Systems Design and Applications, Proceedings of the 17th International Conference on Intelligent Systems Design and Applications (ISDA 2017), Delhi, India, 14–16 December 2017*; Springer: Cham, Switzerland, 2018; pp. 650–660. [CrossRef]
7. Shahrazad, H. Knowledge economy: Characteristics and dimensions. *Manag. Dyn. Knowl. Econ.* **2017**, *5*, 203–225.
8. Baneres, D.; Rodriguez-Gonzalez, M.E.; Serra, M. An Early Feedback Prediction System for Learners At-Risk within a First-Year Higher Education Course. *IEEE Trans. Learn. Technol.* **2019**, *12*, 249–263. [CrossRef]
9. Imran, M.; Latif, S.; Mehmood, D.; Shah, M.S. Student Academic Performance Prediction using Supervised Learning Techniques. *Int. J. Emerg. Technol. Learn.* **2019**, *14*, 92–104. [CrossRef]
10. Phua, E.J.; Batcha, N.K. Comparative analysis of ensemble algorithms' prediction accuracies in education data mining. *J. Crit. Rev.* **2020**, *7*, 37–40.
11. Abu, A. Educational data mining & students' performance prediction. *Int. J. Adv. Comput. Sci. Appl.* **2016**, *7*, 212–220.
12. Romero, C.; Ventura, S. Educational Data Mining: A Review of the State of the Art. *IEEE Trans. Syst. Man Cybern. Part. C (Appl. Rev.)* **2010**, *40*, 601–618. [CrossRef]
13. Arun, D.K.; Namratha, V.; Ramyashree, B.V.; Jain, Y.P.; Choudhury, A.R. Student academic performance prediction using educational data mining. In Proceedings of the 2021 International Conference on Computer Communication and Informatics (ICCCI), Coimbatore, India, 27–29 January 2021; pp. 1–9.
14. Alturki, S.; Alturki, N. Using Educational Data Mining to Predict Students' Academic Performance for Applying Early Interventions. *J. Inf. Technol. Educ. Innov. Pract.* **2021**, *20*, 121–137. [CrossRef]
15. Trautwein, U.; Lüdtke, O.; Marsh, H.W.; Köller, O.; Baumert, J. Tracking, grading, and student motivation: Using group composition and status to predict self-concept and interest in ninth-grade mathematics. *J. Educ. Psychol.* **2006**, *98*, 788–806. [CrossRef]
16. Li, F.; Zhang, Y.; Chen, M.; Gao, K. Which Factors Have the Greatest Impact on Student's Performance. *J. Phys. Conf. Ser.* **2019**, *1288*, 012077. [CrossRef]
17. Francis, B.K.; Babu, S.S. Predicting Academic Performance of Students Using a Hybrid Data Mining Approach. *J. Med. Syst.* **2019**, *43*, 162. [CrossRef]
18. Md Zubair Rahman, A.M.J. Model of Tuned J48 Classification and Analysis of Performance Prediction in Educational Data Mining. 2018. Available online: http://www.ripublication.com (accessed on 5 July 2021).
19. Tomasevic, N.; Gvozdenovic, N.; Vranes, S. An overview and comparison of supervised data mining techniques for student exam performance prediction. *Comput. Educ.* **2019**, *143*, 103676. [CrossRef]
20. Aucejo, E.M.; French, J.; Ugalde Araya, M.P.; Zafar, B. The impact of COVID-19 on student experiences and expectations: Evidence from a survey. *J. Public Econ.* **2020**, *191*, 104271. [CrossRef] [PubMed]
21. Zollanvari, A.; Kizilirmak, R.C.; Kho, Y.H.; Hernandez-Torrano, D. Predicting Students' GPA and Developing Intervention Strategies Based on Self-Regulatory Learning Behaviors. *IEEE Access* **2017**, *5*, 23792–23802. [CrossRef]

22. Abu Amrieh, E.; Hamtini, T.; Aljarah, I. Mining Educational Data to Predict Student's academic Performance using Ensemble Methods. *Int. J. Database Theory Appl.* **2016**, *9*, 119–136. [CrossRef]
23. Hutt, S.; Gardener, M.; Kamentz, D.; Duckworth, A.L.; D'Mello, S.K. Prospectively predicting 4-year college graduation from student applications. In Proceedings of the LAK '18: International Conference on Learning Analytics and Knowledge, Sydney, Australia, 7–9 March 2018; pp. 280–289. [CrossRef]
24. Xu, J.; Moon, K.H.; van der Schaar, M. A Machine Learning Approach for Tracking and Predicting Student Performance in Degree Programs. *IEEE J. Sel. Top. Signal. Process.* **2017**, *11*, 742–753. [CrossRef]
25. Shaukat, K.; Luo, S.; Varadharajan, V.; Hameed, I.A.; Chen, S.; Liu, D.; Li, J. Performance Comparison and Current Challenges of Using Machine Learning Techniques in Cybersecurity. *Energies* **2020**, *13*, 2509. [CrossRef]
26. Hassan, H.; Ahmad, N.B.; Anuar, S. Improved students' performance prediction for multi-class imbalanced problems using hybrid and ensemble approach in educational data mining. *J. Phys. Conf. Ser.* **2020**, *1529*, 052041. [CrossRef]
27. Wood, L.; Kiperman, S.; Esch, R.C.; Leroux, A.J.; Truscott, S.D. Predicting dropout using student- and school-level factors: An ecological perspective. *Sch. Psychol. Q.* **2017**, *32*, 35–49. [CrossRef]
28. Nahar, K.; Shova, B.I.; Ria, T.; Rashid, H.B.; Islam, A.H.M.S. Mining educational data to predict students performance. *Educ. Inf. Technol.* **2021**, *26*, 6051–6067. [CrossRef]
29. Madni, H.A.; Anwar, Z.; Shah, M.A. Data mining techniques and applications—A decade review. In Proceedings of the International Conference on Automation and Computing (ICAC), Huddersfield, UK, 7–8 September 2017; pp. 1–7.
30. Hall, M.; Frank, E.; Holmes, G.; Pfahringer, B.; Reutemann, P.; Witten, I.H. The WEKA data mining software: An update. *ACM SIGKDD Explor. Newsl.* **2009**, *11*, 10–18. [CrossRef]
31. Cenitta, D.; Arjunan, R.V.; Prema, K.V. Missing data imputation using machine learning algorithm for supervised learning. In Proceedings of the 2021 International Conference on Computer Communication and Informatics (ICCCI), Coimbatore, India, 27–29 January 2021; pp. 1–5.
32. Alam, T.M.; Shaukat, K.; Hameed, I.A.; Luo, S.; Sarwar, M.U.; Shabbir, S.; Li, J.; Khushi, M. An Investigation of Credit Card Default Prediction in the Imbalanced Datasets. *IEEE Access* **2020**, *8*, 201173–201198. [CrossRef]
33. Kanchan, J.; Saha, S. Incorporation of multimodal multi objective optimization in designing a filter based feature selection technique. *Appl. Soft Comput.* **2021**, *98*, 106823.
34. Krishnan, N.; Karthikeyan, M. IEEE signal processing/computational intelligence/computer joint societies chapter. In Proceedings of the 2014 IEEE International Conference on Computational Intelligence and Computing Research, Coimbatore, India, 18–20 December 2014.
35. Salloum, S.A.; Alshurideh, M.; Elnagar, A.; Shaalan, K. Mining in educational data: Review and future directions. In Proceedings of the Joint European—US Workshop on Applications of Invariance in Computer Vision, Ponta Delgada, Portugal, 9–14 October 2020; pp. 61–70.
36. Sakri, S.; Alluhaidan, A.S. RHEM: A robust hybrid ensemble model for students' performance assessment on cloud computing course. *Int. J. Adv. Comput. Sci. Appl.* **2020**, *11*, 388–396. [CrossRef]
37. Musiliu, B. Single Classifiers and Ensemble Approach for Predicting Student's Academic Performance. 2020. Available online: www.rsisinternational.org (accessed on 10 August 2021).
38. Ali, S.; Smith, K.A. On learning algorithm selection for classification. *Appl. Soft Comput. J.* **2006**, *6*, 119–138. [CrossRef]
39. Rokach, L. Taxonomy for characterizing ensemble methods in classification tasks: A review and annotated bibliography. *Comput. Stat. Data Anal.* **2009**, *53*, 4046–4072. [CrossRef]
40. Livieris, I.E.; Iliadis, L.; Pintelas, P. On ensemble techniques of weight-constrained neural networks. *Evol. Syst.* **2021**, *12*, 155–167. [CrossRef]
41. Ahmad, I.; Yousaf, M.; Yousaf, S.; Ahmad, M.O. Fake News Detection Using Machine Learning Ensemble Methods. *Complexity* **2020**, *2020*, 8885861. [CrossRef]
42. Yang, X.; Lo, D.; Xia, X.; Sun, J. TLEL: A two-layer ensemble learning approach for just-in-time defect prediction. *Inf. Softw. Technol.* **2017**, *87*, 206–220. [CrossRef]
43. Riestra-González, M.; del Puerto Paule-Ruíz, M.; Ortin, F. Massive LMS log data analysis for the early prediction of course-agnostic student performance. *Comput. Educ.* **2021**, *163*, 104108. [CrossRef]
44. Hoque, I.; Azad, A.K.; Tuhin, M.A.H.; Salehin, Z.U. University Students Result Analysis and Prediction System by Decision Tree Algorithm. *Adv. Sci. Technol. Eng. Syst.* **2020**, *5*, 115–122. [CrossRef]
45. Panigrahi, R.; Borah, S. Rank Allocation to J48 Group of Decision Tree Classifiers using Binary and Multiclass Intrusion Detection Datasets. *Procedia Comput. Sci.* **2018**, *132*, 323–332. [CrossRef]
46. Bauer, E.; Kohavi, R. An empirical comparison of voting classification algorithms: Bagging, boosting, and variants. *Mach. Learn.* **1999**, *36*, 105–139. [CrossRef]
47. Li, X.; Zhang, Y.; Cheng, H.; Zhou, F.; Yin, B. An Unsupervised Ensemble Clustering Approach for the Analysis of Student Behavioral Patterns. *IEEE Access* **2021**, *9*, 7076–7091. [CrossRef]
48. Ashraf, M.; Zaman, M.; Ahmed, M. An Intelligent Prediction System for Educational Data Mining Based on Ensemble and Filtering approaches. *Procedia Comput. Sci.* **2020**, *167*, 1471–1483. [CrossRef]
49. Shaukat, K.; Luo, S.; Varadharajan, V.; Hameed, I.A.; Xu, M. A Survey on Machine Learning Techniques for Cyber Security in the Last Decade. *IEEE Access* **2020**, *8*, 222310–222354. [CrossRef]

50. Sun, Y.; Li, Z.; Li, X.; Zhang, J. Classifier Selection and Ensemble Model for Multi-class Imbalance Learning in Education Grants Prediction. *Appl. Artif. Intell.* **2021**, *35*, 290–303. [CrossRef]
51. Schapire, R.E. A brief introduction to boosting. *Ijcai* **1999**, *99*, 1401–1406.
52. Shaukat, K.; Masood, N.; Mehreen, S.; Azmeen, U. Dengue Fever Prediction: A Data Mining Problem. *J. Data Min. Genom. Proteom.* **2015**, *6*, 3. [CrossRef]
53. Adejo, O.W.; Connolly, T. Predicting student academic performance using multi-model heterogeneous ensemble approach. *J. Appl. Res. High. Educ.* **2018**, *10*, 61–75. [CrossRef]
54. Dutta, S.; Bandyopadhyay, S.K. Forecasting of Campus Placement for Students Using Ensemble Voting Classifier. *Asian J. Res. Comput. Sci.* **2020**, 1–12. [CrossRef]
55. Alabi, E.O.; Adeniji, O.D.; Awoyelu, T.M.; Fasae, O.D. Hybridization of Machine Learning Techniques in Predicting Mental Disorder. *Int. J. Hum. Comput. Stud.* **2021**, *3*, 22–30.
56. Wasif, M.; Waheed, H.; Aljohani, N.R.; Hassan, S.-U. Understanding student learning behavior and predicting their performance. In *Cognitive Computing in Technology-Enhanced Learning*; IGI Global: Hershey, PN, USA, 2019; pp. 1–28. [CrossRef]
57. Emmanuel, A.A.; Aderoju, M.A.; Falade, A.A.F.; Atanda, A. An appraisal of online gambling on undergraduate students' academic performance in university of Ilorin, Nigeria. *Int. J. Innov. Technol. Integr. Educ.* **2019**, *3*, 45–54.
58. Yousafzai, B.K.; Hayat, M.; Afzal, S. Application of machine learning and data mining in predicting the performance of intermediate and secondary education level student. *Educ. Inf. Technol.* **2020**, *25*, 4677–4697. [CrossRef]
59. Alam, T.M.; Mushtaq, M.; Shaukat, K.; Hameed, I.A.; Sarwar, M.U.; Luo, S. A Novel Method for Performance Measurement of Public Educational Institutions Using Machine Learning Models. *Appl. Sci.* **2021**, *11*, 9296. [CrossRef]
60. Ajibade, S.-S.M.; Ahmad, N.B.B.; Shamsuddin, S.M. Educational Data Mining: Enhancement of Student Performance model using Ensemble Methods. *IOP Conf. Ser. Mater. Sci. Eng.* **2019**, *551*, 012061. [CrossRef]
61. Ragab, M.; Aal, A.M.K.A.; Jifri, A.O.; Omran, N.F. Enhancement of Predicting Students Performance Model Using Ensemble Approaches and Educational Data Mining Techniques. *Wirel. Commun. Mob. Comput.* **2021**, *2021*, 6241676. [CrossRef]
62. Saleem, F.; Ullah, Z.; Fakieh, B.; Kateb, F. Intelligent Decision Support System for Predicting Student's E-Learning Performance Using Ensemble Machine Learning. *Mathematics* **2021**, *9*, 2078. [CrossRef]

Review

A Comparative Analysis of Big Data Frameworks: An Adoption Perspective

Madiha Khalid * and Muhammad Murtaza Yousaf

Department of Software Engineering, Faculty of Computing and Information Technology, University of the Punjab, Lahore 54000, Pakistan; murtaza@pucit.edu.pk
* Correspondence: madiha.khalid@pucit.edu.pk; Tel.: +92-42-111-923-923 (ext. 554)

Abstract: The emergence of social media, the worldwide web, electronic transactions, and next-generation sequencing not only opens new horizons of opportunities but also leads to the accumulation of a massive amount of data. The rapid growth of digital data generated from diverse sources makes it inapt to use traditional storage, processing, and analysis methods. These limitations have led to the development of new technologies to process and store very large datasets. As a result, several execution frameworks emerged for big data processing. Hadoop MapReduce, the pioneering framework, set the ground for forthcoming frameworks that improve the processing and development of large-scale data in many ways. This research focuses on comparing the most prominent and widely used frameworks in the open-source landscape. We identify key requirements of a big framework and review each of these frameworks in the perspective of those requirements. To enhance the clarity of comparison and analysis, we group the logically related features, forming a feature vector. We design seven feature vectors and present a comparative analysis of frameworks with respect to those feature vectors. We identify use cases and highlight the strengths and weaknesses of each framework. Moreover, we present a detailed discussion that can serve as a decision-making guide to select the appropriate framework for an application.

Keywords: big data frameworks; fault tolerance; stream processing systems; distributed frameworks; Spark; Hadoop; Storm; Samza; Flink; comparative analysis; a survey; data science

Citation: Khalid, M.; Yousaf, M.M. A Comparative Analysis of Big Data Frameworks: An Adoption Perspective. *Appl. Sci.* **2021**, *11*, 11033. https://doi.org/10.3390/app112211033

Academic Editor: Kamran Shaukat

Received: 25 October 2021
Accepted: 12 November 2021
Published: 22 November 2021

Publisher's Note: MDPI stays neutral with regard to jurisdictional claims in published maps and institutional affiliations.

Copyright: © 2021 by the authors. Licensee MDPI, Basel, Switzerland. This article is an open access article distributed under the terms and conditions of the Creative Commons Attribution (CC BY) license (https://creativecommons.org/licenses/by/4.0/).

1. Introduction

Over the years, data has been generated from millions of data sources at an astonishing rate. Perhaps, the most substantial byproduct of the digital revolution is the generation of an explosive amount of data. This incredible data growth is predicted in a report generated by The Internet Data Center (IDC). In 2012, the IDC estimated that the digital data would be grown by 300 times between 2005 and 2020, which means it will increase from 130 exabytes to 20,000 exabytes [1]. More recently, IDC has predicted in its white paper that by 2025, the digital data will grow by 175 zettabytes [2]. This increasingly growing amount of data is often referred to as *'big data'* [3]. Data is a valuable asset in our information society. Extracting meaningful information from these high volume datasets has become a fundamental activity for industrial and academic communities. Business organizations use big data analytics to analyze customer behaviors and trends that can be capitalized. The high availability of data is also greatly changing the trends in scientific communities. Science has moved towards a data-oriented quest, where the data-intensive computations yield discoveries in science.

Analyzing large scale data may also result in unexpected outcomes that can help to improve the quality of life in many ways. For example, by analyzing the number of flu-related queries, Google Flu Trend can detect regional flu outbreaks faster than the Center for Disease Control and Prevention [4]. Similarly, Google uses large amounts of data to solve complex problems. The data generated by Global Positing System (GPS) is used to avoid traffic jams, define routes, and determine optimal paths between locations. IBM uses real-time traffic data to accurately predict the arrival times of buses in London [5]. All these data-oriented advancements are achieved mainly due to the emergence of new technologies that provide powerful functions and controls to programmers, so that they can focus on data processing and information extraction instead of managing resources and low-level parallelism details.

Since datasets have grown to an order of magnitude which is difficult to perceive, to put this into perspective, Figure 1 shows some real-world examples to illustrate large data scales. Such voluminous and incremental datasets make it impossible to store and process them in a reasonable amount of time using traditional computing techniques. To Address this challenge, parallel computing environments and technologies have emerged as a prime solution. These parallel computing environments offer increasingly powerful ways to analyze and process large scale data for real-time analysis. However, the complexity of such parallel computing environments and their characteristics hinders the maximum productive utilization of these platforms. Some of the concerns include resolving dependencies, load balancing, scheduling and scalability. The problem poses an additional challenge when we add an almost certain possibility of machine failure and fluctuation of workloads that may be caused by temporary suspension or activation of computing nodes. These challenges resulted in the development and evolution of several big data processing frameworks.

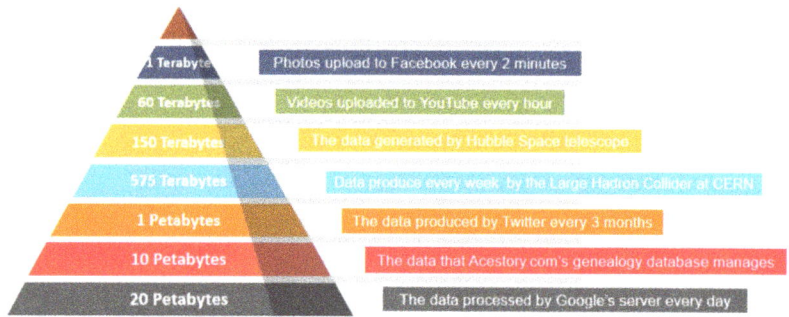

Figure 1. Understanding the data deluge.

Hadoop MapReduce is one of the earliest frameworks that empowers the use of inexpensive commodity machines for big data analytics in place of expensive high-end systems. The early adoption of Hadoop MapReduce by research communities caused the rapid evolution of the system, which laid the foundation for the development of several other frameworks. Among those frameworks, some are based on Hadoop distributions, while others are self-developed.

Big data analytics is a rewarding tech trend in business communities and enterprise software development. Consequently, big data processing is fundamental to the business models of many companies. The availability of a number of big data frameworks makes it difficult for practitioners and researchers to decide which framework will better serve the needs of a particular application. Therefore, selecting an appropriate big data processing framework for a particular application is a non-trivial task. In order to choose the right framework for a particular application, one must consider the architectural features, the data processing model, semantics of fault tolerance and performance guarantees of the framework. These considerations will help determine whether or not a framework will best meet the needs of an application. Therefore, it is important to have a study that discusses and compares the most prominent and widely used big data frameworks.

This article provides an in-depth review of the five most popular and widely adopted big data frameworks in the open-source landscape, i.e., Hadoop, Spark, Storm, Samza and Flink. We identify some key features and group the logically related features together to form a feature vector. The frameworks discussed in this study are then compared based on seven feature vectors. We also identify the key strengths and limitations of these frameworks. We discover the use cases where each of these frameworks ideally fits in. The main contributions of this work are as follows:

- A comprehensive overview of the most widely used open-source frameworks with an architectural perspective. We discussed the different fault-tolerance mechanisms, the scheduling schemes, and the data flow models used by each of these frameworks.
- Comparative analysis of the frameworks with respect to identified feature vectors.
- Identification of key strengths and weaknesses of each of the frameworks under consideration. We presented a detailed discussion that serves as a guide for selecting the appropriate framework for an application.
- We pointed out the application use cases where each of the frameworks ideally fits in.

For convenient referencing, Table 1 provides a list of acronyms used in this article. The rest of the paper is organized as follows: Section 2 surveys existing literature studies and highlights the differences of our work from existing studies. Section 3 discusses the requirements of a distributed framework. Section 4 presents the architectural details along with the identified requirements of the presented frameworks. Section 5 discusses feature vectors and comparative analysis of the frameworks with respect to those feature vectors. Section 6 presents a comprehensive discussion and point out the findings of the comparison. Finally, in Section 7, we present our conclusion. Figure 2 outlines the overall organization of the paper.

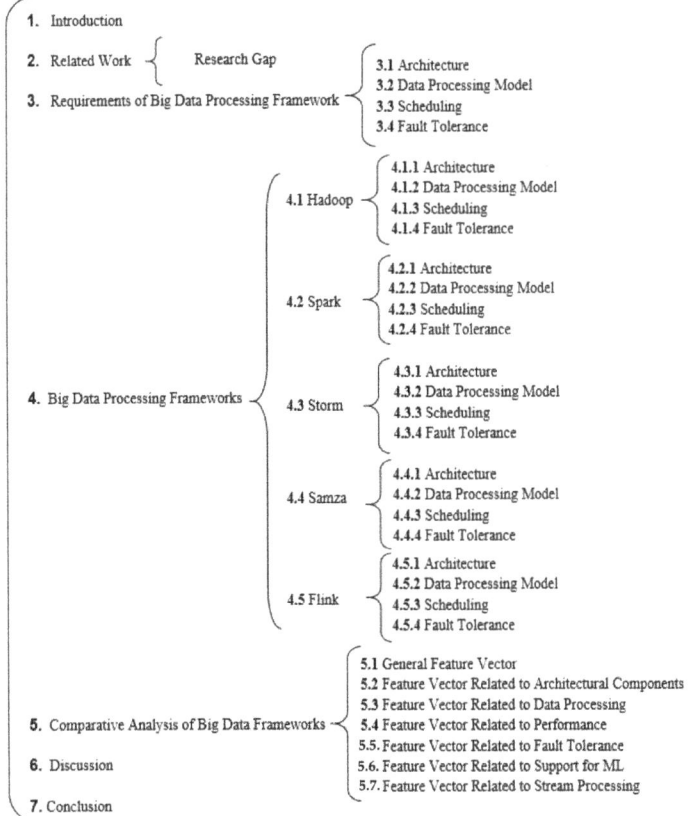

Figure 2. Organization of the paper.

Table 1. List of acronyms used in this article.

ACLs	Access Control Lists
AMP	Advanced Materials Processing
API	Application Programming Interface
AWS	Amazon Web Services
CPU	Central Processing Unit
DAG	Directed Acyclic Graph
FIFO	First In First Out
GPS	Global Positioning System
HDFS	Hadoop Distributed File System
I/O	Input/Output
IDC	Internet Data Center
ML	Machine Learning
NM	Node Manager
RDDs	Resilient Distributed Datasets
RM	Resource Manager
SSL	Secure Sockets Layer
TLS	Transport Layer Security
YARN	Yet Another Resource Negotiator

2. Related Work

There are various studies published in the literature that compares different big data frameworks. In this section, we will discuss some of the significant and recent research contributions on the topic. Figure 3 depicts a timeline view of the research works discussed.

Chen and Zhang [6] focused on the problems and challenges of big data and the techniques to address these problems. The authors discussed a number of methodologies to handle large scale data such as cloud computing, granular computing, quantum computing and bio-inspired computing. Singh and Reddy [7] presented a comprehensive analysis of big data platforms, including HPC clusters, Hadoop ecosystem, peer-to-peer networks, GPUs, multicore CPUs and field programmable gate arrays (FPGAs). Morais [8] provided a theoretical survey of Hadoop, Spark and Storm. The author compared two frameworks Spark and Storm, based on five parameters, processing model, latency, fault tolerance, batch framework integration and supported languages. Hesse and Lorenz [9] carried out a conceptual survey of stream processing systems. The discussion is generally focused on some fundamental differences related to stream processing systems. Landset et al. [10] discussed open-source tools for machine learning with big data in the Hadoop ecosystem. The authors discussed machine learning tools and their compatibility with MapReduce, Spark, Flink, Storm and H_2O. They evaluated a number of machine learning frameworks based on scalability, ease of use, and extensibility. Authors in [11] compared big data frameworks on a number of performance parameters based on some empirical evidence from the available literature. Bajaber et al. [12] presented a taxonomy and investigation of open challenges in big data systems. The authors discussed big data systems, their SQL processing support and graph processing support. The research focuses on identifying research problems and opportunities for innovations in future research.

A survey of the state-of-the-art stream processing systems is presented in [13]. Authors discussed mechanisms for resource elasticity to adapt to the needs of streaming services in cloud computing. The research also explores the problems and existing solutions associated with effective resource management. The research indicators are limited to the elasticity aspect of stream processing systems. Inoubli [14] compared big data frameworks on the basis of experimental evaluation. Another study [15] empirically compared the performance of popular big data frameworks on a number of applications that include WordCount, Kmeans, PageRank, Grep, TeraSort, and connected components. Authors demonstrated that Spark outperformed Flink and Hadoop for WordCount and k-means, while Flink performed well for PageRank. Both Spark and Flink yield similar results on rest of the applications. In [16], researchers measured the performance of Spark and

Hadoop using WordCount and a logistic regression program. The results showed that Spark outperformed Hadoop.

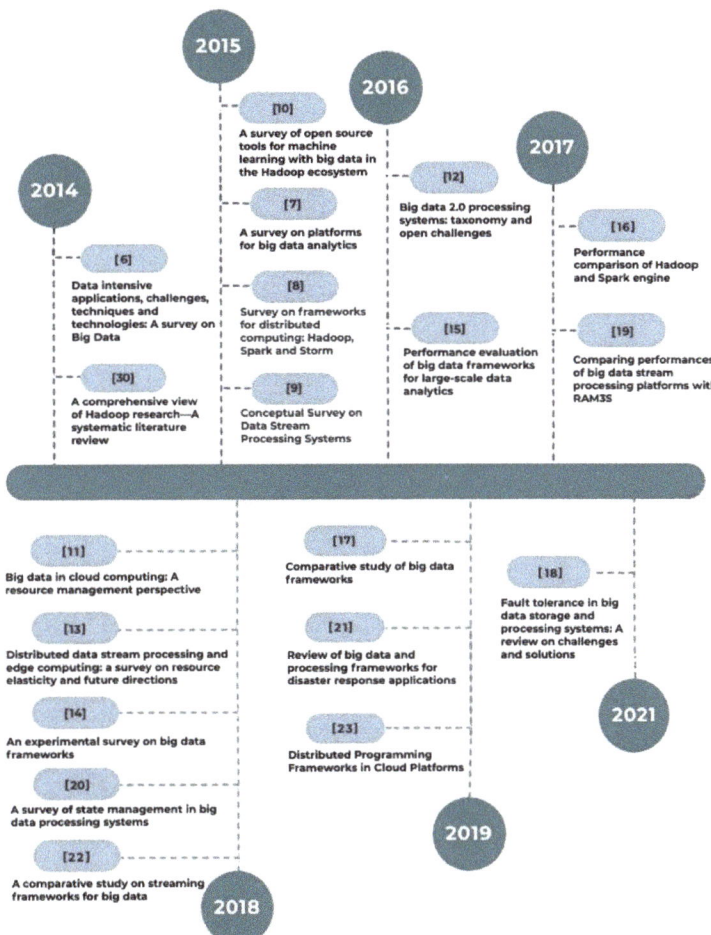

Figure 3. A timeline view of the research works reviewed.

Gupta and Parveen [17] surveyed popular big data frameworks on the basis of a few primitive parameters. Saadoon et al. [18] highlighted common problems and potential solutions related to fault tolerance in big data systems. The study presented a thorough discussion based on the findings derived from existing studies. Bartolini and Patella [19] conducted a study that used sustainable input rate as a measure of efficiency to compare big data frameworks. Authors empirically proved that Storm outperformed both Flink and Spark in local cluster setting as well as in cloud environment. In [20] authors focused state management techniques in big data systems such as Flink, Heron, Samza, Spark, and Storm. Cumbane [21] reviewed big data frameworks for disaster response applications. This research also discussed the similarities and differences of big data frameworks. However, the focus of the study revolves around the application of big data systems in the response phase of a disaster. Inoubli et al. [22] surveyed popular stream processing frameworks and an experimental evaluation of resource consumption. Patil [23] discussed big data frameworks and empirically compared Spark and Flink with TeraSort benchmark using execution time, network usage and throughput as performance measures.

Research Gap

There are some research gaps in the aforementioned literature works. The architectural aspects of big data frameworks are not thoroughly explored, which could have significantly assisted in suitability assessment. Several researchers [14–17,19,22,23] focused on the performance comparison of the big data frameworks. A number of studies are dedicated to reviewing big data frameworks concerning a specific aspect or in the context of a specific application domain [10,12,20–22]. The studies that made architectural comparisons considered only a limited number of features. Although the architectural and related aspects of some big data frameworks have been explored recently, no guidance is provided to help developers and practitioners select a suitable framework for their application. Furthermore, the existing studies do not elaborate on the comparative analysis that can help to build meaningful preference about the frameworks for a particular application. There is a need to cover all architectural aspects related to the core functionality of a big data framework. A detailed comparative analysis based on the comprehensive feature set will help choose a suitable big data framework for an application. This clearly gives a motivation to explore the most widely used big data frameworks and the important architectural features in qualitative assessment.

3. Requirements of a Big Data Processing Framework

This section specifies the four important requirements of a big data processing framework that we chose to focus on.

3.1. Architecture

Almost all big data processing frameworks distribute workloads across multiple processors, which requires partitioning and distribution of data files, managing data storage in a distributed file system, and monitoring actual processing performed by multiple processing nodes in parallel. The architecture of a framework is designed to handle all these responsibilities. It typically serves as a reference blueprint for available infrastructure that defines various logical roles and describes how the system will work, the components used, and how the data will flow. Most of the big data framework architectures include four major modules: resource management, scheduling, execution, and storage [24]. The architecture should outline the entire data life cycle starting from the data source till the generation and storage of results for future use [25]. This architecture must ensure fault tolerance, scalability, and high availability.

3.2. Data Processing Model

The data processing model defines how the data is processed and how the computations are represented in the system. Generally, the data is processed either in batch mode or in the form of a continuous stream. In a batch processing system, the processing is done on a block of data that is stored over a period of time. Whereas, in a stream processing system, the processing is done on a continuous stream of data as it arrives. Computations are also represented in different forms, for example, Hadoop processes computations in map-reduce functions. Alternatively, data and computations can also be realized as a logical directed acyclic graph (DAG).

3.3. Scheduling

In a big data processing system, a lot of CPU cycles, network bandwidth, and disk I/O are required. Therefore, it is important to schedule tasks efficiently such that it minimizes the overall execution time and maximizes resource utilization. The primary goal of task scheduling is to schedule independent and dependent tasks and the optimal reduction of the number of task migrations, thereby reducing computation time while increasing resource utilization.

3.4. Fault Tolerance

In distributed computing, faults can occur at various levels, such as node failures, process failures, network failures, and resource constraints. Although the failure probability of a single component is relatively low, when a large number of such components work together, the probability of component failure at any given time cannot be ignored. In fact, in large scale computing, failure is not an exception rather a norm. Fault tolerance is an attribute that enables the system to continue working if one or more components fail.

4. Big Data Processing Frameworks

Parallel and distributed computing has emerged as a prime solution for the processing of very large datasets. Yet, their complexity and some of their features may prevent its maximum productive utilization to common users. Data partitioning and distribution, scalability, load balancing, fault tolerance, and high availability are among the major concerns. Various frameworks have been released to abstract these functions and provide users with high-level solutions. These frameworks are typically classified according to their data processing approach, i.e., batch processing and stream processing (as shown in Figure 4). MapReduce has emerged as one of the earliest programming models for batch processing. Today, it is recognized as a pioneer system in big data analytics. In 2004, under the influence of an ever-increasing amount of data on the web, Google developed Google File System [26] and MapReduce [27]. In a MapReduce program, the user specifies the computation in the form of two functions map and reduce, which can be executed in parallel on multiple computing nodes and easily scaled to large clusters. The Map function takes in a key/value pair and generates a collection of intermediate key/value pairs. The Reduce function combines all the intermediate values assigned to the same intermediate key. The runtime system is responsible for data partitioning, distribution of data and computation across the cluster, handling machine failures, and managing necessary communications among computing nodes.

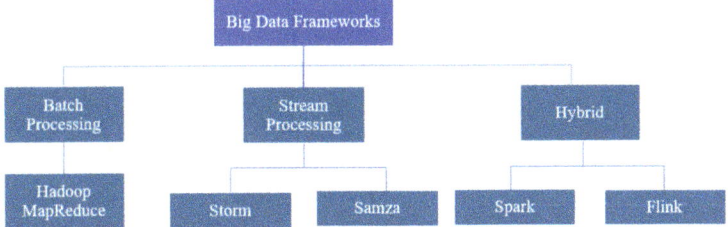

Figure 4. Classification of big data processing frameworks.

Efforts have been made to convert these technologies into open-source software, which resulted in the development of Apache Hadoop [28] and Hadoop file system [29], that laid the foundation for other big companies like Yahoo!, IBM, Twitter, LinkedIn, Oracle and HP to invest in building solutions for large scale data processing. MapReduce and its related distributions had established them as a sound solution to batch workloads. However, a well-defined processing model for distributed stream processing was still lacking. Consequently, a number of reliable and popular open-source frameworks were developed, such as Sparks, Storm, Samza and Flink. This section sheds light on the five most prominent and widely adopted big data processing frameworks.

4.1. Hadoop

Apache Hadoop [28] is the most widely used implementation of the map reduce programming model. Being an open-source implementation, Hadoop is equally popular in the researchers and industrial community. However, the major reason for its increasing adoption is its inherent characteristics such as load balancing, fault tolerance, and scalability.

The framework was first developed by a yahoo employee Doug Cutting and a professor of the University of Michigan, Mike Cafarella [30]. Later, it evolved over several years to reach its current stable version. Since its initial release, Hadoop gained the increasing attention of researchers and was adopted by several industry giants such as Yahoo!, Amazon, Facebook, eBay, and Adobe, which caused the rapid evolution of the framework [30].

4.1.1. Architecture

The overall architecture of Hadoop consists of two major components Hadoop Distributed File System (HDFS) [29] and Yet Another Resource Negotiator (YARN) [31]. HDFS is Hadoop's very own distributed file system which provides high throughput access to application data across thousands of machines in a fault tolerant manner. While YARN is responsible for resource management and scheduling. Figure 5 illustrates the architecture of Apache Hadoop.

In HDFS, data is stored in the form of files that are divided into data blocks. Each block is stored in one of the nodes in the Hadoop cluster. Thus, each node in the cluster stores a part of a file. Data blocks are replicated to ensure high availability and fault tolerance. HDFS is primarily based on two daemons called NameNode and DataNode. The HDFS cluster consists of one master node and several slave nodes. The master runs the NameNode daemon that is responsible for managing the file system and regulating file access to users. While slave runs DataNode daemon that stores data blocks and serves read/write requests from a user.

YARN was introduced by Yahoo! and Hortonworks in 2012 [31], and it became part of Hadoop as Hadoop 2.x [30]. In Hadoop 2.x, YARN takes the role of distributed application manager and MapReduce stays as pure computational framework. It has two major components named Resource Manager (RM) and Node Manager (NM). Resource Manager is a master daemon that is responsible for scheduling and resource management, while, Node Manager is a slave daemon that is responsible for managing containers and monitoring resource usage on a single node. It periodically monitors the health status of the host node and reports the same to RM.

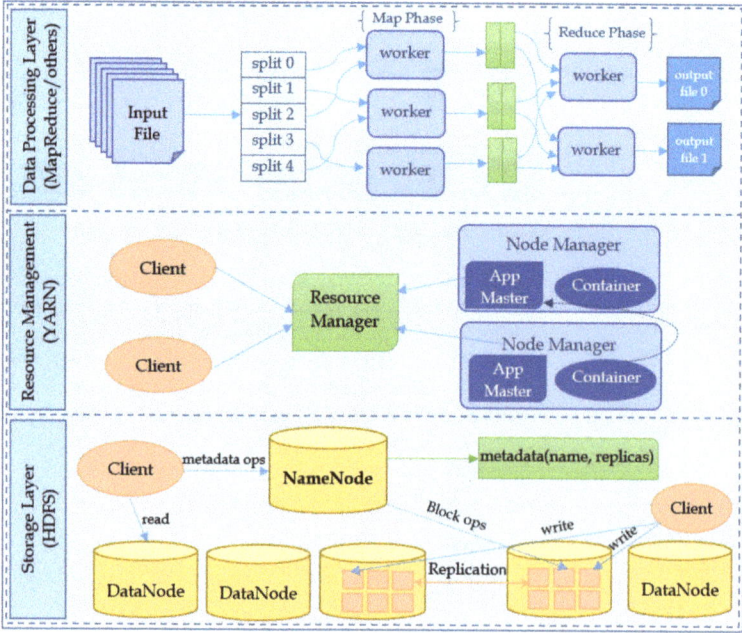

Figure 5. Apache Hadoop architecture.

4.1.2. Data Processing Model

Apache Hadoop is well suited for batch processing of unstructured data. Prior to Hadoop 2.x, there were two layers in the Hadoop, MapReduce layer for data processing and cluster management while HDFS layer for data storage. Therefore, MapReduce was the only data processing framework for Hadoop 1.x. Later, with the emergence of Hadoop 2.x, data processing and resource management are separated into two layers that enable Hadoop to work with other data processing platforms such as Crunch (Apache Crunch: http://crunch.apache.org) (accessed on 12 June 2021), Tez [32], Pig [33] and Cascading (Cascading: https://www.cascading.org) (accessed on 12 June 2021). However, majorly the data processing is done using the MapReduce paradigm.

4.1.3. Scheduling

Scheduler in Hadoop is part of YARN resource manager and is purely responsible for scheduling resources to run applications. YARN scheduler offers three pluggable scheduling policies, FIFO, Capacity and Fair. FIFO is the default scheduling policy that serves resource requests on a first come, first serve basis. This scheduling policy is not suitable for shared clusters as larger applications will occupy all the resources resulting longer waiting times for other applications in the queue. The Capacity Scheduler, originally developed by Yahoo!, allows large clusters to be shared with multiple tenants while providing each tenant with a minimum capacity guarantee. On the contrary, the Fair scheduler, developed by Facebook, does not reserve resources as per capacity rather, it dynamically balances resources among all outstanding jobs. The idea is to share the available resources among submitted jobs such that each job will get, on average, an equal share of resources.

4.1.4. Fault Tolerance

Apache Hadoop is highly fault tolerant. HDFS layer ensures fault tolerance using data replication. Data blocks stored in DataNodes are replicated and distributed across the cluster to provide reliability and high availability. Prior to the 2.x, the NameNode was a single point of failure in an HDFS cluster, with the release of Hadoop 2, HDFS high availability enables multiple standby NameNodes to run on a single HDFS cluster in an active/passive configuration. A failure can arise at three levels: task level, slave node level, master node level. If a task fails at the slave node, it reports back to the resource manager before exiting which in return allocates the failed task to another machine in the cluster and marks up the free slot on slave for another task. If a task fails at the master node, that task can be restarted in the same node from the last check point state since the master takes periodic check points of all the master data structures. When a slave node fails, the RM at the master node will detect this failure by timing out its heartbeat response. The RM will assign failed node tasks to some other idle node in the cluster and remove the failed node from a pool of resources. If the fault is transient, the NM at slave cleans up its local state, resynchronize itself with RM and redo its work done during the fault. RM failure was a single point of failure before Hadoop 2.x. However, the high availability feature enables running a redundant resource manager in standby mode that takes up in case of active resource manager failure.

4.2. Spark

Apache Spark is a cluster computing framework originally developed by Matei Zaharia at UC Barkley in 2009 and later donated to Apache Foundation in 2013 [34]. Previously, Hadoop was deficient for iterative working sets that are reused across multiple parallel operations. Hence, the primary design goal of Spark is to extend the MapReduce model to support interactive queries and iterative jobs efficiently. Spark introduced Resilient Distributed Datasets [35] for in-memory processing to speed up computations. Since its inception, several communities have contributed to building a sound echo system around it, especially a rich set of APIs initially available in Scala and later available in Java, Python,

R and SQL. Spark is one of the first frameworks to support distributed batch processing and stream processing along with iterative queries.

4.2.1. Architecture

Apache Spark has a layered architecture in which all Spark components and layers are loosely interconnected, as shown in Figure 6. Spark has a rich set of high-level libraries, which includes SparkSQL [36] for the processing of structured data, Spark streaming [37] for real-time stream processing, MLlib [38] for machine learning algorithms, GraphX [39] for graph processing and SparkR [40] for big data analysis from R shell. Spark core is responsible for task scheduling, fault recovery, interacting with storage systems and memory management. The spark core engine is based on the master slave architecture. The master node has the driver program that executes the main function of the user application. The driver program creates the spark context. The spark context connects with the cluster manager and acquires the executors on worker nodes and distributes tasks to the executors. The worker nodes are salve nodes that actually executes the tasks and return the result to spark context. Every worker node launches a process known as executor to run tasks and provide in-memory storage for Resilient distributed datasets (RDDs). RDDs are in-memory partitioned sets of data that are distributed over multiple nodes across the cluster. Spark can be deployed as a Standalone server or run on top of a cluster manager like Mesos [41] or YARN. Spark does not have its storage mechanism rather. It can work with any Hadoop compatible data sources such as HBase, HDFS, Casandra and Hive etc. [34].

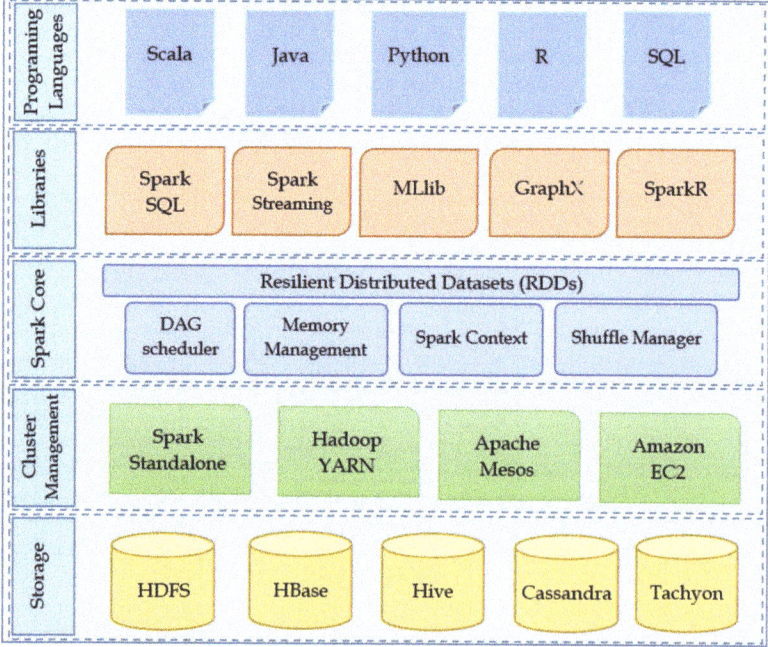

Figure 6. Layered architecture of Spark.

4.2.2. Data Processing Model

Unlike Hadoop, Spark is suitable for stream processing as well as batch processing. Spark works with RDDs and DAG to run operations. All Spark jobs are eventually converted into a Directed Acyclic Graph prior to execution. In contrast to MapReduce, where there are only two stages of computations map stage and reduce stage, Spark has multiple stages of computations that forms a DAG.

4.2.3. Scheduling

The internal scheduling of tasks within a Spark application is done either using a FIFO scheduler or a Fair scheduler. FIFO is the default scheduler that may cause significant delay to process later tasks if the earlier tasks are long running. Fair scheduler mitigates this problem by assigning tasks round robin fashion. FAIR Scheduler also supports grouping tasks into pools. In addition, different scheduling parameters (such as weights) can be configured for each pool. This is useful for creating higher priority pools for certain tasks. For scheduling across multiple applications over the cluster, Spark relies on the cluster managers that it runs on. For a multi-user environment in the cluster, Spark offers both static and dynamic scheduling. With static partitioning of resources, on startup each application is given its maximum required resources for its lifetime. Spark's standalone cluster mode, coarse-grained Mesos mode and YARN use static partitioning. In standalone mode, by default, applications run in FIFO order, and each application will try to use all available nodes. Spark also have a mechanism to dynamically allocate resources based on the demand of applications. This enables applications giving up on resources even during the execution if they are not in use and applications can request them back if they are needed.

4.2.4. Fault Tolerance

Since, spark processes data in a fault-tolerant file system (such as HDFS), so any RDD built from fault-tolerant data will be fault-tolerant. Also, it inherits the fault-tolerance of highly resilient cluster managers such as YARN and apache mesos, as it runs on top of them. Another main semantic of fault tolerance in Apache Spark is that all Spark RDDs are immutable and the dependencies between the RDDs are recorded through the lineage graph in the DAG. Hence, each RDD remembers that how it was created from previous RDD. In case of failure, RDDs can be recovered by using lineage information. If a worker node fails, the executors on that worker node will be killed along with the data in its memory. With the help of a lineage graph, these tasks can be re-executed on another worker node. If the master node fails, the cluster manager can restart the application.

4.3. Storm

Apache Storm is a distributed processing framework for real-time data streams. Storm was originally developed by Nathan Martz of BackType, which was acquired by Twitter in 2011. Storm became open-source in 2012 and became part of Apache projects later in 2014. Since its inception, Storm has been widely recognized and adopted by some of the big names in the industry, such as Twitter, Yahoo!, Alibaba, Groupon, WeatherChannel, Baidu and Rocket Fuel [42]. Apache Storm is designed to process and analyze large amounts of unbounded data streams that may come from various sources and publish real-time updates on the user interface or other locations without storing any real data. Storm is highly scalable in nature and provides low latency with an easy to use interface through which developers can program virtually in any programming language [43]. To achieve this language independence, Apache Storm uses Thrift definition to define and deploy topologies.

4.3.1. Architecture

The Apache Storm is based on the master/slave architecture. The Storm architecture allows only one master node. The physical architecture of Storm consists of three main components. Nimbus, Zookeeper and supervisor (as shown in Figure 7a). Nimbus is a master daemon that distributes work among all available workers. The key responsibilities of Nimbus include assignment of tasks to working nodes, tracking the progress of tasks, and rescheduling of the tasks to other working nodes in case of failure. Actual processing is performed by worker nodes. Each worker node can run one or more worker processes. At any given time, a single machine may be running multiple worker processes. Each worker node has a supervisor process running on it which communicates with Nimbus.

The supervisor coordinates the status of the currently running topology and announces any available slots to take up possibly more work. Nimbus monitors the topologies that need to be mapped and does the mapping between those topologies and supervisors when needed. Zookeeper [44] is used for all coordination between Nimbus and the Supervisors.

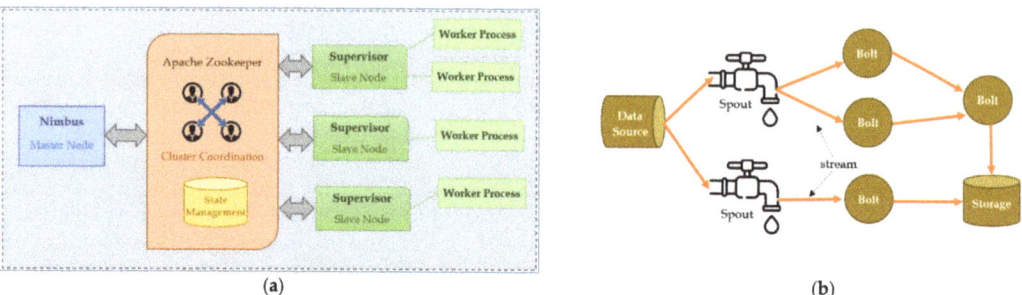

Figure 7. Apache Storm (**a**) Architecture of Apache Storm; (**b**) An illustration of Storm Topology.

4.3.2. Data Processing Model

The basic data processing model of Storm consists of four abstractions, topology, spouts, bolts, stream. In Storm, a stream is an unbounded sequence of tuples, where tuples are named lists of values, that can be of any type including strings, integers, floating-point numbers, etc. The logic of any real time storm application is presented in the form of a topology, which is a network of bolts and spouts. Figure 7b illustrates a storm topology. Spouts are source of stream that essentially connects with a data source such as Kafka [45] or Kestrel. It continuously receives data and converts it to stream of tuples and pass them to bolts. Bolts are the processing units of a storm application that can perform a variety of tasks.

4.3.3. Scheduling

Apache Storm has four built-in schedulers: Default, Isolation, Multitenant, and Resource Aware [46]. The default Storm scheduler is fair scheduler that takes into account each node when scheduling tasks. It implements a simple round-robin strategy with the goal of producing an even distribution of work among workers. Isolation scheduling enables safe sharing of a cluster among many topologies. In isolation scheduling, the user can specify which topologies should be isolated, which means topologies marked isolated are running on a dedicated set of nodes in the cluster, and other topologies will not be able to run on those nodes. These isolated topologies have priority in the cluster, when there is competition with the non-isolated topology, resources are allocated to the isolated topology. When the isolated topology requires resources, the resources are taken away from the non-isolated topologies. The multitenant scheduler is designed for a multitenant storm cluster. It allocates resources on per user basis. Whereas, the resource aware scheduler works in two phases. In the first phase, task selection is performed by obtaining a list of unassigned tasks. In the later phase, it selects a node for each task based on resource-aware considerations such as CPU, memory, physical distance and network bandwidth. Other than built-in schedulers, there are a number of scheduling techniques proposed in the literature [46–51] that focuses on improving latency, network traffic, and throughput.

4.3.4. Fault Tolerance

The Nimbus and Supervisors are designed to fail-fast, yet resilient and stateless daemons, with all of their data stored in Zookeeper or on the local discs, thus, preventing any catastrophic loss in case of processes or processor failure. This design artifact is the key to Storm's fault-tolerance. Even if the Nimbus process fails, the workers can still make progress. However, without Nimbus, workers will not be reassigned to other machines when necessary. Furthermore, the Supervisors can restart the worker processes if they fail. If a supervisor fails and unable to send a heartbeat to Nimbus, or the task assigned to a supervisor is timed out, then the Nimbus will reschedule that task to another slave node. Additionally, Storm offers reliable spouts to replay the stream in case it is failed to be processed.

4.4. Samza

Samza [52], developed in-house at LinkedIn in 2013 and later donated to Apache Software Foundation. It is based on a unified design for the stateful processing of batched data and high volume real time data streams. Samza is designed to support high throughput (millions of messages per sec) for data streams while providing quick fault recovery and high reliability. To achieve these design goals, samza uses some key abstractions, such as partitioned streams, changelog capturing and local state management. Samza is now adopted by several big companies including LinkedIn, VMWare, Uber, Netflix, and TripAdvisor [53].

4.4.1. Architecture

Samza has a layered architecture that consists of three layers. Figure 8 depicts three layers of Samza architecture. A streaming layer which is responsible for providing replayable data source such as Apache Kafka, AWS Kinesis, or Azure EventHub. The execution layer which is responsible for scheduling and resource management, and processing layer which is responsible for data processing and flow management. The streaming layer and execution layer are pluggable components. Data streaming can be provided by any existing data sources. Similarly, cluster management and scheduling can be done by Apache YARN or Mesos. However, Samza has built-in support for Apache Kafka data streaming and Apache YARN for job execution. The execution model of a Samza Job is based on publish/subscribe task concept. It listens to a data stream from Kafka topic, processes the message when it arrives, and then sends its output to another stream. The data stream in Kafka consists of several partitions based on a key value pair. Samza tasks consume data streams and can run multiple tasks in parallel to consume all partitions of the stream in parallel. Samza tasks are executed in the YARN containers. YARN distributes containers on multiple nodes in the cluster and distributes tasks evenly among the containers. After execution the output can be sent to another stream for further processing. Unlike common stream processing systems, Samza is based on a decentralized model where there is no system level master to coordinate activities rather every job has a lightweight coordinator to manage it.

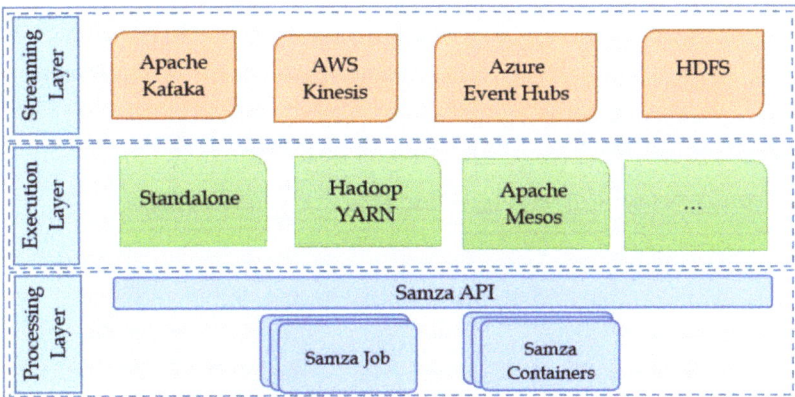

Figure 8. The layered architecture of Samza.

4.4.2. Data Processing Model

The data processing model of Samza builds upon two strong pillar: streams and jobs. Streams are primarily the inputs and outputs of the samza Jobs. A stream in Samza is a multi-part, ordered, multi-subscriber message sequence that is replay-able and lossless by design. User programs in Samza are processed in the form of Samza jobs. A Samza job is the code that consumes and processes a series of input streams and produce one or more output streams. These jobs are represented in the form of a directed graph of operators (vertices) connected by data streams (edges). The job and streams are further broken down into smaller execution units of parallelism, called tasks and partitions. Each task receives data from one or more partitions for each worker input stream. With this break down of stream to partitions and jobs to parallel tasks, samza achieves a linear scalability with number of containers [52].

4.4.3. Scheduling

For task scheduling and resource negotiation, Samza relies on pluggable cluster managers like YARN and Mesos.

4.4.4. Fault Tolerance

To ensure fault tolerance, each task in Samza runs a changelog-capturing service in the background that records incremental changes at a known place in the native file system. A failed task can be restarted by replaying the changelog. When a container restarts after a failure, it looks for the latest checkpoints and begins accepting messages from the latest checkpoint offset, this ensures at least once processing guarantees. This changelog mechanism is more efficient in comparison with full state check pointing, where a snapshot of the entire state is stored [52]. For further efficiency gains, the change log updates do not use the main computation hot path. Updates are stored in batches and sent to Kafka periodically in the background using spare network bandwidth. Re-scheduling a task after failure improves efficiency by Host Affinity mechanism that reduces the overhead of accessing changelog remotely, however, this overhead is unavoidable in case of permanent/long term machine failures.

4.5. Flink

Apache Flink is a distributed processing framework for stateful processing of unbounded and bounded streams of data. Flink is considered as next generation large scale data processing framework that is designed to work in all popular cluster environments with low latency and high throughput. Flink was initiated in 2009 at Technical University of Berlin with the name Stratosphere [54]. In 2014, as an Apache incubator project, Stratosphere became an open-source project with the name "Flink". Flink is known to process data hundred times faster than MapReduce [55]. Due to its highly flexible windowing mechanism, Flink programs can calculate early and approximate results, as well as delayed and accurate results through the same process, so there is no need to combine different systems for the two use cases [56].

4.5.1. Architecture

Flink has a layered architecture that consists of four layers (Figure 9). Primarily, Flink is a stream processing engine that doesn't offer a storage and resource management system of its own, instead it is designed to read data from various streaming and various storage systems. The core of Flink is a distributed data flow engine that receives user programs in the form of a DAG. The DAG in Flink is a parallel data flow graph which contains a series of tasks that produce and consume data streams. Flink has two main APIs: The DataSet API for processing bounded data streams i.e., batch processing and the DataStream API for processing potentially unbounded data streams. DataStream and DataSet APIs are interfaces that programmers can use to define jobs. When compiling the program, these APIs will generate a data flow graph.

The Flink runtime mainly consists of three processes: Job Manager, Task Manager and Client. The client receives the application code, converts it into a data flow graph, and then sends it to the JobManager. This conversion stage will also create serializers and other type-specific code. In addition, the program will go through a cost-based query optimization phase. JobManager is the master process that controls the execution of a single application. It is responsible for all activities that need to be centrally coordinated, such as distributed execution of data streams, monitoring the status and progress of each task, scheduling new tasks and coordinating checkpoints. Task Managers are the worker/slave processes that actually processes the data stream. Each application is managed by a different JobManager that receives the application from client. JobManager then requests the necessary resources from the ResouceManager. When it receives enough TaskManager, tasks will be distributed to the executing TaskManagers.

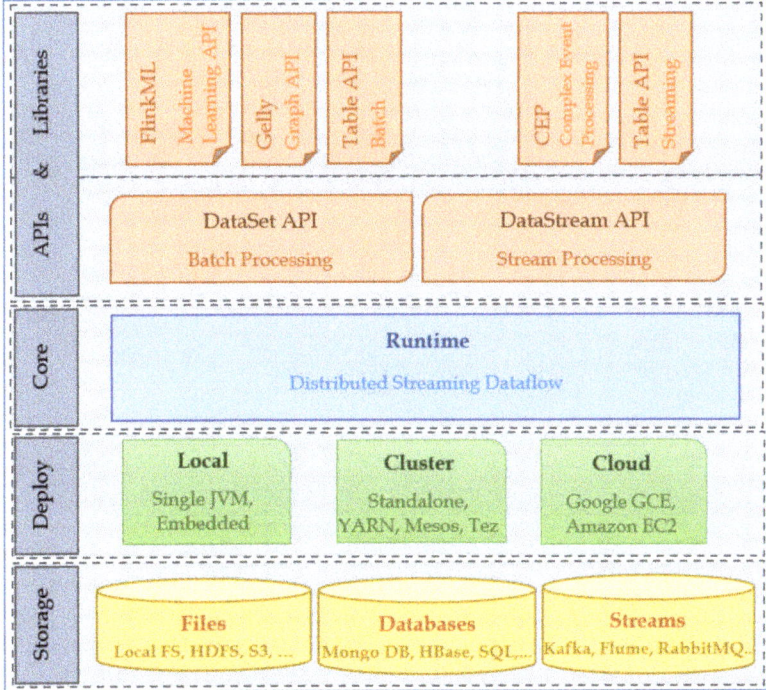

Figure 9. Apache Flink architecture.

4.5.2. Data Processing Model

All the Flink programs are compiled and converted into a common representation i.e., the data flow graph. The data flow graph is then executed by the Flink's execution engine, which is a common layer under the DataSet and DataStream APIs. The data flow graphs are executed in data-parallel manner. In a data flow graph, each edge represents a stream of data, and each vertex represents an operator that uses application defined logic to process data. Usually, there are two types of vertices, called source and sinks as depicted in Figure 10. The source consumes external data and injects it into the application, while the sink is meant to capture the results generated by the operators.

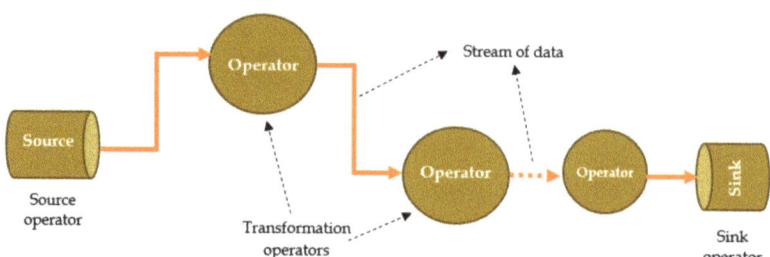

Figure 10. A data flow graph in Flink. Here, edges represent data streams and each vertices represent operators.

4.5.3. Scheduling

There are three scheduling strategies in Flink for resource allocation: all at once/eager scheduling, lazy from sources scheduling and pipelined region scheduling. All at once/eager scheduling tries to allocate required resources at once when the job starts. This strategy is primarily targeted for streaming jobs because in case of batch processing, acquiring all resources in advance will lead to resource underutilization as any resources allocated to subtasks that could not run at any time due to blocking results will be idle and therefore considered wasted. In order to solve the blocking effect and ensure that consumers are not deployed before completing the operations of the respective producers, Flink provides different scheduling strategy for batch processing. The lazy from source scheduling, starts from source and deploys subtasks according to their topological order, this ensures that a subtask can only be deployed if all of its inputs are ready. One limitation of this approach is that it operates on individual tasks and thus treating all tasks in a similar fashion, without considering the subtasks that are non-blocking and can be executed in parallel. To address this limitation, the pipelined region scheduling is introduced in Flink, that analyzes Job graph and identify pipelined regions before deploying tasks and subtasks. It schedules each region only when all of its predecessors are executed thereby making all of its inputs ready. If there are enough available resources, JobManager will try to execute as many pipeline regions in parallel as possible [57].

4.5.4. Fault Tolerance

Flink provides reliable execution with exactly-once consistency guarantees. It takes regular distributed snapshots of data stream and operator states. These snapshots serve as consistent checkpoints, in case of failure, the system can fall back to these checkpoints. Flink's mechanism for taking these snapshots is introduced in [58] which is inspired by the standard Chandy-Lamport's asynchronous distributed snapshot algorithm [59]. A general assumption made by the Flink's fault tolerance mechanism is that the data source is replay able. In addition to checkpoints recovery mechanism that is automatically triggered upon failure, Flink also provides SavePoint mechanism which is manually triggered and managed by the user. SavePoints support pause-and-resume jobs and scheduled backup. If a TaskManager fails, JobManager requests ResourceManager for more processing slots, restores the state of failed process using checkpoints, and re-executes it on another processing slot. However, a failure at JobManager is critical, since JobManager monitors the execution of streaming applications and manages related metadata. Flink supports a high-availability mode, which is based on Apache ZooKeeper that stores all necessary metadata on a reliable remote storage system. When the JobManager fails, a new or a standby JobManager takes over the work of the failed JobManager by requesting the Zookeeper to yield JobGraph, metadata and state handles of last successful check point of the application from the remote storage.

5. Comparative Analysis of Big Data Frameworks

This section presents a comparative analysis of the big data frameworks discussed above. We identified various parameters and features to compare big data systems that include scalability, fault tolerance, data processing model, support for programming languages, data storage, resource management, throughput, latency, scheduling, and maturity. To provide a clear representation of the related concepts, the related features are grouped to form a feature vector. To this end, seven distinct feature vectors are defined: general features, performance related features, fault tolerance, data processing, architectural features, machine learning support, and stream processing. These feature vectors are summarized in Table 2 and discussed in the following subsections.

Table 2. Description of feature vectors.

Feature Vectors	Components of Feature Vector
General features	Main backers, maturity, implementation language, support for programming languages.
Architectural features	Architecture model, data storage, resource management, scheduling, security.
Data processing	Data processing model, execution model, processing mode, support for in-memory processing.
Performance	Latency, throughput, scalability.
Fault tolerance	Failure identification, failure handling, high availability.
Machine learning	Native support, compatibility, supported ML algorithms
Stream processing	Processing guarantees, state management, data source, processing format, stream primitives

5.1. General Feature Vector

This feature vector holds general characteristics of frameworks such as, main backers, maturity, implementation language, support for programming languages. Table 3 summarizes the comparison of the frameworks against general features. Every framework has some strong backing of a well-established business company, for example Hadoop is primarily backed by Google and Yahoo, Spark is backed by AMP Lab, whereas Storm's main backers are BackType and Twitter, Samza and Flink are backed by LinkedIn and dataArtisans respectively. As regards language support, it can be seen that each framework supports a number of programming languages with Storm topping the list with the support of widest range of languages because Storm uses Thrift [60] definition to define and deploy topologies. Since Thrift has code generation support for any high level programming language so Storm topologies can also be defined using any programming language, thus making Storm more developer friendly than its competitors. Maturity is a significant parameter from adoption perspective, it is generally preferred that the framework is mature and well tested. Currently, Hadoop has overcome its unstable stage and it has now developed more reliable and stable among its less mature counter parts. On the other hand, as of today, Flink is still in its early stages of evolution, many features are continuously being modified making Flink a little difficult to understand as a beginner, because there may be less community support and limited active forums to discuss Flink-related queries.

Table 3. Comparison of big data frameworks with respect to general features.

	Hadoop	Spark	Storm	Samza	Flink
Main backers	Google, Yahoo!	AMP Lab	Backtype, Twitter	LinkedIn	dataArtisans
Implementation language	Java	scala	clojure	scala, java	java, Scala
Programming language support	most of the high level languages	java, Scala, python, R	any programming language	JVM languages	java, Scala, python, R
Maturity	very high	high	high	medium	low

5.2. Feature Vector Related to Architectural Components

Since, big data frameworks distribute workloads across multiple processors, that requires splitting and distributing data files, managing the storage of data in a distributed file system, scheduling tasks across the available computing and ensuring security. In this feature set we grouped together architecture related features such as architecture model, resource manager, storage, scheduling and security. Table 4 summarizes the comparison of the frameworks against architecture related features. It can be seen that four of most popular frameworks are based on master/slave architecture, whereas, Samza has no system wide master, instead Samza's architecture is based on publish/subscribe model. Most of the frameworks under discussion support resource management through Hadoop YARN and Apache Mesos. All the frameworks provide reliable and fault tolerant computing through different abstractions. Many big data applications are migrating from in-house storage and preferred to be deployed in cloud environment where different users can easily access or maintain privacy-sensitive data that leads to privacy and security risks. To provide authorization and authentication for computing nodes, Hadoop and Storm use the Kerberos authentication protocol [61]. Spark uses a password-based configuration as well as Access Control Lists (ACLs) to ensure security. Flink uses Kerberos and TLS/SSL authentication and Samza has no built-in support for security.

Table 4. Comparison of big data frameworks with respect to architectural features.

	Hadoop	Spark	Storm	Samza	Flink
Architecture Model	master-slave	master-slave	master-slave	publish-subscribe	master-slave
Resource Manager	YARN	stand alone, YARN, Mesos	YARN, Mesos	stand alone, YARN, Mesos	stand alone, YARN, Mesos
Storage	HDFS	HDFS, HBase, Hive, Casandra	HDFS	HDFS	HDFS, streams databases,
Scheduling	Fair, FIFO, Capacity	FIFO, Fair	default, isolation, multitenant, resource aware	YARN scheduler	all at once, lazy from source, pipelined region
Security	Kerberos authentication protocol	Password based shared secret configuration, Access Control Lists (ACLs)	Kerberos authentication protocol	no built-in security	Kerberos and TLS/SSL authentication

5.3. Feature Vector Related to Data Processing

Data processing in big data frameworks define how the data is processed and how the computations are represented in the system. Hadoop is a batch processing system that is best suited for large scale data processing. Storm and Samza are stream processing systems. Spark and Flink are hybrid systems that can handle batch as well as streaming data. Stream processing frameworks can handle virtually unlimited data volumes. However, they generally process streaming data in one of the two ways, native streaming that processes data items as they arrive or micro-batching which processes very small batches of incoming data. Spark and Storm uses micro-batching while Samza and Flink uses native streaming. Table 5 compares big data frameworks on the basis of data processing features.

Table 5. Comparison of big data frameworks with respect to feature vector related to data processing.

	Hadoop	Spark	Storm	Samza	Flink
Execution Format	batch only	batch and stream	stream only	stream only	batch and stream
Data Processing Model	MapReduce	DAG	Topology	DAG of operators	data flow graph
Processing Mode	batch processing	micro-batching	micro-batching	native streaming	native streaming
In-memory processing	No	Yes	Yes	yes	yes

5.4. Feature Vector Related to Performance

This feature vector includes performance metrics and those parameters that have a significant impact on the performance of a big data framework. This includes latency that defines how quickly a data item can be processed, throughput and scalability. The desired value of latency is as low as possible and the desired value for throughput is as high as possible. Scalability defines the ability of a system to adapt to change in workloads by involving additional resources. Scalability can be achieved either by making existing resources stronger and faster so that they can efficiently handle increased workload (referred as scale-up) or adding more resources in parallel to spread out the increased load (referred as scale-out). Comparison of big data frameworks with respect to performance related features is shown in Table 6.

Table 6. Comparison of big data frameworks with respect to performance related features.

	Hadoop	Spark	Storm	Samza	Flink
Latency	high (seconds)	low (few seconds)	very low (sub seconds)	very low (sub seconds)	very low (sub seconds)
Throughput	high	High	medium	high	high
Scalability	high	Moderate	moderate	low	high

5.5. Feature Vector Related to Fault Tolerance

To improve the reliability and performance of big data systems, the adoption of fault tolerant systems has grown over the years. The need for highly fault tolerant systems arise due to the frequent failures caused by the complexity, scale and heterogeneity of underlying systems. Fault detection is the starting point of any fault-tolerant mechanism, that enables faults to be detected as soon as they appear within the system. In large-scale systems, stable fault detection methods such as heartbeat mechanism and fault prediction are used. Most big data frameworks are based on the heartbeat detection approach [18]. After fault detection, fault recovery is used to restore the faulty component's normal behavior. Data replication is typically used to ensure the reliability of storage systems. Google File System and HDFS both storage systems employed this method for fault tolerance and high availability. Redundant processing and redundant storage of in-processing metadata is used to recover faults that occur during the data processing. Checkpointing is another approach to ensure fault tolerance in big data systems which is used by stream processing engines or real time transactions where low latency is desired. Table 7 presents a comparison of frameworks on the basis of feature vector related to fault tolerance.

Table 7. Comparison of big data frameworks with respect to features related to fault tolerance.

	Hadoop	Spark	Storm	Samza	Flink
Fault detection	heart beat mechanism	heart beat mechanism	heart beat mechanism	Keeping in-memory record of all emitted tuples and tracks them within a configured timeout	heart beat mechanism
Fault Recovery	Data Replication	RDD lineage	Tuples acknowledgement, Zookeeper	Change log capturing	Light weight distributed snapshots
High availability	Redundant standby NameNodes and ResourceManagers	Multiple masters with Zookeeper	Running multiple standby Nimbus servers	Relies on YARN's high availability mode	Stores JobGraph and all necessary metadata on a reliable remote storage system

5.6. Feature Vector Related to Support for Machine Learning

Machine learning is a powerful tool that enables the use of data to make predictions and help to make decisions. The core of machine learning is data that empowers the underlying models. The emerging technologies of big data processing heavily incorporate machine learning tools to help make smarter and more informed decisions based on data.

Since machine learning concepts and algorithms are increasingly used in big data analytics, thus almost all of the frameworks are complemented with machine learning libraries and toolkits. Though, no special platform or library is required to execute machine learning tasks on Hadoop clusters, yet, a set of machine learning packages that can be run on Hadoop includes Mahout, H$_2$O, Distributed Weka and Oryx [10]. Spark and Flink have their native machine learning libraries. Spark's MLlib aims to simplify machine learning tasks for Spark. Its core functions include clustering, classification, collaborative filtering and regression. Additionally, it also includes algorithms for dimension reduction, transformation, optimization and feature extraction [10]. FlinkML is Flink's native machine learning library which was released in April 2015. It aims at providing extensible machine learning tools and algorithms for the development of complex machine learning applications. Storm and Samza both do not offer native machine learning library. However, both have compatibility with SAMOA [62]. As can be seen from Table 8, that all five frameworks have support for either native or in compatibility mode for machine learning tools that implements clustering, classification and regression algorithms. However, H$_2$O is the only machine learning platform considered in this paper that implements deep learning algorithms, consequently, those frameworks that can be integrated with H$_2$O offers deep learning algorithms.

Table 8. Support for machine learning tools and algorithms in big data frameworks.

Frameworks	Machine Learning Tools		Machine Learning Algorithms				
	Native ML Support	Compatibility	Deep Learning	Clustering	Collaborative Filtering	Classification	Regression
Hadoop	Mahout	Distributed Weka, Oryx, H$_2$O, SAMOA	✔	✔	✔	✔	✔
Spark	MLlib	Distributed Weka, H$_2$O, Mahout, Oryx	✔	✔	✔	✔	✔
Storm	-	SAMOA, H$_2$O	✔	✔	✗	✔	✔
Samza	-	SAMOA	✗	✔	✗	✔	✔
Flink	FlinkML	SAMOA	✗	✔	✔	✔	✔

5.7. Feature Vector Related to Stream Processing

The streaming frameworks apply computations on the data as it enters the system. This requires a different processing model from batch processing. Rather than defining the operations that are applied to the entire dataset, stream processors define the operations that will be applied to individual data items or extremely small batches of data. These operations usually maintain no or minimal state in between record. However, some frameworks provide some mechanism to maintain state. There are some important features that revolve around stream processing frameworks, such as state management, processing guarantees, stream primitives etc. Table 9 compares the stream processing frameworks on the basis of these features.

Table 9. Comparison of big data frameworks with respect to features related to stream processing.

	Spark	Storm	Samza	Flink
Processing Guarantees	exactly once	at least once	at least once	exactly once
Data Source	HDFS, DBMS, Kafka	Spout	Kafka	HDFS, DBMS, Kafka
Processing Format	micro-batches	micro-batches	continuous flow streaming	continuous flow streaming, batched, micro-batched
Stream Primitives	Dstream	Tuple	message	datastream
State Management	stateful	stateless	stateful operators	stateful operators

6. Discussion

Hadoop MapReduce leverages disk storage. As each task needs to access the disk to read and write multiple times, so it is usually very slow. However, since disk space is typically one of the copious resources on a server, which means, MapReduce can process huge datasets. This also means that MapReduce jobs can usually be executed on less expensive hardware than some alternatives because it doesn't use in-memory computations. This makes Hadoop best suited for very large datasets where execution time is not a constraint. Hadoop MapReduce is highly scalable, it can scale up to thousands of nodes (Hadoop cluster at Yahoo! is reported to have 42,000 nodes [11]). Hadoop not only has a strong ecosystem but is also often used as a building block for other frameworks. Several frameworks and execution engines integrate Hadoop to use the capabilities of HDFS and YARN.

Spark is significantly faster than Hadoop due to its in-memory data structure RDDs and DAG scheduling. It supports both batch and stream processing models, which gives the advantage of managing multiple processing workloads from a single cluster. In addition to its core capabilities, Spark has a sound set of libraries for machine learning, interactive queries, and iterative jobs, etc. It is largely acknowledged in developer communities that Spark tasks are easier to write than MapReduce, which has a significant impact on performance [63]. Spark uses micro-batches for processing which means it buffers data as it enters the system. Though, the buffer is capable of keeping a large amount of data but waiting for the buffer to be flushed can cause a significant increase in latency, thereby making Spark streaming a less suitable choice for the applications where low latency is required. However, Spark is a good fit for applications where high throughput is more desired than latency. Also, because Spark uses in-memory computations and memory is often more expensive than disk, Spark may be more expensive than disk-based frameworks. However, faster execution means tasks can be finished early, which can completely offset the cost of working in a paid work environment. Yet, in a multitenant environment, Spark may be a less considerate neighbor as compared to Hadoop due to its extensive resource usage.

Storm is one of the most trusted solutions for the near real-time workloads that need to be processed with minimal latency. Storm is usually a good choice when processing time has a direct impact on the user experience, for example during interactive web sessions. Storm provides at least once processing guarantee, which means that every message is guaranteed to be processed, but some messages may be processed more than once. However, after the release of Trident, it supports exactly once processing guarantee. Storm does not support batch processing, though, Storm with Trident offers the flexibility of using micro-batches as an alternative to pure streaming. For interoperability, Storm integrates with the YARN and can be easily connected to existing Hadoop implementations. Strom is polyglot and supports more programming languages than any other framework.

Samza is heavily reliant on Kafka to ensures some unique features to the system. For example, Kafka provides replicated storage with notably low latency and a low-cost multi-subscription model for each data partition. Samza's fault tolerance mechanism has a strong contribution coming from Kafka. Results are also written back to Kafka that can be ingested by later stages. Writing the results directly to Kafka also helps eliminating backpressure problem [63]. Backpressure occurs when the peak load causes data to flow faster than the real-time processing speed of the components, resulting in processing downtime and possible data loss. Kafka is capable of holding data for longer time periods that enable components to read and process data at their convenience. The strong coupling between samza and Kafka leads to the loosely coupled processing stages. Samza is suitable for organizations in which multiple teams may need to access data streams at different stages of processing because several subscribers can consume the output of each stage. Samza can store state with the help of a fault-tolerant check pointing system and offers at-least once processing guarantees. This makes it provide inaccurate recovery of the aggregated state such as counts because, in case of failure, data can be delivered multiple times.

Like Spark, Flink is also a hybrid framework that provides low-latency streaming and supports traditional batch processing tasks. However, Spark is not preferred for streaming in many use cases due to its micro-batch processing style. While Flink provides real stream processing with low latency and high throughput. Flink treats batch processing as a special case of streaming i.e., bounded data stream. This is contrary to other frameworks approach, where batch-processing is the primary processing model and streaming is used as a subset of it. Unlike other frameworks that relies on Java garbage collector, Flink has its own memory management mechanism that handles garbage collection, partitioning and caching. While running in the Hadoop stack, it is designed to be a fair neighbor and only consumes the resources it needs at any given time. Flink's language and rich API support is limited to Java and Scala thereby, making it not a good fit if more support for high level APIs is needed.

To summarize the discussion above, there is no best fit for all solution, rather every framework has its own strengths and weaknesses. Which framework is most appropriate for a project is dependent largely on the nature of data being processed, the time constraints, and the type of processing that is intended in that particular project. There is a trade-off between implementing the best fit for all system and dealing with highly focused projects, and similar considerations apply when comparing innovative but new systems with well-tested and mature solutions. Table 10 presents the application use cases where each of the discussed frameworks ideally fits in.

Table 10. Application use cases where each of the frameworks ideally fits in.

Big Data Frameworks	Best Fit Application Use-Cases
Hadoop	Applications that require batch processing of very large datasets where execution time is not a hard constraint
Spark	Applications with batch or streaming workloads where high throughput is more desired than latency
Storm	Streaming applications where extremely low latency is desired with at least once processing guarantees
Samza	Streaming applications that require multiple teams to access same data streams at different stages of processing
Flink	Applications with batch or streaming workloads where extremely low latency is desired with exactly once processing guarantees
Spark	Applications with batch or streaming workloads where high throughput is more desired than latency
Storm	Streaming applications where extremely low latency is desired with at least once processing guarantees

7. Conclusions

In the presence of a number of available big data processing frameworks selecting most appropriate framework according to application context is non-trivial. To choose the appropriate framework for an application, one must consider a number of features and characteristics of the system. In the literature, several studies have performed comparisons of big data frameworks but these lack detailed comparison of architecture with respect to the core functionality of its components. No specific guidance is provided to help developers and practitioners in the selection of a suitable framework for their application. Furthermore, the classification of features that are used for comparative analysis is lacking. To fill this research gap, our work aims to provide a comprehensive review of most popular big data frameworks in an attempt to highlight the strengths and weaknesses of each framework. The features used for comparative analysis are logically classified the into seven feature vectors. The frameworks are thoroughly compared with respect to identified feature vectors. Furthermore, we pointed out the application use cases where each of the frameworks ideally fit in and a detailed discussion is presented that can serve as a decision making guide to select the appropriate framework for an application.

This work differs from existing studies in number of ways. First, a detailed-oriented review of big data frameworks is presented with respect to four significant aspects: architecture, fault tolerance, data processing model and scheduling. Second, this paper presents a purposeful discussion related to the core characteristics of big data frameworks. The findings can help in selecting the most competent and preferable system according to particular scenario or application requirement.

We believe that our work will benefit the researchers and practitioners in the following ways:

- In the literature, the qualitative comparisons were performed in bits and pieces and architecture of the frameworks were discussed and analyzed briefly. Furthermore, the classification of features that are used for comparative analysis is lacking. In this paper, we have logically classified the features into seven feature vectors. We thoroughly compared the frameworks in terms of identified feature vectors.
- Although, the official documentation of the frameworks contains information about the architecture of the framework, but this information cannot be used to compare the frameworks because there is no consistent view under which the information is presented for each framework. The documentation varies from framework to framework on the basis of the format on which the information is presented and the characteristics are considered. Hence, there is no consistent view available through which one can compare these frameworks and conclude some frameworks selection guidelines. We have analyzed the popular big data frameworks in detail under a consistent view of feature vectors. That is, all the frameworks are compared and discussed on the basis of the four significant aspects and seven feature vectors. Thus, we have presented the information in systematic way. The readers can easily assess the pros and cons of each framework under a consistent view. Since, the information has been structured in a systematic way therefore, it is easy to perform a cross-comparison of the systems.

Author Contributions: M.K. was responsible for conceptualization and methodology of the work; M.K. and M.M.Y. participated in writing and editing the manuscript and analyzing data. All authors have read and agreed to the published version of the manuscript.

Funding: This research received no external funding.

Institutional Review Board Statement: Not applicable.

Informed Consent Statement: Not applicable.

Data Availability Statement: Not applicable.

Conflicts of Interest: The authors declare no conflict of interest.

References

1. Reinsel, J.G. The Digital Universe in 2020: Big Data, Bigger Digital Shadows, and Biggest Growth in the Far East. Internet Data Cent, IDC: iView: IDC Analyze the Future 2007. 2012, pp. 1–16. Available online: http://www.emc.com/collateral/analyst-reports/idc-the-digital-uni (accessed on 22 June 2021).
2. Reinsel, D.; Gantz, J.; Rydning, J. The Digitization of the World—From Edge to Core. Internet Data Cent. 2018, pp. 1–28. Available online: https://www.seagate.com/files/www-content/our-story/trends/files/idc-seagate-dataage-whitepaper.pdf (accessed on 22 June 2021).
3. Chebbi, I.; Boulila, W.; Farah, I.R. Big Data: Concepts, challenges and applications. In *Computational Collective Intelligence, Lecture Notes in Computer Science*; Springer: Cham, Switzerland, 2015; Volume 9330, pp. 638–647.
4. Dugas, A.F.; Jalalpour, M.; Gel, Y.; Levin, S.; Torcaso, F.; Igusa, T.; Rothman, R.E. Influenza forecasting with Google Flu Trends. *PLoS ONE* **2013**, *8*, 2. [CrossRef]
5. Maier, M. Towards a Big Data Reference Architecture. Ph.D. Thesis, Eindhoven University of Technology, Eindhoven, The Netherlands, 2013.
6. Chen, P.C.L.; Zhang, C.Y. Data-intensive applications, challenges, techniques and technologies: A survey on Big Data. *Inf. Sci.* **2014**, *275*, 314–347. [CrossRef]
7. Singh, D.; Reddy, C.K. A survey on platforms for big data analytics. *J. Big Data* **2015**, *2*, 8. [CrossRef] [PubMed]
8. Morais, T. Survey on Frameworks for Distributed Computing: Hadoop, Spark and Storm. In Proceedings of the 10th Doctoral Symposium in Informatics Engineering—DSIE'15, Porto, Portugal, 29–30 January 2015.
9. Hesse, G.; Lorenz, M. Conceptual Survey on Data Stream Processing Systems. In Proceedings of the IEEE 21st International Conference on Parallel and Distributed Systems (ICPADS), Melbourne, VIC, Australia, 14–17 December 2015; pp. 797–802. [CrossRef]

10. Landset, S.; Khoshgoftaar, T.M.; Richter, A.N.; Hasanin, T. A survey of open source tools for machine learning with big data in the Hadoop ecosystem. *J. Big Data* **2015**, *2*, 1–36. [CrossRef]
11. Ullah, S.; Awan, M.D.; Khiya, M.S.H. Big data in cloud computing: A resource management perspective. *Sci. Program.* **2018**, *8*, 1–7. [CrossRef]
12. Bajaber, F.; Elshawi, R.; Batarfi, O.; Altalhi, A.; Barnawi, A.; Sakr, S. Big data 2.0 processing systems: Taxonomy and open challenges. *J. Grid Comput.* **2016**, *14*, 379–405. [CrossRef]
13. Assunção, M.D.d.; Veith, A.d.S.; Buyya, R. Distributed data stream processing and edge computing: A survey on resource elasticity and future directions. *J. Netw. Comput. Appl.* **2018**, *103*, 1–17. [CrossRef]
14. Inoubli, W.; Aridhi, S.; Mezni, H.; Maddouri, M.; Nguifo, E.M. An experimental survey on big data frameworks. *Future Gener. Comput. Syst.* **2018**, *86*, 546–564. [CrossRef]
15. Veiga, J.; Expósito, R.R.; Pardo, X.C.; Taboada, G.L.; Tourifio, J. Performance evaluation of big data frameworks for large-scale data analytics. In Proceedings of the IEEE International Conference on Big Data, Washington, DC, USA, 5–8 December 2016; pp. 424–431.
16. Hazarika, A.V.; Ram, G.J.S.R.; Jain, E. Performance comparison of Hadoop and spark engine. In Proceedings of the I-SMAC (IoT in Social, Mobile, Nalytics and Cloud), Palladam, India, 10–11 February 2017; pp. 671–674.
17. Gupta, H.K.; Parveen, D.R. Comparative study of big data frameworks. In Proceedings of the International Conference on Issues and Challenges in Intelligent Computing Techniques (ICICT), Ghaziabad, India, 27–28 September 2019; pp. 1–4. [CrossRef]
18. Saadoon, M.; Hamid, S.H.A.; Sofian, H.; Altarturi, H.H.M.; Azizul, Z.H.; Nasuha, N. Fault tolerance in big data storage and processing systems: A review on challenges and solutions. *Ain Shams Eng. J.* **2021**, in press. [CrossRef]
19. Bartolini, I.; Patella, M. Comparing performances of big data stream processing platforms with RAM3S. In Proceedings of the 25th Italian Symposium on Advanced Database Systems (SEBD), Squillace Lido, Italy, 25–29 June 2017; pp. 145–152.
20. To, Q.C.; Soto, J.; Markl, V. A survey of state management in big data processing systems. *VLDB J.* **2018**, *27*, 847–872. [CrossRef]
21. Cumbane, S.P.; Gidófalvi, G. Review of big data and processing frameworks for disaster response applications. *ISPRS Int. J. Geo-Inf.* **2019**, *8*, 387. [CrossRef]
22. Inoubli, W.; Aridhi, S.; Mezni, H.; Maddouri, M.; Nguifo, E. A comparative study on streaming frameworks for big data. In Proceedings of the 44th International Conference on Very Large Databases: Workshop LADaS-Latin American Data Science, Rio De Janeiro, Brazil, 27–31 August 2018; pp. 1–8.
23. Patil, A. Distributed Programming Frameworks in Cloud Platforms. *Int. J. Recent Technol. Eng.* **2019**, *7*, 1–9.
24. Demchenko, Y.; de Laat, C.; Membrey, P. Defining Architectural Components of the Big Data Ecosystem. In Proceedings of the International Conference on Collaboration Technologies and Systems (CTS), Minneapolis, MN, USA, 19–23 May 2014; pp. 104–112. [CrossRef]
25. Park, E.; Sugumaran, V.; Park, S. A Reference Model for Big Data Analytics. In Proceedings of the 9th IEEE Annual Ubiquitous Computing, Electronics & Mobile Communication Conference (UEMCON), New York, NY, USA, 8–10 November 2018; pp. 382–391. [CrossRef]
26. Ghemawat, S.; Gobioff, H.; Leung, S. The Google file system. In Proceedings of the Nineteenth ACM Symposium on Operating Systems Principles (SOSP '03), Bolton Landing, NY, USA, 19–22 October 2003; pp. 29–43.
27. Dean, J.; Ghemawat, S. MapReduce: Simplified data processing on large clusters. *Commun. ACM* **2008**, *51*, 107–113. [CrossRef]
28. White, T. *Hadoop: The Definitive Guide*; O'Reilly Media: Newton, MA, USA, 2009.
29. Shvachko, K.; Kuang, H.; Radia, S.; Chansler, R. The Hadoop distributed file system. In Proceedings of the 26th IEEE Symposium on Mass Storage Systems and Technologies (MSST), Incline Village, NV, USA, 3–7 May 2010; pp. 1–10.
30. Polato, I.; Goldman, R.R.A.; Kon, F. A comprehensive view of Hadoop research—A systematic literature review. *J. Netw. Comput. Appl.* **2014**, *46*, 1–25. [CrossRef]
31. Vavilapalli, V.K.; Murthy, A.C.; Douglas, C.; Agarwal, S.; Konar, M.; Evans, R.; Graves, T.; Lowe, J.; Shah, H.; Seth, S.; et al. Apache Hadoop YARN: Yet another resource negotiator. In Proceedings of the 4th Annual Symposium on Cloud Computing, Santa Clara, CA, USA, 1–3 October 2013; pp. 1–16.
32. Saha, B.; Shah, H.; Seth, S.; Vijayaraghavan, G.; Murthy, A.; Curino, C. Apache Tez: A unifying framework for modeling and building data processing applications. In Proceedings of the ACM SIGMOD International Conference on Management of Data, Melbourne, VIC, Australia, 31 May–4 June 2015; pp. 1357–1369.
33. Olston, C.; Reed, B.; Srivastava, U.; Kumar, R.; Tomkins, A. Pig Latin: A not-so-foreign language for data processing. In Proceedings of the International Conference on Management of Data (SIGMOD '08), Vancouver, BC, Canada, 9–12 June 2008; pp. 1099–1110.
34. Salloum, S.; Dautov, R.; Chen, X.; Peng, P.X.; Huang, J. Big data analytics on Apache Spark. *Int. J. Data Sci. Anal.* **2016**, *1*, 145–164. [CrossRef]
35. Zaharia, M.; Chowdhury, M.; Das, T.; Dave, A.; Ma, J.; McCauley, M.; Franklin, M.J.; Shenker, S.; Stoica, I. Resilient distributed datasets: A fault-tolerant abstraction for in-memory cluster computing. In Proceedings of the 9th USENIX NSDI'12 USENIX Association, San Jose, CA, USA, 25–27 April 2012.
36. Armbrust, M.; Xin, R.S.; Lian, C.; Huai, Y.; Liu, D.; Bradley, J.K.; Meng, X.; Kaftan, T.; Franklin, M.J.; Ghodsi, A.; et al. Spark SQL: Relational data processing in spark. In Proceedings of the International Conference on Management of Data (SIGMOD '15), Melbourne, VIC, Australia, 31 May–4 June 2015; pp. 1383–1394.

37. Zaharia, M.; Das, T.; Li, H.; Hunter, T.; Shenker, S.; Stoica, I. Discretized streams: Fault-tolerant streaming computation at scale. In Proceedings of the 24th ACM Symposium on Operating Systems Principles (SOSP '13), Farminton, PA, USA, 3–6 November 2013; pp. 423–438.
38. Meng, X.; Bradley, J.; Yavuz, B.; Sparks, E.; Venkataraman, S.; Liu, D.; Freeman, J.; Tsai, D.; Amde, M.; Owen, S.; et al. Mllib: Machine learning in apache spark. *J. Mach. Learn. Res.* **2016**, *17*, 1–7.
39. Xin, R.S.; Gonzalez, J.E.; Franklin, M.J.; Stoica, I. GraphX: A resilient distributed graph system on Spark. In Proceedings of the 1st Int. Workshop on Graph Data Management Experiences and Systems (GRADES '13), New York, NY, USA, 23 June 2013; Volume 2, pp. 1–6.
40. Venkataraman, S.; Yang, Z.; Liu, D.; Liang, E.; Falaki, H.; Meng, X.; Xin, R.; Ghodsi, A.; Franklin, M.; Stoica, I.; et al. SparkR: Scaling R programs with Spark. In Proceedings of the International Conference on Management of Data (SIGMOD '16), San Francisco, CA, USA, 26 June–1 July 2016; pp. 1099–1104.
41. Hindman, B.; Konwinski, A.; Zaharia, M.; Ghodsi, A.; Joseph, A.D.; Katz, R.; Shenker, S.; Stoica, I. Mesos: A platform for fine-grained resource sharing in the data center. In Proceedings of the 8th USENIX Conference on Networked Systems Design and Implementation (NSDI '11), Boston, MA, USA, 30 March–1 April 2011; pp. 295–308.
42. Toshniwal, A.; Taneja, S.; Shukla, A.; Ramasamy, K.; Patel, J.M.; Kulkarni, S.; Jackson, J.; Gade, K.; Maosong, F.; Donham, J.; et al. Storm@twitter. In Proceedings of the ACM International Conference on Management of Data (SIGMOD '14), Snowbird, UT, USA, 22–27 June 2014; pp. 147–156.
43. Iqbal, M.H.; Soomro, T.R. Big data analysis: Apache Storm perspective. *Int. J. Comput. Trends Technol.* **2015**, *19*, 9–14. [CrossRef]
44. Hunt, P.; Konar, M.; Junqueira, F.; Reed, B. ZooKeeper: Wait-free coordination for internet-scale systems. In Proceedings of the USENIX Annual Technical Conference, Boston, MA, USA, 23–25 June 2010; pp. 1–11.
45. Kreps, J.; Narkhede, N.; Rao, J. Kafka: A distributed messaging system for log processing. In Proceedings of the SIGMOD Workshop on Networking Meets Databases, Athens, Greece, 12 June 2011.
46. Muhammad, A.; Aleem, M. A3-Storm: Topology, traffic, and resource-aware storm scheduler for heterogeneous clusters. *J. Supercomput.* **2021**, *77*, 1059–1093. [CrossRef]
47. Cardellini, V.; Grassi, V.; Presti, F.L.; Nardelli, M. Optimal operator placement for distributed stream processing applications. In Proceedings of the 10th ACM International Conference on Distributed and Event-based Systems (DEBS '16), Irvine, CA, USA, 20–24 June 2016; pp. 69–80.
48. Aniello, L.; Baldoni, R.; Querzoni, L. Adaptive online scheduling in Storm. In Proceedings of the 7th ACM international conference on conference on Distributed event-based systems, Arlington, TX, USA, 29 June–3 July 2013; pp. 207–218.
49. Peng, B.; Hosseini, M.; Hong, Z.; Farivar, R.; Campbell, R. R-Storm: Resource-aware scheduling in Storm. In Proceedings of the 16th Annual Middleware Conference (Middleware '15), Vancouver, BC, Canada, 7–11 December 2015; pp. 149–161.
50. Xu, J.; Chen, Z.; Tang, J.; Su, S. T-Storm: Traffic-aware online scheduling in Storm. In Proceedings of the 34th International Conference on Distributed Computing Systems (ICDCS 13), Madrid, Spain, 30 June–3 July 2014; pp. 535–544.
51. Jian, T.; Xu, J. A predictive scheduling framework for fast and distributed stream data processing. In Proceedings of the IEEE International Conference on Big Data, Santa Clara, CA, USA, 29 October–1 November 2015; pp. 333–338.
52. Noghabi, S.A.; Paramasivam, K.; Pan, Y.; Ramesh, N.; Bringhurst, J.; Gupta, I.; Campbell, R.H. Samza: Stateful scalable stream processing at LinkedIn. *Proc. VLDB Endow.* **2017**, *10*, 1634–1645. [CrossRef]
53. Apache Samza. Available online: http://samza.apache.org/powered-by/ (accessed on 22 June 2021).
54. Alexandrov, A.; Bergmann, R.; Ewen, S.; Freytag, J.C.; Hueske, F.; Heise, A.; Kao, O.; Leich, M.; Leser, U.; Markl, V.; et al. The stratosphere platform for big data analytics. *VLDB J.* **2014**, *23*, 939–964. [CrossRef]
55. Armoogum, S.; Li, X. Big data analytics and deep learning in bioinformatics with Hadoop. In *Deep Learning and Parallel Computing Environment for Bioengineering Systems*; Academic Press: Cambridge, MA, USA, 2018; pp. 17–36.
56. Carbone, P.; Katsifodimos, A.; Ewen, S.; Markl, V.; Haridi, S.; Tzoumas, K. Apache Flink: Stream and batch processing in a single engine. *IEEE Data Eng. Bull.* **2015**, *36*, 28–38.
57. Zagrebin, A. Improvements in Task Scheduling for Batch Workloads in Apache Flink. Available online: https://flink.apache.org/2020/12/15/pipelined-region-sheduling.html#the-new-Pipelined-region-scheduling (accessed on 2 June 2020).
58. Carbone, P.; Fora, G.; Ewen, S.; Haridi, S.; Tzoumas, K. Lightweight asynchronous snapshots for distributed dataflows. *arXiv* **2015**, arXiv:1506 08203.
59. Chandy, K.M.; Lamport, L. Distributed snapshots: Determining global states of distributed systems. *ACM Trans. Comput. Syst.* **1985**, *3*, 63–75. [CrossRef]
60. Apache Thrift. Available online: https://thrift.apache.org/ (accessed on 22 June 2021).
61. Zhang, X.; Liu, C.; Nepal, S.; Dou, W.; Chen, J. Privacy-preserving layer over MapReduce on cloud. In Proceedings of the 2nd International Conference on Cloud and Green Computing, CGC, Xiangtan, China, 1–3 November 2012; pp. 304–310.
62. Morales, G.D.F.; Bifet, A. SAMOA: Scalable advanced massive online analysis. *J. Mach. Learn. Res.* **2015**, *16*, 149–153.
63. Ellingwood, J. Hadoop, Storm, Samza, Spark, and Flink: Big Data Frameworks Compared. Digital Ocean. 2016. Available online: https://www.digitalocean.com/community/tutorials/hadoop-storm-samza-spark-and-flink-big-data-frameworks-compared (accessed on 12 August 2021).

Article

Cognitive Biases on the Iran Stock Exchange: Unsupervised Learning Approach to Examining Feature Bundles in Investors' Portfolios

Adele Ossareh, Mohammad Saeed Pourjafar and Tomasz Kopczewski *

Faculty of Economic Science, University of Warsaw, 00-241 Warsaw, Poland; a.ossareh@student.uw.edu.pl (A.O.); m.pourjafar@student.uw.edu.pl (M.S.P.)
* Correspondence: tkopczewski@wne.uw.edu.pl

Featured Application: Better stock market investment strategies; understanding the financial crisis in terms of cognitive biases of investors; teaching stock market investors about their cognitive errors.

Abstract: This paper innovatively analyses the joint occurrence of cognitive biases in groups of stock exchange investors. It considers jointly a number of common fallacies: confirmation bias, loss aversion, gambler's fallacy, availability cascade, hot-hand fallacy, bandwagon effect, and Dunning–Kruger effect, which have hitherto been studied separately. The paper aims to highlight the diverse range of investor's profiles which are characterised by such fallacies, and the considerable differences observed based on their age, stock market experience and perception of market trends. The analysis is based on k-means and hierarchical clustering, feature importance and Principal Component Analysis, which were applied to data from the Tehran Stock Exchange. There are a few essential findings which contribute to the existing literature. Firstly, the results show that gender does not have a role to play in diversifying the investors' profiles. Secondly, cognitive biases are bundled, and we distinguish four investors' profiles; thus, they should be analysed jointly, not separately. Thirdly, the exposure to cognitive biases differs significantly due to the individual features of investors. The group most vulnerable to almost all analysed biases are inexperienced investors, who are pessimistic about market developments and have invested a large amount. Fourthly, the ages of investors are essential only in connection with other factors such as experience, market perception and investment exposure. Young (20–40 years), experienced investors with huge investments (+1000 mln rials/+24,000 USD) are mostly less exposed to all biases and much less risk-averse. Additionally, older (50+) and experienced investors (5–10 years) who are more optimistic about trends (hot hand bias) were affected much less by cognitive biases, only showing vulnerability to the Dunning–Kruger effect. Fifthly, more than 40% of investors apply consultation and technical analysis approaches to succeed in trading. Finally, from a methodological perspective, this study shows that unsupervised learning methods are effective in profiling investors and bundling similar behaviours.

Keywords: cognitive bias; stock market; behavioural finance; investor's profile; Teheran Stock Exchange; unsupervised learning; clustering

Citation: Ossareh, A.; Pourjafar, M.S.; Kopczewski, T. Cognitive Biases on the Iran Stock Exchange: Unsupervised Learning Approach to Examining Feature Bundles in Investors' Portfolios. *Appl. Sci.* **2021**, *11*, 10916. https://doi.org/10.3390/app112210916

Academic Editor: Suhuai Luo

Received: 9 October 2021
Accepted: 14 November 2021
Published: 18 November 2021

Publisher's Note: MDPI stays neutral with regard to jurisdictional claims in published maps and institutional affiliations.

Copyright: © 2021 by the authors. Licensee MDPI, Basel, Switzerland. This article is an open access article distributed under the terms and conditions of the Creative Commons Attribution (CC BY) license (https://creativecommons.org/licenses/by/4.0/).

1. Introduction

The psychological characteristics of stock market investors has always been a point of interest for behavioural scientists who seek to unfold the decision-making processes of investors based on their attitudes and specific attributes. Transactions on the stock market are based on information, while the way in which the information is processed directly impacts the behaviour of the financial system. The central assumption that financial and economic models are based on the rationality of investors is far from the reality. In fact, traditional theoretical models have failed to justify investors' cognitive biases. This phenomenon in financial markets which causes stock prices to deviate from their fundamental values consequently attracts arbitrageurs and creates stock market bubbles and causes capital flight. Economists have underlined that these fallacies have a considerable impact when they result in collective actions, that is, when they are replicated and enforced by the actions of other investors [1,2]. In the case of financial markets, this may bring about instability or even crises.

Economic and psychological literature (e.g., [3]) lists almost 100 different cognitive biases; however, not all of them refer to investors' behaviour in financial markets. We selected seven of them: confirmation bias, loss aversion, gambler's fallacy, availability cascade, hot-hand fallacy, bandwagon effect, and Dunning–Kruger effect. These are often listed as the most critical fallacies occurring in financial markets. However, the literature thus far has primarily analysed them individually, which has created an important research gap. This paper considers the joint cognitive biases affecting stock exchange investors; this is the main area of innovation in the research. We propose the hypothesis that these bundles of cognitive biases are heterogeneous among different groups of investors, and that this may form the foundations of some specific market distortions.

As many researchers have shown (e.g., [4,5]), inter-cultural differences affect the economic and investment decision-making process. Economic and cultural systems, involvement in financial issues, wealth, attitude to risk and many other factors influence behavioural patterns. This means that the results of studies on financial markets can not necessarily be extrapolated to other markets; in fact, all cultural environments need special attention. What is more, international, and intercultural comparisons are necessary for understanding the degree to which these environments are specific. There is a relative wealth of studies contained within the literature on well-developed financial markets and the behaviour of their investors, while studies on less-developed markets are sparser. Teheran Stock Exchanges of investors on the Tehran Stock Exchange (TSE) are gaining increasingly more attention in the literature. Indeed, one can find studies focusing on the following: IPOs (Initial Public Offering) [6], confirmation of the existence of these effects [7,8], correlation of personality characteristics with conservatism and availability biases [9], targeting of a deeper understanding of individual investment decisions and portfolios [10–12]; demonstration of the correlation between overconfidence and trading volume [13]; and an examination of intuitive thinking [14] and mental accounting [15]. However, these studies mostly report the existence of these effects but do not explain interactions between cognitive biases. This paper fills this gap by examining bundles of cognitive biases evident in the behaviour of Iranian stock exchange investors. It delivers further insight to the international community with regard to this niche financial market. An important aspect of studies on cognitive biases and investors' behaviour beyond the cultural environment is the research methodology. The most common stream of research focuses on analysing stock prices and volumes and drawing conclusions on psychological attitudes and failures indirectly by assuming the behavioural patterns (e.g., [16]). Such studies usually examine time series and their correlations and co-integration (e.g., [17]). The second, much more infrequent stream of research concentrates on surveying investors in the market directly. Our research method develops this direct approach by examining investors' behavioural attitudes and such profile metrics as gender, age, investment amount, and portfolio experience. Individual data require adequate quantitative analytics. This study proposes the use of unsupervised learning methods, such as clustering and dimension reduction, which enable a more detailed analysis of investors' profiles to be conducted. This methodology may reveal which cognitive biases occur either jointly or separately, and whether personal and professional concerns have a significant role to play in their occurrence.

Contributions: This study fills a research gap and proposes a few contributions in behavioural economics and finance:

1. It uses the joint analysis of cognitive biases observed among stock market investors to derive investors' behavioural profiles;
2. It examines bundles of cognitive biases present among TSE investors;
3. It provides methodological solutions based on individual data using unsupervised learning methods better to understand bundles of cognitive biases and investors' profiles.

The remainder of the paper is as follows. Section 2 presents the literature review on seven analysed cognitive biases, Section 3 gives a summary of the study design, Section 4 describes details of the quantitative analysis, Section 5 discusses the results, and Section 6 provides the conclusions.

2. Cognitive Biases in the Stock Market: Literature Review

This section presents and discusses the most commonly observed cognitive biases that occur in the decision-making process of stock exchange investors. Those mental effects are the basis of this study and are empirically tested in the analytical part of this paper.

Cognitive bias can be defined as a systematic error in the thought process that occurs when people handle and interpret the data and knowledge at their disposal, affecting their judgements and conclusions [3]. Even though the human brain is well developed and highly complex, it is nevertheless subject to limitations. Cognitive biases are often the result of the brain's attempt to automate the processing of information and make the interpretation of such information more understandable and straightforward. However, there are some situations in which these biases have a substantial impact on the decision-making process, which is the main focus of this study.

This study considers the seven most common fallacies that investors in the stock market commit in their financial decisions: confirmation bias, loss aversion, gambler's fallacy, availability cascade, hot hand fallacy, the bandwagon effect, and the Dunning–Kruger effect. These fallacies are the central focus of the paper. They are discussed below and addressed in a further part of the study in the form of a questionnaire. There also exists a number of other fallacies which were not covered in this text: mental accounting, adjustment bias, affinity bias, anchoring bias, cognitive dissonance bias, herd behaviour bias, hindsight bias, the illusion of control, incentive-caused bias, limited attention span (or bounded rationality), neglect of probability, outcome bias, overconfidence bias, over-simplification tendency, recency bias, a paradox of choice, regret bias (or endowment bias), representativeness bias, restraint bias, self-attribution bias, self-control bias, and snakebite effect. A wider list can be found in [3].

Confirmation bias—following [18], "confirmation bias is the tendency to seek out information that supports our beliefs and ignore information that contradicts them." In the stock market, it is likely that investors overlook information that is not entirely aligned with their ideas, especially when they acquire information that confirms their beliefs. However, through comprehensive research, McKenzie [19] has shown that even simply asking confirmatory questions can lead to a false sense of confirmation among investors. Investors' reactions to good and bad information depends on their attitudes; pessimistic investors undervalue good news and over-react to bad news. Conversely, optimistic investors over-react to good news and respond too optimistically to bad news [20]. This diversity in the handling of information causes deep divisions among traders and may explain particularly diverse behaviours in stock markets [21]. This cognitive bias was addressed in Q7 of the survey: "If you hear that the company which you invested in is on the verge of declaring bankruptcy, you consider selling your stocks".

Loss aversion is observed among investors who must choose between guaranteed, low-return investments and riskier, high-return investment. As Tversky and Kahneman [22] have shown in their experiments (confirmed recently in [23]), such investors are more sensitive to losses than gains. This leads to numerous perspectives on every individual choice and asset price in stock markets. Loss aversion influences the financial markets by impacting the risk attitudes of investors. It essentially occurs when investors continue to hold onto losing investments for much longer than they should and end up suffering much more significant losses than they otherwise would have. Investors do not acknowledge a loss as being such until it is realised; they can avoid mentally and emotionally coming to terms with the truth of their loss as long as they have not yet closed out the trade. This cognitive bias was addressed in Q8 of the survey: "You prefer to choose a low-return, guaranteed investments rather than a more promising investment with higher risk".

Availability cascade is recognised as a self-reinforcing cycle in which a specific idea or belief gains rapid currency in popular discourse; its rising popularity makes people more likely to believe it and to spread it further among society. This bias mainly occurs due to the combined effects of two distinct components: informational cascades and reputational cascades [24] (in the case of stock exchange investors, this would start with the verification of decision based on the findings of social media reports and announcements broadcasted by news agencies). When these two types of cascades happen simultaneously on a large scale and strengthen each other, a phenomenon is triggered whereby a piece of news or information is repeated and widely circulated. The result is an availability cascade, where investors regularly spread a specific chunk of data or a particular belief while increasing the opportunity for others to do likewise.

Accordingly, an availability cascade is a kind of positive-input framework, since the greater the number of individuals bringing attention to an idea, and the more time they spend doing so, the more others are inclined to do the same. In particular, when the rising prevalence of a specific belief is such that it reaches a specific minimum amount and passes this threshold, the attention it draws is sufficient to set off a chain response, which makes it increasingly indisputable.

Pollock et al. [25] have examined how the recency and availability of information regarding others' actions within and between different communities have a significant role to play in the allocation of attention and evaluations. They have demonstrated how widely available and recent information interacts to influence people's attention and evaluation, which is a foundation of the availability heuristic. They have also shown that market investors use the information gained from others' activities to handle the unpredictability of the market. By definition, it advances directional research on how imitative characteristics affect market activities. Their study emphasised how the public impact is conveyed through homogenised practices, social networks, and learning. Yet, they illustrated a more widespread procedure of social effects based on the core activities carried out by a group of market investors, their collaborative motion and direction, and the market roles of various actors. Their study also offers "additional insights into the cognitive biases of persistence and change in social systems that may not be apparent when a researcher is studying these systems from a purely structural point of view or considering interactions within a single community." This cognitive bias was addressed in Q10 of the survey: "You read in the news that the company you invested in experienced a high level of trading on specific days. You buy more stocks of the company in the upcoming days".

Gambler's fallacy is the expectation that a random sequence of outcomes should exhibit systematic reversals and that a long series of the same results are of low probability. It occurs very regularly, especially for inexperienced investors. Kenton [26] explained it as a phenomenon that takes place when an individual wrongly believes that a particular stochastic event is less likely to occur based on the outcome of a preceding event or series of events. This evaluation is incorrect, since past occurrences do not change the probability that certain events will occur in the future. Hon-Snir [27] describes this bias as "an (incorrect) belief in negative autocorrelation of a non-auto correlated random sequence. For example, individuals who are prone to the gambler's fallacy believe that after three red numbers appearing on the roulette wheel, a black number is 'due' that is, it is more likely to appear than a red number". The history of this behaviour goes back to 1796 according to a published paper by Wilcox [28]. It was first identified in the laboratory and under controlled circumstances in the literature on probability matching. It was observed in real life in a Las Vegas casino in 1913; for this reason, it is known as the Monte Carlo fallacy. The gambler's fallacy is caused by the representativeness heuristic (Tversky and Kahneman [29]). Examples of this fallacy include the instance where a group of experienced investors were asked a couple of questions [30] in order to identify their thinking methodology and, consequently, their decision-making approaches; there are also documents revealing that market "signals" considered by practical analysts are compatible with a number of cognitive fallacies, including gambler's fallacy. In general, the gambler's fallacy is considered to be a well-known phenomenon, both in the laboratory and in the real world, including stock market decisions and behaviour. This cognitive bias was addressed in Q9 of the survey: "The price of the company which you invested in has decreased in the last six months, thus you expect it to increase in the next six months".

Hot hand fallacy is the opposite of gambler's fallacy; it is the belief in excessive persistence rather than reversals [31]. It assumes that a long series of the same results will last longer still. It relies on the intuition accumulated from past events and the transposition of their results into future outcomes. With hot hand fallacy, though, one may think that a winning streak will continue in the future so that it can be interpreted as a false uninterrupted success sequence. Rabin and Vayanos [32] have built a theoretical model for the analysis of both hot hand and gambler's fallacies and have proven that both cognitive biases may strongly impact the behaviour of financial markets. It was also shown by way of experiment that it is gender-dependent and that female-only groups are more prone to this bias than male-only groups [33]. This cognitive bias was addressed in Q11 of the survey: "As the returns of the company you invested in have risen over the last six months, you would expect them to continue to rise over the next six months".

Bandwagon effect (or groupthink) is part of a larger group of cognitive biases or errors in thinking that influence people's judgments and decisions [34]. Cognitive biases are often designed to help people think and reason more quickly, but they often introduce miscalculations and mistakes. "If potential investors pay attention not only to their own information about a new issue, but also to whether other investors are purchasing, bandwagon effects, or informational cascades, may develop" [35]. This phenomenon is similar to the herd behaviour of agents and can be observed in the stock market decision-making process when investors try to include themselves in a large cluster of investors, so they feel relatively safe and secure regarding their investment (since everyone else is walking the same path). In reference to financial markets, the bandwagon effect can be observed when an investor who discovers that the total trading proportion for the company they invested in was more than expected would consider increasing the sum of their stock market share. This cognitive bias was addressed in Q12 of the survey: "Over the past two months, the total trading proportion for the company you invested in was more than expected, so you consider increasing the sum of your stock market holdings".

The Dunning–Kruger effect is observed when people tend to overestimate their own competency, which leads to overconfidence and underestimation of the limits of their own understanding [36]. This fallacy is especially dangerous in situations where agents assume that they have sufficient knowledge for predicting and managing their stock portfolios. It can also be more time-consuming for investors to behave in this way. In our question, we asked about the impossibility of making a profit from the market, which is based on the Dunning–Kruger curve; this stage is identified as a "valley of despair", and it occurs after the initial stage on which most investors entering the field think that they are relatively knowledgeable about every aspect of the stock market. This cognitive bias was addressed in Q13 of the survey: "Making a profit from investing in the stock market is very difficult and at some point, becomes impossible".

3. Survey Design

This research is based on a collection of individual data, such as the answers from TSE investors to a particular set of questions. The questions surveyed their attitudes towards specific cognitive fallacies in the context of financial investment. Some crucial aspects of the survey design are discussed below.

Firstly, in addition to a good sample, an effective survey design requires the **robust design of questions** that can reliably reflect people's thoughts, experiences, and public actions. Accurate random samples and high response rates may not be possible if the information obtained is subject to uncertainty or bias. The fundamental development of suitable measures includes writing suitable questions and then arranging them in a questionnaire format. The questionnaire constitutes a multi-stage process that highlights and scrutinizes many details simultaneously. The task of designing the questionnaire is not a straightforward one, since questions can be asked in various formats and to different levels of detail. Questions posed earlier in the survey can also affect how participants respond to later questions. The survey design process becomes more intricate when it involves the estimation and measuring of the degree of psychological biases. It is necessary for us to scrutinise all aspects of design, including verifying the order of questions, in order to ensure that the respondents answer each question accurately, which ultimately gives us the means for our study. All these aspects were considered when designing a questionnaire (see Appendix A) which addresses the cognitive fallacies discussed.

Secondly, one should understand the **institutional environment** of interviewees. The research was conducted on the Iranian Stock Exchange. There are a wide variety of entities active in the Iranian capital market (Figure 1). There are four exchanges, comprising two equity markets, TSE (Tehran Stock Exchange) and IFB (Iran Fara Bourse), and two commodity markets, IME (Iran Mercantile Exchange) and IRENEX (Iran Energy Exchange). They are supported by institutions such as CSDI (Central Securities Depository of Iran), and IDS (Information Dissemination Services), and associations such as IIIA, SEBA, and TSETMC (Tehran Securities Exchange Technology Management Co.). Since November 2005, the Tehran market has been in its fourth stage of development, oriented towards attracting small investors and financing companies. As of September 2021, TSE's total market capitalisation was USD 1,427,595,000 (CEIC data). As these markets play a constructive role in the allocation of resources and national capital, they are heavily relied upon for the economic development of society. TSE has a similar structure to other markets of its size and impact, which increases the transferability of results.

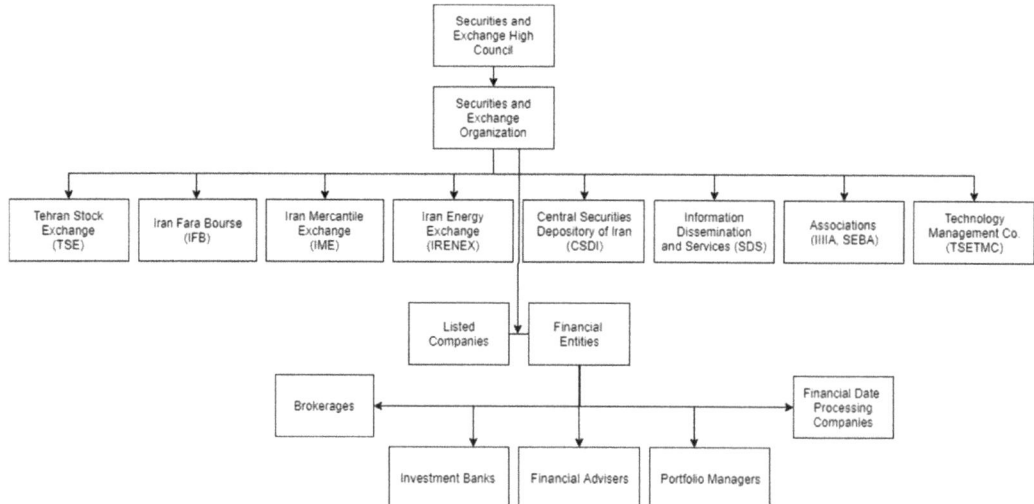

Figure 1. Iran's capital market structure.

Thirdly, the survey should mimic the **behavioural conditions** of decision-makers; this may lead to a high degree of consistency in the questionnaire and participants' natural reactions. The psychological aspect of decision-making in the stock markets cannot be overlooked, since many investors tend to bypass rationality and, at some point, rely solely on intuition. These effects, which can also be referred to as fallacies, are based on feelings, emotions, and intuition, rather than on rational considerations, and they often result in inferior financial performance [27]. Additionally, cognitive biases can be understood as "hard wired" actions [37], making us all liable to take shortcuts, oversimplify complex decisions and be overconfident in our decision-making processes. Therefore, understanding the cognitive fallacies of the stock market holders can lead to better decision being made, which is fundamental to lowering risk and improving investment returns over time. Furthermore, investors can often be misled, simply due to the order or manner in which they have received information or the circumstances under which they make a decision; therefore, being aware and mindful of these biases can ultimately lead to optimal investment judgments being made. Consequently, survey questions were kept as direct and straightforward as possible and were pilot tested for wording and transparency of meaning. They were also inspired by other questions which already had an established place in the literature.

Fourthly, the **operational details** of the survey are of high importance for the validation of results. The sample comprises 104 surveyed investors, the stock market holders in TSE (Tehran Stock Exchange). The study aims to analyse their behaviour based on the most well-known examples and cases of cognitive biases. In order to measure the tendency to exhibit these expected behaviours, we dedicated specific questions in the survey to analysing these biases. After some initial general questions regarding gender, age, experience, the preferred method of approach in the stock market and the amount of the stock market holder's investment, we asked questions that analysed the behaviour of the investor in terms of cognitive biases. We also included a question addressing investor's overall views of Iran's economic situation, which we believe can link the underlying approach of the investor—being either optimistic or pessimistic—to their individual thought process, which ultimately influences their choices around selling or buying stocks and mutual funds. Furthermore, the questions were based on the Likert scale for multiple choice answers, since this is the most widely used psychometric approach for asking the investors about their opinions or feelings about different stock market situations in a survey. Details of the survey are in the Appendix A. As will be shown in the following sections, this approach enables a valuable and reliable research sample to be obtained, in turn allowing conclusions to be drawn on the bundling of cognitive biases.

Fifthly, we present **threats to validity**. We have analysed the existing research that (1) considered cognitive biases of investors on financial markets, (2) examined seven selected biases jointly, (3) analysed individual data from investors' surveys, and (4) examined the behavioural studies for Tehran Stock Exchange. We have screened the databases of Web of Science, Scopus, IEEE Xplore, ACM Digital Library, Science Direct, and Springer Link. Additionally, we ran forward and backward searches in Google Scholar and Research Gate. We looked for multiple combinations of "stock exchange", "financial market", "Tehran Stock Exchange", "confirmation bias", "loss aversion", "availability cascade", "gambler's fallacy", "hot hand", "bandwagon effect", "Dunning–Kruger effect". We focused on papers published since 2017 in the first round and since 2010 in the second round. The usefulness of the research was assessed based on the abstract. We found many papers that dealt with a given cognitive bias separately, which was not our interest. We did not find any papers which either analysed seven cognitive biases jointly or used unsupervised learning methods. All other papers presenting interesting approaches and findings were mentioned as references.

4. Study Results

The analysis presented below was conducted in three ways. Firstly, we followed the traditional statistical approach of testing the hypothesis on equality of means in subgroups by features, also crossed with gender, age and market experience. This allowed us to gain a greater understanding of the one- and two-dimensional relationships between perceptions and the personal attributes of investors. Secondly, we ran a Principal Component Analysis (PCA) to reduce features with similar information in order to determine the strength and direction of cognitive biases. We also carried out clustering of observations using a dendrogram and k-means to separate groups of features revealing similar behaviour; the role of these factors in building clusters of features was tested using the variable importance method. Thirdly, we applied clustering of features using a dendrogram and k-means to separate groups of investors revealing similar behaviour; we put the investors' profiles showing similar behavioural patterns into the following subgroups: age, invested amount, market experience and market perception. All computations and graphics were conducted using R software.

4.1. Hypothesis Testing

The data collected show that in most cases, the outputs precisely matched expectations. In some instances, the findings from the data revealed truths that could not be seen directly. Some cases were surprising and went beyond any logical explanation. We observed that the dataset is heterogeneous, and simple generalisation could distort the results. The study avoids giving universal attributes to the whole sample of investor respondents. Instead, significant biases in profiled groups were measured in selected characteristics such as gender, age, investment amount, and years of experience on the stock market. Not all attributes are significant in all cases. We used a t-test for equality of means. For pair comparisons, we applied the standard version of the test, while for multiple comparisons, we used the Bonferroni correction.

Firstly, we **compared the results in groups by gender** by testing the differences in biases between male and female investors (Table 1). The only meaningful differences in biases observed between the two genders were in the cases of gambler's fallacy and availability heuristics (where the p-value of the t-test for equality of group means is below the significance threshold of 0.05). We surveyed the investors about the availability cascade based on the information from the news. It was revealed that women are more likely to make a decision based on a mental shortcut that relies on immediate examples (such as a news report that mentions a high level of trading on specific days for the company they invested in), while men are less likely to fall into this bias. However, even if the aforementioned two effects were observed, it was found that gender does not play a role in clustering or building investors' profiles.

Table 1. Fallacies based on gender.

	Female Mean	Male Mean	t Statistics	p-Value
Confirmation	4.133	3.721	0.867	0.364
Loss aversion	3.594	3.131	−0.992	0.341
Gambler's	3.647	3.406	−8.435	0.000 *
Availability	3.112	2.861	−5.967	0.000 *
Hot hand's	3.058	3.091	−0.481	0.440
Bandwagon	3.295	2.898	1.065	0.329
Dunning-Kruger	3.459	3.282	−3.077	0.054

Second, we determined **which bias is the strongest**. A notable finding was that the most common fallacy for both genders was confirmation bias. Many investors were not keen to verify the information gained prior to action and considered immediate action, even if said information could turn out to be false. The investors fell into availability bias in the same way. Both availability and confirmation bias serve as evidence that the information to which investors have been exposed greatly affects the way they respond in the stock market (even though all investors need reliable information to continue to make stable investments). Conversely, it demonstrates how dangerous it is to surround investors with targeted information, which may lead to designed and planned actions which favour certain agencies and companies. The existence of these biases means that news, advertisements, and the media all have a considerable influence on the way investors make decisions.

Third, we explicitly asked investors about their **dedicated approaches to succeeding in TSE** in order to better understand these methods and confirm these patterns in the direct answers to the question: "Which approach do you use in your stock analysis?". It is reasonable to expect that results would differ from those found in the experiments we had already conducted. The possible choices were as follows: Technical, Fundamental, News, Consultation, Self-Strategy and No Strategy; more than one choice was allowed. The results are presented in Figure 2. The two most commonly chosen methods were Consultation and Technical analysis, each of these being applied by more than 40% of investors of both genders. Our results can be compared with the analysis conducted by Davis [38], who studied the role of the mass media in investor relations and found there to be a slow decline in the importance of financial news media in the investment process. However, he argued that financial news nevertheless plays a significant role in trading in the city and can, at times, still have a powerful impact on investment patterns. It can also be observed from Figure 2 that News was, for men, a more popular method than fundamental analysis, but equally as popular as No Strategy. Here, we reached similar results, albeit not for different periods (differing from [38], which compares the effects of mass media over time); however, we reached the conclusion that men are more likely to rely on news than women.

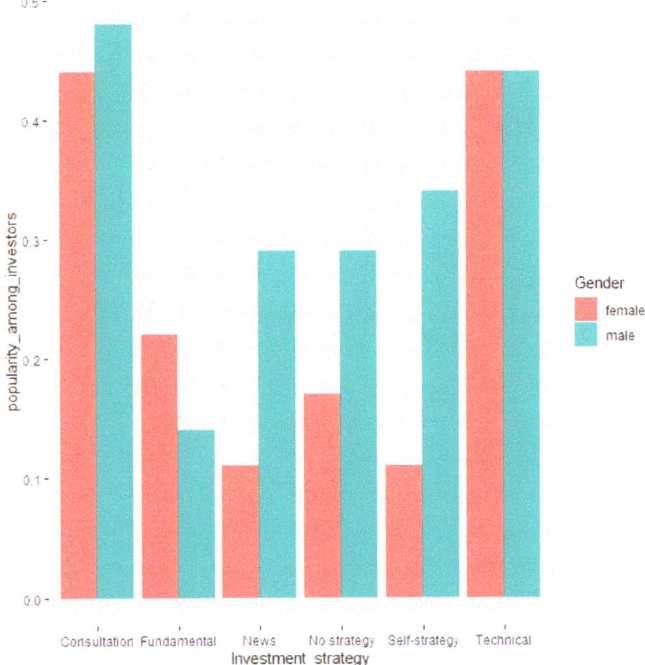

Figure 2. Adopted investment approaches on TSE based on gender.

Fourth, we analysed questionnaires with regard to the **age of investors**. For better segmentation, we divided the investors into three age groups (Table 2). People in the age group ">45" are less likely to fall into confirmation bias than the two younger groups. Most of the groups of investors that appear to commit confirmation bias fall into the 36–45 age group. Additionally, it is noticeable that loss aversion is much higher in this age group (36–45) than in other age groups. The loss aversion question was designed to measure whether the investors prefer lower- risk investments to higher–risk ones. It emerged that, as we had expected, the youngest groups favour riskier investments. Even though the age group ">45" is quite close to the youngest, the difference between them is still significant.

Table 2. Fallacies based on age.

	Age				
	<35	36–45	>45	Statistics	p-Value
Confirmation	3.738 [a]	4.006 [a]	3.478 [b]	22.725	0.001 *
Loss aversion	2.965 [a]	3.604 [b]	2.996 [c]	26.905	0.000 *
Gambler's	3.173	3.524	3.939	6.777	0.170
Availability	2.714	3.024	3.109	2.112	0.485
Hot hand's	2.690 [a]	3.237 [b]	3.729 [b]	39.264	0.000 *
Bandwagon	2.849	2.975	3.214	6.508	0.163
Dunning-Kruger	3.213	3.288	3.591	4.414	0.283

Note: letters in superscripts indicate significantly different groups.

There can also be observed significant differences in the hot hand fallacy between age groups. As can be recalled from the definition, both hot hand and gambler's fallacies involve the conclusion of future outcomes based on past events. In theory, it is reasonable to assume that these two phenomena will occur in parallel. If a person feels that the past values of their assets will affect future values, then their thought process would align with both hot hand and gambler's fallacies. However, we observed that a subtle difference between these two biases means that they may not necessarily occur together. In the case of the hot hand fallacy, there is no change of direction. It assumes a consistent series of outcomes in the future; if a company's returns have risen over the past two months, then this trend will continue into the future without any change. On the other hand, the gambler's fallacy states that if returns have decreased over the past two months, they are bound to increase in the future. Thus, the latter fallacy is based on a notable shift in circumstances. We assumed the hypothesis that both the gambler's and hot hand fallacies have the same mean, and they are equally preferred. However, based on the data, we rejected the null hypothesis, and we can assert that investors favoured consistency in their stock returns (hot hand) over changes to them (gambler's) (Table 3).

Table 3. Comparing gambler's fallacy and hot hand fallacy.

Gambler's	Hot Hand's	Statistics	p-Value
3.085	3.446	49.000	0.000

Fifth, an important consideration is that we have used **positive framing** in asking both questions, that is, we have asked them in such a manner that the outcomes lean towards a better situation; if it is increasing, then it will continue to grow (hot hand), and if it is decreasing, then it is due to increase (gambler's). For both biases, we observed some optimistic responses since most investors agreed with them. In another question, we asked investors to give their opinions regarding Iran's economy, that is, whether or not it is growing. The majority of investors either strongly disagreed (48.3%) or disagreed (32.2%), which in total is 80.5%. This highlights the fact that the stock market is not the economy, and there could well be a considerable disconnection between these two. The paper "Economic Forces and the Stock Market" [39] shows it is not always the case that macroeconomic variables systematically and directly affect stock market returns. To shed more light on the situation in Iran and in recent times, Goodman's [40] article in New York Times "Iran's Economy Is Bleak. Its Stock Market Is Soaring" justifies these findings and has been correlated with aspects of geopolitics such as U.S sanctions and macroeconomics.

Sixth, we have analysed **fallacies with regard to investors' experience** on the stock market. The first bias that is noticeable in Table 4 is the Dunning–Kruger effect. Investors who are more experienced in the TSE are more likely to agree with our statement in the survey about the obstacles to make a profit in the stock market. There was more agreement among more experienced investors than those in the other two groups with fewer years of experience. As investors become more acquainted with the ups and downs of the stock market, they would think and behave differently with regard to making a profit in the long term.

Table 4. Fallacies based on years of experience on the stock market.

	Years of Experience on the Stock Market					
	<3	3–5	5–10	>10	Statistics	p-Value
Confirmation	4.065	3.603	3.469	3.550	7.124	0.201
Loss aversion	3.417 [a]	2.790 [b]	3.394 [ab]	3.090 [ab]	15.744	0.025 *
Gambler's	3.394	3.502	3.380	3.613	10.107	0.087
Availability	2.910 [a]	2.858 [a]	2.928 [b]	2.932 [ab]	12.524	0.047 *
Hot hand's	2.932	3.109	3.239	3.459	11.334	0.072
Bandwagon	2.936 [a]	3.147 [a]	2.622 [b]	3.005 [a]	16.226	0.020 *
Dunning-Kruger	3.228 [ab]	3.035 [a]	3.774 [ab]	3.776 [b]	11.823	0.044 *

Note: letters in superscripts indicate significantly different groups.

Similarly, in the case of the bandwagon effect, investors with greater experience (the 5–10 years group) are more immune to this bias than those in other groups. Additionally, loss aversion was more prevalent in groups with more experience, where investors preferred low returns and steady profits over riskier and higher returns. As expected, the confirmation bias among less experienced investors (especially those with less than three years of experience) is higher than among more experienced ones.

4.2. Direction and Strength of Biases

The previous section revealed the patters of biases based on individual characteristics such as gender, age, and experience, but examined them separately. The analysis below goes further by discussing the behaviour of fallacies in groups (clusters). By grouping the biases together and comparing them with each other, one can measure which biases are crucial to explaining the variability within our data. For this purpose, we first implemented the Principal Component Analysis (PCA) method to reduce the dimensions of our independent variables and to then extract the variables that contribute the most to the dispersion of our individual investors. This analysis is oriented towards discovering whether any cognitive biases or investors' features overlap in terms of informational content. PCA analysis, based on eigenvectors, finds the synthetic variables—the axes of highest variability of data. The first and second eigenvectors are typically analysed and plotted, while their explanatory power results from the percentage of variance explained. The contribution of the variable to the following principal components is to make a ranking of their importance. The second method applied here, clustering of observations, allows for explicit groups of similar factors to be obtained. Unsupervised learning algorithms, such as k-means, require setting a priori the number of clusters; this parameter is crucial for the final grouping. There are many criteria for selecting the most appropriate number of clusters [41], while their recommendations are often very diverse, as shown in practice. Each dataset requires individual treatment due to differing degrees of clusterability. An efficient approach is to inspect the hierarchical clustering, for which the dendrogram presents all available partitioning (from separation of all observations into individual [bottom] clusters called singletons to collection of all data into a single [top] cluster). Vertical lines illustrate the number of clusters at a given height (on the y axis) and support the clustering decision with regard to clusterability. To assure the robustness of division into groups, the dendrogram clusters are compared with k-means clusters. The following two measures of quality were applied: silhouette statistic, which examines whether the centroids of an object's own cluster are closer than centroids of the second-closest cluster (fine partitioning if all individual silhouette values are non-negative); and variable importance, which checks for each variable the degree to which partitioning changes when the examined variable is shuffled (a variable is important when, due to mixing of its values, the misclassification rate on the x-axis is high).

As a result, explanatory variables in the first two principal components of PCA cumulatively account for 34% of the variation in our data set (Table 5). This result proves that reducing dimensions in this dataset is a challenging, due to a relatively low information overlap among analysed variables.

Table 5. Principal components eigenvalues.

	Eigenvalue	Percentage of Variance	Cumulative Percentage of Variance
comp 1	2.3832053	19.860044	19.86004
comp 2	1.7042055	14.201712	34.06176

In this two-dimensional PCA, the hot hand fallacy, together with availability and confirmation, seem to be the variables that explain the most variance. At the same time, the amount of investment is the least important variable (see Figure 3). Those factors also had a higher range of variation among investors, which therefore explains the greater degree of dispersion observed than with the other biases and characteristics. With regard to gender, even if the different biases discussed tend to be more apparent in female subgroups, one can see that the overall variation in responses in the dataset did not have much to do with gender. Much more influential than gender is the age of investors and amount of experience in the financial market. It must be said that answers for the questions on Dunning-Kruger, gender, investment, and Iran's economy were very similar across different investors in the context of a two-dimensional PCA.

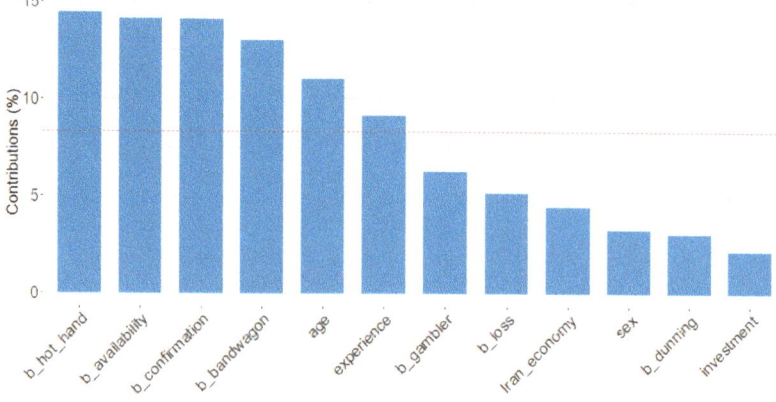

Figure 3. Contribution of variables in PCA.

Two dimensional-visualisation of PCA (Figure 4) can help identify the strength and direction of biases and other variables so that they can be grouped. Positively related variables are grouped together, while negatively related variables are positioned on the opposite sides of the plot origin in opposing quadrants. The distance between variables and the origin determines the quality of the variables on the factor map. Variables that are far away from the origin are well represented on the factor map. Thus, one can conclude that the perception of Iran's economy is negatively correlated with most factors. The reaction for the bandwagon effect and availability cascade is very similar.

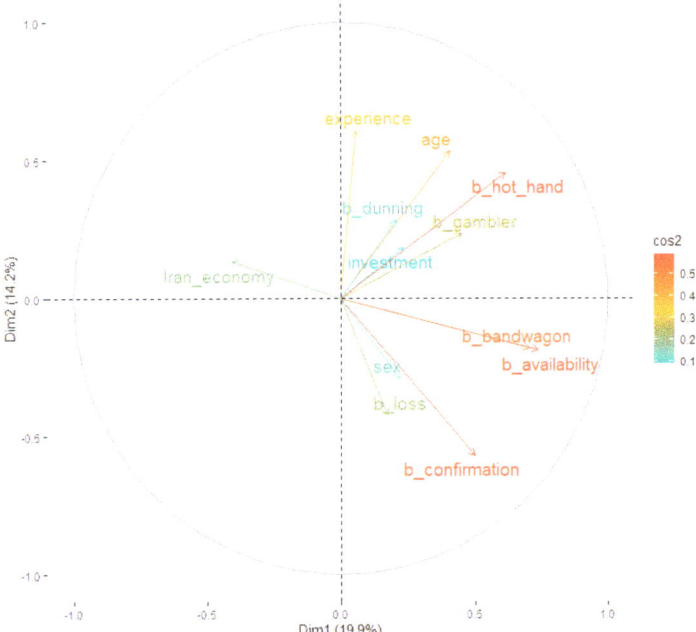

Figure 4. Quality and direction of representation for variables.

As well as PCA dimensions reductions, individual data can be clustered with k-means and visualised in 2D space (Figure 5). With an optimal number of clusters k = 3 selected using the dendrogram approach, one can check the groupings and separation of variables. K-means clustering with Euclidean distance showed that confirmation bias and investment amount form one group; gender, age and assessment of Iran's economy form the second group; and the remaining biases (availability, bandwagon, loss aversion, hot-hand, Dunning–Kruger and gambler's), together with experience, form the third group. This partitioning is stable both in k-means and in the dendrogram, while the silhouette statistic proves its high quality. Feature Importance, a method for diagnosing the impact of a given variable on cluster formation, plays a role similar to significance in parametric statistics. One can see that the most influential factor for partitioning is loss aversion bias, followed by experience and gambler's bias. The three least important factors are gender, age, and perception of Iran's economy, and they build their own cluster. The conclusion is that diversification of investors likely results mostly from experience and somehow inherited risk aversion, while gender and age are not decisive factors.

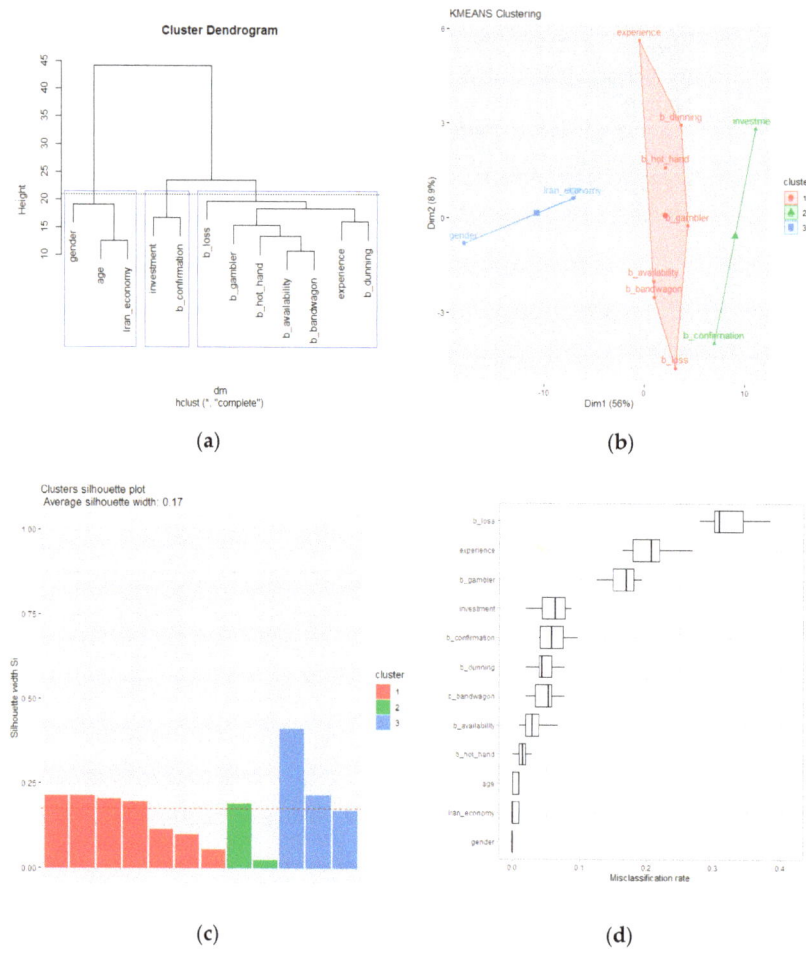

Figure 5. Clustering of variables: (**a**) dendrogram in hierarchical clustering; (**b**) PCA-reduced dimensions of k-means clustering; (**c**) silhouette statistic; (**d**) feature importance. Note: K-means output (**b**) was PCA-reduced for 2D visualisation purposes; labels of x and y axes show the variance around the first and second principal components. Feature importance (**d**) is measured through misclassification rate; the higher the misclassification rate, the more important given feature.

4.3. Individual Investors' Profiles

The dataset from the survey is a two-dimensional table with observations (people) and their features. Previous analysis has focused on clustering of observations to obtain groups of features. The following approach is the opposite; it involves clustering of features to obtain groups of observations that constitute investors' profiles. The data were numeric; thus, the k-means algorithm is sufficient, and extensions as k-modes for qualitative data or k-prototypes for mixed data are unnecessary. We also considered using Self-Organising Maps to detect clusters [42], but the results were not straightforward in interpretation. We ran pre- and post- clustering diagnostics to validate the results. In the pre-clustering analysis, we considered an optimal number of clusters using the silhouette statistic, the gap statistic, inertia and a dendrogram. In the post-clustering analysis, we examined the significance of differences in group means using a pairwise *t*-test with the Bonferroni *p*-value correction, using tabular and visual inspection tools. We also calculated the ratio of average values inside and outside the cluster, which shows whether values within the cluster are significantly higher or lower than those in the rest of the sample.

In the pre-clustering phase, the silhouette statistic recommended two clusters only, the gap statistic recommended a single cluster, inertia advised 14 clusters, while the dendrogram separated four visible groups. As in the previous section, we used results from the dendrogram, which performed the best with this dataset regarding sample size and inherited clusterability. A number of clusters are visible as vertical groupings (Figure 6). Distinctive division of observations into four clusters was possible at the height of ca. 8. The second feasible partitioning at height = 6.5 generated nine groups, which for 104 observations was too many. Partitioning below height = 6 are almost random and drive the system to singletons.

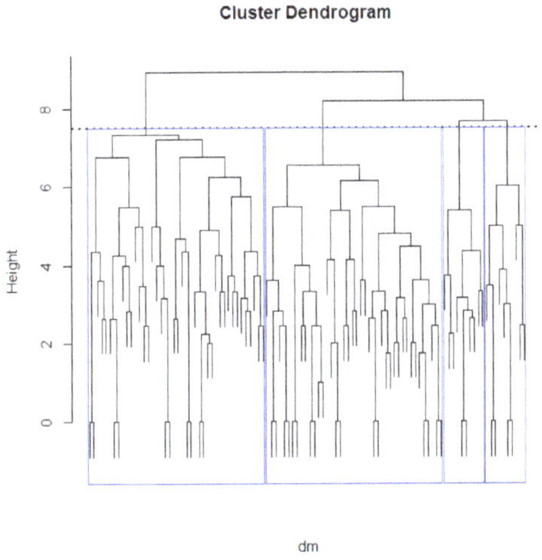

Figure 6. Hierarchical clustering with the dendrogram.

In the post-clustering phase, each of the four obtained clusters conducted for each of the 12 variables involved a test for equality of means inside and outside the cluster. We examined the significance of the differences between inside- and outside-cluster values to determine the significant and important disparities only (Table 6). This helped us to find the significant drivers of each cluster and to validate the quality of partitioning.

Table 6. Predominant investors' profiles.

	Cluster_1	Cluster_2	Cluster_3	Cluster_4
experience	0.675	0.797	0.736	1.902
age	0.000	0.000	0.706	1.414
gender	0.000	0.000	0.000	0.000
investment	1.129	0.552	1.192	1.106
Iran_economy	0.793	0.000	0.000	0.000
b_confirmation	1.206	0.000	0.000	0.845
b_loss	1.490	1.229	0.597	0.000
b_gambler	1.259	0.831	0.848	0.000
b_availability	1.363	0.845	0.762	0.000
b_hot_hand	1.304	0.675	0.839	1.200
b_bandwagon	1.438	0.000	0.758	0.000
b_dunning	0.000	0.000	0.000	1.170

Note: Non-zero values were reported in cases showing significant differences between the cluster and the rest of the observations. Values in tables are a ratio of average values within the cluster to average values outside the cluster.

The four derived clusters, which constitute the predominant investors' profiles, can be characterised as follows (Table 6) (values in brackets are ratios of values within the cluster to those outside the cluster):

Cluster 4: Experienced, older investors (age and experience are higher than average) who invested more than average (1.11). These investors are less liable to fall into confirmation bias (0.85); instead, they look for reliable information prior to making decisions. They also reveal higher instances of both hot hand bias (1.2) (showing an optimistic attitude in terms of sticking with trends) and Dunning–Kruger bias (1.17) (betraying realistic awareness of the difficulty of making a profit on the stock exchange at certain times).

Cluster 1: Less experienced investors who invested large amounts (1.13) and are pessimistic about stock trends (0.79). These investors are vulnerable to all analysed biases except for Dunning–Kruger. However, they are most susceptible to loss aversion bias (1.49)– among all cluster groups, they are the group most concerned with not wanting to risk too much.

Cluster 2: Less experienced investors (experience 0.797) who invested only a small amount (investment 0.55). They are afraid of loss (loss bias 1.23) and are risk-averse, but are vulnerable to gambler's (0.83), hot hand (0.67), and availability cascade (0.85). This means that they are less sensitive to information stimuli and do not tend to make predictions based on their emotions.

Cluster 3: Less experienced investors (experience 0.736) who invested a large amount (investment 1.19) and are relatively young (0.706). They behave similarly to investors from cluster 2, with two differences: they are much less vulnerable to both loss aversion bias (0.597), which makes them risk-lovers, and much less susceptible to bandwagon bias (0.758). One can conclude that this group of young investors are non-emotional and love risk.

This summary demonstrates that risk-seeking is a predominant characteristic among young investors. A pessimistic attitude to general market trends makes investors vulnerable to all possible biases. There is no division by gender—females exhibit the same behaviour as males. Among inexperienced groups of investors (clusters 1, 2, 3), two contradictory biases can be seen to occur in parallel; gambler's and hot hand biases are jointly declared (either strongly or weakly). This may be interpreted as irrationality on the part of investors or their poor understanding of market trends and forecasting methods. The overall conclusion is that vulnerability of investors to various biases is a complex phenomenon. This study reveals the existence of (at least) four factors significant for cognitive biases: experience, age, the value of the investment, and market perception. Interestingly, a greater level of experience in the stock market means a more limited number of biases that may be manifested; however, by no means are they eliminated entirely.

5. Discussion of Results

From a methodological perspective, this study encountered a few challenges in data analysis, the most significant one being a moderate sample size. Even if datasets of more than 100 observations are not considered a small sample, they require careful treatment and validation to assure stability and robustness of results. We applied robust statistical solutions, such as a t-test based on t-Student distribution, which is dedicated to moderate samples. In the clustering procedure, we considered a few alternative methods. The multitude of available clustering criteria results from their various characteristics and usefulness addressing a diverse range of problems; thus, deciding what to use requires research expertise and robustness checks. The examined dataset was only clusterable to a moderate degree, and a trial to extract a large number of groups failed due to instability. The comprehensive analysis of possible groupings allowed robust partitioning, with significantly different values of variables. ANOVA and pairwise tests of differences in means among cluster groups revealed significantly diverse characteristics among obtained investors' profiles. For validity checking, we ran alternative partitioning (not reported in detail); the results were similar, statistically weaker, and led to satisfying conclusions. In the validation procedure, we also considered bootstrapping to improve the statistical features of the sample; however, the results did not alter significantly, which confirms the robustness of outputs from pure data.

From a conceptual perspective, this approach is innovative in a number of ways. Firstly, the cognitive biases were considered jointly, not separately; secondly, the problem was approached directly from individual survey data, not indirectly from market data; thirdly, unsupervised learning methods such as clustering and PCA were applied (rather than time-series, as has been used in the majority of studies). This innovative approach also presents methodological challenges in designing survey questionnaires and analytical paths. The lack of other similar studies using these methods limits the possibility of comparison with existing state-of-the-art. On the other hand, it opens the door for further scientific discussion on profiling of investors and understanding how their attitudes and perceptions can influence the market in the form of collective, non-rational behaviour.

From an empirical perspective, we believe that the obtained profiles of investors present an interesting cross section of competencies, behaviour, rationality, and cognitive biases. Moreover, the size of groups suggests that TSE investors are widely diversified and that these groups have a significant impact on the financial market. Going forward, a challenge for the scientific community will be to validate these results by comparing them with studies on other markets or on the same market in the following years. This may help understand the unexplainable patterns in financial markets and more accurately predict potential financial crises.

6. Limitations and Future Directions

The presented study is the first trial evident in the international literature to bundle investors' cognitive biases. However, the conclusions from this research are far from being generalised to all world financial markets. The local specificity of Iranian investors has some evident similarities to other markets, but without a doubt, it also has significant differences due to cultural and economic diversified systems. Thus, the main limitation of this study is the narrow possibility to classify investors universally on the other markets by using classes and categories from this analysis.

The major limitation of this study is also a future direction for further research. The impossibility of using this classification of investors on the other markets opens the door for similar analyses in different countries. This comparative stream of research would be important because of at least two reasons. Firstly, international studies on cognitive biases among investors could present how much the Iranian financial market is similar or different to other markets. Understanding the homogeneities and heterogeneities of investors' profiles are essential in designing institutions and mechanisms for financial markets. Secondly, a study for the single market cannot test the correlation between the strength of cognitive biases and financial crises. The broader understanding of differences between investors, as well as of the degree of participation in the market of given groups (with specific biases), can be an important factor in explaining non-rational behaviours and other non-typical phenomena. The research design developed in this paper can be used universally.

7. Conclusions

In this research, we aimed to reveal the various cognitive biases present among investors in the Tehran Stock Exchange (TSE), taking into account such factors as age, gender, and experience in order to reveal the underlying reasons for investors' behaviour in the stock market. We measured the most common cognitive fallacies by asking 104 investors to fill out the survey in which each question was related to a different cognitive bias. We observed that different groups of investors—these groups being defined by their attributes—react differently in their decision-making processes towards achieving success in their stock market journeys. Our hypothesis that cognitive biases occur to varying degrees between groups defined by age, experience and money invested is true. However, we obtained clear evidence that gender does not have an impact on cognitive biases and choices. Therefore, one cannot generalise when forming opinions and making judgements without taking into account the personal characteristics of investors.

The survey data were analysed with the use of the unsupervised learning methods as PCA and k-means clustering. We analysed clusters of features and clusters of individual observations. We found similarities in behaviour among analysed personal characteristics and biases; level of experience is a significant factor in almost all cognitive biases, while the amount invested is related to confirmation bias. When clustering, the strongest drivers of partitions were loss aversion, experience, and gambler's bias, while the weakest were gender, perception of the market situation and age. However, they were never observed to act individually; thus, the final investor's profile depends on the specific bundle of features. In clusters of individual values, we applied a t-test to examine whether within-cluster values differed significantly from other values. We found out that the relationships between some factors are not linear but multi-dependent and exogenous. We discovered that even those biases that tend to be similar in theory (gambler's fallacy and hot hand fallacy in this case of this study) do not necessarily behave and influence the investors in the same way. One can conclude that cognitive biases occur jointly; investors exhibit similar behaviours in terms of confirmation, availability, loss and bandwagon biases, which is partly supported by their level of experience and their perception of the overall situation.

This study raises a few issues. Firstly, cognitive biases in behavioural finance appear jointly and depend on the personal characteristics of investors. Secondly, investors' profiles are influenced by age, stock market experience and perception of market trends, but not by gender. Thirdly, inexperienced investors who are pessimistic about market developments and have invested a great amount are the group most vulnerable to almost all analysed biases. Fourthly, young investors who are more optimistic about general trends are, for the most part, less susceptible to all biases. Fifth, older and experienced investors are not affected by loss aversion bias, gambler's fallacy, availability cascade bias or bandwagon bias. Sixth, one can put together an investor's profile using unsupervised learning methods, such as k-means, feature importance and PCA.

This study opens the door for further analysis, specifically around joint cognitive biases which are known in the literature. It proves that making generalisations about investors' behaviour without referring to their characteristics blurs the picture of real transmission channels of perceptions into decisions on the financial market. It also demonstrates that unsupervised learning methods serve as useful analytical approaches, even in the case of cognitive science questionnaires.

Despite a relatively simple survey being used, the use of new data science methods enabled consistent and interpretable results to be gained and the clustering of cognitive biases to be identified. Repeating this type of research across different markets would allow certain differences in behaviour resulting from these markets' cultural and institutional differences to be identified. Perhaps the grouping of cognitive errors in given groups of investors is a common phenomenon, but the characteristics of the market behaviour are determined by the proportions in which these errors occur.

Author Contributions: Conceptualization, A.O. and M.S.P.; methodology, T.K., A.O. and M.S.P.; software, A.O., M.S.P. and T.K.; validation, T.K.; formal analysis, T.K.; investigation, A.O. and M.S.P.; resources, A.O. and M.S.P.; data curation, A.O. and M.S.P.; writing—original draft preparation, A.O. and M.S.P.; writing—review and editing, T.K.; visualisation, A.O., M.S.P. and T.K.; supervision, T.K. All authors have read and agreed to the published version of the manuscript.

Funding: This research received no external funding. The APC was funded by University of Warsaw, Poland.

Institutional Review Board Statement: Not applicable.

Informed Consent Statement: Informed consent was obtained from all subjects involved in the study.

Data Availability Statement: Survey data supporting reported results can be found at https://github.com/tomvar/Cognitive_Biases_on_the_Iran_Stock_Exchange, accessed on 13 November 2021. They can be accessed and used without any restrictions.

Conflicts of Interest: The authors declare no conflict of interest.

Appendix A
Design of survey questions

Q1	What is your gender?	Female (1) Male (0)	
Q2	Which approach do you use in your stock analysis?	Technical (A) Fundamental (B) News (C) Consultation (D) Self-Strategy (E) No Strategy (F)	
Q3	How many years of experience do you have in TSE?	<1 (1) [1,3) (2) [3,5) (3) [5,10) (4) +10 (5)	
Q4	Which age group do you belong to?	20–35 years (1) 36–45 years (2) 46–60 years (3) 61–70 years (4) 70+ years (5)	
Q5	How much money have you invested in stocks? (In million of Rial)	<200 (1) [200–500) (2) [500–800) (3) [800–1000) (4) >=1000 (5)	
Q6	Iran's economy is growing rapidly.	Strongly disagree (1) Disagree (2) Neutral (3) Agree (4) Strongly agree (5)	Assessment of general market tendency
Q7	If you hear that the company which you invested in is on the verge of declaring bankruptcy, you consider selling your stocks.		Confirmation Bias
Q8	You prefer to choose a low-return, guaranteed investment rather than a more promising, higher-risk investment.		Loss aversion
Q9	The price of the company which you invested in has decreased in the last six months, thus you expect it to increase in the next six months.		Gambler's fallacy
Q10	You read in the news that the company you invested in has experienced a high level of trading on specific days. You buy more stocks of the company in the upcoming days.		Availability Cascade
Q11	Since the returns of the company you invested in have risen over the last six months, you would expect them to continue rising over the next six months.		Hot hand fallacy
Q12	Over the past two months, the total trading proportion for the company you invested in was more than expected, so you consider increasing the sum of your stock market holdings.		Bandwagon effect
Q13	Making a profit from investing in the stock market is very difficult and at some point becomes impossible.		Dunning–Kruger Effect

References

1. Keynes, J.M. The General Theory of Employment. In *Interest and Money*; Harcourt Brace and Co.: New York, NY, USA, 1936.
2. Akerlof, G.A.; Shiller, R.J. *Animal Spirits: How Human Psy-Chology Drives the Economy, and Why It Matters for Global Capital-Ism*; Princeton University Press: Princeton, NJ, USA, 2009.
3. Blawatt, K.R. Appendix A: List of Cognitive Biases. In *Marconomics*; Emerald Group Publishing Limited: Bingley, UK, 2016; pp. 325–336.
4. Henrich, J. Does Culture Matter in Economic Behavior? Ultimatum Game Bargaining among the Machiguenga of the Peruvian Amazon. *Am. Econ. Rev.* **2000**, *90*, 973–979. [CrossRef]
5. Weber, E.U.; Hsee, C. Cross-cultural differences in risk perception, but cross-cultural similarities in attitudes towards perceived risk. *Manag. Sci.* **1998**, *44*, 1205–1217. [CrossRef]
6. Araghi, M.; Esmaeili, B. Overreaction and representativeness heuristic in initial public offering: Evidence from Tehran Stock Exchange. *Manag. Sci. Lett.* **2014**, *4*, 287–294.
7. Khoshsirat, M.; Salari, M. a study on behavioral finance in Tehran stock exchange: Examination of herd formation. *Eur. J. Econ. Financ. Adm. Sci.* **2011**, *32*, 168–183.
8. Saadatzadeh, H.B.; Abdi, R.; Mohammadzadeh, S.H.; Narimani, M. The role of cognitive bias in the behavior of investors (teachers) in the stock market. *J. Sch. Psychol.* **2021**, *10*, 44–66.
9. Moradi, M.; Mostafaei, Z.; Meshki, M. A study on investors' personality characteristics and behavioral biases: Conservatism bias and availability bias in the Tehran Stock Exchange. *Manag. Sci. Lett.* **2013**, *3*, 1191–1196. [CrossRef]
10. Heybati, F.; Roodposhti, F.R.; Moosavi, S.R. Behavioral approach to portfolio selection: The case of Tehran Stock Exchange as emerging market. *Afr. J. Bus. Manag.* **2011**, *5*, 7593–7602.
11. Abdorrahimian, M.H.; Torabi, T.; Sadeghisharif, S.J.; Darabi, R. Behavioral Decision Making Pattern for Individual Investors in Tehran Stock Exchange. *J. Invest. Knowl.* **2018**, *7*, 113–130.
12. Jamshidi, N.; Ghalibaf, A.H. Dynamics of the Behavior of Individual Investors in Tehran Stock Exchange. *J. Financ. Manag. Perspect.* **2019**, *9*, 101–120.
13. Mousavi, S.M.; Aghababaei, M.E. The effect of Overconfidence on Investors Behaviors: Evidences from Tehran Stock Exchange. *Financ. Knowl. Secur. Anal.* **2017**, *10*, 25–37.
14. Osoolian, M.; Hasannejad, M.; Sadeghi Sharif, S.J.; Hamzenejadi, Y. Intuitive Thinking, Behavioral Biases and Performance of Professional Investors in Tehran Stock Exchange. *Financ. Res. J.* **2021**, *23*, 17–39.
15. Shams, M.F.; Kordlouie, H.; Dezfuli, H.K. The Effect of Mental Accounting on Sales Decisions of Stockholders in Tehran Stock Exchange. *World Appl. Sci. J.* **2012**, *20*, 842–847.
16. Klein, A. A direct test of the cognitive bias theory of share price reversals. *J. Account. Econ.* **1990**, *13*, 155–166. [CrossRef]
17. Metwally, A.H.; Darwish, O. Evidence of the overconfidence bias in the Egyptian stock market in different market states. *Int. J. Bus. Econ. Dev.* **2015**, *3*, 3.
18. Lazaroff, P. How Investors Suffer from Confirmation Bias. 2016. Available online: https://www.forbes.com/sites/peterlazaroff/2016/09/28/confirmation-bias/jfb9d17944b7d2 (accessed on 17 April 2018).
19. McKenzie, C.R.M. Increased sensitivity to differentially diagnostic answers using familiar materials: Implications for confirmation bias. *Mem. Cogn.* **2006**, *34*, 577–588. [CrossRef]
20. Duong, C.; Pescetto, G.; Santamaria, D. How value–glamour investors use financial information: UK. evidence of investors' confirmation bias. *Eur. J. Financ.* **2014**, *20*, 524–549. [CrossRef]
21. Cafferata, A.; Tramontana, F. A financial market model with confirmation bias. *Struct. Chang. Econ. Dyn.* **2019**, *51*, 252–259. [CrossRef]
22. Tversky, A.; Kahneman, D. Advances in Prospect Theory: Cumulative Representation of Uncertainty. *Choices Values Fram.* **2000**, *5*, 44–66. [CrossRef]
23. Yang, L. Loss Aversion in Financial Markets. *J. Mech. Inst. Des.* **2019**, *4*, 119–137. [CrossRef]
24. Kuran, T.; Sunstein, C.R. Availability cascades and risk regulation. *Stanf. Law Rev.* **1998**, *51*, 683. [CrossRef]
25. Pollock, T.G.; Violina, P.R.; Patrick, G. Maggitti, Market watch: Information and availability cascades among the media and investors in the US IPO market, Academy of Management: Briarcliff Manor, NJ, USA. *Acad. Manag. J. AMJ* **2008**, *51*, 335–358, ZDB-ID 221859-8.
26. Kenton, W. Investopedia. Available online: https://www.investopedia.com/terms/g/gamblersfallacy.asp (accessed on 2 February 2021).
27. Hon-Snir, S.; Kudryavtsev, A.; Cohen, G. Stock Market Investors: Who Is More Rational, and Who Relies on Intuition? *Int. J. Econ. Financ. Arch.* **2009**, *4*, 5.
28. Wilcox, J.W. The gambler's ruin approach to business risk. *Sloan Manag. Rev.* **1976**, *18*, 33.
29. Tversky, A.; Kahneman, D. Belief in the law of small numbers. *Psychol. Bull.* **1971**, *76*, 105. [CrossRef]
30. Zielonka, P. Technical analysis as the representation of typical cognitive biases. *Int. Rev. Financ. Anal.* **2004**, *13*, 217–225. [CrossRef]
31. Gilovich, T.; Vallone, R.; Tversky, A. The hot hand in basketball: On the misperception of random sequences. *Cogn. Psychol.* **1985**, *17*, 295–314. [CrossRef]
32. Rabin, M.; Vayanos, D. The gambler's and hot-hand fallacies: Theory and applications. *Rev. Econ. Stud.* **2010**, *77*, 730–778. [CrossRef]

33. Stöckl, T.; Huber, J.; Kirchler, M.; Lindner, F. Hot hand and gambler's fallacy in teams: Evidence from investment experiments. *J. Econ. Behav. Organ.* **2015**, *117*, 327–339. [CrossRef]
34. Leibenstein, H. Bandwagon, snob, and Veblen effects in the theory of consumers' demand. *Q. J. Econ.* **1950**, *64*, 183–207. [CrossRef]
35. Welch, M. Collaboration: Staying on the bandwagon. *J. Teach. Educ.* **1998**, *49*, 26–37. [CrossRef]
36. Kruger, J.; Dunning, D. Unskilled and unaware of it: How difficulties in recognising one's own incompetence lead to inflated self-assessments. *J. Personal. Soc. Psychol.* **1999**, *77*, 1121. [CrossRef]
37. Douglas, D. Rod Bush and Radical Pedagogy. *Hum. Archit. J. Sociol. Self-Knowl.* **2019**, *12*, 1.
38. Davis, A. The role of the mass media in investor relations. *J. Commun. Manag.* **2006**, *10*, 7–17. [CrossRef]
39. Chen, N.-F. Economic Forces and the Stock Market. *J. Bus.* **1986**, *59*, 383–403. [CrossRef]
40. Goodman, P. Iran's Economy Is Bleak. Its Stock Market Is Soaring, The New York Times. 2020. Available online: https://www.nytimes.com/2020/02/13/business/iran-stock-market.html (accessed on 5 October 2021).
41. Charrad, M.; Ghazzali, N.; Boiteau, V.; Niknafs, A. NbClust: An R package for determining the relevant number of clusters in a data set. *J. Stat. Softw.* **2014**, *61*, 1–36. [CrossRef]
42. Stefanovič, P.; Kurasova, O. Visual analysis of self-organising maps. *Nonlinear Anal. Model. Control.* **2011**, *16*, 488–504. [CrossRef]

Article

Machine Translation in Low-Resource Languages by an Adversarial Neural Network

Mengtao Sun [1,*], Hao Wang [2], Mark Pasquine [3] and Ibrahim A. Hameed [1]

1. Department of ICT and Natural Sciences, Norwegian University of Science and Technology, 6009 Ålesund, Norway; ibib@ntnu.no
2. Department of Computer Science, Norwegian University of Science and Technology, 2815 Gjøvik, Norway; hawa@ntnu.no
3. Department of International Business, Norwegian University of Science and Technology, 6009 Ålesund, Norway; mapa@ntnu.no
* Correspondence: mengtao.sun@ntnu.no

Abstract: Existing Sequence-to-Sequence (Seq2Seq) Neural Machine Translation (NMT) shows strong capability with High-Resource Languages (HRLs). However, this approach poses serious challenges when processing Low-Resource Languages (LRLs), because the model expression is limited by the training scale of parallel sentence pairs. This study utilizes adversary and transfer learning techniques to mitigate the lack of sentence pairs in LRL corpora. We propose a new Low resource, Adversarial, Cross-lingual (LAC) model for NMT. In terms of the adversary technique, LAC model consists of a generator and discriminator. The generator is a Seq2Seq model that produces the translations from source to target languages, while the discriminator measures the gap between machine and human translations. In addition, we introduce transfer learning on LAC model to help capture the features in rare resources because some languages share the same subject-verb-object grammatical structure. Rather than using the entire pretrained LAC model, we separately utilize the pretrained generator and discriminator. The pretrained discriminator exhibited better performance in all experiments. Experimental results demonstrate that the LAC model achieves higher Bilingual Evaluation Understudy (BLEU) scores and has good potential to augment LRL translations.

Keywords: machine learning; adversarial machine learning; imbalanced datasets; transfer learning

Citation: Sun, M.; Wang, H.; Pasquine, M.; A. Hameed, I. Machine Translation in Low-Resource Languages by an Adversarial Neural Network. *Appl. Sci.* **2021**, *11*, 10860. https://doi.org/10.3390/app112210860

Academic Editor: Valentino Santucci

Received: 6 October 2021
Accepted: 12 November 2021
Published: 17 November 2021

Publisher's Note: MDPI stays neutral with regard to jurisdictional claims in published maps and institutional affiliations.

Copyright: © 2021 by the authors. Licensee MDPI, Basel, Switzerland. This article is an open access article distributed under the terms and conditions of the Creative Commons Attribution (CC BY) license (https://creativecommons.org/licenses/by/4.0/).

1. Introduction

Traditional Neural Machine Translation (NMT) models directly learn and fit the correspondence between source and target language pairs through deep neural networks. This approach is based on a sequence-to-sequence (Seq2Seq) architecture which is comprised of encoder and decoder networks. At present, the most popular NMT models such as RNNsearch [1] and Transformer [2] have designs based on the Seq2Seq model architecture. RNNsearch has achieved remarkable translative scores due to its ability to supplement a human-like attention mechanism between the encoder and decoder. RNNsearch achieved several state-of-the-art records up to 2018 and is still widely used in machine translation today. In 2017, a novel architecture known as Transformer was introduced and outperformed existing models in different natural language processing tasks. Recently, researchers have developed a new embedding method based on Transformer, i.e., Bidirectional Encoder Representations from Transformers (BERT) [3]. However, the aforementioned approaches require a large amount of parallel bilingual data for training. For It is laborious for Low-Resource Languages (LRL) to build an adequate corpus for training satisfactory models.

Ruder [4] systematically summarized the necessity of working on LRL information processing. In addition to linguistic diversity, models developed for LRLs can generally help strengthen the featurization, cope with overfitting problems, and facilitate useful applications. For this purpose, there has been much research focusing on LRLs. Zoph et al. [5]

analyzed the relevance in translations by exploiting the pretrained model through the transfer encoder and decoder, but the performances of LRLs were unstable when using different High-Resource Language (HRL) models. To cope with the instability, Maimaiti et al. [6] presented a multi-round transfer learning approach, which alleviated the unpredictability of cross-lingual and generative training to some extent. Moreover, Cheng [7] utilized a pivot language to bridge the language pairs and train a joint network of NMT, i.e., A→B, B→C. Ren et al. [8] introduced a triangle architecture where a small language was an intermediate variable in the translation process between rich languages, dividing the translation process into two translation processes. Their models use the rich bilingual pairs in an HRL corpus to improve the performance of LRL translation.

This study presents research on adversarial learning, which achieves a higher performance in image generation [9]. It incorporates rival losses during training and can yield more explicit images. Recently, this has also been applied to NLP tasks. However, no study has investigated how adversarial learning applies to and influences LRL translation. We seek better feature extraction in the small-scale training of sentence pairs to obtain more accurate translations in complex systems. Moreover, we also take advantage of transfer learning in our proposed model to further improve NMT performance.

There are some challenges to consider when attempting to implement this strategy. First, it is problematic to utilize adversary and Seq2Seq together, as the performances of both techniques need to be analyzed and evaluated. Second, it is challenging to improve translation scores in cross-lingual transfer learning [5,6]. Third, it is challenging to develop a new method combining a pretrained model. Therefore, the proposed system should be developed as an end-to-end differentiable model.

This study proposes a novel Low resource, Adversarial, and Cross-lingual Neural Machine Translation (LAC) model for NMT. The proposed model focuses mainly on LRLs and is expected to overcome the limitations of Seq2Seq, leverage the capabilities of multilingual NMT, and produce high-quality translations. To be more specific, the contributions of this study are summarized as follows:

- A novel translation model, LAC, is designed. Compared to Seq2Seq, this model takes advantage of the adversary technique, reduces the required size of the corpus, and significantly enhances the experimental results on LRLs;
- The LAC model is designed to be end-to-end differentiable and transferable. A pretrained discriminator demonstrated a stronger ability for feature extraction and achieved a higher accuracy in terms of Bilingual Evaluation Understudy (BLEU) scores compared to a non-transferred LAC system;
- The effectiveness of the generator and discriminator in the LAC model is investigated. From the exploratory experiments, the results are analyzed in an interpretable manner.

2. Related Work
2.1. Adversarial Neural Networks

Despite wide usage in image generation, adversarial learning was only proposed for NMT in 2018. Wu et al. [10] utilized the adversary technique to strengthen the Seq2Seq-NMT, namely an Adversarial Neural Machine Translation, which outperformed traditional architectures. Cao et al. [11] also pointed out that the adversary technique supplemented the rival losses to enhance the feature selection from a sequence. The text limitation is that token samples are discrete and undifferentiable, making it inoperable to backpropagate the errors from the discriminator D to the generator G. As a result, G parameters cannot be updated. Recent studies focused on solving the undifferentiability problem by using a lingual adversary technique to address this problem. SeqGAN [12] focused on the differentiation problem using a policy gradient algorithm. Inspired by reinforcement learning, SeqGAN bypasses the generator differentiation problem by directly performing a gradient policy update. A decisional error gradient (instead of an error gradient) was conveyed to train the generator G. Wu et al. [10] used the same strategy to address the gradient problem in a generator. Their model successfully applied adversarial learning to an NMT and achieved better translation scores.

Nevertheless, with reinforcement learning, tuning the parameters requires many experiments in different language models. Lee et al. [13] introduced alternative methods to make the input of D continuous from discrete samplings, e.g., using the hidden states of a generator before activation [14] or substituting the activation function of a generator such as Gumbel-softmax [15]. In this way, the output of G will be the tokens' distributions rather than the tokens' samplings. Press et al. [16] successfully adopted this approach in adversarial text generation systems, which share some similarities with NMT systems. In this work, we use the method mentioned in [14,16], using the hidden states of a generator before activation. An A-NMT uses a pre-trained NMT model as the generator in the most primitive state. However, warm starting seems to reduce generalization in deep neural networks [17]. In addition, it cannot be well adopted in transfer learning of LRL corpora. In the proposed LAC model, the discriminator and generator are designed to facilitate training from scratch. For other related adversarial models, Yi et al. [18] proposed adversarial transfer learning to alleviate the low resource conditions of an acoustic model. Dai et al. [19] put forward a novel metric-based GAN, which used the distance-criteria to distinguish between real and fake samples. Dong et al. [20] presented a semi-supervised adversarial training process for cross-lingual text classification, where the labeled data from one language could be applied to a completely different language classification. We also refer to various solutions for imbalance datasets. Alam [21] proposed a new model specified for imbalanced datasets of credit card default prediction. Khushi utilize the testing results of 20+ class imbalance models with three types of classifiers to detect the best imbalance techniques for medical datasets [22]. Some works explore the risk factors in machine learning models that influence the class identification in an imbalanced dataset [23–25].

2.2. Low Resource Languages Machine Translation

Existing methods of low resource languages machine translation are based on lingual features and transfer learning. For lingual features, Li et al. [26] utilized subword segmentation in Tibetan neural machine translation. The structure of Tibetan words consists of two levels. First, Tibetan words consist of a sequence of syllables, and then a syllable consists of a sequence of characters. According to this special word structure, they proposed two methods for Tibetan to extract the lingual features for machine translation. Tran et al. [27] proposed a new method for word segmentation in Vietnam-Chinese machine translation. They improved the word tokens for isolated Chinese and Vietnamese pairs, made the word boundaries of two languages more symmetric, and achieved 1-1 alignments. As a result, the performance improved by using the embeddings of new word tokens. Choi et al. [28] pointed out that Korean and Japanese share the same grammatical structure for transfer learning. They built an unsupervised machine translation system based on the similarity of the two languages. Nguyen et al. [29] performed Zero-shot reading comprehension by cross-lingual transfer learning. They analyzed the influences of grammatical structure on the model performance and concluded that similar grammatical sentences could improve the effectiveness in cross-lingual transfer learning.

3. Adversarial Model

3.1. GAN

The seminal paper on adversarial training by Goodfellow et al. proposed a Generative Adversarial Network (GAN) in 2014 [9]. The new adversarial model first produces an over expected explicit image without human intervention. Here, we briefly review the three types of GANs originally proposed for adversarial training.

3.1.1. Basic GAN

We denote the randomly initialized Gaussian distribution as Yz, real distribution as Yr, and model distribution as Yg. The goal is to learn the mapping from Yz to Yg and make the distance between Yr and Yg as close as possible, i.e., $x \in Yz$ with distribution $x \sim p_{Yz}(x)$ will be mapped into the domain $\hat{x} \in Yg$ with distribution $\hat{x} \sim p_{Yg}(\hat{x})$, $\hat{x} = G(x)$. The objective function is expressed as:

$$\min_G \max_D \mathcal{L}(G,D) = \underbrace{\mathbb{E}_{x \sim p_{Yr}}[\log D(x)]}_{Lr} + \underbrace{\mathbb{E}_{G(x) \sim p_{Yg}}[1 - \log D(G(x))]}_{Lg} \quad (1)$$

The inputs of D are two types of data, $\{x\}$ and $\{\hat{x}\}$, in turn. The inputs of G are $\{x\}$. Here, D determines the gradients of G. In the most common training, we maximize D in k times, minimize G one time every epoch, and $k = 10$ is the default. Lr and Lg are marked in Figure 1a.

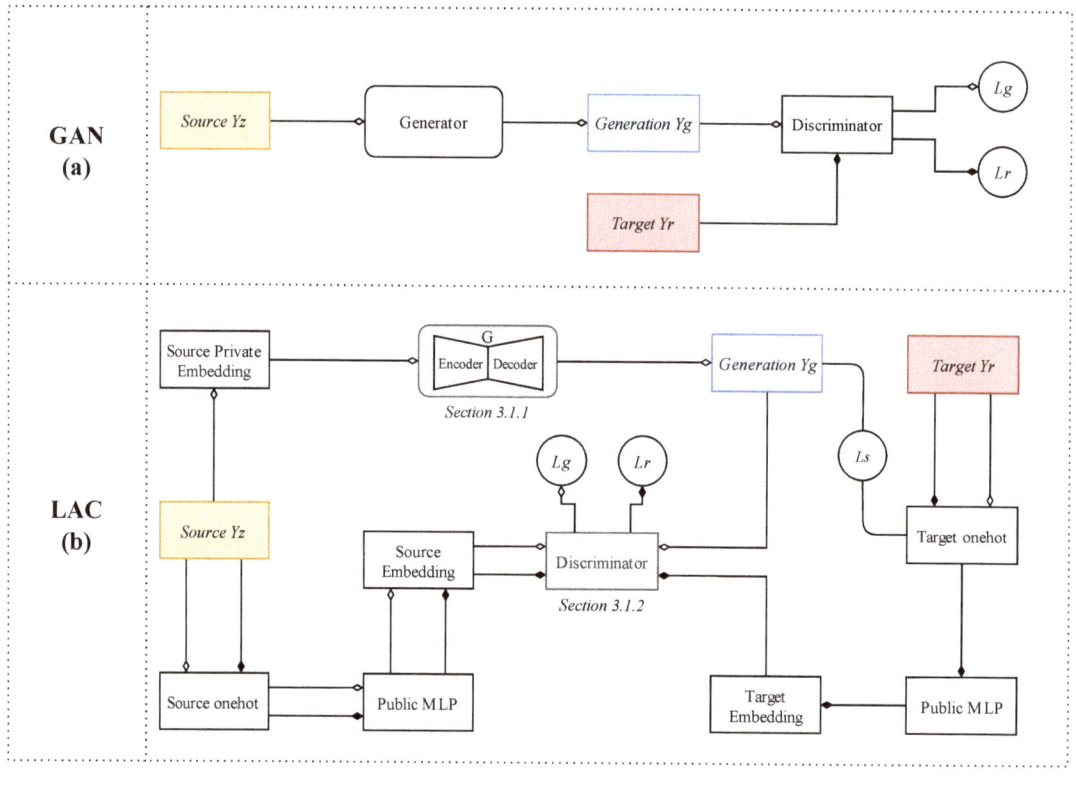

Figure 1. Comparison of the GAN and LAC models. (**a**): GAN: for image generation, the Source, Generation, and Target are randomly initialized noises, generated images, and real images, respectively. (**b**): LAC: the Source, Generation, and Target are the source language, generated translation, and human translation, respectively. Lg, Lr are the adversarial losses, Ls is the translation loss. Batches run along the White (◇) and Black (◆) routes in turn.

GANs have successfully generated images, yielding realistic images that can even fool the human eye. Nevertheless, this type of structure depends heavily on data distributions. It is not stable and often difficult to train without distribution overlaps between generated and real images. Arjovsky et al. [30] proposed the Wasserstein GAN (WGAN) to address these challenges.

3.1.2. WGAN

The loss functions in a GAN are approximated to calculate the Jensen–Shannon (JS) divergence of two distributions. This can easily become locally saturated, leading to the problem of gradient vanishing. Therefore, Arjovsky et al. [30] proposed the Wasserstein distance, substituting the JS divergence with continuity and differentiability. The objective function of a WGAN is expressed as:

$$\min_{G} \max_{D \in |f(D)|_L \leq 1} \mathcal{L}(G, D) = \underbrace{\mathbb{E}_{x \sim p_{Yr}}[D(x)]}_{Lr} - \underbrace{\mathbb{E}_{G(x) \sim p_{Yg}}[D(G(x))]}_{Lg} \quad (2)$$

where $|f|_L \leq 1$ is a 1-Lipschitz constraint. In a WGAN, the 1-lipschitz constraint is implemented by clipping a compact space $[-c, c]$ on the parameters of the discriminator.

In a WGAN, the optimization of $\max_{D \in |f(D)|_L \leq 1} \mathcal{L}(G, D)$ is equal to the Wasserstein distance of $(G(x), x)$. In other words, it uses a neural network to approach the Wasserstein distance. Formally:

$$\text{Wasserstain distance} = \max_{D \in |f(D)|_L \leq 1} \mathcal{L}(G, D)$$

i.e., $\max_{D \in |f(D)|_L \leq 1} \mathcal{L}(G, D)$ measures the difference between $x \sim p_{Yr}$ and $G(x) \sim p_{Yg}$.

3.1.3. WGAN-GP

Weight clipping is purely used to meet the 1-Lipschitz condition. In later training, most of the WGAN weights normally become plus or minus c, which is not satisfactory in some cases. Gulrajani et al. introduced an improved WGAN with a gradient penalty (WGAN-GP) instead of weight clipping [31]. The WGAN-GP penalizes the gradient norm of the discriminator by using the following objective function:

$$\min_{G} \max_{D} \mathcal{L}(G, D) = \underbrace{\mathbb{E}_{x \sim p_{Yr}}[D(x)]}_{Lr} - \underbrace{\mathbb{E}_{G(x) \sim p_{Yg}}[D(G(x))]}_{Lg} + \lambda \underbrace{\mathbb{E}_{\tilde{x} \sim p_{\tilde{x}}}\left[\left(\|\nabla_{\tilde{x}} D(\tilde{x})\|_2 - 1\right)^2\right]}_{\text{Gradient Penalty}} \quad (3)$$

where λ is the penalty coefficient. $p_{\tilde{x}}$ is the sampling distribution that uniformly samples along straight lines between pairs of points sampled from the data distribution p_{Yr} and generator distribution p_{Yg}. This method performs better than the standard WGAN and achieves stable training on various GAN architectures.

3.2. LAC

As depicted in Figure 1a, the entire GAN system is composed of a discriminator D and generator G, which play minimax games with each other. Two adversarial losses are used to optimize the parameters of G and D in turn. G yields fake samples to confuse the discriminator D and adjusts its parameters according to the recognition in terms of D. In contrast, the goal of the discriminator D is to identify the fake samples generated by G as accurately as possible and adjust its parameters accordingly. Adversarial training and GAN are different concepts. A GAN is used for unsupervised learning, which can generate explicit images without human intervention. Our proposed LAC model is classified as supervised learning. We incorporated the rival losses of a GAN for machine translation because they were helpful for LRL translation.

The LAC model comprises a generator G and a discriminator D, as shown in Figure 1b. The source language and human translations are embedded by a public Multi-Layer Perceptron (MLP). An MLP is a class of feed-forward neural networks. It can be comprised of different layers, and its purpose is to map the one-hot representation of a token into context embedding, which aligns with the work done by Mikolov et al. [32]. Here, we utilize a 1-layer feed-forward neural network for simplicity. The public feed-forward network is used for the source and target languages. To avoid underrepresenting, we set the hidden units to 5000. We define the distribution of the source language Yz, human translation Yr, and generated translation Yg. The inputs to the discriminator are (Yz, Yg) and (Yz, Yr) in turn, yielding two types of adversarial losses Lg and Lr, respectively, as shown in Figure 1b. The distribution of (Yz, Yg) and (Yz, Yr) is as close as possible, based on WGAN-GP. That is, embedding $u \in Yz$ with distribution $u \sim p_{Yz}(u)$ will be mapped into the domain $\hat{v} \in Yg$ with distribution $\hat{v} \sim p_{Yg}(\hat{v})$, $\hat{v} = G(u)$.

The distribution of Yg and Yr is also as close as possible. That is, $\hat{v} \in Yg$ approaches $v \in Yr$ with distribution $v \sim p_{Yr}(v)$ as close as possible. We constrain v, $\hat{v}$, and u in the same dimension. The adversarial losses Lg, Lr are generated from D to measure the Wasserstein distance of $(Yz, Yg) - (Yz, Yr)$. The translation consistency loss Ls measures the distance of $(Yg) - (Yr)$. The objective function is expressed as:

$$\min_G \max_D \mathcal{L}(G, D) = \underbrace{\mathbb{E}_{u \sim p_{Yz}, v \sim p_{Yr}(v)}[D(u, v)]}_{Lr} - \underbrace{\mathbb{E}_{u \sim p_{Yz}, G(u) \sim p_{Yg}(G(u))}[D(u, G(u))]}_{\text{Adversarial loss (Lg)}}$$
$$+ \lambda \underbrace{\mathbb{E}_{u \sim p_{Yz}, \tilde{v} \sim p_{\tilde{v}}}\left[\left(\left\|\nabla_{\tilde{v}} D\left(u, \tilde{v}\right)\right\|_2 - 1\right)^2\right]}_{\text{Gradient Penalty}} - \mu \underbrace{\mathbb{E}_{v \sim p_{Yr}(v), G(u) \sim p_{Yg}(G(u))}[v \log G(u)]}_{\text{Translation Loss (Ls)}} \quad (4)$$

where λ is the penalty coefficient. Distribution $p_{\tilde{v}}$ is the linear interpolation between distributions Yg and Yr in terms of WGAN-GP. Coefficient μ controls the translation weight. $v \log G(u)$ is the cross-entropy of the real and generated translations. We found that cross entropy greatly outperformed Mean Absolute Error and Mean Square Error in machine translation. In a word, Equation (4) consists of adversarial rival loss of WGAN-GP and cross-entropy loss between machine translation and ground truth.

4. LAC Configuration

4.1. Generator

Traditional Seq2Seq NMT models consist of an encoder and decoder, two components of a recurrent neural network. A Gated Recurrent Unit (GRU) [33] is a typical recurrent neural network proposed to solve long-term memory problems and gradients in backpropagation. Compared with Long-Short Term Memory, GRU can greatly improve training efficiency. Therefore, current researchers are more inclined to use GRU.

RNNsearch was proposed in 2014 and is an attention mechanism that makes the decoder conditionally focus on the fraction of hidden states of the encoder. This generally enhances the translation performance. We utilized the RNNsearch as a generator, comprised of a GRU encoder, attention mechanism, and GRU decoder. According to WGAN-GP, we adopted an extra fully-connected layer after data passes through the RNNsearch to produce a logit as output. We also adopted "teacher forcing" to train the LAC model, i.e., using human translation v_{t-1} to calculate generation $\hat{v}_t$.

To recap briefly, given source u and the human translation v_{t-1} in last time step, the generated translation $\hat{v}_t$ is:

$$\hat{v}_t = \text{FC}(h_t; d) \quad (5)$$

$$h_t = \text{RNNsearch}(h_{t-1}, v_{t-1}, c_t) \quad (6)$$

where h_t is the hidden state from the decoder at time t, and c_t is the context embedding from the encoder and attention mechanism. d is the number of neurons, which is in accordance with the vocabulary scale in human translation.

From Equation (4), we minimize the generator loss as follows:

$$G\_loss = -\mathbb{E}_{u \sim p_{Yz}, G(u) \sim p_{Yg}(G(u))}[D(u, G(u))] - \mu \mathbb{E}_{v \sim p_{Yr}(v), G(u) \sim p_{Yg}(G(u))}[v \log G(u)] \quad (7)$$

4.2. Discriminator

Given source u, human translation v, generated translation $\hat{v}$, pairs (u, v) and $(u, \hat{v})$ are separately fed into the discriminator to yield a translative matching degree. Ideally, the output will be greater in (u, v) and smaller in $(u, \hat{v})$. A residual convolutional neural network (CNN) [34] was designed to classify the input pairs based on their hierarchical properties, as shown in Figure 2.

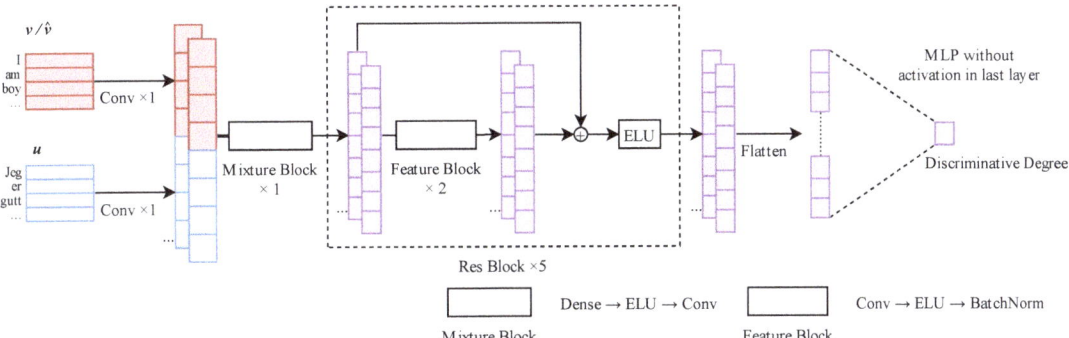

Figure 2. Structure of Discriminator D. Red and blue represent the $(u, \hat{v})$ and (u, v) pairs, respectively, and purple denotes the mixture hidden states.

The discriminator consists of three types of blocks: *Mixture*, *Res*, and *Feature*. For a *Mixture Block*, two types of embeddings in the input pair separately pass a private convolutional layer, and then are concatenated. This block includes dense exponential linear units (ELU) [35] and a convolutional layer in sequence to fuse their embeddings thoroughly. An ELU activation function tends to converge errors to zero faster and produce more accurate results in real tasks than the rectified linear unit (RELU) [36]. For the *Res Block*, the residual connection converges faster under the premise of the same number of layers. After removing a few layers, the performance of the residual network will not be significantly affected [37].

Moreover, Balduzzi et al. [38] pointed out that the residual network could solve the problem of the shattering gradient. Inside the *Res Block*, the *Feature Blocks* contain 1D Convolution, ELU, and a batch normalization layer in line. The hidden state goes into an MLP after being flattened. Here, MLP is a 3-layer feedforward network consisting 256 neurons in the first and second layer with ELU activation, 1 neuron in the third layer without activation. It is noteworthy that the activation function is removed in the last layer of the MLP, based on WGAN-GP. The blocks and layers are depicted in Figure 2.

From Equation (4), we minimize the discriminator loss as follows:

$$D\_loss = -\mathbb{E}_{u\sim p_{Yz}, v\sim p_{Yr}(v)}[D(u,v)] + \mathbb{E}_{u\sim p_{Yz}, G(u)\sim p_{Yg}(G(u))}[D(u,G(u))] - \lambda \mathbb{E}_{u\sim p_{Yz}, \tilde{v}\sim p_{\tilde{v}}}\left[\left(\left\|\nabla_{\tilde{v}} D\left(u, \tilde{v}\right)\right\|_2 - 1\right)^2\right] \quad (8)$$

5. Experiments

This section describes the corpora across different source languages translated to English and the baseline methods applied for comparison. We also detail the hyperparameter configuration of the proposed model.

5.1. Dataset

The Tatoeba Dataset comprises short and clean parallel language pairs from 81 languages for the English translation and has been widely used for rare language NMT research [39,40]. LRL is a comparable concept that HRL reflects according to:

(1) The dataset only comprises limited bilingual sentence pairs.
(2) The languages do not have a good pretrained model, or the relative studies are insufficient.

As shown in Table 1, by the number of sentence pairs used in this work, 7 types of translations are selected: tur-eng, aze-eng, ind-eng, tgl-eng, dan-eng, nob-eng and kor-eng. Among them, the following 5 datasets are very low resources: aze-eng, ind-eng, tgl-eng, nob-eng and kor-eng. Here, tur and aze are cognate, and they have similar grammatical structures. dan and nob are cognate, and they have similar grammatical structures. ind, tgl and kor are isolated languages, and they have quite different grammatical structures.

Table 1. Attributions of Translation Corpora.

Language Codes	Full Names	Avg Sentence Length	Train	Val	Test
tur-eng	Turkish-English	8.05	7.0 k	2.0 k	2.0 k
aze-eng	Azerbaijani-English	7.01	2.2 k	0.4 k	0.4 k
ind-eng	Indonesian-English	8.36	2.2 k	0.4 k	0.4 k
tgl-eng	Tagalog-English	8.34	2.2 k	0.4 k	0.4 k
dan-eng	Danish-English	8.94	7.0 k	2.0 k	2.0 k
nob-eng	Norwegian-English	9.14	2.2 k	0.4 k	0.4 k
kor-eng	Korean-English	7.27	2.2 k	0.4 k	0.4 k

To help the source language better align with the target language, the data is processed as follows. Two special tags, "<start>" and "<end>", are inserted at the beginning and end of sentences to signal the start and termination of the translation system, respectively. The words are changed to lowercase and stop words and stop punctuations are removed. All the languages are processed in the same way. We set the max length of a sentence to 9 words, based on an average sentence length. Examples of words before and after preprocessing are shown in Table 2.

Table 2. Examples of Tatoeba Corpus before and after preprocessing.

Language Codes	Before		After	
	Source	Target	Source	Target
tur-eng	Tom şirketin %30'unun sahibi.	Tom owns 30% of the company.	<start> tom şirketin 30 unun sahibi . <end>	<start> tom owns 30 of the company . <end>
aze-eng	Ağzınızı açın!	Open your mouth!	<start> ağzınızı açın ! <end>	<start> open your mouth ! <end>
ind-eng	Aku membayar $200 untuk pajak.	I paid $200 in taxes.	<start> aku membayar 200 untuk pajak . <end>	<start> i paid 200 in taxes . <end>
tgl-eng	"Terima kasih." "Sama-sama."	"Thank you." "You're welcome."	<start> terima kasih. sama sama . <end>	<start> thank you. You re welcome . <end>
dan-eng	Vores lærer sagde at vand koger ved 100 °C.	Our teacher said that water boils at 100 °C.	<start> vores lærer sagde at vand koger ved 100 °C . <end>	<start> our teacher said that water boils at 100 °C . <end>
nob-eng	Du hater virkelig ekskona di, gjør du ikke?	You really do hate your ex-wife, don't you?	<start> du hater virkelig ekskona di, gjør du ikke ? <end>	<start> you really do hate your ex wife, don t you ? <end>
kor-eng	게임은 2:30에 시작해.	The game starts 2:30.	<start> 게임은 2 30 에 시작해 . <end>	<start> the game starts 2 30 . <end>

5.2. Parameters

We set source embeddings, target embeddings, and source private embeddings as 128 dimensions for the LAC model. The vocabulary list was limited to 5 K words for each source and 4 K words for the target (English). The generator contained 768 units in the GRU layer. The structure of the discriminator shown in Figure 2 has 128 units in each CNN layer in terms of embeddings. The loss here is calculated on a 128 batch size. If the batch size is too small, the randomness will be higher in training. We used the Adam optimizer with a learning rate of 0.001 for the training from scratch in the generator and discriminator. The learning rate was set to 0.0001 when transfer learning.

5.3. Metrics

BLEU scores are often used as the fundamental metric for the evaluation of NMT systems. Ref. [41] analyzed previous criteria and argued that current BLEU methods could not adequately judge translations with a low presence of outliers. Instead, Character n-gram F-score (ChrF) [42] was more powerful in efficacy. We used word-level BLEU as our testing metric because it provided some useful confidence conclusions on translation results. We also used F3 values of n-gram (ChrF3) to monitor the training progress, where the result was the macro-averaged value of $n = 2$ to $n = 6$.

5.4. Baseline Models

Our baselines include two stages. First, we verified the effectiveness of our proposed LAC model by comparing it with four types of Seq2Seq based neural networks. Second, we compared the LAC model in non-transfer training with a transfer pre-trained Generator, Discriminator, and both. In the deep learning era, traditional machine learning methods are getting weaker at present [43,44]. Therefore, we perform several latest studies on machine translation as baselines. The baseline models are:

RNNsearch: This method is based on word-level sequences. We applied a bidirectional GRU for the encoder, and the attention structure in [1] with another bidirectional GRU for the decoder.

RNNsearch + Unknown (UNK) Replace: As mentioned in [45], using a very large target vocabulary without increasing the training complexity can become difficult. A good solution is replacing the low frequent vocabulary with a special unified UNK token. In low-resource translation, from Turkish to English, this can determine the influence of a low frequent vocabulary on a sentence pair.

BERT: BERT is a pretrained text representative model. More details can be found from the research [2] and [3]. Zhu et al. [46] incorporated BERT into Transformer for NMT. In this study, BERT was directly employed as the encoder to replace a bidirectional GRU (bi-GRU) encoder.

ALBERT: BERT is primarily reliant on large graphic and tensor processing memory. To address this problem, a lite BERT (ALBERT) was proposed as a substitution. With lower complexity, this model shows stronger results in several benchmarks [47].

6. Results

This section discusses the main results of our proposed LAC model for the machine translation task across different LRLs. The proposed model achieved the best results compared with several typical models. We also probe the effectiveness and transferability of the LAC model using explanatory experiments.

6.1. Main Results

6.1.1. Comparison of Baseline Models

A comparison of baseline models was applied to a Turkish-English dataset, as shown in Table 3.

Table 3. Comparison of baseline models.

First Proposed	Details	BLEU
RNNsearch. 2015 [1]	GRU_encoder + Att. + GRU_decoder	33.6
RNNsearch + UNK Replace. 2015 [45]	RNNsearch + UNK Replace	32.8
BERT. 2019. [3] 2020. [46]	BERT_encoder + RNNsearch	34.7
ALBERT. 2020 [47]	ALBERT_encoder + RNNsearch	35.8
LAC-RNNsearch	Adversary (RNNsearch, D)	**37.9**

In our experiment, the traditional RNNsearch model obtained a 33.6 BLEU score in Turkish-English Translation dataset. RNNsearch with UNK Replace cannot help to generalize and obtain better features when lacking sentence pairs, resulting in a decreased BLEU score of 0.8. BERT and its variants show more powerful capabilities and achieved a higher results. Compared to RNNsearch, BERT and ALBERT obtained 1.1 and 2.2 increases in BLEU scores. We incorporated RNNsearch with adversary and conducted the training from scratch. The BLEU score improved by 4.3 with less training data and outperformed the pretrained BERT and ALBERT models.

6.1.2. Comparison of Languages (aze/ind/tgl/kor/nob-eng)

We selected LRLs for our experiments comprised of limited sentence pairs only. The results on the aze/ind/tgl/kor/nob-eng datasets are shown in Table 4.

Table 4. Comparison of low-resource Corpora.

Language Codes	RNNsearch	LAC-RNNsearch
aze-eng	20.4	**20.7**
ind-eng	17.7	**19.3**
tgl-eng	22.0	**22.8**
kor-eng	17.6	**17.7**
nob-eng	14.4	**15.3**

The pretrained embeddings are not available in low resource corpora, so that all the language models were trained from scratch. The RNNsearch was used as the baseline, and the proposed LAC model demonstrated an average enhancement compared with these results. We can see that LAC model has an increment of 0.3 in aze-eng, 1.6 in ind-eng, 0.8 in tgl-eng, 0.1 in kor-eng and 0.9 in nob-eng.

6.2. Transfer Learning

We transfer tur-eng as HRL to aze-eng model, and transfer dan-eng as HRL to nob-eng model. Because the two HRLs has the same grammatical structure as their related LRLs. The transferability of the LAC model was tested with a separated transfer generator, separated discriminator, and both the generator and discriminator, as seen in Tables 5 and 6, respectively. The BLEU scores indicate a positive impact when a pre-trained discriminator was used.

Table 5. Transfer learning of LAC from tur-eng to aze-eng.

aze–eng	BLEU	ChrF3
Non-transfer	20.7	19.4
Transfer G	18.5	16.6
Transfer D	**21.2**	**23.9**
Transfer G and D	18.8	17.1

Table 6. Transfer learning of LAC from dan-eng to nob-eng.

nob–eng	BLEU	ChrF3
None-Transfer	15.3	26.9
Transfer G	15.6	24.7
Transfer D	**15.8**	**29.2**
Transfer G and D	15.5	25.5

The ChrF3 scores from pretrained components in different training steps are shown in Figure 3, which demonstrate that our proposed LAC model can consistently improve translations when the training steps are increased. #D denotes the transfer discriminator, #G denotes the transfer generator, and #D #G denotes both.

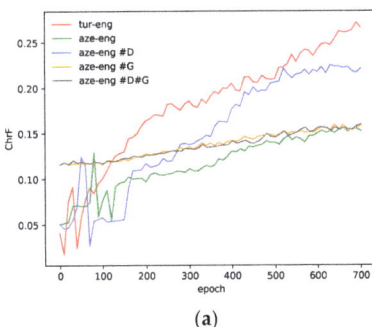
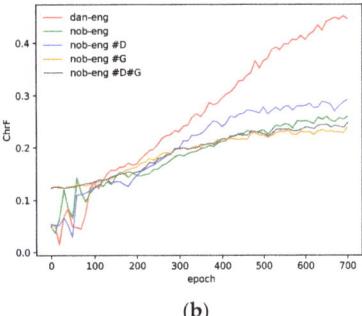

(a)   (b)

Figure 3. ChrF3 scores during the training: (**a**) transfer tur-eng to aze-eng, and (**b**) transfer tur-eng to aze-eng. The red line (—) is the reference language. The green (—), blue (—), gold (—), and gray (—) lines represent the non-transfer, transfer Generator, Discriminator, and both, respectively.

Figure 3a shows the change of ChrF3 with increasing steps. Overall, the translation performance of the tur-eng model is better than for the aze-eng model. #G and #D #G demonstrated better performance early compared with training from scratch. They continued to improve slowly but were surpassed by the pretrained discriminator in a later stage. The BLEU score of the discriminator surpassed those of the non-transfer, #G, and #D #G after approximately 300 epochs and then maintained the lead position.

Our hypothesis is also proven in the dan-eng to nob-eng transfer learning experiment. Applying a pretrained discriminator in other languages achieved a higher ChrF3 score than using other pretrained components, as shown in Figure 3b. #G and #D#G had no positive or negative influences on the training progress compared with non-transfer training.

6.3. Case Study

Four translations of different models in Azerbaijan-English and Norwegian-English were generated, provided in Tables 7 and 8. We observed that the proposed LAC model improved and generated better translations, while the RNNsearch remained in a fixed pattern. Because the dataset is very limited, RNNsearch translation tended to be shorter, sentences were not as diverse, and it usually reduplicated common words. In four modes of the LAC model, #D produced the most informative translation. As a result, the generator will receive more useful information and produce more human-like translations by transfer discriminator.

Table 7. Azerbaijan-English.

Epoch	100	200	300	700
Source		Sizin mənə nə edəcəyimi deməyə haqqınız yoxdur.		
Ground Truth		You have no right to tell me what to do.		
RNNsearch	.	i .	i think i think i think i think	i think that what do you know tom
LAC	i m the know i m the know	i m a good to go to go	i don t know you re not your	you have three children are you want to
LAC #G	door tom	door tom	is have you ?	is have you ?
LAC #D #G	door tom	door tom	is have you the .	is have you ?
LAC #D	i m a m a m a m	you re you re you re you re	you have to be your problem to do	you have no right to tell me what
Source		Sən Avstriyanın harasında böyümüsən?		
Ground Truth		Where in Austria did you grow up?		
RNNsearch	.	i .	tom is the dog .	tom is monday .
LAC	i m a know the know the know	i m not a good to go to	you can t want you have a good	where in austria ?
LAC #G	do you house the tom	do you .	do you re ?	do my to tom
LAC #D #G	do you like tom	do you very the tom	do you re ?	do my to tom
LAC #D	i m a m a m a m	you ?	where are you in japan ?	where in austria did you grow up ?
Source		Mən maşında idim.		
Ground Truth		I was in the car.		
RNNsearch	.	i .	i have a good .	i ate the library .
LAC	i m a m a m a m	i m a good .	tom has a good .	i think of the cat .
LAC #G	is briefly .	i happy is .	i m s t .	i m s t .
LAC #D #G	is briefly .	i happy is .	i m s t .	i m s t .
LAC #D	i m a was .	i m a i m a i m	i was in the driver .	i was in the car .
Source		Əminəm ki, Tom sənə nifrət etmir.		
Ground Truth		I'm sure Tom doesn't hate you.		
RNNsearch	.	i .	i m not a good .	i m sure tom will you like it
LAC	i m the know i m the know	i m a good to go to go	i don t know you re not your	i m sure tom doesn t hate you
LAC #G	i will the he	i will the you very the he	i m s the you her you re	i m s the to be you her
LAC #D #G	i will the he	i will the the the the the the	i m s the you her the you	i m s the you the to be
LAC #D	i m a m a m a m	i m a tom s a tom is	i m here .	i m sure tom doesn t hate you

Table 8. Norwegian-English.

Epoch	100 (10)	200 (20)	300 (30)	700 (70)
Source		Jeg betraktet Tom som en venn.		
Ground Truth		I regarded Tom as a friend.		
RNNsearch	i .	i .	i ve been a lot of the truth	i ve been to be a friend .
LAC	i m a lot of a lot of	i m a lot of the tom is	i m sure tom is a friend in	i wonder tom will have a friend .
LAC #G	i if tom to tom	i was into . .	i was tom .	i m and tom a lot it tom
LAC #D #G	i that	i ve tom . .	i was t to to .	i m tom a friend .
LAC #D	i m to i m to i m	i m a lot of the tom s	i tom tom a friend .	i assumed tom was a friend .
Source		Er det noe du ikke forteller oss?		
Ground Truth		Is there something you're not telling us?		
RNNsearch	i .	i .	i ve been to be a lot of	what is it s someone know that you
LAC	i m a lot of a lot of	are you have a lot of this is	is there is you re not his life	is there something you re not telling me
LAC #G	i do about you the .	are s you you the .	are s you t you the .	are s you t you that ?
LAC #D #G	i do people you the .	are s you the .	are s you the .	are s you that you you that you
LAC #D	tom is a lot .	are you have to do you are you	is there s something to do not to	is there something you re not telling me
Source		Jeg skulle ønske det var mer jeg kunne ha gjort.		
Ground Truth		I wish there was more I could've done.		
RNNsearch	i .	i .	i wish i wish i wish i wish	i wish i wish i wish i wish
LAC	i ve	i m not to be a lot of	i wish there s more than i was	i wish there was more than i was
LAC #G	do wish the .	i wish . .	i wish i do i could the .	i wish there do i could the .
LAC #D #G	i wish the .	i wish . .	i wish i had the .	i wish there will more do more more
LAC #D	i m i m i m i m	i m a lot of i ve been	i wish it was more than i was	i wish there were more than i could
Source		Tom skal gjøre det i morgen.		
Ground Truth		Tom will be doing that tomorrow.		
RNNsearch	i .	i .	i m a lot of the lot of	you re supposed to be happy to be
LAC	tom s a lot of a lot of	tom is a lot .	tom will be happy to be the truth	tom will do that .
LAC #G	he t with really	tom your with i that with i that	tom a lot know find	tom will really tomorrow .
LAC #D #G	he t with he t	tom . .	tom a lot know a lot it ,	tom will it tomorrow
LAC #D	tom is the lot .	tom s a lot of the room .	tom is do that .	tom will do that tomorrow .

6.4. Ablation Study

The contribution of different components was observed in the LAC model. Ablation experiments were performed on the tur-eng dataset and the results are displayed in Table 9. When we substituted the encoder-decoder of the generator using RNN, there was a 2.4%

decrease. The performance decreased by 2.9% if the attention mechanism was removed. From these results, we found that the generator played an important role in the LAC model.

Table 9. Ablation Study of LAC in Turkish-English Sentence Pairs.

Model	BLEU
LAC	37.9
G_RNN	35.5
G_No Attention	35.0
D_ReLu Nonlinearity	36.5
D_ res block × 1	35.6

The importance of the discriminator was also demonstrated. The activation function caused a 1.4% decline with the RELU replacement. Moreover, the results demonstrated that the LAC model with a single res block layer, i.e., reducing the ability of discriminator, the result has a 2.3% drop in BLEU score.

6.5. Wasserstein Distance

The Wasserstein distance of training progress in each step is shown in Figure 4.

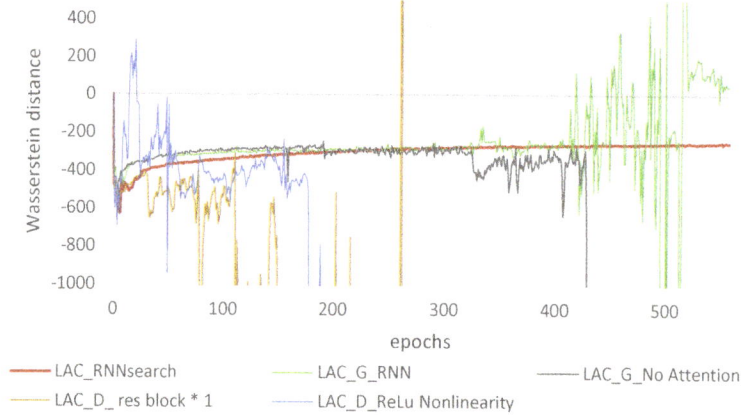

Figure 4. Wasserstein distance during the training on the validation dataset, plotted by every epoch.

The critic ability is reduced in the ablation study against the discriminator (i.e., the gold and blue lines). The Wasserstein distance cannot be accurately measured as the curve is diverging. That is, the discriminator is unable to detect generated and real translation. As a result, the rival loss cannot be used to improve the translation.

The ablation study reduces the translative ability against the generator (i.e., the green and gray lines). The curve started to diverge after 300 epochs because the generator was well fitted and could produce some translations. That is, the generated and real translations were not separable from the discriminator. Additionally, due to the weak translative ability, the generator could only produce the most common words.

The optimization showed smooth and incremental converging progress in our proposed LAC model (the red line). The LAC model achieved the best BLEU score based on translative and critical abilities, as shown in Sections 6.1 and 6.2.

From Figure 4, the LAC model incorporates the knowledge from adversarial systems and human translation. It got the better translation features and produced the best translation score in low-resource languages machine translations.

6.6. Steps of Message Passing

The ChrF3 curve of the LAC during different step numbers was plotted to demonstrate the influence of epochs during the update process and the performances with and without an adversary. Figure 5 illustrated the ChrF3 scores for four LRLs when the step number was increased.

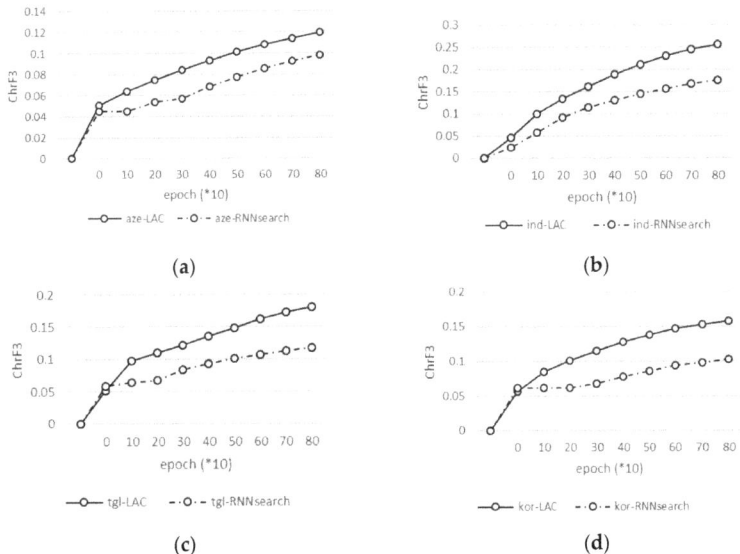

Figure 5. ChrF3 training curves for four languages: (**a**) aze-eng, (**b**) ind-eng, (**c**) tgl-eng, and (**d**) kor-eng. LAC-RNNsearch and RNNsearch are denoted by the solid and dotted lines, respectively.

The results indicate that the number of update steps is crucial to the performance of the LAC model, which increased on all four datasets. The ChrF3 of the LAC model not only outperformed RNNsearch in the testing, but it was larger at each step for all four LRLs. The generator learned an extra rival loss from the discriminator, aggregating the global information from the machine and human translations in each step. LAC model can therefore capture more valuable information through the adversary.

7. Conclusions

This study proposed a new machine translation model based on an adversarial mechanism, named LAC. The results of the LAC are significantly stronger than those of the traditional machine translation models without an adversarial mechanism. LAC does not have an over-complex structure, but it shows better evaluations compared with the latest models. Furthermore, the higher performance are widely shown in multiple languages, indicating that the adversary can effectively improve the model capabilities.

Typically, transfer learning is not suitable for machine translation even though the languages have similar grammar. In this experiment, we analyzed the transferability of LAC inter similar languages. First, we used both pretrained discriminator and generator from a relative and higher resource language. Then we used a separate pretrained discriminator and generator. We found that using a separate pretrained discriminator shows better performance. Similarly, in case studies, a separate pretrained discriminator produced more fluent and correct sentences. It manifested that the LAC model has the potential in cross-lingual transfer learning compared with traditional models.

We analyzed the impact of different components in the LAC network by ablation experiments. In conclusion, no matter the ability of discriminator or generator is reduced, the translation results eventually became worse. Furthermore, from the Wasserstein distance curves (i.e., convergence curves) of ablation experiments, we found that reducing the capabilities of the discriminator or generator will eventually make the LAC model non-convergent. It showed that the original LAC model incorporates the useful adversarial features from discriminator and generator. The performance of the LAC model is the result of the interaction of discriminator and generator.

Finally, we tested the translation performance of the model in different iteration steps, and we found that the LAC model was better than the translation system without an adversarial mechanism during iteration. It shows that the adversarial mechanism can improve the model's ability in any step, and the improvement is stable.

In summary, experimental results showed that LAC has good potential in LRL translations. For future works, we will explore how to improve and leverage the discriminator and generator so that the translation performance can be further improved. In addition, we will work on how to reduce the computational costs of adversarial training.

Author Contributions: Methodology, M.S.; software, M.S.; validation, M.S.; formal analysis, M.S.; investigation, M.S.; data curation, M.S.; writing—original draft preparation, M.S.; writing—review and editing, H.W., M.P. and I.A.H.; visualization, M.S.; supervision, H.W., M.P. and I.A.H.; project administration, H.W., M.P. and I.A.H.; funding acquisition, H.W., M.P. and I.A.H. All authors have read and agreed to the published version of the manuscript.

Funding: This research was funded by Norwegian University of Science and Technology.

Institutional Review Board Statement: Not applicable.

Informed Consent Statement: Not applicable.

Data Availability Statement: Data available in a publicly accessible repository that does not issue DOIs. Publicly available datasets were analyzed in this study.

Conflicts of Interest: The authors declare no conflict of interest.

References

1. Bahdanau, D.; Cho, K.; Bengio, Y. Neural machine translation by jointly learning to align and translate. In Proceedings of the International Conference on Learning Representations, San Diego, CA, USA, 7 May 2015.
2. Vaswani, A.; Shazeer, N.; Parmar, N.; Uszkoreit, J.; Jones, L.; Gomez, A.N.; Kaiser, Ł.; Polosukhin, I. Attention is all you need. In Proceedings of the Advances in Neural Information Processing Systems Conference, Long Beach, CA, USA, 4 December 2017; pp. 5998–6008.
3. Devlin, J.; Chang, M.W.; Lee, K.; Toutanova, K. Pre-training of deep bidirectional transformers for language understanding. In Proceedings of the 2019 Conference of the North American Chapter of the Association for Computational Linguistics, Minneapolis, MN, USA, 2 June 2019.
4. Ruder, S.; Vulić, I.; Søgaard, A. A survey of cross-lingual word embedding models. *J. Artif. Intell. Res.* **2019**, *65*, 569–631. [CrossRef]
5. Zoph, B.; Yuret, D.; May, J.; Knight, K. Transfer learning for low-resource neural machine translation. In Proceedings of the Conference on Empirical Methods in Natural Language Processing, Austin, TX, USA, 1 November 2016. [CrossRef]
6. Maimaiti, M.; Liu, Y.; Luan, H.; Sun, M. Multi-Round Transfer Learning for Low-Resource NMT Using Multiple High-Resource Languages. *ACM Trans. Asian Low-Resour. Lang. Inf. Process.* **2019**, *18*, 4. [CrossRef]
7. Yong, C. Joint Training for Neural Machine Translation. Ph.D. Thesis, IIIS Department, Tsinghua University, Beijing, China, 2014.
8. Ren, S.; Chen, W.; Liu, S.; Li, M.; Zhou, M.; Ma, S. Triangular architecture for rare language translation. In Proceedings of the 56th Annual Meeting of the Association for Computational Linguistics, Melbourne, Australia, 15 July 2018. [CrossRef]
9. Goodfellow, I.; Pouget-Abadie, J.; Mirza, M.; Xu, B.; Warde-Farley, D.; Ozair, S.; Courville, A.; Bengio, Y. Generative adversarial networks. *Commun. ACM* **2020**, *63*, 139–144. [CrossRef]
10. Wu, L.; Xia, Y.; Tian, F.; Zhao, L.; Qin, T.; Lai, J.; Liu, T.Y. Adversarial neural machine translation. In Proceedings of the Asian Conference on Machine Learning (ACML 2018), Beijing, China, 14 November 2018; pp. 534–549.
11. Cao, P.; Chen, Y.; Liu, K.; Zhao, J.; Liu, S. Adversarial transfer learning for Chinese named entity recognition with self-attention mechanism. In Proceedings of the 2018 Conference on Empirical Methods in Natural Language Processing, Brussels, Belgium, 31 October 2018; pp. 182–192. [CrossRef]
12. Yu, L.; Zhang, W.; Wang, J.; Yu, Y. Seqgan: Sequence generative adversarial nets with policy gradient. In Proceedings of the Thirty-first AAAI Conference on Artificial Intelligence, San Francisco, CA, USA, 4 February 2017. [CrossRef]

13. Lee, H.; Yu, T. ICASSP 2018 tutorial: Generative adversarial network; Its applications to signal processing; Natural language processing. In Proceedings of the ICASSP 2018, Calgary, AB, Canada, 15 April 2018. [CrossRef]
14. Zhang, Y.; Gan, Z.; Fan, K.; Chen, Z.; Henao, R.; Shen, D.; Carin, L. Adversarial feature matching for text generation. In Proceedings of the 34th International Conference on Machine Learning, Sydney, Australia, 6 August 2017; Volume 70, pp. 4006–4015.
15. Nie, W.; Narodytska, N.; Patel, A. Relgan: Relational generative adversarial networks for text generation. In Proceedings of the International Conference on Learning Representations, Vancouver, BC, Canada, 30 April 2018.
16. Press, O.; Bar, A.; Bogin, B.; Berant, J.; Wolf, L. Language generation with recurrent generative adversarial networks without pre-training. In Proceedings of the 34th International Conference on Machine Learning, Sydney, Australia, 6 August 2017.
17. Ash, J.T.; Adams, R.P. On the difficulty of warm-starting neural network training. *arXiv* **2019**, arXiv:1910.08475.
18. Yi, J.; Tao, J.; Wen, Z.; Bai, Y. Language-Adversarial Transfer Learning for Low-Resource Speech Recognition. *IEEE/ACM Trans. Audio Speech Lang. Proc.* **2019**, *27*, 621–630. [CrossRef]
19. Dai, G.; Xie, J.; Fang, Y. Metric-based generative adversarial network. In Proceedings of the 25th ACM International Conference on Multimedia (MM '17), Mountain View, CA, USA, 23–27 October 2017; Association for Computing Machinery: New York, NY, USA, 2017; pp. 672–680. [CrossRef]
20. Dong, X.; Zhu, Y.; Zhang, Y.; Fu, Z.; Xu, D.; Yang, S.; de Melo, G. Leveraging adversarial training in self-learning for cross-lingual text classification. In Proceedings of the 43rd International ACM SIGIR Conference on Research, Development in Information Retrieval, Virtual Conference, China, 25–30 July 2020; Association for Computing Machinery: New York, NY, USA, 2020; pp. 1541–1544. [CrossRef]
21. Alam, T.M.; Shaukat, K.; Hameed, I.A.; Luo, S.; Sarwar, M.U.; Shabbir, S.; Li, J.; Khushi, M. An investigation of credit card default prediction in the imbalanced datasets. *IEEE Access* **2020**, *8*, 201173–201198. [CrossRef]
22. Khushi, M.; Shaukat, K.; Alam, T.M.; Hameed, I.A.; Uddin, S.; Luo, S.; Yang, X.; Reyes, M.C. A Comparative Performance Analysis of Data Resampling Methods on Imbalance Medical Data. *IEEE Access* **2021**, *9*, 109960–109975. [CrossRef]
23. Alam, T.M.; Shaukat, K.; Mahboob, H.; Sarwar, M.U.; Iqbal, F.; Nasir, A.; Hameed, I.A.; Luo, S. A Machine Learning Approach for Identification of Malignant Mesothelioma Etiological Factors in an Imbalanced Dataset. *Comput. J.* **2021**, bxab015. [CrossRef]
24. Latif, M.Z.; Shaukat, K.; Luo, S.; Hameed, I.A.; Iqbal, F.; Alam, T.M. Risk factors identification of malignant mesothelioma: A data mining based approach. In Proceedings of the 2020 International Conference on Electrical, Communication, and Computer Engineering (ICECCE), Istanbul, Turkey, 12–13 June 2020; pp. 1–6.
25. Yang, X.; Khushi, M.; Shaukat, K. Biomarker CA125 Feature engineering and class imbalance learning improves ovarian cancer prediction. In Proceedings of the 2020 IEEE Asia-Pacific Conference on Computer Science and Data Engineering (CSDE), Gold Coast, Australia, 16–18 December 2020; pp. 1–6.
26. Li, Y.; Jiang, J.; Yangji, J.; Ma, N. Finding better subwords for Tibetan neural machine translation. In Proceedings of the Transactions on Asian and Low-Resource Language Information Processing, Gold Coast, Australia, 16–18 December 2021; Volume 20, pp. 1–11.
27. Tran, P.; Dinh, D.; Nguyen, L.H. Word re-segmentation in Chinese-Vietnamese machine translation. *ACM Trans. Asian Low-Resour. Lang. Inf. Process.* **2016**, *16*, 1–22. [CrossRef]
28. Choi, Y.-S.; Park, Y.-H.; Yun, S.; Kim, S.-H.; Lee, K.-J. Factors Behind the Effectiveness of an Unsupervised Neural Machine Translation System between Korean and Japanese. *Appl. Sci.* **2021**, *11*, 7662. [CrossRef]
29. Nguyen, T.Q.; Chiang, D. Zero-shot reading comprehension by cross-lingual transfer learning with multi-lingual language representation model. In Proceedings of the EMNLP, Hong Kong, China, 3 November 2019.
30. Arjovsky, M.; Chintala, S.; Bottou, L. Wasserstein generative adversarial networks. In Proceedings of the International Conference on Machine Learning, Sydney, Australia, 6 August 2017; pp. 214–223.
31. Gulrajani, I.; Ahmed, F.; Arjovsky, M.; Dumoulin, V.; Courville, A. Improved training of Wasserstein GANs. In Proceedings of the Advances in Neural Information Processing Systems Conference, Long Beach, CA, USA, 4 December 2017; pp. 5767–5777.
32. Mikolov, T.; Sutskever, I.; Chen, K.; Corrado, G.S.; Dean, J. Distributed representations of words and phrases and their compositionality. In Proceedings of the Advances in Neural Information Processing Systems Conference, Lake Tahoe, NV, USA, 5 December 2013.
33. Cho, K.; van Merriënboer, B.; Gulcehre, C.; Bahdanau, D.; Bougares, F.; Schwenk, H.; Bengio, Y. Learning phrase representations using RNN encoder–decoder for statistical machine translation. In Proceedings of the 2014 Conference on Empirical Methods in Natural Language Processing (EMNLP 2014), Doha, Qatar, 25–29 October 2014; pp. 1724–1734. [CrossRef]
34. He, K.; Zhang, X.; Ren, S.; Sun, J. Deep residual learning for image recognition. In Proceedings of the IEEE conference on Computer Vision and Pattern Recognition (CVPR 2016), Las Vegas, NV, USA, 27–30 June 2016; pp. 770–778. [CrossRef]
35. Clevert, D.A.; Unterthiner, T.; Hochreiter, S. Fast and accurate deep network learning by Exponential Linear Units (ELUs). In Proceedings of the International Conference on Learning Representations (ICLR 2016), San Juan, Puerto Rico, 2 May 2016.
36. Kim, J.; Won, M.; Serra, X.; Liem, C.C. Transfer learning of artist group factors to musical genre classification. In Proceedings of the Web Conference 2018 (WWW '18), Lyon, France, 23 April 2018; pp. 1929–1934. [CrossRef]
37. Veit, A.; Wilber, M.J.; Belongie, S. Residual networks behave like ensembles of relatively shallow networks. In Proceedings of the Advances in Neural Information Processing Systems (NIPS 2016), Barcelona, Spain, 5 December 2016; pp. 550–558.
38. Balduzzi, D.; Frean, M.; Leary, L.; Lewis, J.P.; Ma, K.W.D.; McWilliams, B. The shattered gradients problem: If resnets are the answer, then what is the question? In Proceedings of the 34th International Conference on Machine Learning (ICML'17), Sydney, Australia, 6 August 2017; Volume 70, pp. 342–350.

39. Fu, Z.; Xian, Y.; Geng, S.; Ge, Y.; Wang, Y.; Dong, X.; Wang, G.; de Melo, G. ABSent: Cross-lingual sentence representation mapping with bidirectional GANs. In Proceedings of the Thirty-Fourth AAAI Conference on Artificial Intelligence (AAAI 2020), New York, NY, USA, 7 February 2017. [CrossRef]
40. Tran, C.; Tang, Y.; Li, X.; Gu, J. Cross-lingual retrieval for iterative self-supervised training. In Proceedings of the Advances in Neural Information Processing Systems Conference (NIPS 2020), Virtual Conference, 6 December 2020.
41. Mathur, N.; Baldwin, T.; Cohn, T. Tangled up in BLEU: Reevaluating the Evaluation of Automatic Machine Translation Evaluation Metrics. In Proceedings of the 58th Annual Meeting of the Association for Computational Linguistics (ACL 2020), Virtual Conference, 5 July 2020. [CrossRef]
42. Popović, M. chrF: Character n-gram F-score for automatic MT evaluation. In Proceedings of the Tenth Workshop on Statistical Machine Translation (EMNLP 2015 Workshop), Lisbon, Portugal, 17 September 2015; pp. 392–395. [CrossRef]
43. Shaukat, K.; Luo, S.; Varadharajan, V.; Hameed, I.A.; Xu, M. A Survey on Machine Learning Techniques for Cyber Security in the Last Decade. *IEEE Access* **2020**, *8*, 222310–222354. [CrossRef]
44. Shaukat, K.; Luo, S.; Varadharajan, V.; Hameed, I.A.; Chen, S.; Liu, D.; Li, J. Performance Comparison and Current Challenges of Using Machine Learning Techniques in Cybersecurity. *Energies* **2020**, *13*, 2509. [CrossRef]
45. Jean, S.; Cho, K.; Memisevic, R.; Bengio, Y. On using very large target vocabulary for neural machine translation. In Proceedings of the 53rd Annual Meeting of the Association for Computational Linguistics and the 7th International Joint Conference on Natural Language Processing (ACL-IJCNLP 2015), Beijing, China, 26 July 2015. [CrossRef]
46. Zhu, J.; Xia, Y.; Wu, L.; He, D.; Qin, T.; Zhou, W.; Li, H.; Liu, T.Y. Incorporating BERT into neural machine translation. In Proceedings of the International Conference on Learning Representations (ICLR 2020), Virtual Conference, 30 April 2020.
47. Lan, Z.; Chen, M.; Goodman, S.; Gimpel, K.; Sharma, P.; Soricut, R. ALBERT: A lite BERT for self-supervised learning of language representations. In Proceedings of the International Conference on Learning Representations (ICLR 2020), Virtual Conference, 30 April 2020.

Article

Selection of the Right Undergraduate Major by Students Using Supervised Learning Techniques

Alhuseen Omar Alsayed [1,2,*], Mohd Shafry Mohd Rahim [1], Ibrahim AlBidewi [3], Mushtaq Hussain [4], Syeda Huma Jabeen [5], Nashwan Alromema [6], Sadiq Hussain [7] and Muhammad Lawan Jibril [8]

1. Department of Computer Science, School of Computing, Faculty of Engineering, Universiti Teknologi Malaysia, Johor Bahru 81310, Johor, Malaysia; shafry@utm.my
2. Deanship of Scientific Research, King Abdulaziz University, Jeddah 21589, Saudi Arabia
3. Department of Information Technology, Faculty of Computing and Information Technology, King Abdulaziz University, Jeddah 21589, Saudi Arabia; ialbidewi@kau.edu.sa
4. Department of Computer Science and Information Technology, Virtual University of Pakistan, Lahore 54000, Pakistan; mushtaq.hussain@vu.edu.pk
5. Brainnettom Center, Institute of Automation, University of Chinese Academy of Sciences, Beijing 100190, China; hjabeen2@gmail.com
6. Department of Computer Science, Faculty of Computing and Information Technology in Rabigh (FCITR), King Abdulaziz University, Jeddah 21589, Saudi Arabia; nalromema@kau.edu.sa
7. Examination Branch, Dibrugarh University, Dibrugarh 786004, India; sadiq@dibru.ac.in
8. Department of Computer Science, Federal University of Kashere, Barri 771103, Gombe State, Nigeria; lawan.jibril@fukashere.edu.ng
* Correspondence: nuriy3@graduate.utm.my; Tel.: +966-543-169-128

Abstract: University education has become an integral and basic part of most people preparing for working life. However, placement of students into the appropriate university, college, or discipline is of paramount importance for university education to perform its role. In this study, various explainable machine learning approaches (Decision Tree [DT], Extra tree classifiers [ETC], Random forest [RF] classifiers, Gradient boosting classifiers [GBC], and Support Vector Machine [SVM]) were tested to predict students' right undergraduate major (field of specialization) before admission at the undergraduate level based on the current job markets and experience. The DT classifier predicts the target class based on simple decision rules. ETC is an ensemble learning technique that builds prediction models by using unpruned decision trees. RF is also an ensemble technique that uses many individual DTs to solve complex problems. GBC classifiers and produce strong prediction models. SVM predicts the target class with a high margin, as compared to other classifiers. The imbalanced dataset includes secondary school marks, higher secondary school marks, experience, and salary to select specialization for students in undergraduate programs. The results showed that the performances of RF and GBC predict the student field of specialization (undergraduate major) before admission, as well as the fact that these measures are as good as DT and ETC. Statistical analysis (Spearman correlation) is also applied to evaluate the relationship between a student's major and other input variables. The statistical results show that higher student marks in higher secondary (hsc_p), university degree (Degree_p), and entry test (etest_p) play an important role in the student's area of specialization, and we can recommend study fields according to these features. Based on these results, RF and GBC can easily be integrated into intelligent recommender systems to suggest a good field of specialization to university students, according to the current job market. This study also demonstrates that marks in higher secondary and university and entry tests are useful criteria to suggest the right undergraduate major because these input features most accurately predict the student field of specialization.

Keywords: machine learning; learning analytics; student field forecasting; imbalanced datasets; explainable machine learning; intelligent tutoring system

1. Introduction

Today, higher education institutions face considerable difficulties, such as the absence of government funding, competitive job markets, admission processes, student strength, and selections of student specializations [1,2]. Student specialization selection is an area of educational research that has received little attention, although it is critical in recognizing students' interests and preparing them for a future career [3]. Student specialization is a worldwide educational problem that needs to be investigated. For example, in the USA, approximately 30% of year-one students do not return for their second year, and more than $9 billion is spent on these students [4]. Furthermore, the completion rates of 4-year degrees in the US are approximately 50% [5]. These alarming figures require every possible effort to support students and higher education institutions in this critical issue. According to a study conducted by the United States Departments of Education (NCES), of the 98% of students that declared a bachelor's degree major in 2011–2012, 33% changed their major by 2014 during their third year of study [6]. Moreover, approximately 35% of college students who declared their majors to be STEM programs and 29% of students who declared their majors to be STEM-related programs eventually changed their majors after 2 years of study [7].

Student specialization selection can indicate the choice of an appropriate specialization/major that leads to a high level of satisfaction, success in allotment, graduation within a time frame, or other more specific milestones [8]. In an educational institution, the selection of the right undergraduate major by students is a major challenge when progressing to an academic level because students do not know about the job market and the demand for the required skills.

1.1. Student Field Specialization (Undergraduate Major Course)

Field specialization selection means selecting the right undergraduate major for students, for example, engineering, computer science, and management [9,10]. Universities are required to fulfill students' academic disciplines. One essential goal of universities is to aid student admission into their desired college specialization. What student admission means varies depending on the context of the university requirements, students' academic results, and other related factors [11,12]. Universities provide student admission centers and student counselors or advisors to help students meet their educational needs. Recommending suitable colleges and fields (suitable undergraduate majors) based on students' attributes and preferences is one service that could be provided by admission departments. However, due to the growing numbers of fields, students, and available skills, these advisors sometimes fail to help students with their selections [3,13,14]. Due to the substantial amount of work required by these advisors, who are not able to handle this situation, students have insufficient knowledge about how to select an appropriate field (major) in their undergraduate program that fits their preferences, personality, subjects of interest, and career type that he or she likes [3,13,14].

1.2. Significance of Predicting Student Field Specialization

The undergraduate major (field specialization) is an important research topic because an incorrect undergraduate major selection affects students' academic lives, learning, and careers [15]. Students in every country face challenges in selecting the right undergraduate major. From the time students decide to continue their higher education, they are confronted with decisions concerning their education, many of which can be challenging. When students attend college, they choose a major based on several factors, such as their friends, parents, future opportunities, and, most importantly, the student advisory center. Some students are not fully aware of the importance of their academic abilities and job market demands [16]. They may depend on others' opinions, which may lead to the incorrect and unsuitable major selection. Incorrect academic decisions have a considerable and direct impact on students' success and future lives [17]. If a student chooses an unsuitable academic major and continues to have low grades and fails to raise his or her CGPA within a year, the student will be dismissed from college.

Thus, the choice of a field (student major) for a new student can be a difficult decision; therefore, universities need to use a student intelligent counseling system because the correct student feedback has been shown to decrease the course dropout rate and increase graduation rate [18]. Long et al. [19] indicated that improving and enhancing the matching of students with their university specialization could substantially assist in decreasing the level of study discontinuation among younger students, which would also contribute to opening up spots for other potential students and in decreasing the inefficient utilization of public resources and funds for higher education. Therefore, this paper addressed the field of specialization suggestion problem by suggesting appropriate study fields for students at early stages, according to the current job market, education history, and career goals for the students. Hence, it is desirable to develop sophisticated forms of intelligent recommendation tools to help students in selecting an appropriate field of specialization

1.3. Machine Learning Techniques Used in an Education Predictive Model

Artificial intelligence (AI) is an important concept in the field of science and is currently a promising technological revolution. It uses machines to develop a concept of intelligence that is more like the human brain. There have been various fields that have taken advantage of implementing AI in their day-to-day business processes. In the area of computer sciences, the concept of artificial intelligence is widely utilized, and it is considerably related to the concept of machine learning (ML). ML is a sub-field of AI that identifies complex and hidden patterns or knowledge from large amounts of data and then makes smart decisions on unseen data [20]. One of the key features of ML is a training model utilizing different dependent and independent variables, which further depends on different utilized learning algorithms types (supervised, semisupervised, or unsupervised). ML is mostly used for predictions in many field to provide solutions to questions such as global solar radiation [21], weather predictions [22], flight time deviation [23], mortality rates in COVID-19 patients [24], predict bank failures [25], credit default prediction in bank [26], cyber security [27], bankruptcy prediction [28], filter e-learning contents [29] and efficient processes for manufacturing industries [8]. It can also be used for predicting rates in student dropouts in any course [17] and for understanding unique student learning styles [30]. Moreover, ML algorithms can assist the educational sector by constantly evaluating student academic performance. Due to the vast and dynamic implementation of ML, as well as its capability to learn from any dataset and to predict and classify future transactions, we have selected multiple ML algorithms for use in this study.

In recent years, research interest in the application of ML in education has increased, particularly among higher-education institutions. A recent study discovered that educational-related decisions are frequently made based on educational management stakeholders'/ students' impressions and experience, rather than based on knowledge-rich data. Unfortunately, it is a challenging task to make a suitable choice of the subject matter at an early stage due to the convoluted interaction of a variety of factors [31–33]. ML approaches are designed to make necessary educational information readily available to knowledge consumers. ML techniques have also been shown to be beneficial in improving outcomes at several educational institutions and student management centers by making necessary educational information readily available to students and other individuals [34,35]. In the past 10 years, investigations on ML and education data mining [EDM] have played a significant role in exploring educational problems [31,36], such as understanding student performance [37,38] and educational institution performance [39]. These techniques have also been used to predict student engagement and difficulty in online education [40,41] and in recommending suitable colleges and courses [9,42–45]. ML is increasingly prevalent and vital in educational contexts, in terms of predicting and identifying quality educational-related problems for students and decision-makers, as well as in enhancing other managerial services pertaining to streamlining students' needs. Furthermore, numerous research studies on education have predicted admission to universities, student allotment, and admission into their desired colleges/majors by using ML techniques [33,46,47].

The current study investigated the best ML classifier that is suitable for building student field specialization intelligent systems, which can predict student study fields based on student academic history and the job market. Predicting student study fields is a classification problem; therefore, we verified the performance of common ML classification algorithms, such as Decision Tree (DT), extra tree classifiers [ETC], random forest (RF) classifiers, and gradient boosting classifiers [GBC], and Support Vector Machine [SVM], on the current study dataset. The performances of these algorithms are good, based on categorical data [48]. Additionally, these algorithms are easily described, understandable, and implemented [48]. The current study also verified the performance of the SVM on the current study dataset because it can examine both linear and nonlinear data [49].

1.4. Innovation of the Current Study

The current study investigated the student field of specialization by using students' previous histories and job market information utilizing different ML techniques. ML approaches have been employed to accurately forecast college selection and select the best fit student major by means of common classification algorithms with diverse feature sets [1]. To achieve our current study goal, we trained different common ML models (extra tree classifiers [ETC], random forest [RF] classifiers, decision tree [DT] classifiers, gradient boosting classifiers [GBC], and support vector machine [SVM]) based on the current job market and students' previous histories. The results showed that RF and GBC predicted student majors with higher accuracy, as compared to DT, SVM, and ETC. Based on the Spearman correlation method, the study concluded that higher marks in higher secondary levels, entry tests, and universities, are good criteria for suggesting student field specialization. Furthermore, student work experiences and job placements are additional factors that are strongly related to student field specializations. In addition, these ML models and features could be of high value in developing an intelligent system to easily recommend a specialization to potential applicants who are often unsure of their desired fields of specialization. Finally, this paper differs from other research in this area of predicting student field specializations because it is based on the job market and student histories and experiences.

The current study investigated the following research questions.

Question 1: Can we model the student undergraduate major path choice according to the job market and student academic history by applying different ML algorithms, and if so, which ML classifier offers optimal performance in predicting student undergraduate major selection?

Question 2: How is a student's undergraduate major path choice associated with that student's previous academic performance and the job market?

Contributions: This study possesses contributions as enlisted below in the domain of selection of majors by students.

1. The research utilized Kaggle repositories to devise a ML approach in selecting the field of specialization by students for future endeavors.
2. Several supervised learning techniques with 10-k fold cross-validation were utilized and yielded that RF, SVM, and GBC were the suitable classifiers for predicting student undergraduate major.
3. The influential factors related to selecting the right undergraduate major were also showcased. According to my knowledge, no work has been done to find student influential factors.
4. The findings may be integrated into the intelligent field recommender system for predicting suitable fields for students according to the job market.

The rest of this paper is organized as follows. The literature review of the student study field is discussed in Section 2. The research materials and methods are discussed in Section 3, which contains all of the details of our proposed framework of the student study field selection system. Section 4 describes the experiment and discusses the results of the current study, where the performances of different ML algorithms are tested on the current study dataset. Finally, Section 5 presents the conclusions and future work of the current study.

2. Literature Review

Several studies have been conducted to investigate student field specialization (student major) using ML. Past research has used different ML techniques and input features to study the relationship between student data and student majors. Alshaikh et al. [3] built a recommendation system to suggest suitable colleges for KAU students based on the students' grades, college specializations, and enrollment requirements. They applied this system to a dataset of 960 KAU preparatory students in 2017. Two methods were used to evaluate the accuracy of the k-nearest-neighbor algorithm. In the first method, the dataset was split into two datasets, 20% of the dataset for testing and the remaining 80% for training, which generated 70.83% accuracy. The second approach applied k-fold cross-validation, where the dataset was split into K smaller sets and the test was applied K times. Pupara et al. [50] have proposed an accurate institutional recommender system (RS) that was developed by combining decision tree and association rule methodologies. The RS is intended to assist students in selecting acceptable colleges based on their context and educational institution information using a mobile device. Ezz and Elshenawy [9] presented an adaptive recommendation system for predicting a suitable engineering department for students enrolled in an engineering preparatory year college using classification methods such as SVM, k-nearest neighbor (KNN), linear regression (LR), quadratic discriminant analysis (QDA), and RF. The system recommends a suitable engineering department among seven engineering departments for each student based on his academic performance and the proposed system has an average accuracy of 82.57%. In the study of Salaki et al. [51], 3 ML algorithms, namely, naïve Bayes (NB), RF, and sequential minimal optimization (SMO), were trained on a dataset collected from three different educational colleges in Bangladesh to identify and select the best groups of educational majors to streamline the selection of a suitable direction for new students. The results showed that RF had the best performance, with 84.9% accuracy, 84.9% precision, 84.6% sensitivity, and an F-measure of 84.3%. In a study conducted by Fiarni et al. [52], an academic decision support system was built in the IS department to classify and recommend IS sub-majors for students using a C4.5 decision tree classifier and a rule-based approach. Bautista et al. [10] adopted 8 methods (namely, the J48 tree classifier, logistic function classifier, naïve Bayes (NB), nominal regression, decision tree CHAID, neural network multilayer perceptron, neural network radial basis function, and nearest neighbor) to recommend a suitable specialization for engineering students. The first three methods were tested in Weka and achieved accuracies of 80.5%, 64.30%, and 60.11%, respectively. The last 5 experiments conducted in SPSS, yielded accuracies of 64.00%, 68.20%, 71.30%, 61.00%, and 71.20%. Moreover, the J48 tree classifier performed the best, with the highest accuracy of 80.5%. A study conducted by Kularbphettong and Tongsiri [53] aimed to develop a decision support system for student major selection using two ML methods, J48 and Bayesian network algorithms (BNs). Their results showed that BNs performed the best, with 92.13%, 0.93, and 0.91 accuracy, precision, and F-measure, respectively. Meng and Fu [35] applied 8 classification methods, namely, SVM, decision tree (DT), naïve Bayes (GNB), RF, gradient boosting decision tree (GBDT), convolutional neural network (CNN), collaborative filtering (CF), and recurrent neural network (RNN), to recommend appropriate college majors. RF performed best, with an accuracy of 97.87% and an f-score of 96.60%. Wei et al. [54] proposed an improved SVM-based prediction system model for predicting second major selection. Their experimental results indicated that the proposed method performed best, with an accuracy of 87.36%, AUC of 0.8735, the sensitivity of 85.37%, and specificity of 89.33%, Sethi et al. [55] conducted a study to predict the appropriate study stream for students in higher secondary education. They found that the neural network (NN) outperformed the other approaches with a classification accuracy of 86.72%, the sensitivity of 0.92, specificity of 0.82, and MCC of 0.72. Abosamra et al. [56] examined various types of ML predictions models on a dataset, which gave the best choice as a (NN) architecture that provides 6.26 an average root mean squared error, and a mean absolute error of 5.74 based on a scale of 0 to 100.

The artificial neural network (ANN) method was adopted by Latifah et al. [57] to predict suitable student specialization in a dataset of 314 students based on student records from the iGracias Integrated Academic Information System at Telkom University in 2016, and they achieved an accuracy of 94.81%. The NB method and analytic hierarchy process (AHP) techniques were adopted by Zubaedah et al. [58] to build a decision support system to predict suitable specialization in technical faculty in Indonesia. A rule-based classification algorithm (PART) was adopted by Tamiza et al. [59] to propose an intelligent model for selecting and predicting suitable university specialization. The model achieved an accuracy of 73.7%. Iyer and Variawa [60] built a system model to guide first-year undeclared/undecided engineering students to predict suitable engineering majors. They found that the RF approach outperformed the other classification algorithms, with the highest accuracy of 57%. AlAhmar [61] developed a rule-based expert system that suggested majors for students at the undergraduate level. Kamal et al. [62] has used RF classifiers to analyze students' personality and intelligence across various majors and academic programs and predict suitable college majors for students based on academic results, personality, and level of intelligence with an accuracy of level one at 96.1% and 94.72% at second level respectively, moreover, they have investigated that their framework has potential to recommend a student towards future higher degree options.

Although the attractiveness of higher education institutions in many areas of student field of study selection has been extensively researched, there is a paucity of evidence available for modeling the relationship between these factors and intelligent recommendation of student fields based on the job market and student history and experience. To our knowledge, no studies have been conducted on the use of any ML algorithm specifically designed for the purpose of predicting student specialization and identifying the extent to which various parameters contribute to the determination of the specialization of students. As a result of this discovery, we were inspired to conduct our current study. As a result, the current research has implications for higher education, students, and the labor market.

3. Materials and Methods

In the current study, we developed an intelligent system for the field of specialization selection. We trained and tested various ML models on a student dataset because such techniques are suitable for categorical data. The proposed framework has the following stages: data preprocessing, visualization model selection modules, and model deployment. Figure 1 shows all the steps of the proposed framework. Overall, this section provides all the implementations of the student study field intelligent system in the form of the below sub-section.

3.1. Data Description

The data collection consists of several steps. Before the implementation process, consistent and appropriate educational data are required to achieve acceptable results. In this experiment, the dataset was published in Kaggle [63]. The details are shown in Table 1. This dataset was collected from MBA students of CMS Business School in January 2020 and was published on the Kaggle website [63]. This dataset contains placement data of students, including secondary school, higher secondary school, and entry test scores. The dataset also includes work experience, degree percentage, and salary offered by the organization. The salary information represents the importance of the field in the job market. The degree percentage shows the student's interest in the field. The current database contains 216 student records and 19 input features. The first experimental dataset is shown in Table 1, and the target variable is specialization.

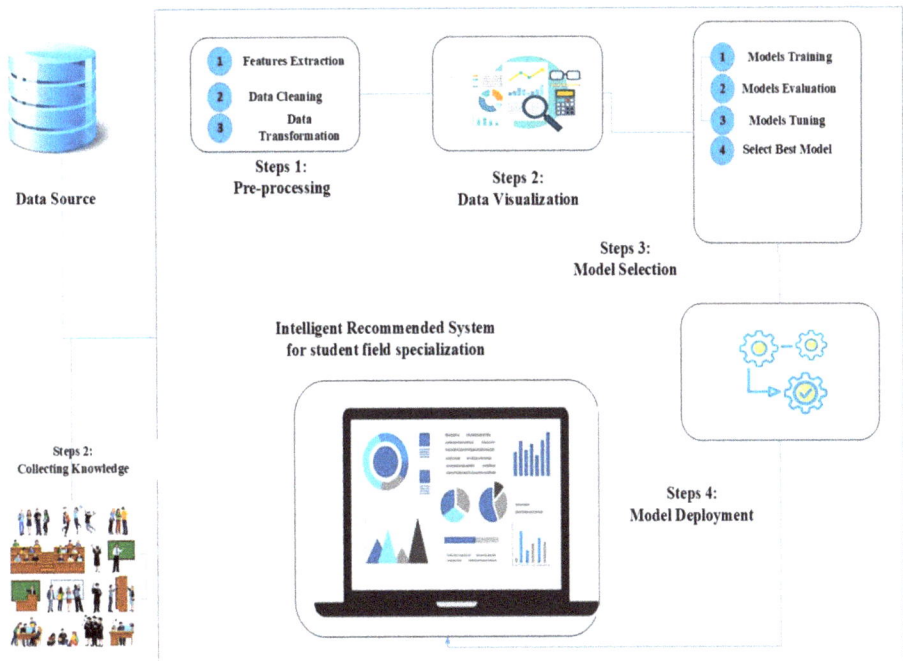

Figure 1. Intelligent recommender system for student field recommendation.

Table 1. First experiment dataset description.

Features Name	Description	Data Type
Gender	Student Gender (Male/Female)	Categorical
SSC_P	Student secondary school percentage	Numeric
SSC_b	Student secondary school board studied (Class 10)	Categorical
HSC_P	Higher secondary school percentage (Class 12)	Numeric
hsc_b	Higher secondary school board studied (Class 12)	Categorical
hsc_s	High secondary school (Class 12) specialization	Categorical
degree_p	Degree percentage	Numeric
degree_t	Degree type	Categorical
workex	Work experience	Categorical
etest_p	Score on entrance test	Numeric
specialization	Degree specialization	Categorical
mba_p	Student percentage in MBA	Numeric
status	Student placement status	Categorical
salary	Student salary	Numeric
ssc_p_catg	Student secondary school percentage in 3 categories (85%+, 60–85%, <60%)	Categorical
hsc_p_catg	Higher secondary school percentage in three categories (85%+, 60–85%, <60%)	Categorical
mba_p_catg	Student percentage in MBA in 3 categories ((85%+, 60–85%, <60%)	Categorical
degree_p_catg	Degree percentage in 3 categories (85%+, 60–85%, <60%)	Categorical
etest_p_catg	Percentage on entrance test in 3 categories (85%+, 60–85%, <60%)	Categorical

3.2. Proposed Framework

Undergraduate major selection is a crucial and challenging decision for the university and the student during the process of admission to fulfill their future success. Due to bad counseling by the admission office center in the university, students go into the wrong study field; as a result, student learning will be affected [15]. Every country faces problems with students selecting the right undergraduate major course, and past studies have indicated that institutions have seen a significant increase in the number of students enrolling as undeclared. In reality, it is estimated that over 50% of students enter college undecided and that approximately 75% of students change their majors at least once before they complete their degree [64,65].

This study builds a student major intelligent system that provides feedback to students and universities about study field selection based on the data extracted from the university database. Finding and building an intelligent system model of students' field of specialization could be of high value in developing an intelligent system to easily recommend a specialization to potential applicants who are often unsure of their desired field of specialization. In the current study, we verified the performance of different supervised ML techniques to predict students' fields of specialization based on student history and the job market. High-performance ML algorithms can provide a high degree of support to student major intelligent systems. Based on performance, the student major intelligent system can provide various support to educational institutions on many issues, such as (1) helping the university administration staff in making quick decisions about students' fields of study; (2) recommending personalized study fields according to students preferences and the job market; (3) decreasing the workload for the admission office; (4) enrolling students according to their preferences and job markets; (5) identifying at-risk students and chances of success of students at early stages; and (6) intervening with the student at early stages so that course dropout rates will decrease, as well as to ensure that students go into the right study fields. Figure 1 shows the basic architecture of the intelligent system for student field of specialization recommendation. The proposed student field intelligent system framework has four major phases, which are shown below.

Step 1 Pre-processing: In the first phase known as Phase-1 (preprocessing), raw information (216 student records) was collected from a university database, as shown in Table 1. Subsequently, we applied different preprocessing techniques by using the Python module, such as removing missing records, deleting irrelevant student records, normalization, outlier detection, and hot encoding. To increase the proposed system performance, we also created new features by creating different categories at different education levels (ssc_p_catg, hsc_p_catg, mba_p_catg, degree_p_catg and etest_p_catg). To remove the missing records, we used different missing record techniques. Sometimes, ML techniques do not process the categorical technique; therefore, we applied the hot encoding technique. Additionally, the cleaned data were normalized because the ML model does not work correctly on non-normalized data. Finally, the preprocessing module converted the data into an acceptable form for the ML models, and the data were ready for the next phase. The current study dataset contained 19 input features (previous exam history, salary, and experiences of students), and the explanation of our current study dataset is shown in Table 1. Specialization is the target variable (Y) that finds the class of independent variables. When students belong to Management and Human resource management (HR) study fields (Mk and HR) then target variable (Y) is set "1" and if students belong to Management and Finance study field then target variable (Y) is set to "0".

Step 2 Data Visualization: In the second phase (data visualization), the clean data were visualized by using a different Python library, which shows how important the input feature is in predicting student study fields. This visualization is used to better understand the current study data.

Steps 3 Model Selection: In the third Phase (model selection modules), different supervised ML techniques were trained and tested using a 10-fold cross-validation method on the clean data by using the Scikit-learn Python library. It is a free ML library of python. In this library, we can easily implement ML algorithms. The current study ML algorithms were trained and tuned on training data and tested on test data using 10-fold cross-validation. After training, the model will find a pattern between input features and out variables or find the best model on the current study dataset. In addition, to select high-performance models, different performance metrics, such as accuracy and a true positive rate, were used. Finally, ML models with high accuracy are selected for intelligent field systems:

Step 4 Model Deployment: In Phase four, an intelligent field of specialization system was developed with the help of a high-performance ML model (RF, GBC, and SVM) because RF, GBC, and SVM predict field specialization with high accuracy. Consequently, intelligent detection of the student field of specialization provides decision-makers, academic advisors, students, and other individuals with knowledge and person-specific information, which is intelligently filtered or presented at the appropriate time, to improve education and the student's best-fit specialization field [3,14,35,66,67]. Additionally, the proposed intelligent field of specialization system will help university admission offices in daily activities.

4. Results and Discussion

Consequently, the selection of an appropriate and suitable field of study is a paramount issue for both students and educational institutes. Therefore, in this section, we investigated the student field (student major) of specialization selection using different ML techniques based on student academic history and the current job market. We also visualized the current dataset to further understand the input variables and performed several experiments using Python to answer the research questions.

We performed data visualization using Python to further understand the experimental dataset. These visualization results show the importance of input attributes in predicting field specialization. Figure 2 shows that higher secondary students who obtained jobs mostly majored in commerce and science. This result further indicates that commerce and science fields are currently in the greatest demand.

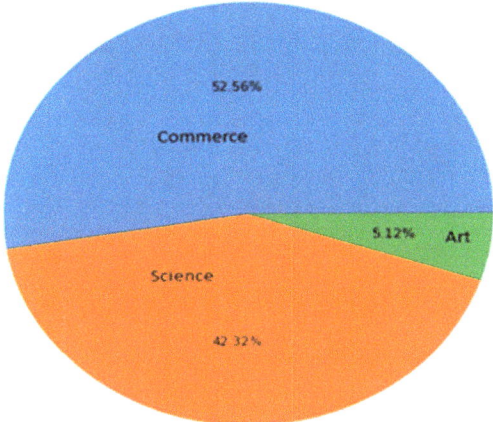

Figure 2. The proportion of different student fields of specialization in higher secondary school.

Figure 3 shows that commerce and management students in higher secondary schools mostly take science and technology fields as postgraduates.

In Figure 4, the blue portion (1) represents Mkt and finance, and the yellow portion (0) represents the Mkt and HR. Figure 4 indicates that 55.81% of students take the MKT& Finance program in postgraduate education, and others take the MKT & HR field.

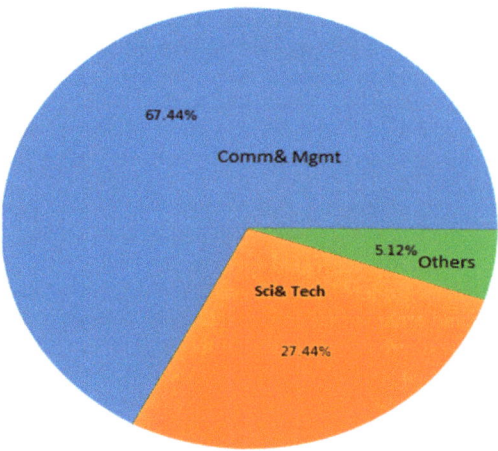

Figure 3. The proportion of different student fields of specialization in degree.

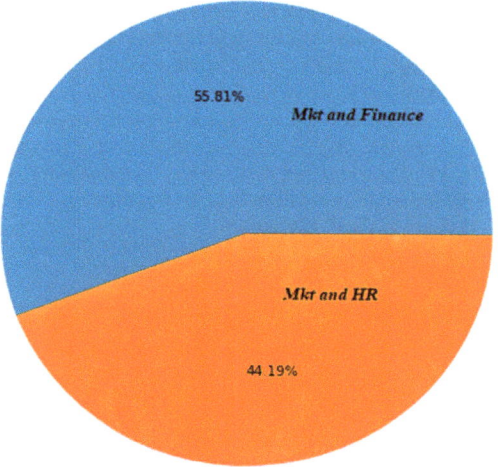

Figure 4. The proportion of different student fields of specialization in postgraduate education.

At this step, we have obtained considerable knowledge about the data and can easily build models. Although there are lots of studies related to the selection of majors by students and its influential factors [1–7,68], studies with a machine learning approach in this domain are limited [7]. In this study, we investigate the student study field based on student job markets, student academic history, and job experience. As the number of factors, size of the datasets, methods applied varied in different studies, it is impractical to compare these studies. Some of these studies were listed in Table 2. To find an appropriate ML model and student factors for our proposed recommendation system, this study conducts two experiments on datasets using the Python Sklearn library. Sklearn is a Python library that is used to train and deploy ML models. In this section, we investigate the following research question:

Table 2. Related studies are based on major influence factors for the recommendation of the future domain.

Reference	Year of Publication	Country	No of Participants	Some of the Most Influential Factors in Selecting Major	Methods Used
[69]	2006	USA	89	personal interest in the subject matter, long-term salary prospects, probability of working in the field after graduation, starting salary, and prestige of the profession	Average Importance
[70]	2017	Korea	816	collaborative learning; technology-based learning; self-regulated learning; hands-on activities; belief in major benefits	Cronbach's Alpha, exploratory factor analysis (EFA), and confirmatory factor analysis (CFA)
[71]	2016	Korea	195	Gender, Grade, Acquaintance's recommendation, Daily hours of study, Place of residence	Fisher's exact test, t-test, one way ANOVA, Mann Whitney test, and ANCOVA
[14]	2019	Saudi Arabia	239 prospective participants and 392 university participants	the outcome of student's qualification exams and overall high school grades	Fuzzy Expert System
[72]	2015	Indonesia	40	value of national examination, the value of the placement test, and value of School Exams	Fuzzy Multiple Attribute Decision Making (FMADM)
[73]	2011	Iran	465	Students' interest and decision	Structural Equation Modeling
[74]	2004	USA	114	Financial aid, previous education, potential career/degree characteristics, and information sources.	chi-square and analysis of variance for mean differences
[55]	2020	India	550	Marks in Board exam, Family income, Scholarship, etc.	SVM, k-nearest neighbor and Neural Networks

Question 1: Can we model the student undergraduate major path choice according to the job market and student academic history by applying different ML algorithms, and if so, which ML classifier offers optimal performance in predicting student undergraduate major selection?

The first experiment was conducted to explore this question. In the first experiment, we applied several Tree based ML models (DT algorithm, RF algorithm, extra tree classifier, and XGBoost) and SVM to our dataset by using their default parameters. Decision-tree has been widely implemented in various domains, such as in medical fields [75], marketing prediction tasks [76], and education [77,78], due to its various well-known attractive features [79]. Features such as simplicity, comprehensive calculations, no required parameters, and the capability of handling mixed types of data, encouraged us to select DT in this study. Random forests are used in this study due to being easy and stable with many interesting properties. One of these interesting properties is that they provide a powerful computation of variables [80]. The extra tree classifier is one of the learning algorithms that can aggregate the results of multiple de-correlated decision trees collected in a "forest" to output its classification result. It has been applied in this study because it is similar to RF; however, it is faster, and its method in the construction of the decision tree in the forest is optimal. The tree-based algorithm is simple and requires less data; additionally, it is easy to understand and easily implemented [81,82]. Conversely, deep learning (artificial neural network) is complex, computationally expensive, and requires more data [83]. Additionally, we did not use the naive Bayes algorithm, which is a very commonly used algorithm to solve real-life problems because it overlooked how to calculate probabilities [84]. We used SVM because the performance is good using small datasets [85,86]. Moreover, it does not apply a strict requirement on the number of samples and sample points; additionally, it can process error distributions and can be easily promoted. XGBoost was used in this study because it has higher predictive accuracy than other ML algorithms, such as SVM and DT [87,88]. Our dataset contains both numeric and categorical attributes. Therefore, the selected model must perform well on categorical data. For the first experimental dataset, we used 19 input features, which are shown in Table 1, and the target variable was *specialization*. First, we converted the target variable (specialization) into a binary form (0,1) by using python, wherein "0" denotes marketing and finance (Mk&Fin) and "1" represents the Market and Human resources Field (Mk&HR). As ML algorithms cannot directly work on categorical data, and to convert input features in digital form, we used a hot encoding technique. Hot encoding is a technique that can map categorical data into integers; as a result, the Ml algorithm can produce better results. Hot encoding is useful when there is no relationship between the variables. The 10-fold cross-validation method was used to increase the generalization ability of the models and to ensure that the model behavior was optimal. Furthermore, accuracy, true positive rate (TPR), false-positive rate (FPR), and receiver operating characteristic (ROC) curve were used as evaluation metrics. The accuracy represents the percentage of correct predictions of the model given unseen data. In ML, the TPR is also known as recall or sensitivity and indicates the percentage of actual positive values that are correctly predicted by the model. Finally, the ROC curve plots the TPR of the model [89]. The current study performance metrics are shown below.

$$TPR = TP/TP + FN$$

$$FPR = FP/FP + TN$$

$$Accuracy = TP + TN/TP + TN + FP + FN$$

Notes: TP (true positive), FN (false negative), TN (true negative), FP (false positive).

DT algorithms belong to the supervised category of ML algorithms. A DT is simple and easily understandable. We selected this technique because it is widely used by researchers due to its simplicity. In addition, a DT has some great advantages, such as representing rules that could be easily understood and interpreted by users [81]. This type of algorithm performs well for categorical and numerical attributes and does not require complex data preparation. In short, ML classifiers and their outputs are easy to understand for individuals with a non-analytical background [90]. The default parameters (ccp_alpha = 0.0, criterion = 'gini', min_samples_split = 2) are used to train the DT model, and an accuracy of 55% was obtained by DT using 10-fold cross-validation. Table 3 shows that the DT correctly classifies student specialization with a TPR of 0.87 and an FPR of 0.71.

Table 3. Confusion matrix of the decision tree classifier.

	TN = 10 (0.29)	FP = 25 (0.71)
Actually (0)	FN = 4 (0.13)	TP = 26 (0.87)
Actually (1)	Predicted (0)	Predicted (1)

In the second step of the first experiment, RF classifiers were used to predict student specialization given a student placement dataset. The RF classifier is a supervised learning algorithm that applies to both classification and regression problems [80]. RF creates multiple DTs from random sample data and then gives predictions on high-accuracy trees [91,92]. The RF classifier predicts the student field specialization with the following default parameters (bootstrap = True, ccp_alpha = 0.0, criterion = 'gini', max_depth = 15, max_features = 'auto',max_leaf_nodes = 10). The TPR of RF is 0.70, and the FPR is 0.20, as shown in Table 4.

Table 4. Confusion matrix of the random forest classifier.

	TN = 28 (0.80)	FP = 7 (0.20)
Actually (0)	FN = 9 (0.30)	TP = 21 (0.70)
Actually (1)	Predicted (0)	Predicted (1)

Extra tree classifiers (ETC) are used in the third step to predict the student's field of specialization. ETC is an ensemble learning technique that collects the result of multiple trees. The approach is similar to an RF classifier, but the tree construction method differs. The accuracy of the ETC classifier on the student dataset is 0.52. During training, the ETC Classifier used the default parameters (n_estimators = 100, random_state = 0) to predict student specialization with high accuracy. The TPR and FPR of the ETC classifier were 0.53 and 0.49, respectively, as shown in Table 5.

Table 5. Confusion matrix of the extra tree classifier.

	TN = 18 (0.51)	FP = 17 (0.49)
Actually (0)	FN = 14 (0.47)	TP = 16 (0.53)
Actually (1)	Predicted (0)	Predicted (1)

In the fourth step of the first experiment, we used the SVM classifier. SVM is a supervised learning algorithm that is mostly used for classification problems. SVM finds the hyperplane that divides a dataset into two classes [93]. SVM classifiers perform well on clean and small datasets. Furthermore, SVM is faster than other machine learning techniques [93]. The best accuracy (52%) of SVM was achieved with the following default parameters (random_state = 0, tol = 1×10^{-5}), as shown in Table 6. The TPR and FPR of SVM are 0.53 and 0.49, respectively, as shown in Table 7.

Table 6. Experimental results of the machine learning models on the current study dataset.

Model	Accuracy
Decision Tree Algorithm	0.5538
Random Forest Algorithm	0.7538
Extra Trees Classifier	0.5231
Support Vector Machine	0.5231
XGBoost	0.6154

Table 7. Confusion matrix of the support vector machine (SVM).

	TN = 18 (0.51)	FP = 17 (0.49)
Actually (0)	FN = 14 (0.47)	TP = 16 (0.53)
Actually (1)	Predicted (0)	Predicted (1)

Finally, we used the XGBoost classifier to predict student specializations by using default parameters (base_score = 0.5, booster = 'gbtree', colsample_bylevel = 1, learning_rate = 0.1). XGBoost is a popular boosting technique in ensemble ML, and its performance is good on structured and tabular data. XGBoost is also called GBC. XGBoost uses parallel tree boosting to solve real-life data science problems. We used this technique because its impact has been widely recognized in many machine learning and data mining challenges, where it has become a commonly used and popular tool among Kaggle's competitors and data scientists [87]. XGBoost predicts the student's specialization with an accuracy of 61%, and the TPR and FPR of the XGBoost classifier are 0.57 and 0.35, respectively, as shown in Table 8.

Table 8. Confusion matrix of the XGBoost classifier.

	TN = 23 (0.66)	FP = 12 (0.34)
Actually (0)	FN = 13 (0.43)	TP = 17 (0.57)
Actually (1)	Predicted (0)	Predicted (1)

In the first experiment, the TPR and accuracy of the RF and GBC classifiers were higher than DT, SVM, and ETC, and the FPR was lower than that of DT, SVM, and ETC, as shown in Figure 5, which indicates that the performance of these classifiers in predicting field specializations is good, compared to that of the alternatives. Sometimes, accuracy is misleading when the dataset is imbalanced [94–96]. In other words, if the ratio of some classes is less than that of others in the dataset, we used the ROC curve and TPR, which is also called recall. We used ROC to further understand the performance of the models. The ROC is an evaluation metric that represents the performance of an ML model in the form graph [97] by plotting the TPR and FPR of the model. Figure 5 shows that the TPR of the RF and GBC classifiers was high, compared to that of the DT, SVM, and ETC. The results also showed that RF and GBC classifiers are appropriate classifiers to build student field recommendation systems because they can handle ordinal, non-ordinal, and categorical data and are also good choices for skewed and multimodal data [98]. Moreover, the RF and GBC classifier ensemble method outperforms simple DT classifiers. The previous study showed that the performance of SVM in small data is good and faster [93]. Furthermore, DT and ETC are unstable and have high sensitivities for overfitting classifiers [15].

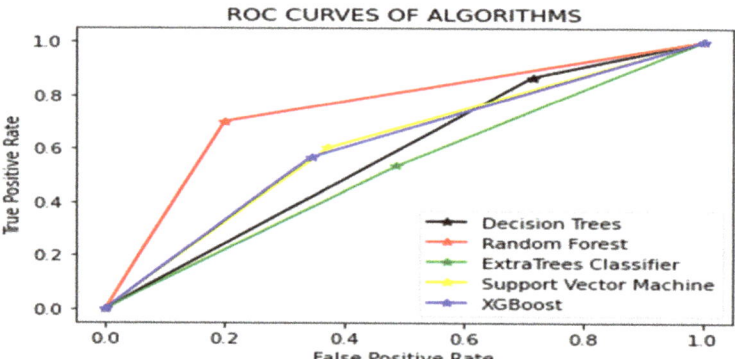

Figure 5. ROC curves of all the classifiers.

Question 2: How is a student's undergraduate major path choice associated with that student's academic performance and the job market?

We performed a second experiment to investigate the second research question. The second experiment investigated how a student's field of specialization was associated with that student's previous academic history, salary, and experience. First, we observed the baseline characteristics of different selected variables, such as secondary education percentage, higher secondary education percentage, degree percentage, MBA percentage, and employability test percentage. Then, we performed statistical analysis (Spearman correlation) to assess the relationship between a student's major and other input variables. The Spearman correlation shows how closely two variables are related. Table 9 shows the Spearman correlation between student field specialization and other input variables of the current study. The statistical results show that higher student marks in higher secondary (hsc_p), university degree (Degree_p), and entry test (etest_p) play a significant role in student field of specialization, and we can easily suggest study fields according to these features. Furthermore, student work experience (work_exp) and job placement (status) also impact student field specialization. Several interesting observations are obtained from the above statistical analysis. First, students at the high secondary stage are very excited about their field in university (undergraduate level) or undergraduate major path choice. At this level, every student wants to go into a good study field. In other words, students place high importance on student field specialization decisions. Second, students who get admitted to their favorite field graduate with higher grades. Third, the student field of specialization also affects student work experience and market salary. Fourth, students who applied for their favorite field may receive high marks on their university entry test. Fifth, students who graduate in their favorite field have a high chance of getting a job. In addition, the student marks percentage in a higher secondary, university degree, and entry test is useful criteria for study field suggestion. The result also demonstrates that student marks percentage in higher secondary, university degree, entry test assignment, and other factors are beneficial to the intelligent recommendation system. Using these variables, the proposed recommender system correctly predicts student field specialization according to their marks and preferences.

Table 9. Spearman correlation between student specialization and other input variables.

Input Features	r	p Value	Mean	Std
gender	−0.106	0.12	0.64651	0.47917
ssc_p	−0.17	0.01	67.3034	10.8272
ssc_b	−0.05	0.45	0.46047	0.499598
hsc_p	−0.24	0.00	66.3332	10.8975
hsc_b	0.002	0.97	0.6093	0.48905
hsc_s	0.17	0.01	1.37209	0.58098
degree_p	−0.21	DOT00	66.3702	7.35874
degree_t	0.08	0.21	0.6	0.89024
workex	−0.19	0.00	0.34419	0.47621
etest_p	−0.23	0.00	72.1006	13.276
mba_p	−0.1	0.12	0.44186	5.83339
status	−0.25	0.00	0.68837	0.46424
ssc_p_catg	0.15	0.02	0.50698	0.84759
hsc_p_catg	0.16	0.01	0.45116	0.80081
mba_p_catg	0.1	0.14	0.37674	0.4857
degree_p_catg	0.24	0.00	0.3814	0.78158
etest_p_catg	−0.011	0.86	0.641860	0.80716
Salary	−0.14	0.07	288,655.405	93,457.45

The current study results show that we can design a recommendation system for predicting the field of specialization using RF, GBC, and SVM classifiers. The proposed recommendation system will offer a variety of functions to students and college/university staff, such as recommending appropriate fields of study for students, ranking highly demanding fields in the coming and current years, and predicting the future salary of recommended fields. The results also show that higher secondary education is an appropriate stage to enter a good study field. Moreover, having a suitable specialization might affect students' academic performance and job salary, which could assist in lessening their anxiety and confusion and could lead to significantly better study program completion and increase graduation rates in the future. Having early awareness of the estimated number of incoming freshmen per study specialization program could also be of high value to the college administration. With this great insight, they would be able to allocate required resources per specialization field and better prepare schedules.

5. Conclusions

Unsuitable field of specialization selection for new graduate students has serious consequences for students and universities. Choosing an appropriate field of specialization is a critical determinant of a student's future academic and work progression. The current study used a machine learning and statistical approach to investigate the student study field. In this study, we extracted data from the Kaggle repository, which is publicly available for research purposes, and then converted these data into a form that is acceptable for ML models. We then applied several supervised learning techniques (DT, RF, ETC, and GBC) to our dataset and evaluated them using a 10-fold cross-validation method. The findings showed that RF and, GBC predict student study fields with accuracy 0.75% and 0.61 respectively. The results indicate that RF and GBC are the most appropriate, classifiers to integrate into the intelligent field recommender system for predicting suitable fields for students according to the job market because the performance of these classifiers is good on less training data Additionally, the intelligent field recommender system will help educational institutions to suggest study fields according to the current job market and demand. Using this recommendation system, students can select a field that is according to the job market. The study also demonstrated that the student field of specialization selection is mostly dependent on the percentage of marks in higher secondary, university, and entry tests. Student work experience and student job placement also affect the student's field of study. Furthermore, student mark percentage in higher secondary, university, and entry tests are appropriate criteria for all higher education institution admission departments to select the right undergraduate major path choice.

This experiment aims to investigate whether these data could be used to suggest an appropriate study field for students. This study used student academic data and job market data from the Kaggle repository. The student's field of specialization is a complex problem that also depends on other factors, such as country and student family background. Therefore, these factors must be further investigated.

The Current study limitations: There are some limitations, for example, the current study has limited specializations, records, and input features. In the future, we will use design surveys to assess other factors or input features related to the student field of specialization. Additionally, the accuracy of RF, GBC, and SVM models will be further improved by increasing the number of observations and hyperparameter tuning. Then, we will build an intelligent field recommendation system using collaborative filtering to recommend suitable fields to students according to their preferences and the job market. This proposed system will help the university admission system make quick decisions about student field recommendations.

Author Contributions: Conceptualization, A.O.A. and M.S.M.R.; Methodology, M.H., S.H.J. and S.H.; Software, M.H.; Validation, M.H., M.S.M.R. and M.L.J.; Formal Analysis, A.O.A. and M.H., S.H.J.; Investigation, A.O.A. and S.H.J.; Resources, A.O.A.; Data Curation, M.H.; Writing—Original Draft Preparation, A.O.A. and N.A.; Writing—Review & Editing, A.O.A., S.H.J. and M.H.; Visualization, M.H.; Supervision, M.S.M.R., I.A. and M.H.; Project Administration, A.O.A., M.H. and N.A. All authors have read and agreed to the published version of the manuscript.

Funding: This research work is funded under the project number IFPIP:536-830-1442.

Institutional Review Board Statement: Data is being taken from an authorized open source site (Kaggle).

Informed Consent Statement: Not applicable.

Data Availability Statement: The current study data are publicly available online (https://www.kaggle.com/benroshan/factors-affecting-campus-placement 7 November 2021) for research purposes. No participants' personal information (e.g., name or address) was included in this study.

Acknowledgments: The authors extend their appreciation to the Deputyship for Research & Innovation, Ministry of Education in Saudi Arabia for funding this research work through the project number IFPIP:536-830-1442 and King Abdulaziz University, DSR, Jeddah, Saud Arabia.

Conflicts of Interest: The authors have no conflict of interest.

References

1. Mengash, H.A. Using Data Mining Techniques to Predict Student Performance to Support Decision Making in University Admission Systems. *IEEE Access* **2020**, *8*, 55462–55470. [CrossRef]
2. Fong, S.; Si, Y.-W.; Biuk-Aghai, R. Applying a hybrid model of neural network and decision tree classifier for predicting university admission. In Proceedings of the 2009 7th International Conference on Information, Communications and Signal Processing (ICICS), Macau, China, 8–10 December 2009; IEEE: Piscataway, NJ, USA, 2009; pp. 1–5.
3. Alshaikh, K.; Bahurmuz, N.; Torabah, O.; Alzahrani, S.; Alshingiti, Z.; Meccawy, M. Using Recommender Systems for Matching Students with Suitable Specialization: An Exploratory Study at King Abdulaziz University. *Int. J. Emerg. Technol. Learn.* **2021**, *16*, 316–324. [CrossRef]
4. Aulck, L.; Velagapudi, N.; Blumenstock, J.; West, J. Predicting student dropout in higher education. In Proceedings of the 33rd International Conference on Machine Learning (ICML) Workshop on #Data4Good: Machine Learning in Social Good Applications, New York, NY, USA, 24 June 2016; pp. 16–20.
5. Elbadrawy, A.; Polyzou, A.; Ren, Z.; Sweeney, M.; Karypis, G.; Rangwala, H. Predicting Student Performance Using Personalized Analytics. *Computer* **2016**, *49*, 61–69. [CrossRef]
6. Leu, K. *Beginning College Students Who Change Their Majors within 3 Years of Enrollment*; NCES: Washington, DC, USA, 2017.
7. Atuahene, F. An analysis of major and career decision-making difficulties of exploratory college students in a Mid-Atlantic University. *SN Soc. Sci.* **2021**, *1*, 80. [CrossRef]
8. Yeyie, P. Selecting Program of Study for Undergraduate Students in the Valley View University, Kumasi. *Soc. Educ. Res.* **2021**, *2*, 315–330. [CrossRef]
9. Ezz, M.; Elshenawy, A. Adaptive recommendation system using machine learning algorithms for predicting student's best academic program. *Educ. Inf. Technol.* **2019**, *25*, 2733–2746. [CrossRef]
10. Bautista, R.; Dumlao, M.; Ballera, M. Recommendation system for engineering students' specialization selection using predictive modeling. In Proceedings of the Third International Conference on Computer Science, Computer Engineering, and Social Media (CSCESM2016), Thessaloniki, Greece, 13–15 May 2016; SDIWC: Lodz, Poland, 2016; pp. 34–40.
11. Al-Shalabi, L. A Data Mining Model for Students' Choice of College Major Based on Rough Set Theory. *J. Comput. Sci.* **2019**, *15*, 1150–1160. [CrossRef]
12. Eydi, M.; Moradi, Z.; Randian, R.; Rahdari, A.; Aliabadi, A. A Model to Determine Effective Factors on Pharmacy Major Selection (A Case Study: Students of Zabol University of Medical Sciences). *J. Pharm. Res. Int.* **2017**, *17*, 1–8. [CrossRef]
13. Reddy, M.Y.S.; Govindarajulu, P. College recommender system using student'preferences/voting: A system development with empirical study. *Int. J. Comput. Sci. Netw. Secur.* **2018**, *18*, 87–98.
14. Alghamdi, S.; Alzhrani, N.; Algethami, H. Fuzzy-Based Recommendation System for University Major Selection. In Proceedings of the 11th International Joint Conference on Computational Intelligence, Vienna, Austria, 17–19 September 2019; SCITEPRESS—Science and Technology Publications: Setúbal, Portugal, 2019; pp. 317–324.
15. Hattie, J.; Timperley, H. The Power of Feedback. *Rev. Educ. Res.* **2007**, *77*, 81–112. [CrossRef]
16. Kazi, A.S.; Akhlaq, A. Factors affecting students' career choice. *J. Res. Reflect. Educ.* **2017**, *2*, 187–196.
17. Astorne-Figari, C.; Speer, J.D. Are changes of major major changes? The roles of grades, gender, and preferences in college major switching. *Econ. Educ. Rev.* **2019**, *70*, 75–93. [CrossRef]
18. Bettinger, E.P.; Baker, R.B. The Effects of Student Coaching. *Educ. Eval. Policy Anal.* **2014**, *36*, 3–19. [CrossRef]
19. Long, M.; Ferrier, F.; Heagney, M. *Stay, Play or Give It Away? Students Continuing, Changing or Leaving University Study in First Year*; Centre for the Economics of Education and Training, Monash University: Melbourne, Australia, 2006.
20. Sharma, S.; Gupta, Y.K. Predictive analysis and survey of COVID-19 using machine learning and big data. *J. Interdiscip. Math.* **2021**, *24*, 175–195. [CrossRef]
21. Ağbulut, Ü.; Gürel, A.E.; Biçen, Y. Prediction of daily global solar radiation using different machine learning algorithms: Evaluation and comparison. *Renew. Sustain. Energy Rev.* **2021**, *135*, 110114. [CrossRef]
22. Haupt, S.E.; Cowie, J.; Linden, S.; McCandless, T.; Kosovic, B.; Alessandrini, S. Machine Learning for Applied Weather Prediction. In Proceedings of the 2018 IEEE 14th International Conference on e-Science (e-Science), Amsterdam, The Netherlands, 29 October–1 November 2018; IEEE: Piscataway, NJ, USA, 2018; pp. 276–277.
23. Stefanovič, P.; Štrimaitis, R.; Kurasova, O. Prediction of Flight Time Deviation for Lithuanian Airports Using Supervised Machine Learning Model. *Comput. Intell. Neurosci.* **2020**, *2020*, 8878681. [CrossRef] [PubMed]

24. Subudhi, S.; Verma, A.; Patel, A.B.; Hardin, C.C.; Khandekar, M.J.; Lee, H.; McEvoy, D.; Stylianopoulos, T.; Munn, L.L.; Dutta, S.; et al. Comparing machine learning algorithms for predicting ICU admission and mortality in COVID-19. *Npj Digit. Med.* **2021**, *4*, 87. [CrossRef]
25. Gogas, P.; Papadimitriou, T.; Agrapetidou, A. Forecasting bank failures and stress testing: A machine learning approach. *Int. J. Forecast.* **2018**, *34*, 440–455. [CrossRef]
26. Alam, T.M.; Shaukat, K.; Hameed, I.A.; Luo, S.; Sarwar, M.U.; Shabbir, S.; Li, J.; Khushi, M. An investigation of credit card default prediction in the imbalanced datasets. *IEEE Access* **2020**, *8*, 201173–201198. [CrossRef]
27. Shaukat, K.; Luo, S.; Varadharajan, V.; Hameed, I.A.; Xu, M. A survey on machine learning techniques for cyber security in the last decade. *IEEE Access* **2020**, *8*, 222310–222354. [CrossRef]
28. Alam, T.M.; Shaukat, K.; Mushtaq, M.; Ali, Y.; Khushi, M.; Luo, S.; Wahab, A. Corporate bankruptcy prediction: An approach towards better corporate world. *Comput. J.* **2020**, *65*. [CrossRef]
29. Javed, U.; Shaukat, K.; Hameed, I.A.; Iqbal, F.; Alam, T.M.; Luo, S. A review of content-based and context-based recommendation systems. *Int. J. Emerg. Technol. Learn.* **2021**, *16*, 274–306. [CrossRef]
30. Shin, J.C.; Harman, G. New challenges for higher education: Global and Asia-Pacific perspectives. *Asia Pac. Educ. Rev.* **2009**, *10*, 1–13. [CrossRef]
31. Anoopkumar, M.; Rahman, A.M.J.M.Z. A review on data mining techniques and factors used in educational data mining to predict student amelioration. In Proceedings of the International Conference on Data Mining and Advanced Computing (SAPIENCE), Ernakulam, India, 16–18 March 2016; IEEE: Piscataway, NJ, USA, 2016; pp. 122–133.
32. Isma'Il, M.; Haruna, U.; Aliyu, G.; Abdulmumin, I.; Adamu, S. An Autonomous Courses Recommender System For Undergraduate Using Machine Learning Techniques. In Proceedings of the 2020 International Conference in Mathematics, Computer Engineering and Computer Science (ICMCECS), Ayobo, Nigeria, 18–21 March 2020; IEEE: Piscataway, NJ, USA, 2020; pp. 1–6.
33. Tan, L.; Main, J.B.; Darolia, R. Using random forest analysis to identify student demographic and high school-level factors that predict college engineering major choice. *J. Eng. Educ.* **2021**, *110*, 572–593. [CrossRef]
34. Dhar, J.; Jodder, A.K. An Effective Recommendation System to Forecast the Best Educational Program Using Machine Learning Classification Algorithms. *Ingénierie Des Syst. Egrave Mes Inf.* **2020**, *25*, 559–568. [CrossRef]
35. Meng, Y.; Fu, M. CMRS: Towards Intelligent Recommendation for Choosing College Majors. In Proceedings of the 2020 4th International Conference on Advances in Image Processing, Chengdu, China, 13–15 November 2020; pp. 152–157.
36. Baskota, A.; Ng, Y.-K. A Graduate School Recommendation System Using the Multi-Class Support Vector Machine and KNN Approaches. In Proceedings of the 2018 IEEE International Conference on Information Reuse and Integration (IRI), Salt Lake City, UT, USA, 6–9 July 2018; IEEE: Piscataway, NJ, USA, 2018; pp. 277–284.
37. Baker, R.S.; Yacef, K. The State of Educational Data Mining in 2009: A Review and Future Visions. *J. Educ. Data Min.* **2009**, *1*, 3–17. [CrossRef]
38. Shaukat, K.; Nawaz, I.; Aslam, S.; Zaheer, S.; Shaukat, U. Student's performance in the context of data mining. In Proceedings of the 2016 19th International Multi-Topic Conference (INMIC), Islamabad, Pakistan, 5–6 December 2016; pp. 1–8.
39. Alam, T.M.; Mushtaq, M.; Shaukat, K.; Hameed, I.A.; Umer Sarwar, M.; Luo, S. A Novel Method for Performance Measurement of Public Educational Institutions Using Machine Learning Models. *Appl. Sci.* **2021**, *11*, 9296. [CrossRef]
40. Hussain, M.; Zhu, W.; Zhang, W.; Abidi, S.M.R. Student Engagement Predictions in an e-Learning System and Their Impact on Student Course Assessment Scores. *Comput. Intell. Neurosci.* **2018**, *2018*, 6347186. [CrossRef] [PubMed]
41. Hussain, M.; Zhu, W.; Zhang, W.; Abidi, S.M.R.; Ali, S. Using machine learning to predict student difficulties from learning session data. *Artif. Intell. Rev.* **2018**, *52*, 381–407. [CrossRef]
42. El-Qulity, S.A.; Mohamed, A.; Bafail, A.O.; Abdelaal, R.M.S. A Multistage Procedure for Optimal Distribution of Preparatory-Year Students to Faculties and Departments: A Mixed Integer Nonlinear Goal Programming Model with Enhanced Differential Evolution Algorithm. *J. Comput. Theor. Nanosci.* **2016**, *13*, 7847–7863. [CrossRef]
43. Sahin, A.; Waxman, H.C.; Demirci, E.; Rangel, V.S. An Investigation of Harmony Public School Students' College Enrollment and STEM Major Selection Rates and Perceptions of Factors in STEM Major Selection. *Int. J. Sci. Math. Educ.* **2020**, *18*, 1249–1269. [CrossRef]
44. Powar, V.; Girase, S.; Mukhopadhyay, D.; Jadhav, A.; Khude, S.; Mandlik, S. Analysing recommendation of colleges for students using data mining techniques. In Proceedings of the 2017 International Conference on Advances in Computing, Communication and Control (ICAC3), Mumbai, India, 1–2 December 2017; IEEE: Piscataway, NJ, USA, 2017; pp. 1–5.
45. Xiao, M.; Yi, H. Building an efficient artificial intelligence model for personalized training in colleges and universities. *Comput. Appl. Eng. Educ.* **2021**, *29*, 350–358. [CrossRef]
46. Awaliyah, M.M.; Kurniawati, A.; Rizana, A.F. Profile matching for students specialization in industrial engineering major. *IOP Conf. Ser. Mater. Sci. Eng.* **2020**, *830*, 032063. [CrossRef]
47. Pertiwi, D.A.; Daniawan, B.; Gunawan, Y. Analysis And Design of Decision Support System in Major Assignment at Buddhi High School Using AHP and SAW Methods. *Tech-E* **2019**, *3*, 13–21. [CrossRef]
48. Bhargava, N.; Sharma, G.; Bhargava, R.; Mathuria, M. Decision tree analysis on J48 algorithm for data mining. *Int. J. Adv. Res. Comput. Sci. Softw. Eng.* **2013**, *3*, 1114–1119.
49. Hsu, C.W.; Chang, C.C.; Lin, C.J. *A Practical Guide to Support Vector Classification*; Department of Computer Science and Information Engineering, National Taiwan University: Taipei, Taiwan, 2003; pp. 1–16.

50. Pupara, K.; Nuankaew, W.; Nuankaew, P. An institution recommender system based on student context and educational institution in a mobile environment. In Proceedings of the 2016 International Computer Science and Engineering Conference (ICSEC), Chiang Mai, Thailand, 14–17 December 2016; IEEE: Piscataway, NJ, USA, 2016; pp. 1–6.
51. Salaki, R.J.; Kawet, C.R.; Manoppo, R.; Tumimomor, F. Decision support systems major selection vocational high school in using fuzzy logic android-based. In Proceedings of the International Conference on Electrical Engineering, Informatics, and Its Education (CEIE) 2015, Malang, Indonesia, 3 October 2015; CEIE: Fairfax, Virginia, 2015; pp. 1–6.
52. Fiarni, C.; Sipayung, E.M.; Tumundo, P.B. Academic Decision Support System for Choosing Information Systems Sub Majors Programs using Decision Tree Algorithm. *J. Inf. Syst. Eng. Bus. Intell.* **2019**, *5*, 57–66. [CrossRef]
53. Kularbphettong, K.; Tongsiri, C. Mining educational data to support students' major selection. *Int. J. Educ. Pedagog. Sci.* **2014**, *8*, 21–23.
54. Wei, Y.; Ni, N.; Liu, D.; Chen, H.; Wang, M.; Li, Q.; Cui, X.; Ye, H. An Improved Grey Wolf Optimization Strategy Enhanced SVM and Its Application in Predicting the Second Major. *Math. Probl. Eng.* **2017**, *2017*, 9316713. [CrossRef]
55. Sethi, K.; Jaiswal, V.; Ansari, M.D. Machine Learning Based Support System for Students to Select Stream (Subject). *Recent Adv. Comput. Sci. Commun.* **2020**, *13*, 336–344. [CrossRef]
56. Samra, G.E.A.; Faloudah, A. Machine Learning based Marks Prediction to Support Recommendation of Optimum Specialization and Study Track. *Int. J. Comput. Appl.* **2019**, *181*, 15–25. [CrossRef]
57. Latifah, S.N.; Andreswari, R.; Hasibuan, M.A. Prediction Analysis of Student Specialization Suitability using Artificial Neural Network Algorithm. In Proceedings of the 2019 International Conference on Sustainable Engineering and Creative Computing (ICSECC), Bandung, Indonesia, 20–22 August 2019; IEEE: Piscataway, NJ, USA, 2019; pp. 355–359.
58. Zubaedah, R.; Lintang, M.; Putra, N.P. Decision Support System for Departemen Selection for Prospective Students using the Naïve Bayes Method and Analytical Hierarchy Process Model at Faculty of Engineering Universitas Musamus. *IOP Conf. Series: Mater. Sci. Eng.* **2021**, *1125*, 012030. [CrossRef]
59. Tamiza, L.; Shahin, G.; Tahboub, R. Intelligent Model for Suitable University Specialization Selection in Palestine. In Proceedings of the 2018 IEEE/ACS 15th International Conference on Computer Systems and Applications (AICCSA), Aqaba, Jordan, 28 October–1 November 2018; IEEE: Piscataway, NJ, USA, 2018; pp. 1–8.
60. Iyer, S.; Variawa, C. Using machine learning as a tool to help guide undeclared/undecided first-year engineering students towards a discipline. In Proceedings of the Canadian Engineering Education Association (CEEA), Ottawa, ON, Canada, 8–12 June 2019; Queen's University Library: Kingston, ON, Canada, 2019; pp. 1–17.
61. AymanAlAhmar, M. A Prototype Rule-based Expert System with an Object-Oriented Database for University Undergraduate Major Selection. *Int. J. Appl. Inf. Syst.* **2012**, *4*, 38–42. [CrossRef]
62. Kamal, N.; Sarker, F.; Mamun, K.A. A Comparative Study of Machine Learning Approaches for Recommending University Faculty. In Proceedings of the 2020 2nd International Conference on Sustainable Technologies for Industry 4.0 (STI), Dhaka, Bangladesh, 19–20 December 2020; IEEE: Piscataway, NJ, USA, 2020; pp. 1–6.
63. Ben, R. Placement_Data_Full_Class.csv. Available online: https://www.kaggle.com/benroshan/factors-affecting-campus-placement (accessed on 22 July 2021).
64. Beggs, J.M.; Bantham, J.H.; Taylor, S. Distinguishing the factors influencing college students' choice of major. *Coll. Stud. J.* **2006**, *42*, 381–395.
65. Strange, C.; Gordon, V.N. The Undecided College Student: An Academic and Career Advising Challenge. *J. High. Educ.* **1986**, *57*, 113. [CrossRef]
66. Damayanti, A.S.; Wibawa, A.P.; Pujianto, U.; Nafalski, A. The Use of Adaptive Neuro Fuzzy Inference System in Determining Students' Suitable High School Major. In Proceedings of the 2018 4th International Conference on Education and Technology (ICET), Malang, Indonesia, 26–28 October 2018; IEEE: Piscataway, NJ, USA, 2018; pp. 1–4.
67. Stein, S.A.; Weiss, G.M.; Chen, Y.; Leeds, D.D. A College Major Recommendation System. In Proceedings of the Fourteenth ACM Conference on Recommender Systems, Virtual Event, Brazil, 22–26 September 2020; pp. 640–644.
68. Chen, L.; Pratt, J.A.; Cole, C.B. Factors Influencing Students' Major and Career Selection in Systems Development: An Empirical Study. *J. Comput. Inf. Syst.* **2016**, *56*, 313–320. [CrossRef]
69. Crampton, W.J.; Walstrom, K.A.; Schambach, T.P. Factors influencing major selection by college of business students. *Issues Inf. Syst.* **2006**, *7*, 226–230.
70. Han, S. Korean Students' Attitudes toward STEM Project-Based Learning and Major Selection. *Educ. Sci. Theory Pract.* **2017**, *17*, 529–548. [CrossRef]
71. Kim, Y.-J.; Yoo, H.; Park, M. Effect of Motive for Major Selection on Major Satisfaction, Campus-life Satisfaction, and Self-directed Learning Ability among Nursing Students. *J. Korea Acad. Coop. Soc.* **2016**, *17*, 261–270. [CrossRef]
72. Khasanah, F.N.; Permanasari, A.E.; SuningKusumawardani, S. Fuzzy MADM for major selection at senior high school. In Proceedings of the 2015 2nd International Conference on Information Technology, Computer, and Electrical Engineering (ICITACEE), Semarang, Indonesia, 16–18 October 2015; pp. 41–45.
73. Rabani, R.; Rabiei, K. Evaluation of Major Selection and its Impact on Educational Satisfaction among Isfahan University Students. *IRPHE* **2011**, *17*, 99–120.
74. Lobb, W.B.; Shah, M.; Kolassa, E.M. Factors Influencing the Selection of a Major: A Comparison of Pharmacy and Nonpharmacy Undergraduate Students. *J. Pharm. Teach.* **2004**, *11*, 45–64. [CrossRef]

75. Ullah, Z.; Saleem, F.; Jamjoom, M.; Fakieh, B. Reliable Prediction Models Based on Enriched Data for Identifying the Mode of Childbirth by Using Machine Learning Methods: Development Study. *J. Med. Internet Res.* **2021**, *23*, e28856. [CrossRef]
76. Nti, I.K.; Adekoya, A.F.; Weyori, B.A. Efficient Stock-Market Prediction Using Ensemble Support Vector Machine. *Open Comput. Sci.* **2020**, *10*, 153–163. [CrossRef]
77. Bresfelean, V.P. Analysis and Predictions on Students' Behavior Using Decision Trees in Weka Environment. In Proceedings of the 2007 29th International Conference on Information Technology Interfaces, Cavtat, Croatia, 25–28 June 2007; IEEE: Piscataway, NJ, USA, 2007; pp. 51–56.
78. Dervisevic, O.; Zunic, E.; Eonko, D.; Buza, E. Application of KNN and Decision Tree Classification Algorithms in the Prediction of Education Success from the Edu720 Platform. In Proceedings of the 2019 4th International Conference on Smart and Sustainable Technologies (SpliTech), Split, Croatia, 18–21 June 2019; IEEE: Piscataway, NJ, USA, 2019; pp. 1–5.
79. Qu, W.; Tan, G.; Zeng, Q.; Xu, X. Based on the SVM university education's quality regression analysis. In Proceedings of the Third International Symposium on Intelligent Information Technology Application, Nanchang, China, 21–22 November 2009; IEEE: Piscataway, NJ, USA, 2009; pp. 306–309.
80. Beaulac, C.; Rosenthal, J.S. Predicting University Students' Academic Success and Major Using Random Forests. *Res. High. Educ.* **2019**, *60*, 1048–1064. [CrossRef]
81. Patil, R.; Tamane, S. A Comparative Analysis on the Evaluation of Classification Algorithms in the Prediction of Diabetes. *Int. J. Electr. Comput. Eng.* **2018**, *8*, 3966–3975. [CrossRef]
82. Hämäläinen, W.; Vinni, M. Classifiers for educational data mining. In *Handbook of Educational Data Mining*; Romero, C., Pechenizkiy, M., Baker, R.S.J.D., Ventura, S., Eds.; Chapman & Hall/CRC Press: Boca Raton, FL, USA, 2010; pp. 57–74.
83. Hern, A. Why Data Is the New Coal. Available online: https://www.theguardian.com/technology/2016/sep/27/data-efficiency-deep-learning (accessed on 24 September 2021).
84. Jeay, S.; Gaulis, S.; Ferretti, S.; Bitter, H.; Ito, M.; Valat, T.; Murakami, M.; Ruetz, S.; Guthy, D.A.; Rynn, C.; et al. A distinct p53 target gene set predicts for response to the selective p53–HDM2 inhibitor NVP-CGM097. *eLife* **2015**, *4*. [CrossRef] [PubMed]
85. Cao, L.; Tay, F. Support vector machine with adaptive parameters in financial time series forecasting. *IEEE Trans. Neural Netw.* **2003**, *14*, 1506–1518. [CrossRef] [PubMed]
86. Huang, S.; Fang, N. Predicting student academic performance in an engineering dynamics course: A comparison of four types of predictive mathematical models. *Comput. Educ.* **2013**, *61*, 133–145. [CrossRef]
87. Asselman, A.; Khaldi, M.; Aammou, S. Enhancing the prediction of student performance based on the machine learning XGBoost algorithm. *Interact. Learn. Environ.* **2021**. [CrossRef]
88. Huo, H.; Cui, J.; Hein, S.; Padgett, Z.; Ossolinski, M.; Raim, R.; Zhang, J. Predicting Dropout for Nontraditional Undergraduate Students: A Machine Learning Approach. *J. Coll. Stud. Retent. Res. Theory Pract.* **2020**. [CrossRef]
89. Kohavi, R.; Provost, F. Glossary of terms. Machine learning—Special issue on applications of machine learning and the knowledge discovery process. *Mach. Learn.* **1998**, *30*, 271–274.
90. Song, Y.-Y.; Lu, Y. Decision tree methods: Applications for classification and prediction. *Shanghai Arch Psychiatry* **2015**, *27*, 130–135. [CrossRef] [PubMed]
91. Jin, Z.; Shang, J.; Zhu, Q.; Ling, C.; Xie, W.; Qiang, B. RFRSF: Employee turnover prediction based on random forests and survival analysis. In *Web Information Systems Engineering—WISE WISE Lecture Notes in Computer Science*; Huang, Z., Beek, W., Wang, H., Zhou, R., Zhang, Y., Eds.; Springer International Publishing: Cham, Switzerland, 2020; pp. 503–515.
92. Cheng, C.; Yan, X.; Sun, F.; Li, L.M. Inferring activity changes of transcription factors by binding association with sorted expression profiles. *BMC Bioinform.* **2007**, *8*, 452. [CrossRef] [PubMed]
93. Shahiri, A.M.; Husain, W.; Rashid, N.A. A Review on Predicting Student's Performance Using Data Mining Techniques. *Procedia Comput. Sci.* **2015**, *72*, 414–422. [CrossRef]
94. Chicco, D.; Jurman, G. The advantages of the Matthews correlation coefficient (MCC) over F1 score and accuracy in binary classification evaluation. *BMC Genom.* **2020**, *21*, 6. [CrossRef]
95. Khushi, M.; Shaukat, K.; Alam, T.M.; Hameed, I.A.; Uddin, S.; Luo, S.; Yang, X.; Reyes, M.C. A comparative performance analysis of data resampling methods on imbalance medical data. *IEEE Access* **2021**, *9*, 109960–109975. [CrossRef]
96. Alam, T.M.; Shaukat, K.; Mahboob, H.; Sarwar, M.U.; Iqbal, F.; Nasir, A.; Hameed, I.A.; Luo, S. A machine learning approach for identification of malignant mesothelioma etiological factors in an imbalanced dataset. *Comput. J.* **2021**. [CrossRef]
97. Bradley, A.P. The use of the area under the ROC curve in the evaluation of machine learning algorithms. *Pattern Recognit.* **1997**, *30*, 1145–1159. [CrossRef]
98. Breiman, L. Random Forests. *Mach. Learn.* **2001**, *45*, 5–32. [CrossRef]

Review

Trends and Directions of Financial Technology (Fintech) in Society and Environment: A Bibliometric Study

Adeel Nasir [1,†], Kamran Shaukat [2,3,*,†], Kanwal Iqbal Khan [4,*], Ibrahim A. Hameed [5,*], Talha Mahboob Alam [6] and Suhuai Luo [2]

1. Department of Management Sciences, Lahore College for Women University, Lahore 54000, Pakistan; adeel.nasir@lcwu.edu.pk
2. School of Information and Physical Sciences, The University of Newcastle, Callaghan, NSW 2308, Australia; suhuai.luo@newcastle.edu.au
3. Department of Data Science, University of the Punjab, Lahore 54890, Pakistan
4. Institute of Business & Management, University of Engineering and Technology, Lahore 54000, Pakistan
5. Department of ICT and Natural Sciences, Norwegian University of Science and Technology, 7491 Trondheim, Norway
6. Department of Computer Science and Information Technology, Virtual University of Pakistan, Lahore 54890, Pakistan; talhamahboob95@gmail.com
* Correspondence: kamran.shaukat@uon.edu.au (K.S.); kanwal.khan@uet.edu.pk (K.I.K.); ibib@ntnu.no (I.A.H.)
† Adeel Nasir and Kamran Shaukat contributed equally to this work.

Abstract: The contemporary innovations in financial technology (fintech) serve society with an environmentally friendly atmosphere. Fintech covers an enormous range of activities from data security to financial service deliverables that enable the companies to automate their existing business structure and introduce innovative products and services. Therefore, there is an increasing demand for scholars and professionals to identify the future trends and directions of the topic. This is why the present study conducted a bibliometric analysis in social, environmental, and computer sciences fields to analyse the implementation of environment-friendly computer applications to benefit societal growth and well-being. We have used the 'bibliometrix 3.0' package of the r-program to analyse the core aspects of fintech systematically. The study suggests that 'ACM International Conference Proceedings' is the core source of published fintech literature. China leads in both multiple and single country production of fintech publications. Bina Nusantara University is the most relevant affiliation. Arner and Buckley provide impactful fintech literature. In the conceptual framework, we analyse relationships between different topics of fintech and address dynamic research streams and themes. These research streams and themes highlight the future directions and core topics of fintech. The study deploys a co-occurrence network to differentiate the entire fintech literature into three research streams. These research streams are related to 'cryptocurrencies, smart contracts, financial technology', 'financial industry stability, service, innovation, regulatory technology (regtech)', and 'machine learning and deep learning innovations'. The study deploys a thematic map to identify basic, emerging, dropping, isolated, and motor themes based on centrality and density. These various themes and streams are designed to lead the researchers, academicians, policymakers, and practitioners to narrow, distinctive, and significant topics.

Keywords: fintech; financial technology; blockchain; deep learning; regtech; environment; social sciences

Citation: Nasir, A.; Shaukat, K.; Iqbal Khan, K.; A. Hameed, I.; Alam, T.M.; Luo, S. Trends and Directions of Financial Technology (Fintech) in Society and Environment: A Bibliometric Study. *Appl. Sci.* **2021**, *11*, 10353. https://doi.org/10.3390/app112110353

Academic Editor: Jianbo Gao

Received: 9 October 2021
Accepted: 1 November 2021
Published: 4 November 2021

Publisher's Note: MDPI stays neutral with regard to jurisdictional claims in published maps and institutional affiliations.

Copyright: © 2021 by the authors. Licensee MDPI, Basel, Switzerland. This article is an open access article distributed under the terms and conditions of the Creative Commons Attribution (CC BY) license (https://creativecommons.org/licenses/by/4.0/).

1. Introduction

As the world is entering the digitalisation age, many organisations are adopting and investing in new technologies to cope with societal and environmental needs. The financial industry is not so different; it evolves day by day with various fintech technologies. Fintech is the combination of financial technology used to enhance financial operations' effectiveness and efficiency. Its rise has changed the ways of businesses of commercial banking systems [1]. It is implied that it is an emerging area of finance with a significant contribution to technology [2,3]. Nowadays, it has become an industry that successfully takes advantage of the recent development of information technology tools such as cloud computing, big data, the internet of things, social computing, etc. [4]. This advancement supports the existing business structure but also helps the financial service industry to introduce new processes, systems, products, and services that can enhance their efficiency [5]. The companies are intended to restructure their businesses and are more inclined towards hybrid client interactions and more customer self-services, [6], particularly during Covid-19.

The latest fintech technology trends include categorising and assessing various artificial intelligence technologies based on their availability and maturity [7]. Furthermore, it provides studies such as the contextualisation of users' facilities and experience of the web interface in the financial service industry [8], machine learning tools in electronic finance market trading [9], and advanced modelling for stock movements [10] and settlement models with renewable energy that are based on blockchain technology [11]. The researchers believe that there is a need to develop a conceptual framework to understand the perspectives of Fintech [12]. Few researchers presented the Fintech framework based on the flow of money theories applied in the E-commerce system. However, still required is a suitable conceptual framework developed in the context of relevant fields [13]. As well, there is a still need to identify the core contributors in the field of computer, social, and environmental sciences, as well as the future research streams and themes that will lead the scholars to make a significant contribution in the area. Therefore, the purpose of the current study is to conduct a bibliometric analysis for the period of 2010 to 2021.

The current study highlights various influential and conceptual aspects of fintech technology in computer, social, and environmental sciences from the last decade. The significant growth of fintech technologies has raised specific questions for academicians and practitioners. These questions are: (1) What are the contributory key authors and journals of the fintech literature? (2) What are core affiliations, sources and contributing countries in the field of fintech and computer, management, and environmental sciences? (3) What key themes does fintech offer in the field of computer, management, and environmental sciences? (4) With the help of research streams offered by fintech literature, what are the future research gaps to fill by researchers, academicians, and practitioners? The workflow of the study is presented in Figure 1.

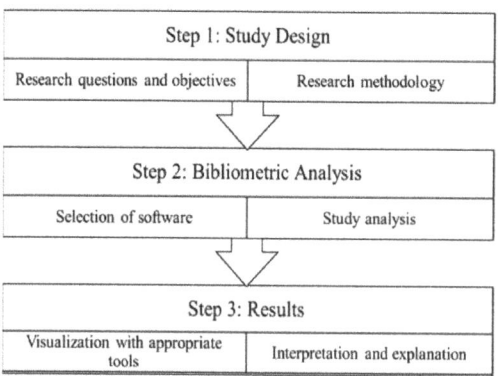

Figure 1. Workflow of study.

2. Study Design and Descriptive Outlook

This study aims to conduct a comprehensive bibliometric analysis to identify the influential and conceptual structure of the fintech literature in computer, social, and environmental sciences. The procedure and steps of studies are shown in Figure 1, using the workflow followed by Nasir et al. [14]. The study proceeds with the study design, where we define our research questions and methodology in step 1. We have used the 'bibliometrix 3.0' package of r-studio to analyse various influential and conceptual aspects of fintech literature [15]. We have used Scopus, emerald, and science direct databases for searching fintech literature. The finalised search query is simply fintech in the computer, social, and environmental science fields. We analysed on 17 March 2021. There is a minimum contribution of fintech literature in the rest of the areas. Furthermore, we have removed the duplicates from our data and ended up with 1556 documents, from which 786 are research articles, 26 are books, 86 are book chapters, 553 are conference papers, 61 are reviews, and 22 are conference reviews and editorials.

Table 1 also highlights the total number of author keywords and keyword plus used by the literature; furthermore, we have taken the literature from 2010 to 2021. The table describes various characteristics such as the collaboration between countries index, authors per documents, and single and multiple-authored documents in fintech literature. Figure 2 represents the annual production of publications per year; fintech is a recent trend globally as, in 2020, there were 724 publications. The growth is substantial, from 1 publication in 2010, to 10 publications in 2015, to 724 publications in 2020. The year 2021 is still ongoing, however, we can see 69 publications in fintech, more than the 30 publications in 2016. The relevant growth in financial technology literature starts in 2017, where we can see 107 publications, followed by 262 in 2018 and 348 in 2019.

Table 1. Main information about fintech literature.

Description	Results
Documents	1556
Sources (Journals, Books, etc.)	759
Keywords Plus (ID)	4453
Author's Keywords (DE)	3454
Period	2010–2021
Average citations per document	3.611
Authors	3483
Author Appearances	4325
Authors of single-authored documents	298
Authors of multi-authored documents	3185
Single-authored documents	373
Documents per Author	0.447
Authors per Document	2.24
Co-Authors per Documents	2.78
Collaboration Index	2.69
Document types	
Article	786
Book	26
Book chapter	86
Conference paper	553
Conference review	22
Editorial	22
Review	61

Figure 2. Annual publications production radar.

3. Bibliometric Analysis

The forthcoming segment represents the holistic bibliometric analysis of fintech literature. The bibliometric analysis is twofold. First, we study dynamic, influential aspects such as core authors having a considerable impact in fintech. We highlight core sources and how they impact the literature on various topics. We propose the main countries and corresponding countries of fintech literature. Then, we discuss primary affiliations or institutions conducting significant research on multiple topics of fintech. We discuss the main contributions of highly ranked documents. We lastly indicate the main keywords in fintech literature.

The second part of the bibliometric analysis provides a conceptual framework. In this section, we discuss various themes and streams of fintech literature. It provides an understanding of the core topics of fintech in computer, social, and environmental sciences, and helps us propose what the future holds for fintech technologies. This section presents a co-occurrence network which creates a matrix of keywords and links them together in various clusters that suggest the main topics. Furthermore, we investigate the thematic map, which divides multiple topics into four quadrants with different characteristics. Finally, from emerging and developing issues, we propose a future research agenda in fintech literature.

3.1. Influential Aspects

3.1.1. Core Sources

Figure 3 represents the top 10 critical influential sources of fintech literature. ACM International Conference Proceedings is the core source in the field. Contemporary research is often presented at the ACM international conference. The core source represents recent studies of diverse, agile tailoring models [16], the advanced mechanism for agricultural marketing and smart contracts using blockchains [17], and the facilitation of decentralised ledger technology for financial derivative markets [18]. The second leading source of fintech literature is Advances in Intelligent Systems and Computing. This journal publishes literature on the digitalisation of the banking and insurance sector [19], introducing the QR-code-based payment systems at fintech future [20] and dynamic uses of blockchain technology such as e-voting [21]. The third primary source is lecture notes in computer sciences that involve literature on fintech innovation with patent data [22], the role of information technology (IT) in developing fintech business model canvases [23], and the use of fintech AI that is interpretable in evaluating the efficiency of lending risk [24]. IEEE access provides literature on the development of a blockchain-based microgrid transaction model for optimised bidding [25], market settlement models based on blockchain technology while securing efficient energy trading mechanisms [26], and contract production and transaction with dynamic technology such as a block-enabled integrated marketing platform [27].

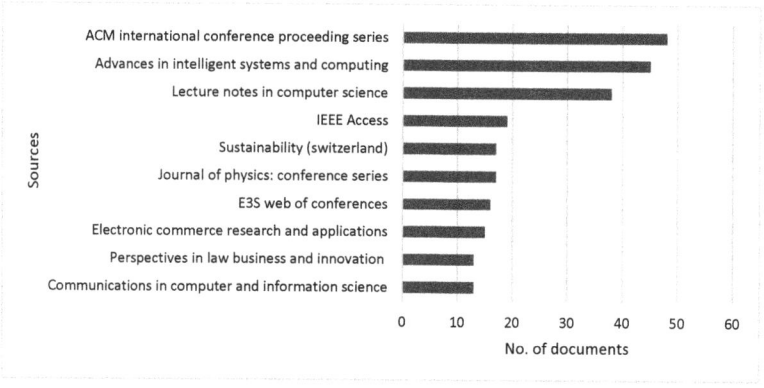

Figure 3. Most relevant sources, according to publications.

Table 2 represents the primary sources listed and arranged based on h-index and g-index. It shows the impact of the journal on fintech literature. Electronic commerce, research, and applications are top-ranked sources for producing fintech literature with an h-index of 7 and a g-index of 13. Its 15 publications have 186 total citations, and the first article on fintech was published in 2015. The journal highlights the key areas of fintech, which are initial coin offerings (ICO) and information asymmetries associated with it [28], the proposed value created by the mobile payment ecosystem [29], and contract signing protocol with blockchain technologies [30]. Financial innovation comes on the second number in the source impact list with an h-index of seven, a g-index of nine, and its total 9 publications having 148 total citations. It covers the main topics of fintech governance and emergence in Peer to Peer (P2P) lending [31,32] and the growth of digital banking in the financial industry [33]. The first article on technological forecasting and social change (ranked third) was published in 2018; however, it comes in third place with 89 total citations with 11 fintech technology publications.

Table 2. Top ten sources with impact.

Source	h_Index	g_Index	m_Index	TC	NP	PY_Start
Electronic commerce research and applications	7	13	1	186	15	2015
Financial innovation	7	9	1	148	9	2015
Technological forecasting and social change	5	9	1.25	89	11	2018
European business organisation law review	5	7	1.25	53	9	2018
Handbook of blockchain, digital finance, and inclusion	5	5	1	38	9	2017
IT professional	5	7	1	150	7	2017
Electronic markets	5	6	1.25	124	6	2018
Industrial management and data systems	5	6	1.25	85	6	2018
Journal of economics and business	5	6	1.25	231	6	2018
Journal of management information systems	5	6	1.25	204	6	2018

3.1.2. Influential Authors in Fintech Literature

This section represents the core authors who contributed significantly to fintech in the computer, social and environmental sciences. Table 3 describes the ranking of the principal authors and divides the order into two panels. Panel A represents ranking according to h, g and m-index, while panel B grades authors according to total citations.

Table 3. Top authors in fintech literature.

Authors	h_Index	g_Index	m_Index	TC	NP	PY_Start
Panel A: Ranked according to h,g,m index						
Arner DW	4	8	0.67	79	10	2016
Buckley RP	4	8	0.80	77	8	2017
Kauffman RI	4	5	0.57	150	5	2015
Li Y	3	7	0.60	51	11	2017
Wang S	3	3	0.60	14	8	2017
Panel B: Ranked according to total citations						
Gomber P	3	3	0.60	223	3	2017
Kauffman RI	4	5	0.57	150	5	2015
Giudici G	1	2	0.25	127	2	2018
Martinazzi S	1	2	0.25	127	2	2018
Adhami S	1	1	0.25	126	1	2018

D.W. Arner is ranked first according to the top five author list in panel A. one of his main contributions is drivers of financial inclusion and compliance with sustainable development goals (SDGs) [34]. Furthermore, his work covers the protection against fraud and detection through digital identity infrastructure to fulfil the obligations of knowing your customers [35]. He also worked on fintech regulations, digitalisation of manual reporting, and compliance processes such as regtech (regulation technology) [36–38]. In panel A, R.P. Buckley (ranked second) collaborated with D.W. Arner in most of his work [39]. His work as the principal author is related to dependence on digital technologies and cybersecurity during the time of the COVID-19 pandemic [40]. With D.W. Arner, he worked on regtech to control systematic risk in financial crisis, data protection rules, and electronic identification legislation [41]. P. Gomber in Panel B has the highest rank concerning the number of citations. His most cited work is related to technology innovation, transformation, and disruption in financial services [42]. The common name in both panels is R.J. Kauffman, with five publications from 2015. He is the second-highest cited author in the field of fintech in computer, social, and environmental sciences. His apparent work represents the computational social sciences [43] and the changing environment concerning payments through cards [44].

The most cited publication is done by S. Adhami, with only one publication in 2018 and with a total number of citations of 126. He is the fifth most highly cited author because he has produced only one publication in fintech technologies. His work is about the ICOs phenomena, and he addressed the success of token offerings [45].

3.1.3. Most Relevant Affiliations

This section deals with the most relevant affiliations. As shown in Figure 4, Bina Nusantara University is the core affiliation, with 33 publications in fintech technology. The university evolved from a computer training institute founded on 21 October 1974 [46]. The affiliation conducts studies on asset baked tokens with blockchain networks [47], consumer protection in lending transactions [48,49], mobile payment application and acceptance [50], and unified theory of acceptance and use of technology [51].

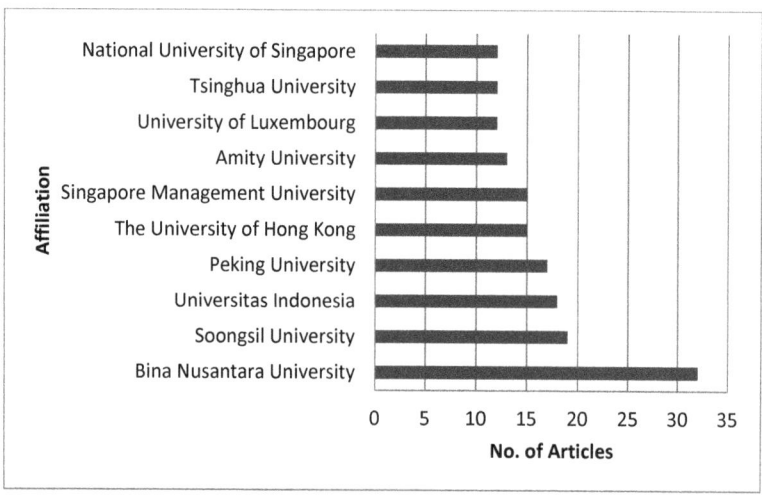

Figure 4. Most relevant affiliations.

Soongsil University is the second-largest affiliation with 18 publications. The university was founded in 1897 by William M. Baird as a private school. Soongsil pioneered a computer science program in Korea, ranked number two in Soul National University [52]. The main topics that Soongsil University covers are small foreign currency remittance with blockchain technology [53], machine learning and adaptive fintech security provision [54], the emergence of mobile-accessible payment services [55,56], and peer to peer (P2P) lending applications [57]. In third place, Universitas Indonesia published 17 documents. The significant studies conducted are related to the effect of fintech on stock returns [58], fintecbased financial instructions, financial performance and consumer behaviour [59] and P2P lending, and women's empowerment [60].

3.1.4. Influential Countries

Concerning Table 4, the USA and China are leading in terms of citations and number of publications. It is seen that China has well over 400 publications, which is 41% higher than the USA's number of publications. Still, on the other hand, in the citations section, the USA has published some of the most fascinating and citable work in fintech and has secured 742 citations. China has 419 publications got 457 citations. There are 114 publications from South Korea; however, the country earned 411 citations. The UK is in the third position in terms of publications; however, UK publications obtained 394 citations. Indonesia and India are in the fourth and fifth positions in terms of publications; however, these countries are not on the citations list. In contrast, Italy and Taiwan are the last two countries in terms of the number of publications. However, a small number of publications from these two countries have significant contributions, as their publications are cited significantly.

Table 4. Core Countries in Terms of Number and Citations.

Country	Total Citations	Country	Number of Publications
USA	742	China	419
China	457	USA	296
South Korea	411	UK	189
United Kingdom (UK)	394	Indonesia	171
Germany	376	India	157
Italy	288	Germany	117
Taiwan	211	South Korea	114
Switzerland	185	Australia	97
Hong Kong	168	Taiwan	87
Spain	144	Italy	75

Figure 5 represents the top 10 corresponding author countries, and it is divided into two parts. The figure's first part shows that the orange colour represents many multiple country publications (MCP). These publications are collaborated on by at least one foreign country author. Bars in green represent single country publications (SCP), where correspondence and collaborations are from the same country [61].

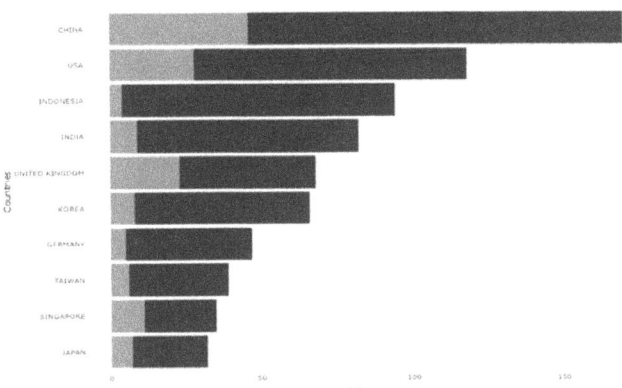

Figure 5. Corresponding author country.

As shown in Figure 5, China has the highest number of both SCP and MCP. The country has produced 170 corresponding articles, of which 124 are SCP, and 46 are MCP.

USA comes in second place with 118 corresponding articles, 90 SCP, and 28 MCP. The exact amount of SCP is produced by Indonesia (ranked third); however, it lacks in MCP with only four publications. India (ranked fourth) and the United Kingdom (ranked fifth) have more inter-country collaboration than Indonesia. India has 9 MCP, and the United Kingdom has 23 MCPs.

3.1.5. Keyword Analysis

Keywords are an essential factor in searching the literature. We have found essential keywords in fintech literature, shown in the shape of word clouds in Figure 6. It is evident that fintech is the main keyword for the literature; our focus is on other keywords representing various topics or fields. In the abstract, financial is the most commonly used keyword in studies relating to technology, market, and blockchain. Similar keywords are found in the study's title; besides, the title covers keywords related to the digital market and banks, as shown in Table 5.

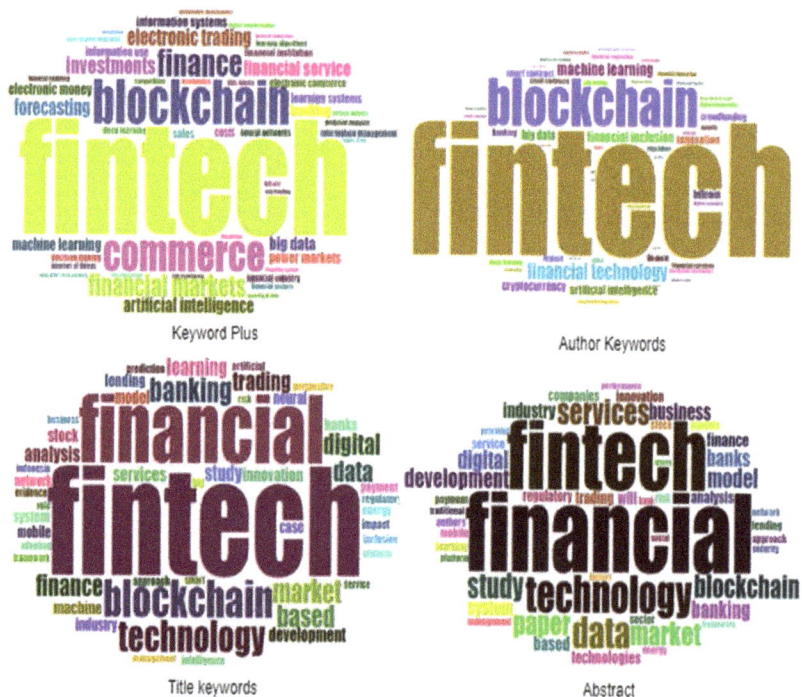

Figure 6. Word clouds.

Keryword plus author represents authentic fintech topics such as financial markets, investments, electronic trading, artificial intelligence, financial services, blockchain, and commerce. In addition to keyword plus author, keywords represent thematic topics in fintech such as blockchain technologies, financial technology, machine learning, financial inclusion, big data, artificial intelligence, and cryptocurrency bitcoin fintech innovation.

This study suggests that author keywords represent significant and authentic keywords compared to other sources, and these keywords cover and analyse a wide variety of topics in fintech. We can find and propose key themes and streams in fintech in computer, social, and environmental sciences by analysing the author's keywords.

Table 5. Research stream of Fintech literature.

Keywords	Clusters	Research Stream
Blockchain, bitcoin, cryptocurrency, entrepreneurial finance, smart contracts, security, internet of things, venture capital, the financial industry	Red	Cryptocurrencies, smart contracts, and financial technology
Fintech, financial inclusion, regulatory sandbox, innovation, financial technology, big data, regulations, regtech, banking, artificial intelligence, financial# (regulations, innovations, service, and stability), digital economy, digitalisation, mobile payment, p2p lending, business model, digital finance.	Blue	Financial industry stability, service, innovation, and regulatory technology (regtech)
Deep learning, machine learning, financial technology, stock market.	Green	Machine learning, deep learning and artificial intelligence

3.2. Conceptual Framework

This section will study various themes and streams that are a significant part of the fintech literature. In addition to tools such as co-occurrence network, thematic map, and thematic evolution, we have proposed a potential future agenda for researchers, educationists, engineers, and policymakers.

3.2.1. Co-Occurrence Network

We have conducted the co-occurrence analysis using the author keyword and identified three main clusters of fintech literature, as shown in Figure 7. These clusters represent distinct research streams which can help the researchers to differentiate the literature significantly. A highly centralised cluster is a blue cluster representing the research stream we have given the name of digital transformation, innovation financial industry, and regulations. There are many topics to seek in this research stream, most prominently, the regulations related to analysing the application and implementation of fintech technologies. Skilful regulations are required for the outbreak of financial innovations throughout the economic systems [62].

Regulatory technology or regtech is a prominent topic that uses information technology for monitoring, compliance, and reporting [39]. Regtech is a better financial solution. Furthermore, certain shared ledger technologies provide potential solutions for finance and banking procedures [63].

Financial regulatory technology would help shape the digital currency's internationalisation by strengthening blockchain's legal context [64]. Tsai et al. [65] introduced the framework for online supply chain finance for small and medium enterprises and suggested replacing it with a traditional supply chain financial mechanism. The innovative regulatory framework streamed by fintech provides a conducive innovative environment, protecting consumer rights and ensuring financial stability with advanced ecosystems [66–72]. The red stream proposed by the co-occurrence network represents the overall research stream of financial technology in cryptocurrencies and smart contracts. Some of the literature is dedicated to the combination of the latest financial technologies and environmental sciences. Le et al. [73] studied the spillovers and connections among green bonds, fintech, and cryptocurrencies, and found long term hedging benefits among them. Many traditional offline activities have been become easy, comfortable, and secure with the penetration of blockchain technology. Rao et al. [21] suggest that the Ethereum blockchain has made e-voting secure and transparent. It has enhanced the scope of smart contracts. Fintech technologies have helped to develop new innovative financial products that transform traditional payment systems into mobile-based application payment systems [74]. Various fields of research are yet to be explored in fintech in relation with the blockchain technology.

Nasir et al. [55] studied blockchain technologies' core theme and research streams, and identified fintech technologies as the key emerging and developing theme. A part of fintech is about making smart contracts, and from the passage of time, the smart contract procedures have evolved significantly. They have become secure, regulated, and user friendly [75,76]. Fintech is making progress in preserving the environment. Hu et al. [77] proposed the trading system that is blockchain distributed carbon emission.

Figure 7. Co-occurrence network.

The green research stream is away from centrality, indicating that some potential topics can set the future research agenda. The stream relates fintech literature with machine learning, deep learning, and stock markets. Certain studies study machine learning techniques to simplify, develop, and increase the online financial market trading systems [6]. Oliveira et al. [78] use machine learning techniques such as the k-mean algorithm, long short term memory (LSTM), and the density-based spatial clustering (DBSC) algorithm to forecast stock market price movements. Abe et al. [79] deploy deep learning on cross-sections of various stock markets with multifactor models and indicate that deep learning is a significant model for the prediction of the cross-section of stock returns. There is a substantial development in the machine and deep learning techniques to propose the prediction model for stock markets [80–82]. Machine learning is also helpful in portfolio risk management [83].

3.2.2. Thematic Map

We have a thematic map (Figure 8) in the study that proposes research themes according to four quadrants. According to Nasir et al. [14], the thematic map divides themes according to two factors (centrality and density). Centrality represents the high volume of work in a specific theme, and density means the importance of a particular theme. The first quadrant in Figure 8 indicates low-density themes with low centrality. These themes are either new, developing, or emerging because they have low density and low centrality. The second quadrant represents basic themes that provide high volume (centrality) but that are less critical (density). The third quadrant represents essential themes in the field; however, less work has been done in such areas. This field should be discussed significantly because these themes can provide potential future directions. The fourth quadrant has themes with both high centrality and density.

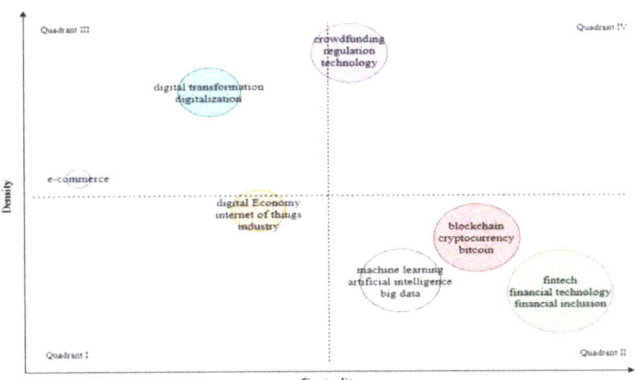

Figure 8. Thematic map.

Digital economy, internet of things, and financial industry-related themes are in the first quadrant. These keywords represent the topic with low centrality and low density. These themes either emerge as a strong future agenda or drop out from the future literature.

In the digital economy, Rozi et al. [84] study innovations and privacy issues for startup companies. In the digital economy era, Jiang et al. [85] analysed the significant risk profile by deploying conditional value at risk models on China's financial banks and found significant systematic risk exposure of small banks compared to big financial institutions. The digital economy is possessed with considerable challenges, such as centralisation of technology, trust, and security; e-commerce transactions are shaping the digital economy's future. Ferrer-Gomila [30] uses the blockchain for contract signing between various parties, making e-commerce transactions easy and cost-effective. One of the emerging topics is industry 4.0. Li et al. [86] use blockchain for immutable, secure, transparent, and auditable peer to peer energy transactions in the industrial internet of things. Moreover, the industrial and financial internet of things is discussed by [87–90].

The basic themes of fintech literature are filled with various significant topics. It is obvious that, for topics related to financial technology, fintech will have strong centrality in the literature. Furthermore, in recent times, blockchain technology for auditable, immutable, transparent, and secure transactions is considered the main fintech tool [91–95]. The blockchain also reduces financial comfort and cost efficiency, as Šapkauskienė [92] studied initial coin offerings of new companies and explained how blockchain reduces cost with ICOs. Machine learning, artificial intelligence, and big data themes are also common in the fintech literature. Significant machine learning literature is related to estimating the movement and pricing of financial assets [96–102]. Kulshrestha et al. [103] deploy technical, fundamental, and artificial intelligence to propose optimal portfolio performance. Big data is about considering various techniques to ensure the quality of the data and its estimations and prediction ability [104]. Fintech has a significant role in shaping the architecture of big data [105].

E-commerce is a highly developed theme; however, its centrality is very low. The growth of e-commerce is significant, and there is a lot to offer by deploying various fintechs such as payment applications, blockchain, bitcoins, price disruption, and channel modelling [106]. Certain issues related to e-commerce business proliferation include online payment models and B2C market supply chain management [107]. There are certain gaps and challenges related to digital wallet payments [108]. Government regulations and understanding of the mobile payment system is another challenge for e-commerce development [109]. Furthermore, fintech contributions in e-commerce is studied by [110–114].

Crowdfunding, regulations, and technology are the motor theme, which indicates high centrality and high density. In contemporary times, raising capital from many people to fund innovative projects is an integral part of startup growth. Jin [115] studies the various patterns of crowdfunding and the various stages of the project. Various technologies and topologies of crowdfunding are studied by [116]. Zetzsche et al. [117] consider studying crowdfunding and propose harmonising or standardising the crowdfunding procedure. It is the stepping stone towards developing and changing businesses' technological environments and significantly achieving entrepreneurial goals [118]. Regtech represents regulation technology and is mainly associated with data protection [41], algorithmic regulations [112], decentralized blockchain [70,118,119], financial markets and risk management [119,120], artificial intelligence [121], anti-money laundering [29], and superior supply chain management [122].

4. Future Research

With the help of fintech literature, we can identify critical areas where further research can be pursued. The following are some recommendations for researchers, policymakers, academicians, and information technology people.

- Using financial technology to achieve sustainable development goals;
- Identify limitations and proliferate industry 4.0 with the internet of things, blockchain, and digital transformation mechanism;
- Will the world see fintech as the opportunity for a new era after the COVID-19 outbreak, or are there challenges ahead;
- Ecommerce proliferation: gap-filling regarding government regulations regarding online payments, supply chain management, blockchain and bitcoin penetration, product differentiation, logistic financial methods, fraud detection, safety policies, law enforcement, ease of startups, and reshaping financial orders;
- Identify and implement various crowdfunding techniques such as blockchain and bitcoin investment with proper regulations to fund multiple new ventures;
- Implementing fintech tools in Islamic banking and finance. Digital transformation of Islamic instruments such as Mudarabah, Musharakah, Islisna, Salam, Ijarah, Sukuk, and Takaful;
- In developing models, applications of fintech technologies, especially blockchains, ensure standard recording, reporting, and companies' disclosure requirements such as technological transformation regarding corporate governance-related recordings [123];
- Using fintech, such as machine learning and neural networks tools, develops banking operations such as know-your-customer, risk management, and forecasting;
- Analysis of Asset pricing models, such as Fama et al.'s [124] three-factor model and five-factor model [125], and other models [126–129], using machine learning [130,131], artificial intelligence [132,133], and deep learning techniques;
- Identify opportunities, gaps, and challenges for implementing and developing regulatory technology.

5. Limitation of Study

- The search query is conducted at one point in time, i.e., 17 March 2021; this is a limitation because these studies may change as new literature may be added on future dates.
- There is limited literature available on fintech literature related to social and environmental sciences. More literature will refine the concept.

6. Conclusions

The study suggests that fintech is the future of business, economy, and information technology, and will help preserve the world's environment. The research indicates various influential and conceptual aspects of the fintech literature from the past decade. We have discovered some of the core factors of fintech literature. It is worth considering that the development of fintech is contemporary, and research has grown substantially in recent years. Among influential aspects, it is observed that the ACM International Conference Proceedings is the core source of fintech publications. It is the source with the highest impact in fintech literature is Electronic commerce research and applications. D.W. Arner is the most prolific author in fintech publications, while P. Gomber can capture the highest number of citations in the field of fintech. With 33 publications, Bina Nusantara University is the top affiliation. Among top countries, China, the USA, and the UK scored in the top three in terms of publications; however, the USA scores total citations.

Overall, China is the core country, ranked first with the highest correspondence in multiple and single country publications. We have addressed conceptual aspects of fintech literature with a co-occurrence network and thematic map. We have shortlisted three main research streams of fintech literature to narrow down. The first research stream is 'cryptocurrency, smart contract, and financial technology.' The second research stream is 'financial industry stability, service, innovation, and regulatory technology (regtech).' The third research stream, which divides the overall fintech literature, is 'machine learning, deep learning, and artificial intelligence.' These research streams have narrowed down the vast literature of fintech into parts to understand mechanics. We further conceptually differentiate the fintech literature in terms of emerging, basic, isolated, and motor themes. We found that blockchain, cryptocurrency, financial inclusions, machine learning, artificial intelligence, and big data-related topics have high centrality and low density in the fintech literature. It may be difficult to find gaps in said topics. E-commerce is a highly anticipated topic as it is isolated with low centrality and high density. The digital economy, internet of things, and financial industry in fintech are emerging and dropping themes. Crowdfunding and regtech are motor themes with high centrality and high importance.

Author Contributions: Conceptualization, A.N. and K.S.; methodology, A.N., K.S., K.I.K., I.A.H. and T.M.A.; software, A.N., K.S., K.I.K., I.A.H. and T.M.A.; validation, A.N. and K.S.; formal analysis, A.N., K.S., K.I.K., I.A.H., T.M.A. and S.L.; investigation, A.N., K.S., K.I.K., I.A.H., T.M.A. and S.L.; resources, I.A.H. and S.L.; data curation, A.N., K.S., K.I.K., I.A.H., T.M.A. and S.L.; writing—original draft preparation, A.N. and K.S.; writing—review and editing, A.N., K.S., K.I.K., I.A.H., T.M.A. and S.L.; visualization, A.N., K.S., K.I.K., I.A.H., T.M.A. and S.L.; supervision, I.A.H. and S.L. All authors have read and agreed to the published version of the manuscript.

Funding: This research received no external funding.

Institutional Review Board Statement: Not applicable.

Informed Consent Statement: Not applicable.

Data Availability Statement: Not applicable.

Conflicts of Interest: The authors declare no conflict of interest.

References

1. Qi, B.Y.; Xiao, J. Fintech: AI powers financial services to improve people's lives. *Commun. ACM* **2018**, *61*, 65–69. [CrossRef]
2. Wang, Y.; Sui, X.P.; Zhang, Q. Can fintech improve the efficiency of commercial banks?—An analysis based on big data. *Res. Int. Bus. Financ.* **2021**, *55*, 101338. [CrossRef]
3. Dranev, Y.; Frolova, K.; Ochirova, E. The impact of fintech M&A on stock returns. *Res. Int. Bus. Financ.* **2019**, *48*, 353–364. [CrossRef]
4. Legowo, M.B.; Subanidja, S.; Sorongan, F.A. Fintech and bank: Past, present, and future. *J. Tek. Komput.* **2021**, *7*, 94–99. [CrossRef]
5. Puschmann, T. Fintech. *Bus. Inf. Syst. Eng.* **2017**, *59*, 69–76. [CrossRef]
6. Nüesch, R.; Alt, R.; Puschmann, T. Hybrid customer interaction. *Bus. Inf. Syst. Eng.* **2015**, *57*, 73–78. [CrossRef]

7. Martínez-Plumed, F.; Gómez, E.; Hernández-Orallo, J. Futures of artificial intelligence through technology readiness levels. *Telemat. Inform.* **2021**, *58*, 101525. [CrossRef]
8. Veilleux, M.; Sénécal, S.; Demolin, B.; Bouvier, F.; Di Fabio, M.-L.; Coursaris, C.; Léger, P.-M. Visualizing a user's cognitive and emotional journeys: A fintech case. In *Design, User Experience, and Usability. Interaction Design*; Lecture Notes in Computer Science (including subseries Lecture Notes in Artificial Intelligence and Lecture Notes in Bioinformatics); Springer: Cham, Switzerland, 2020; Volume 12200, pp. 549–566. [CrossRef]
9. Rabhi, F.A.; Mehandjiev, N.; Baghdadi, A. State-of-the-Art in Applying Machine Learning to Electronic Trading. In *Enterprise Applications, Markets and Services in the Finance Industry*; Lecture Notes in Business Information Processing; Springer: Cham, Switzerland, 2020; Volume 401, pp. 3–20. [CrossRef]
10. Li, W.; Bao, R.; Harimoto, K.; Chen, D.; Xu, J.; Su, Q. Modeling the stock relation with graph network for overnight stock movement prediction. In Proceedings of the IJCAI International Joint Conference on Artificial Intelligence, Yokohama, Japan, 11–17 July 2020; pp. 4541–4547.
11. Oprea, S.-V.; Bara, A.; Andreescu, A.I. Two Novel Blockchain-Based Market Settlement Mechanisms Embedded into Smart Contracts for Securely Trading Renewable Energy. *IEEE Access* **2020**, *8*, 212548–212556. [CrossRef]
12. Erosa, V.E. Online Money Flows: Exploring the Nature of the Relation of Technology's New Creature to Money Supply—A Suggested Conceptual Framework and Research Propositions. *Am. J. Ind. Bus. Manag.* **2018**, *8*, 250–305. [CrossRef]
13. Broto Legowo, M.; Subanija, S.; Sorongan, F.A. Role of FinTech mechanism to technological innovation: A conceptual framework. *Int. J. Innov. Sci. Res. Technol.* **2020**, *5*, 1–6.
14. Nasir, A.; Shaukat, K.; Hameed, I.A.; Luo, S.; Alam, T.M.; Iqbal, F. A Bibliometric Analysis of Corona Pandemic in Social Sciences: A Review of Influential Aspects and Conceptual Structure. *IEEE Access* **2020**, *8*, 133377–133402. [CrossRef]
15. Aria, M.; Cuccurullo, C. Bibliometrix: An R-tool for comprehensive science mapping analysis. *J. Informetr.* **2017**, *11*, 959–975. [CrossRef]
16. Salameh, A.; Bass, J.M. Heterogeneous Tailoring Approach Using the Spotify Model. In *ACM International Conference Proceeding Series*; Association for Computing Machinery: New York, NY, USA, 2020; pp. 293–298.
17. Kumarathunga, M.; Calheiros, R.; Ginige, A. Towards Trust Enabled Commodity Market for Farmers with Blockchain Smart Contracts. In *ACM International Conference Proceeding Series*; Association for Computing Machinery: New York, NY, USA, 2020; pp. 75–82.
18. Paulson-Luna, M.; Reily, K. The Financial Derivative Ecosystem is Old-Decentralized Ledger Technology is its Fountain of Youth. In *ACM International Conference Proceeding Series*; Association for Computing Machinery: New York, NY, USA, 2020; pp. 105–112.
19. Chakravaram, V.; Ratnakaram, S.; Vihari, N.S.; Tatikonda, N. The Role of Technologies on Banking and Insurance Sectors in the Digitalization and Globalization Era—A Select Study. *Adv. Intell. Syst. Comput.* **2021**, *1245*, 145–156. [CrossRef]
20. Nam, G. Bringing the QR Code to Canada: The Rise of AliPay and WeChatPay in Canadian e-Commerce Markets. *Adv. Intell. Syst. Comput.* **2021**, *1290*, 622–628. [CrossRef]
21. Rao, V.; Singh, A.; Rudra, B. Ethereum Blockchain Enabled Secure and Transparent E-Voting. *Adv. Intell. Syst. Comput.* **2021**, *1290*, 683–702. [CrossRef]
22. Xu, L.; Lu, X.; Yang, G.; Shi, B. Identifying fintech innovations with patent data: A combination of textual analysis and machine-learning techniques. In *Sustainable Digital Communities*; Lecture Notes in Computer Science (including subseries Lecture Notes in Artificial Intelligence and Lecture Notes in Bioinformatics); Springer: Cham, Switzerland, 2020; Volume 12051, pp. 835–843. [CrossRef]
23. Mamonov, S. The Role of Information Technology in Fintech Innovation: Insights from the New York City Ecosystem. *Responsible Des. Implement. Use Inf. Commun. Technol.* **2020**, *12066*, 313–324. [CrossRef]
24. Li, L.; Zhao, T.; Xie, Y.; Feng, Y. Interpretable Machine Learning Based on Integration of NLP and Psychology in Peer-to-Peer Lending Risk Evaluation. In *Natural Language Processing and Chinese Computing*; Zhu, X., Zhang, M., Hong, Y., He, R., Eds.; Lecture Notes in Computer Science (including subseries Lecture Notes in Artificial Intelligence and Lecture Notes in Bioinformatics); Springer: Cham, Switzerland, 2020; pp. 429–441.
25. Liu, B.; Wang, M.; Men, J.; Yang, D. Microgrid Trading Game Model Based on Blockchain Technology and Optimized Particle Swarm Algorithm. *IEEE Access* **2020**, *8*, 225602–225612. [CrossRef]
26. Masaud, T.M.; Warner, J.; El-Saadany, E.F. A Blockchain-Enabled Decentralized Energy Trading Mechanism for Islanded Networked Microgrids. *IEEE Access* **2020**, *8*, 211291–211302. [CrossRef]
27. Liao, C.-H.; Lin, H.-E.; Yuan, S.-M. Blockchain-Enabled Integrated Market Platform for Contract Production. *IEEE Access* **2020**, *8*, 211007–211027. [CrossRef]
28. Chen, R.R.; Chen, K. A 2020 perspective on "Information asymmetry in initial coin offerings (ICOs): Investigating the effects of multiple channel signals". *Electron. Commer. Res. Appl.* **2020**, *40*, 100936. [CrossRef]
29. Jocevski, M.; Ghezzi, A.; Arvidsson, N. Exploring the growth challenge of mobile payment platforms: A business model perspective. *Electron. Commer. Res. Appl.* **2020**, *40*, 100908. [CrossRef]
30. Ferrer-Gomila, J.-L.; Hinarejos, M.F. A 2020 perspective on "A fair contract signing protocol with blockchain support". *Electron. Commer. Res. Appl.* **2020**, *42*, 100981. [CrossRef]
31. Tritto, A.; He, Y.; Junaedi, V.A. Governing the gold rush into emerging markets: A case study of Indonesia's regulatory responses to the expansion of Chinese-backed online P2P lending. *Financ. Innov.* **2020**, *6*, 51. [CrossRef]

32. Yan, J.; Yu, W.; Zhao, J.L. How signaling and search costs affect information asymmetry in P2P lending: The economics of big data. *Financ. Innov.* **2015**, *1*, 19. [CrossRef]
33. Li, Y.; Spigt, R.; Swinkels, L. The impact of FinTech startups on incumbent retail banks' share prices. *Financ. Innov.* **2017**, *3*, 26. [CrossRef]
34. Arner, D.W.; Buckley, R.P.; Zetzsche, D.A.; Veidt, R. Sustainability, FinTech and Financial Inclusion. *Eur. Bus. Organ. Law Rev.* **2020**, *21*, 7–35. [CrossRef]
35. Arner, D.W.; Zetzsche, D.A.; Buckley, R.P.; Barberis, J.N. The Identity Challenge in Finance: From Analogue Identity to Digitized Identification to Digital KYC Utilities. *Eur. Bus. Organ. Law Rev.* **2019**, *20*, 55–80. [CrossRef]
36. Donald, D.C. Smart Precision Finance for Small Businesses Funding. *Eur. Bus. Organ. Law Rev.* **2020**, *21*, 199–217. [CrossRef]
37. Donald, D.C. Hong Kong's fintech automation: Economic benefits and social risks. In *Regulating FinTech in Asia*; Perspectives in Law, Business and Innovation; Springer: Singapore, 2020; pp. 31–50. [CrossRef]
38. Arner, D.W.; Barberis, J.; Buckley, R.P. FinTech, regTech, and the reconceptualization of financial regulation. *Northwest J. Int. Law Bus.* **2017**, *37*, 373–415. [CrossRef]
39. Arner, D.W.; Barberis, J.; Buckley, R.P. RegTech: Building a Better Financial System. In *Handbook of Blockchain, Digital Finance and Inclusion*; Elsevier Inc.: Amsterdam, The Netherlands, 2018.
40. Buckley, R.P.; Arner, D.W.; Zetzsche, D.A.; Selga, E.K. Techrisk. *Singap. J. Leg. Stud.* 2020, pp. 35–62. Available online: http://hub.hku.hk/handle/10722/293372 (accessed on 2 September 2021).
41. Buckley, R.P.; Arner, D.W.; Zetzsche, D.A.; Weber, R.H. The road to RegTech: The (astonishing) example of the European Union. *J. Bank. Regul.* **2020**, *21*, 26–36. [CrossRef]
42. Gomber, P.; Kauffman, R.J.; Parker, C.; Weber, B.W. On the Fintech Revolution: Interpreting the Forces of Innovation, Disruption, and Transformation in Financial Services. *J. Manag. Inf. Syst.* **2018**, *35*, 220–265. [CrossRef]
43. Kauffman, R.J.; Kim, K.; Lee, S.-Y.T.; Hoang, A.-P.; Ren, J. Combining machine-based and econometrics methods for policy analytics insights. *Electron. Commer. Res. Appl.* **2017**, *25*, 115–140. [CrossRef]
44. Kauffman, R.J.; Ma, D. Special issue: Contemporary research on payments and cards in the global fintech revolution. *Electron. Commer. Res. Appl.* **2015**, *14*, 261–264. [CrossRef]
45. Adhami, S.; Giudici, G.; Martinazzi, S. Why do businesses go crypto? An empirical analysis of initial coin offerings. *J. Econ. Bus.* **2018**, *100*, 64–75. [CrossRef]
46. History | BINUS UNIVERSITY. Available online: https://binus.ac.id/history/ (accessed on 2 September 2021).
47. Richard; Heryadi, Y.; Lukas; Trisetyarso, A. Leverage from Blockchain in Commodity Exchange: Asset-Backed Token with Ethereum Blockchain Network and Smart Contract. In *Smart Trends in Computing and Communications: Proceedings of SmartCom 2020*; Zhang, Y.-D., Senjyu, T., So-In, C., Joshi, A., Eds.; Smart Innovation, Systems and Technologies; Springer: Singapore, 2021; pp. 301–309.
48. Yuniarti, S.; Rasyid, A. Consumer Protection in Lending Fintech Transaction in Indonesia: Opportunities and Challenges. *Phys. Conf. Ser.* **2020**, *1477*, 052016. [CrossRef]
49. Candra, S.; Nuruttarwiyah, F.; Hapsari, I.H. Revisited the Technology Acceptance Model with E-Trust for Peer-to-Peer Lending in Indonesia (Perspective from Fintech Users). *Int. J. Technol.* **2020**, *11*, 710–721. [CrossRef]
50. Abdullah, E.M.E.; Rahman, A.A.; Rahim, R.A. Adoption of financial technology (Fintech) in mutual fund/ unit trust investment among Malaysians: Unified Theory of Acceptance and Use of Technology (UTAUT). *Int. J. Eng. Technol.* **2018**, *7*, 110–118. [CrossRef]
51. Yohanes, K.; Junius, K.; Saputra, Y.; Sari, R.; Lisanti, Y.; Luhukay, D. Unified Theory of Acceptance and Use of Technology (UTAUT) model perspective to enhance user acceptance of fintech application. In Proceedings of the 2020 International Conference on Information Management and Technology, ICIMTech 2020, Bandung, Indonesia, 13–14 August 2020; Institute of Electrical and Electronics Engineers Inc.: Piscataway, NJ, USA, 2020; pp. 643–648.
52. Soongsil University. Available online: http://www.ssu.ac.kr/web/eng/home (accessed on 2 September 2021).
53. Kim, J.-H.; Jo, S.-I.; Hong, S.-W.; Gim, G.-Y. Small foreign currency remittance based on block chain in Korea and Vietnam. *Asia Life Sci.* 2019, pp. 57–67. Available online: https://scholarworks.bwise.kr/ssu/handle/2018.sw.ssu/34793 (accessed on 2 September 2021).
54. La, H.J.; Kim, S.D. A machine learning framework for adaptive FinTech security provisioning. *J. Internet Technol.* **2018**, *19*, 1545–1553. [CrossRef]
55. Lee, H.J.; Han, K.S. A study on mobile easy payment service based on fintech to reduce smart divide and income gap. *Int. J. Adv. Sci. Technol.* **2018**, *116*, 35–48. [CrossRef]
56. Tran, T.A.; Han, K.S.; Yun, S.Y. Factors influencing the intention to use mobile payment service using fintech systems: Focused on Vietnam. *Asia Life Sci.* 2018, pp. 1731–1747. Available online: https://scholarworks.bwise.kr/ssu/handle/2018.sw.ssu/34383 (accessed on 2 September 2021).
57. Lee, S. Evaluation of mobile application in user's perspective: Case of P2P lending apps in FinTech industry. *KSII Trans. Internet Inf. Syst.* **2017**, *11*, 1105–1115. [CrossRef]
58. Asmarani, S.C.; Wijaya, C. Effects of fintech on stock return: Evidence from retail banks listed in Indonesia stock exchange. *J. Asian Financ. Econ. Bus.* **2020**, *7*, 95–104. [CrossRef]

59. Yulianita Gitaharie, B.; Abbas, Y.; Dewi, M.K.; Handayani, D. *Research on Firm Financial Performance and Consumer Behavior*; Nova Science Publishers, Inc.: Hauppauge, NY, USA, 2020.
60. Saputra, A.D.; Burnia, I.J.; Shihab, M.R.; Anggraini, R.S.A.; Purnomo, P.H.; Azzahro, F. Empowering Women Through Peer to Peer Lending: Case Study of Amartha.com. In Proceedings of the 2019 International Conference on Information Management and Technology, ICIMTech 2019, Jakarta/Bali, Indonesia, 19–20 August 2019; Institute of Electrical and Electronics Engineers Inc.: Piscataway, NJ, USA, 2019; pp. 618–622.
61. Nasir, A.; Shaukat, K.; Khan, K.I.; Hameed, I.A.; Alam, T.M.; Luo, S. What is core and what future holds for blockchain technologies and cryptocurrencies: A bibliometric analysis. *IEEE Access* **2021**, *9*, 989–1004. [CrossRef]
62. Michaels, L.; Homer, M. Regulation and Supervision in a Digital and Inclusive World. In *Handbook of Blockchain, Digital Finance and Inclusion*; Elsevier Inc.: Amsterdam, The Netherlands, 2018.
63. Birch, D.G.W.; Parulava, S. Ambient Accountability: Shared Ledger Technology and Radical Transparency for Next Generation Digital Financial Services. In *Handbook of Blockchain, Digital Finance and Inclusion*; Elsevier Inc.: Amsterdam, The Netherlands, 2018.
64. Ebenhoch, P. Blockchain Compliance. *Jusletter IT*. 2018. Available online: https://jusletter-it.weblaw.ch/en/issues/2018/IRIS/blockchain-complianc_04fc310f86.html__ONCE&login=false (accessed on 2 September 2021).
65. Tsai, C.-H.; Peng, K.-J. The FinTech Revolution and Financial Regulation: The Case of Online Supply-Chain Financing. *Asian J. Law Soc.* **2017**, *4*, 109–132. [CrossRef]
66. Fan, P.S. Singapore Approach to Develop and Regulate FinTech. In *Handbook of Blockchain, Digital Finance and Inclusion*; Elsevier Inc.: Amsterdam, The Netherlands, 2018.
67. Fenwick, M.; Vermeulen, E.P.M.; Corrales, M. Business and regulatory responses to artificial intelligence: Dynamic regulation, innovation ecosystems and the strategic management of disruptive technology. In *Robotics, AI and the Future of Law*; Perspectives in Law, Business and Innovation; Springer: Singapore, 2018; pp. 81–103. [CrossRef]
68. Fenwick, M.; Kaal, W.A.; Vermeulen, E.P.M. Regulation tomorrow: Strategies for regulating new technologies. In *Transnational Commercial and Consumer Law*; Perspectives in Law, Business and Innovation; Springer: Singapore, 2018; pp. 153–174. [CrossRef]
69. Gerlach, J.M.; Rugilo, D. The predicament of fintechs in the environment of traditional banking sector regulation—An analysis of regulatory sandboxes as a possible solution. *Credit Cap. Mark.* **2019**, *52*, 323–373. [CrossRef]
70. Sangwan, V.; Harshita; Prakash, P.; Singh, S. Financial technology: A review of extant literature. *Stud. Econ. Financ.* **2020**, *37*, 71–88. [CrossRef]
71. Makarov, V.O.; Davydova, M.L. On the concept of regulatory sandboxes. In *"Smart Technologies" for Society, State and Economy. ISC 2020*; Lecture Notes in Networks and Systems; Springer: Cham, Switzerland, 2021; pp. 1014–1020.
72. Liao, F. Does china need the regulatory sandbox? A preliminary analysis of its desirability as an appropriate mechanism for regulating fintech in China. In *Regulating FinTech in Asia*; Perspectives in Law, Businsess and Innovation; Springer: Singapore, 2020; pp. 81–95. [CrossRef]
73. Le, T.N.-L.; Abakah, E.J.A.; Tiwari, A.K. Time and frequency domain connectedness and spill-over among fintech, green bonds and cryptocurrencies in the age of the fourth industrial revolution. *Technol. Forecast. Soc. Chang.* **2021**, *162*, 120382. [CrossRef]
74. Petrov, N.A. Main Trends in the Market of Electronic Financial Services in Russia. In *Economic Systems in the New Era: Stable Systems in an Unstable World. IES 2020*; Ashmarina, S.I., Horak, J., Vrbka, J., Suler, P., Eds.; Lecture Notes in Networks and Systems; Springer: Cham, Switzerland, 2021; pp. 708–712.
75. Teeluck, R.; Durjan, S.; Bassoo, V. Blockchain technology and emerging communications applications. In *Security and Privacy Applications for Smart City Development*; Studies in Systems, Decision and Control; Springer: Cham, Switzerland, 2021; pp. 207–256.
76. Mbodji, F.N.; Mendy, G.; Mbacke, A.B.; Ouya, S. Proof of concept of blockchain integration in P2P lending for developing countries. In *Infrastructure and e-Services for Developing Countries. AFRICOMM 2019*; Zitouni, R., Agueh, M., Houngue, P., Soude, H., Eds.; Lecture Notes of the Institute for Computer Sciences, Social-Informatics and Telecommunications Engineering; Springer: Cham, Switzerland, 2020; pp. 59–70.
77. Hu, Z.; Du, Y.; Rao, C.; Goh, M. Delegated Proof of Reputation Consensus Mechanism for Blockchain-Enabled Distributed Carbon Emission Trading System. *IEEE Access* **2020**, *8*, 214932–214944. [CrossRef]
78. De Oliveira, A.D.C.M.; Pinto, P.F.A.; Colcher, S. Stocks Clustering Based on Textual Embeddings for Price Forecasting. In *Intelligent Systems. BRACIS 2020*; Cerri, R., Prati, R.C., Eds.; Lecture Notes in Computer Science (including subseries Lecture Notes in Artificial Intelligence and Lecture Notes in Bioinformatics); Springer: Cham, Switzerland, 2020; pp. 665–678.
79. Abe, M.; Nakagawa, K. Deep Learning for Multi-factor Models in Regional and Global Stock Markets. In *New Frontiers in Artificial Intelligence. JSAI-isAI 2019*; Lecture Notes in Computer Science (including subseries Lecture Notes in Artificial Intelligence and Lecture Notes in Bioinformatics); Springer: Cham, Switzerland, 2020; Volume 12331, pp. 87–102. [CrossRef]
80. Nabipour, M.; Nayyeri, P.; Jabani, H.; Shahab, S.; Mosavi, A. Predicting Stock Market Trends Using Machine Learning and Deep Learning Algorithms Via Continuous and Binary Data; A Comparative Analysis. *IEEE Access* **2020**, *8*, 150199–150212. [CrossRef]
81. Chen, Y.; Liu, K.; Xie, Y.; Hu, M. Financial Trading Strategy System Based on Machine Learning. *Math. Probl. Eng.* **2020**, *2020*, 3589198. [CrossRef]
82. Obthong, M.; Tantisantiwong, N.; Jeamwatthanachai, W.; Wills, G. A survey on machine learning for stock price prediction: Algorithms and techniques. In Proceedings of the FEMIB 2020—2nd International Conference on Finance, Economics, Management and IT Business, Prague, Czech Republic, 5–6 May 2020; SciTePress: Prague, Czech Republic, 2020; pp. 63–71.

83. Lozano-Medina, J.I.; Hervert-Escobar, L.; Hernandez-Gress, N. Risk profiles of financial service portfolio for women segment using machine learning algorithms. In *Computational Science—ICCS 2020. ICCS 2020*; Lecture Notes in Computer Science (including subseries Lecture Notes in Artificial Intelligence and Lecture Notes in Bioinformatics); Springer: Cham, Switzerland, 2020; Volume 12143, pp. 561–574. [CrossRef]
84. Rozi, M.F.; Sucahyo, Y.G.; Gandhi, A.; Ruldeviyani, Y. Appraising Personal Data Protection in Startup Companies in Financial Technology: A Case Study of ABC Corp. In *ACM International Conference Proceeding Series*; Association for Computing Machinery: New York, NY, USA, 2020; pp. 9–14.
85. Jiang, H.; Zhang, J. Discovering systemic risks of China's Listed Banks by CoVaR approach in the digital economy era. *Mathematics* **2020**, *8*, 180. [CrossRef]
86. Li, M.; Hu, D.; Lal, C.; Conti, M.; Zhang, Z. Blockchain-Enabled Secure Energy Trading with Verifiable Fairness in Industrial Internet of Things. *IEEE Trans. Ind. Inform.* **2020**, *16*, 6564–6574. [CrossRef]
87. Yao, S.; Li, J.; Liu, D.; Wang, T.; Liu, S.; Shao, H.; Abdelzaher, T. Deep compressive offloading: Speeding up neural network inference by trading edge computation for network latency. In *SenSys 2020—Proceedings of the 2020 18th ACM Conference on Embedded Networked Sensor Systems*; Association for Computing Machinery, Inc.: New York, NY, USA, 2020; pp. 476–488.
88. Cui, Y.; Pan, B.; Sun, Y. A Survey of Privacy-Preserving Techniques for Blockchain. In *Artificial Intelligence and Security. ICAIS 2019*; Lecture Notes in Computer Science (including subseries Lecture Notes in Artificial Intelligence and Lecture Notes in Bioinformatics); Springer: Cham, Switzerland, 2019; Volume 11635, pp. 225–234. [CrossRef]
89. Gayathri, S.; Mohana, R.S. Optical Character Recognition in Banking Sectors Using Convolutional Neural Network. In Proceedings of the 3rd International Conference on I-SMAC IoT in Social, Mobile, Analytics and Cloud, I-SMAC 2019, Palladam, India, 12–14 December 2019; Institute of Electrical and Electronics Engineers Inc.: Piscataway, NJ, USA, 2019; pp. 753–756.
90. Hasegawa, T. Toward the mobility-oriented heterogeneous transport system based on new ICT environments—Understanding from a viewpoint of the systems innovation theory. *IATSS Res.* **2018**, *42*, 40–48. [CrossRef]
91. Garrido, G.M.; Miehle, D.; Luckow, A.; Matthes, F. A Blockchain-based Flexibility Market Platform for EV Fleets. In Proceedings of the Clemson University Power Systems Conference, PSC 2020, Clemson, SC, USA, 10–13 March 2020; Institute of Electrical and Electronics Engineers Inc.: Piscataway, NJ, USA, 2020.
92. Gupta, S.; Sharma, H.; Hassija, V.; Saxena, V. BitCom: A Commerce Model on Blockchain. In Proceedings of the 6th International Conference on Signal Processing and Communication, ICSC 2020, Noida, India, 5–7 March 2020; Institute of Electrical and Electronics Engineers Inc.: Piscataway, NJ, USA, 2020; pp. 64–70.
93. He, T.; Gui, X.; Zhang, Z.; Zhou, D.; Hu, Z.; Chen, J.; Li, W. Blockchain-Based Distributed Energy Trading Scheme. In Proceedings of the 2020 Asia Energy and Electrical Engineering Symposium, AEEES 2020, Chengdu, China, 29–31 May 2020; Institute of Electrical and Electronics Engineers Inc.: Piscataway, NJ, USA, 2020; pp. 919–924.
94. Ozili, P.K. Contesting digital finance for the poor. *Digit. Policy Regul. Gov.* **2020**, *22*, 135–151. [CrossRef]
95. Liu, J.; Li, X.; Wang, S. What have we learnt from 10 years of fintech research? A scientometric analysis. *Technol. Forecast. Soc. Change* **2020**, *155*, 120022. [CrossRef]
96. Ravikumar, S.; Saraf, P. Prediction of stock prices using machine learning (regression, classification) Algorithms. In Proceedings of the 2020 International Conference for Emerging Technology, INCET 2020, Belgaum, India, 5–7 June 2020; Institute of Electrical and Electronics Engineers Inc.: Piscataway, NJ, USA, 2020.
97. Ampomah, E.K.; Qin, Z.; Nyame, G. Evaluation of tree-based ensemble machine learning models in predicting stock price direction of movement. *Information* **2020**, *11*, 332. [CrossRef]
98. Harahap, L.A.; Lipikorn, R.; Kitamoto, A. Nikkei Stock Market Price Index Prediction Using Machine Learning. *J. Phys. Conf. Ser.* **2020**, *1566*, 012043. [CrossRef]
99. Ismail, M.S.; Md Noorani, M.S.; Ismail, M.; Abdul Razak, F.; Alias, M.A. Predicting next day direction of stock price movement using machine learning methods with persistent homology: Evidence from Kuala Lumpur Stock Exchange. *Appl. Soft Comput. J.* **2020**, *93*, 106422. [CrossRef]
100. Saifan, R.; Sharif, K.; Abu-Ghazaleh, M.; Abdel-Majeed, M. Investigating algorithmic stock market trading using ensemble machine learning methods. *Informatica* **2020**, *44*, 311–325. [CrossRef]
101. Zhang, M. Artificial Intelligence and Application in Finance. In *ACM International Conference Proceeding Series*; Association for Computing Machinery: New York, NY, USA, 2020; pp. 317–322.
102. Chang, J.; Ding, Y.; Tu, W. FollowAKOInvestor: Using Machine Learning to Hear Voices from All Kinds of Investors. In Proceedings of the International Conference on Tools with Artificial Intelligence, ICTAI, Baltimore, MD, USA, 9–11 November 2020; IEEE Computer Society: Washington, DC, USA, 2020; pp. 875–882.
103. Kulshrestha, N.; Srivastava, V.K. Synthesizing Technical Analysis, Fundamental Analysis Artificial Intelligence—An Applied Approach to Portfolio Optimisation Performance Analysis of Stock Prices in India. In Proceedings of the ICRITO 2020—IEEE 8th International Conference on Reliability, Infocom Technologies and Optimization (Trends and Future Directions), Noida, India, 4–5 June 2020; Institute of Electrical and Electronics Engineers Inc.: Piscataway, NJ, USA, 2020; pp. 1185–1188.
104. Wong, K.Y.; Wong, R.K. Big data quality prediction on banking applications: Extended abstract. In Proceedings of the 2020 IEEE 7th International Conference on Data Science and Advanced Analytics, DSAA 2020, Sydney, NSW, Australia, 6–9 October 2020; Institute of Electrical and Electronics Engineers Inc.: Piscataway, NJ, USA, 2020; pp. 791–792.

105. Ceaparu, C. IT solutions for big data processing and analysis in the finance and banking sectors. *Adv. Intell. Syst. Comput.* **2021**, *1243*, 133–144. [CrossRef]
106. Zhang, Q.; Liu, F. Research on channel model and price dispersion of E-commerce market based on blockchain technology. *Wirel. Commun. Mob. Comput.* **2020**, *2020*, 8824754. [CrossRef]
107. Delger, O.; Tseveenbayar, M.; Namsrai, E.; Tsendsuren, G. Current State of E-Commerce in Mongolia: Payment and Delivery. In *Advances in Intelligent Information Hiding and Multimedia Signal Processing*; Pan, J.-S., Li, J., Tsai, P.-W., Jain, L., Eds.; Smart Innovation, Systems and Technologies; Springer: Singapore, 2020; pp. 289–297.
108. Almuhammadi, A. An overview of mobile payments, fintech, and digital wallet in Saudi Arabia. In Proceedings of the 7th International Conference on Computing for Sustainable Global Development, INDIACom 2020, New Delhi, India, 12–14 March 2020; Institute of Electrical and Electronics Engineers Inc.: Piscataway, NJ, USA, 2020; pp. 271–278.
109. Kennedyd, S.I.; Guo, Y.; Fu, Z.; Liu, K. The Cashless Society Has Arrived: How Mobile Phone Payment Dominance Emerged in China. *Int. J. Electron. Gov. Res.* **2020**, *16*, 94–112. [CrossRef]
110. Li, M.; Shao, S.; Ye, Q.; Xu, G.; Huang, G.Q. Blockchain-enabled logistics finance execution platform for capital-constrained E-commerce retail. *Robot. Comput. Integr. Manuf.* **2020**, *65*, 101962. [CrossRef]
111. Ferrer-Gomila, J.-L.; Francisca Hinarejos, M.; Isern-Deyà, A.-P. A fair contract signing protocol with blockchain support. *Electron. Commer. Res. Appl.* **2019**, *36*, 100869. [CrossRef]
112. Najdawi, A.; Chabani, Z.; Said, R.; Starkova, O. Analysing the Adoption of E-Payment Technologies in UAE Based on Demographic Variables. In Proceedings of the 2019 International Conference on Digitization: Landscaping Artificial Intelligence, ICD 2019, Sharjah, United Arab Emirates, 18–19 November 2019; Institute of Electrical and Electronics Engineers Inc.: Piscataway, NJ, USA, 2019; pp. 244–248.
113. Ding, D.; Chong, G.; Chuen, D.L.K.; Cheng, T.L. From Ant Financial to Alibaba's Rural Taobao Strategy—How Fintech Is Transforming Social Inclusion. In *Handbook of Blockhain, Digital Finance and Inclusion*; Elsevier Inc.: Amsterdam, The Netherlands, 2018.
114. Dula, C.; Chuen, D.L.K. Reshaping the Financial Order. In *Handbook of Blockhain, Digital Finance and Inclusion*; Elsevier Inc.: Amsterdam, The Netherlands, 2018.
115. Jin, B.H.; Li, Y.M.; Li, Z.W. Study on crowdfunding patterns and factors in different phases. In Proceedings of the Americas Conference on Information Systems 2018: Digital Disruption, AMCIS 2018, New Orleans, LA, USA, 16–18 August 2018; Association for Information Systems: Atlanta, GA, USA, 2018.
116. Stasik, A.; Wilczyńska, E. How do we study crowdfunding? An overview of methods and introduction to new research agenda. *J. Manag. Bus. Adm. Cent. Eur.* **2018**, *26*, 49–78. [CrossRef]
117. Zetzsche, D.; Preiner, C. Cross-Border Crowdfunding: Towards a Single Crowdlending and Crowdinvesting Market for Europe. *Eur. Bus. Organ. Law Rev.* **2018**, *19*, 217–251. [CrossRef]
118. Ferreira, F.; Pereira, L. Success Factors in a Reward and Equity Based Crowdfunding Campaign. In Proceedings of the 2018 IEEE International Conference on Engineering, Technology and Innovation, ICE/ITMC 2018, Stuttgart, Germany, 17–20 June 2018; Institute of Electrical and Electronics Engineers Inc.: Piscataway, NJ, USA, 2018.
119. Pokrovskaya, M. Risk mitigation based on innovative solutions. In Proceedings of the International Astronautical Congress, IAC. International Astronautical Federation, IAF (2019), Washington, DC, USA, 21–25 October 2019.
120. Miraz, M.H.; Donald, D.C. Application of Blockchain in Booking and Registration Systems of Securities Exchanges. In Proceedings of the 2018 International Conference on Computing, Electronics and Communications Engineering, iCCECE 2018, Southend, UK, 16–17 August 2018; Institute of Electrical and Electronics Engineers Inc.: Piscataway, NJ, USA, 2019; pp. 35–40.
121. Nasir, F.; Saeedi, M. 'RegTech' as a Solution for Compliance Challenge: A Review Article. *J. Adv. Res. Dyn. Control Syst.* **2019**, *11*, 912–919. [CrossRef]
122. Goul, M. Services computing and regtech. In Proceedings of the 2019 IEEE World Congress on Services, SERVICES 2019, Milan, Italy, 8–13 July 2019; Institute of Electrical and Electronics Engineers Inc.: Piscataway, NJ, USA, 2019; pp. 219–223.
123. Singh, H.; Jain, G.; Munjal, A.; Rakesh, S. Blockchain technology in corporate governance: Disrupting chain reaction or not? *Corp. Gov.* **2019**, *20*, 67–86. [CrossRef]
124. Fama, E.F.; French, K.R. The Cross-Section of Expected Stock Returns. *J. Financ.* **1992**, *47*, 427–465. [CrossRef]
125. Fama, E.F.; French, K.R. A five-factor asset pricing model. *J. Financ. Econ.* **2014**, *116*, 1–22. [CrossRef]
126. Nasir, A.; Khan, K.I.; Mata, M.N.; Mata, P.N.; Martins, J.N. Optimisation of Time-Varying Asset Pricing Models with Penetration of Value at Risk and Expected Shortfall. *Mathematics* **2021**, *9*, 394. [CrossRef]
127. Shaukat, K.; Iqbal, F.; Alam, T.M.; Aujla, G.K.; Devnath, L.; Khan, A.G.; Iqbal, R.; Shahzadi, I.; Rubab, A. The impact of artificial intelligence and robotics on the future employment opportunities. *Trends Comput. Sci. Inf. Technol.* **2020**, *5*, 50–54.
128. Shaukat, K.; Alam, T.M.; Hameed, I.A.; Luo, S.; Li, J.; Aujla, G.K.; Iqbal, F. A comprehensive dataset for bibliometric analysis of SARS and coronavirus impact on social sciences. *Data Brief* **2020**, *33*, 106520. [CrossRef] [PubMed]
129. Alam, T.M.; Mushtaq, M.; Shaukat, K.; Hameed, I.A.; Sarwar, M.U.; Luo, S. A Novel Method for Performance Measurement of Public Educational Institutions Using Machine Learning Models. *Appl. Sci.* **2021**, *11*, 9296. [CrossRef]
130. Shaukat, K.; Luo, S.; Varadharajan, V.; Hameed, I.A.; Xu, M. A survey on machine learning techniques for cyber security in the last decade. *IEEE Access* **2020**, *8*, 222310–222354. [CrossRef]
131. Shaukat, K.; Luo, S.; Varadharajan, V.; Hameed, I.A.; Chen, S.; Liu, D.; Li, J. Performance comparison and current challenges of using machine learning techniques in cybersecurity. *Energies* **2020**, *13*, 2509. [CrossRef]

132. Shaukat, K.; Luo, S.; Chen, S.; Liu, D. Cyber Threat Detection Using Machine Learning Techniques: A Performance Evaluation Perspective. In Proceedings of the 2020 International Conference on Cyber Warfare and Security (ICCWS), Islamabad, Pakistan, 20–21 October 2020; pp. 1–6.
133. Shaukat, K.; Masood, N.; Khushi, M. A Novel Approach to Data Extraction on Hyperlinked Webpages. *Appl. Sci.* **2019**, *9*, 5102. [CrossRef]